The Social Origins of Private Life

The Social Origins of Private Life

A History of American Families 1600–1900

STEPHANIE COONTZ

VERSO

London · New York

First published by Verso 1988
© 1988 Verso
All rights reserved

Verso
UK: 6 Meard Street, London W1V 3HR
USA: 29 West 35th Street, New York, NY 10001 12291

Verso is the imprint of New Left Books

British Library Cataloguing in Publication Data
Coontz, Stephanie, *1944–*
   The social origins of private life: a
   history of American families 1600–1900
   (Haymarket series).
   1. United States. Family life. 1600–1900
   I. Title II. Series
   306.8′5′0973

ISBN 0–86091–191–8

US Library of Congress Cataloging in Publication Data
Coontz, Stephanie.
   The social origins of private life.

   (The Haymarket series)
   Bibliography: p.
   Includes index.
   1. Family—United States—History—17th century.
2. Family—United States—History—18th century.
3. Family—United States—History—19th century.
I. Title. II. Series.
HQ535.C64 1988   306.8′5′0973   88–17201
ISBN 0–8609–1191–8
ISBN 0–8609–1907–2 (pbk.)

Typeset by Columns of Reading
Printed in the U.S.A.

Contents

The Haymarket Series

Editors: Mike Davis and Michael Sprinker

The Haymarket Series is a new publishing initiative by Verso offering original studies of politics, history and culture focused on North America. The series presents innovative but representative views from across the American left on a wide range of topics of current and continuing interest to socialists in North America and throughout the world. A century after the first May Day, the American left remains in the shadow of those martyrs whom this series honors and commemorates. The studies in the Haymarket Series testify to the living legacy of activism and political commitment for which they gave up their lives.

Already Published

BLACK AMERICAN POLITICS: From the Washington Marches to Jesse Jackson *by Manning Marable*

PRISONERS OF THE AMERICAN DREAM: Politics and Economy in the History of the US Working Class *by Mike Davis*

MARXISM IN THE USA: Remapping the History of the American Left *by Paul Buhle*

THE LEFT AND THE DEMOCRATS: *The Year Left 1*

TOWARD A RAINBOW SOCIALISM: *The Year Left 2*

RESHAPING THE US LEFT - POPULAR STRUGGLES IN THE 1980s: *The Year Left 3*

CORRUPTIONS OF EMPIRE *by Alexander Cockburn*

FIRE IN THE AMERICAS: Forging a Revolutionary Agenda *by Roger Burbach and Orlando Núñez*

MECHANIC ACCENTS: Dime Novels and Working-Class Culture in 19th-Century America *by Michael Denning*

THE FINAL FRONTIER: The Rise and Fall of the American Rocket State *by Dale Carter*

POSTMODERNISM AND ITS DISCONTENTS: Theories, Practices *Edited by E. Ann Kaplan*

AN INJURY TO ALL: The Decline of American Unionism *by Kim Moody*

Forthcoming

OUR OWN TIME: A History of American Labor and the Working Day *by David Roediger and Philip Foner*

YOUTH, IDENTITY, POWER: The Chicano Generation *by Carlos Muñoz, Jr.*

THE 'FIFTH' CALIFORNIA: The Political Economy of a State-Nation *by Mike Davis*

RANK-AND-FILE REBELLION: Teamsters for a Democratic Union *by Dan Labotz*

THE MERCURY THEATER: Orson Welles and the Popular Front *by Michael Denning*

THE POLITICS OF SOLIDARITY: Central America and the US Left *by Van Gosse*

THE HISTORY OF BLACK POLITICAL THOUGHT *by Manning Marable*

Introduction

Frustrated by the fact that most texts on women treated 'the man's world' as the given and then simply asked where and how women fitted in, I decided to undertake a survey of American gender roles: this was the starting point of the present book. My initial approach was to conceptualize the predominantly male public world as being dependent upon and made possible by woman's private work, and my attention began to focus on the family as the place not only where men and women were brought into interaction but where the private and the public spheres of life intersected and affected each other.

Simultaneously, however, doing research with Peta Henderson on the origins and history of sexual inequality,[1] I began to realize that neither the public–private dichotomy of modern life nor the special association of women with the family was universal. In some societies the private sphere controls the public, and political 'decisions' are subordinate to domestic ones. Thus, for example, male Iroquois sachems declared 'war,' but unless female household heads agreed to arrange provisions for the war party, hostilities could not be commenced. In other societies the distinction between public and private has not existed, or has been qualitatively different from our own. In some groups *men* are thought to have a special association with the family, while women are considered individualistic or unconcerned with family needs. In others, both men and women share responsibility to the family and are intimately involved in interactions with wider networks of kin.

My interest shifted, accordingly, to variations in family life over time. Stimulated by the burgeoning research into family history, I began to look at the family as a culture's way of coordinating personal reproduction with social reproduction – as the socially sanctioned place where male and female reproductive activities condition and are conditioned by the other

1

activities into which human beings enter as they perpetuate a particular kind of society, or try to construct a new one.

As soon as I looked at the family in this way, of course, it ceased to make sense to define it as a private institution, whatever the social ideology about its supposed inviolability or apartness may be. Nor did it make sense to define the family purely in terms of women, ignoring the impact of men on family life and the impact of family life on men. For both men and women, the family offers access to, or attempts to force acceptance of, certain rights and obligations involved in the production and consumption of society's resources. It provides people with an explanation of their rights and obligations that helps link personal identity to social role. At the same time, the family constitutes an arena where people can affect their rights and obligations; it is also, therefore, a place where people resist assignment to their social roles or attempt to renegotiate those roles. The family is thus a major intersection between personal choice and social compulsion. It is, in other words, part of 'the mode of social reproduction.'[2]

In the following chapters I attempt to grapple with some of the connections between the evolution of American families and major transformations in the larger system of social reproduction. This book represents an initial and still tentative synthesis of recent research on the history of the American family rather than an in-depth study of primary sources about a particular time and place. For this reason I can only anticipate correction as more detailed case studies emerge, and there are certainly gaps in my treatment of particular regions and subgroups. I have tried to indicate in the text the limits of many of my generalizations and the variations in family life by class, region, and ethnic group.

The book begins with an overview of the problems in defining the family and understanding the evolution of family life over the past 300 years of Western history. Our tendency to seek a 'proper' or 'natural' family type in history flies in the face of the historical and cross-cultural record, which reveals an astonishing variety of 'successful' family arrangements. I attempt to identify some salient aspects of family change in the West while criticizing linear conceptions or one-sided evaluations of such change. Chapter 2 then discusses Native American kinship and gender systems, which provide a striking illustration of how family arrangements vary in different modes of social reproduction. Native American families took various forms and played specific roles because the larger system of social reproduction was not dependent upon the exchange of private property or the maintenance of state authority. However, in colonial America, as chapter 3 shows, families were based on private property and were the very bedrock of state authority. They were also, however, embedded in a corporate, hierarchical community of households that subordinated family independence to the authority of household and community heads. By the mid eighteenth century, increasing social differentiation and the erosion of corporate controls had begun to change family patterns and the age and gender hierarchies that accompanied them.

In chapter 4, I argue that the American Revolution, the spread of independent household commodity production, and the erosion of traditional justifications of social inequality conferred a new autonomy on individual families and created new relationships between biological and social reproduction. Gender and race began, albeit in different ways, to absorb and disguise other forms of hierarchy and social differentiation. Chapter 5 explores how these new patterns interacted with the spread of wage labor and market production to create new family strategies and gender relations, especially in the northern middle class. The ideal of the independent republican household was challenged after 1815 by accelerated economic, political, and social change. This threatened social order, undermined patriarchal power, eroded the economic independence of the middle-class household — or at least posed a crisis of succession within it — and created a host of new anxieties and opportunities. Middle-class women moved to center stage in the elaboration of new family and gender roles, creating a domestic but not yet a private family in response to changing relations with other classes and regions.

Chapter 6 argues that the dominant middle-class family ideology and practice had become essentially conservative by the mid century, but that polarization occurred as a minority undertook to retain an innovative role in both social and familial relations. This minority played a leading role in the abolition and women's rights movements, aided by the parallel self-organization of Blacks and women workers. After the Civil War, however, most middle-class individuals acquiesced in the compromise that readmitted southern planters into the American power structure. They also opposed attempts by American workers to extend the notion of equality beyond legal and political rights into economic or work relations. Chapters 7 and 8 trace the divergent development of middle-class, working-class, and ethnic families, including the special case of Blacks, from 1870 to 1890. I argue, nonetheless, that the family played a more direct role in social and class reproduction for *all* classes in this period of industrialization than it had done earlier or was to do later.

Finally, chapter 9 forecasts the changes that will be the subject of a subsequent book on the evolution of the twentieth-century family. Using minimal notes, as I will document my points in the later volume, I argue that changes in social reproduction between 1890 and 1920 obviated the need for the family to suppress individualism and play a direct role in class placement, but created new demands on families at the same time. The outcome of those changes was the emergence by the 1920s of a new pattern of family life, associated with the spread of mass production and consumption. The axis of relationship between the family and the economy and state shifted; the internal axis of the family also changed, from the mother–child to the couple relationship. These changes introduced characteristic new tensions and contradictions into family life without diminishing the social centrality of the family to American society. The chapter concludes with a review of the difficulties in making unilinear evaluations about the past and future of family life, suggesting that current family problems stem from dilemmas in the larger system of social reproduction and cannot be solved by a return to some mythical Golden Age of family history.

It is my hope that this book can, if not resolve, at least make us more comfortable with some of the questions and paradoxes surrounding the past and future of the American family. Have we, for example, lost contact with kin as our emotional orientation has concentrated more on the parent–child bond, or have advances in health, transportation, and communication actually amplified the meaning of kin networks in our lives? Have we gained privacy as the nuclear unit has escaped the surveillance and supervision of neighbors and grandparents or lost it as social workers, census takers, and family 'experts' have discovered the 'problems' of family life? Has the breakdown of arbitrary patriarchal authority meant an increase in the autonomy of women and children or an increase in their emotional vulnerability? Is the family a place where non-dominant groups in society can preserve their ethnic or class traditions and organize for social change, or is it a conservative institution that perpetuates social inequality and domination?

I will suggest throughout this book that there has never been a Golden Age of the family and never will be, and that one-sided answers to these questions do not do justice to the complexity of family history. Gains in one aspect of life or for one group in society have been accompanied by losses in other aspects of life or for other groups. Thus, for instance, growing respect for children's autonomy in decision-making in the twentieth century has been accompanied by far greater parental interference in early childhood development, including extraordinary efforts to make sure that children 'share' their experiences, thoughts, and feelings. The expansion of democratic capitalism may have freed families from older political and social hierarchies, but it has subjected them to other hierarchies of consumerism and envy. Although middle-class families gained significant control over schooling for their children in the early twentieth century, the 'invention of juvenile delinquency' at the same time undermined standard legal principles in order to forcibly impose bourgeois behavior on lower-class children, often over the objections of their parents.

A final example of the trade-offs: the increase in the family's ability to resist the interference of neighbors and kin may well have involved a subversion of the confidence needed to resist the advice of 'experts' or government agencies. As one of the 'new' single mothers of the 1980s, I can testify both to the satisfying freedom of being able to set my own patterns with my son and to the constant fear that those patterns are somehow not normal and should correspond to the ideal models laid out in the advice books with which I compulsively surround myself. My own mother, on the other hand, constrained from making major innovations in child-rearing by her parents, her husband, and her network of co-thinkers in neighborhood and political organizations, was also supported by them in resisting standards derived from the state or the mass media. Yet given the social pressures on women in the postwar period, this could hardly have been said to make her confident in her judgment. My hope is that this book will help people see that the family is not an isolated arena in which any of us can achieve full independence or be subjected to complete domination, but is an integral part of the much larger patchwork quilt that shapes our lives even as we stitch in our own designs.

The people around me have certainly shaped my own patterns even as they have generously allowed me the time and space to work on my stitching by myself. Teaching in a small town, at a college that stresses quality undergraduate education above research, I have found myself especially dependent on the written works of other historians. I have tried to make my debts to these authors clear in the notes. But this book has also benefited from the 'interference' of colleagues, students, and family in offering questions, challenges, and advice, as well as from their help in freeing me up for the more individualistic pursuits of the actual research and writing.

Most acknowledgments in academic books bear unwitting testimony to the segregation of 'productive' and domestic work that is discussed in chapter 5. One group of people (often predominantly male) receives thanks for scholarly insights, critical comments, and research. A wholly different group (usually female or family) is thanked for emotional support, personal services, child care, or other relief from the burdens of scholarship. While some of the aid I received was predominantly institutional, such as the leaves kindly provided me by The Evergreen State College, I am happy to say that there are still areas of American life in which the separation of spheres is incomplete. Even my tremendous debts to the circulation, interlibrary loan, and reference staff of TESC are not purely 'public'; much of their help went far beyond the formal demands of their jobs. Most of my obligations are of the preindustrial kind – a complex entanglement of interest and emotion, work and leisure activities, personal support, intellectual criticism, and family/neighborhood services.

Peta Henderson helped me conceptualize my early views on family forms and sex roles and was a rigorous but supportive critic of my work, while also offering her friendship and providing my son with the attention that he often needed while his mother was distracted by the demands of writing. Martha Chubb's commitment to my son meant more than I can say. Nancy Hartsock and Susan Strasser read chapters of my book, discussed the issues with me, and challenged my views on both gender and class. Chris Bose, Barbara Pope, and David Marr read early versions of the first chapter and forced me to clarify some of my ideas. Michael Sprinker's editorial suggestions were invaluable, though occasionally an author's possessiveness prevented me from cutting sections as rigorously as he would have liked. Steve Rose, Linda Malanchuck, Amy Fisher, and Charlotte Raynor offered valuable pointers on the processes of writing, publishing, and remaining human. Various research and teaching assistants, most notably Kim Buselle, Susan Ann Scott, Jim Ascher, Carla Thompson, and Diane Lutz, provided both intellectual and personal support. Bryn Houghton verified notes and did childcare. Adele Smith and Jan Stentz provided secretarial support, and Jan's mastery of the computer is surpassed only by her virtuosity as a jazz singer. My students and colleagues at TESC were generous with academic feedback and personal encouragement: special thanks go to Mike and Ann Beug and Charles Pailthorp. John Finnan, Suzette McCann, and Don Sprague nursed me through computer crises, sometimes at ungodly hours of the night. I have also relied heavily on the extended family networks and fictive kinship ties associated with my stepsiblings, uncle, aunt, and cousin, while my son Kristopher showed remarkable insight into when he needed to be patient with my schedule and when he needed to assert his own demands. Finally, my parents, Pat and Bill Waddington, and my sister, Sharron Coontz, have lovingly reminded me that definitions and conceptions of the family cannot be fully encompassed in abstract theorizing, although they have also proved willing to confront me about the inadequacies of my theories and abstractions.

Notes

1. Stephanie Coontz and Peta Henderson, eds, *Women's Work, Men's Property: The Origins of Gender and Class* (London, 1986).
2. Rayna Rapp, Ellen Ross, and Renate Bridenthal, 'Examining Family History,' *Feminist Studies* 5 (1979), p. 248.

1

Reconceptualizing Family History

This book is a historical and analytical account of the evolution of American families from the seventeenth century to the 1890s. Before attempting to synthesize the ways in which 'the family' has changed, however, it is worth noting the difficulty of identifying a single family unit that permits cross-cultural and historical comparison. In seventeenth and eighteenth century England and America, family was generally defined as all those living under the authority of a household head. 'I lived in Axe Yard, having my wife, and servant Jane, and no more in family than us three,' wrote Samuel Pepys in his diary. Such was still the definition of Everard Peck, of Rochester, New York, in 1820, who wrote home shortly after his marriage: 'We collected our family together which consists of seven persons and we think ourselves pleasantly situated.' Yet by this period many members of the middle class had begun to emphasize the exclusiveness of the parent–child unit, rejecting colonial traditions wherein household heads had made little distinction between children and servants of about the same age. At the same time, European aristocrats continued to define family in terms of those having claim to land and title, regardless of distance in time, geography, or genetic relatedness.[1]

Native Americans had still different conceptions of family: some groups stressed lineal descent, either through the paternal or maternal line; others paid more attention to horizontal ties of kinship than to vertical ones. In all cases, however, Native American family definitions extended well beyond the household and occasionally cut *across* it, with spouses identified as members of different families. Nineteenth-century white women also defined family as extending beyond the household, but they usually referred to predominantly female networks whose concerns were explicitly opposed to the work and political relations organized by Indian kin ties.

Even the biological 'facts' about families are sometimes ambiguous. In many African and traditional Native American societies, a woman could become a female husband and be counted the parent of the children her wife brought to the marriage or afterwards bore by various anonymous lovers. A woman among the Nayar of India could take a *tali* husband whom she might see only at the wedding ceremony; he nevertheless legitimated her future children. Fictive kinship ties were important among Native Americans and Afro-American slaves, while 'going for sisters' or brothers has been an important element of survival among poverty-stricken ghetto residents.[2]

Cross-culturally, families vary so greatly in their gender, marital, and child-rearing arrangements that it is not possible to argue that they are based on universal psychological or biological relations. We are accustomed to thinking of the mother–child relationship as critical to the family, but among the Lakher of Southeast Asia a mother is linked to her child only by virtue of her relationship to the father. If the parents divorce, the mother is considered to have no relationship to her children: she could, theoretically, even marry her son, since the group's incest taboos would no longer be considered applicable. (The widespread practice of brother–sister marriage among ancient Egyptians even throws into doubt the universality of such incest taboos.) Nor is the nuclear family the central reference point for many societies. Among exogamous unilineal kin groups such as the Basoga of East Africa, 'nuclear families tend to be split by the conflicting loyalties of the spouses,' so that children orient to parental lineages rather than to the nuclear family in which they are reared. Among nineteenth-century Cheyenne Indians, the most significant economic and emotional exchanges occurred between children and their uncles or aunts rather than their fathers or mothers.[3]

Following G. P. Murdock, many authors have defined the family as a social unit that shares common residence, economic cooperation, and reproduction. But in groups as diverse as eighteenth-century Austrian peasants and the modern Yoruba, the legally or socially sanctioned family often did not share the same residence, engage in child-rearing, or cooperate economically in either production or consumption. In some tribal societies husbands and wives live apart, while in other societies the basic unit of economic cooperation may be the band, the age group, or the gender group rather than the family. And the history of sexuality surely demonstrates that reproduction often takes place outside the family, a fact which sometimes achieves legal recognition in institutions of concubinage, adoption, and so on.[4]

Sociologists and psychologists have emphasized the family's role as an agent of socialization: Mark Poster suggests that the family is a 'system of love objects' in which psychic structure is decisively formed;

more modestly, Ira Reiss claims that the family is the site of nurturant socialization for the newborn. Yet in preindustrial Europe and colonial America, people frequently turned over at least some of their children to non-relatives for socialization, while in many band-level groups socialzation has traditionally taken place within the group as a whole. In many Native American societies infants might be fed by any lactating woman, rather than exclusively by the mother, while European noblewomen often hired wet nurses for their infants. We also know that many families do *not* nurture their newborns, witness the high rates of infanticide or abandonment in many historical periods; abandonment was often, however, a socially acceptable way of *finding* nurture for a newborn, and the family of procreation did not give up its claims or ties to the child.[5]

Donald Bender believes that we can salvage a universal definition of the family from this jumble of conflicting practices by simply studying the *facts* of kinship, regardless of the function or meaning of kinship to the people involved. Since 'people in all societies recognize kinship relationships and use these relationships as a basis for forming social groups, and because these relationships can be organized in only a certain number of logically possible ways, it is extremely useful to classify kinship groups in terms of structural types.' Bender argues, for example, that the Yoruba of Ondo can be analyzed in terms of '*de facto*' families, even though they do not have '*de jure*' families and even though there are no social groups organized primarily around kinship relations. As Sylvia Yanagisako points out, however, this is analytically absurd. All societies recognize a whole series of categories – by age, height, weight, biological relationships, and so on – but if those categories do not organize or legitimize their social relationships in some way, they do not have much explanatory value for observers of the society. Where families are not legitimized, differentiated, and functional units, they can hardly be said to exist.[6]

But where families *are* legitimized, differentiated units fulfilling certain functions, they cannot be equated with other groups that may perform the same functions on different bases. This is the problem with the opposite approach to finding a universal definition of the family. The *Journal of Home Economics* has dropped kin relations altogether, defining the family 'as a unit of intimate, transacting, and interdependent persons who share some values and goals, resources, responsibility for decisions, and have some commitment to one another over time.'[7] Such a definition, however, makes the word meaningless as a unit of historical or sociological analysis. It excludes the element that has given the family, where it does have legal or moral meaning, such a powerful impact in ordering people's lives – the fact that it is both socially sanctioned and biologically explained.

In modern America, the 'bounded' family is 'a sphere of human relationships shaped by a state that recognizes Families as units that hold property, provide for care and welfare, and attend particularly to the young. . . .'[8] A definition of family that goes beyond kinship or marital relationships is hence attractive to those who wish to extend welfare services and legal rights to units currently denied them by the modern state. But the attempt to extend those rights has generated enormous controversy, which will not be resolved by blithely defining the dispute out of existence. Moreover, it is worth noting that while the move to make, for example, gay households eligible for family assistance is understandable in the current economic climate, it also represents a capitulation to the view that families are, universally, the only legitimate units for emotional commitments, long-term obligations, and social support.

The delineation of a unique place and idea as 'the family,' and the assignment of exclusive emotional, legal, or spatial rights to that unit, is not a universal phenomenon. The Zinacantecos of southern Mexico lack a word differentiating parents and children from other social groupings; instead, they identify the basic social unit as a 'house.' The Yoruba of Ondo fail to define any social groupings purely in terms of kinship. Many band-level societies disperse into small groups organized around a conjugal pair for one season of the year but spend the rest of the year in larger camps or compounds. The small units disappear into the larger at this time, and may be reconstituted with different members in the next season. Lila Leibowitz suggests that these 'minimal dispersal units,' the pairs that ensure the physical reproduction of a group and constitute the smallest unit into which the group can divide and still survive, should not be confused with families. Such units may merely be personal arrangements for biological survival and reproduction, carrying no social sanctions and not functioning as an ideological symbol system. Indeed, a case can be made that some forms of kinship societies are not family systems, since everyone is considered as kin or treated as such and no smaller aggregation of individuals claims exclusive rights, activities, or emotions that demarcate its members from other groups.[9]

Yet if the family is not universal, and if its definition and functions vary widely, the fact remains that the concept of family is extremely widespread. Most societies have used this concept to establish certain kinds of interactions among people, and to prohibit others, on the basis of criteria that are defined as presocial, biologically natural, and therefore less susceptible of voluntary compliance or personal negotiation than other forms of interaction. This is what is fundamentally misleading about Carl Degler's assertion that the family 'is at bottom nothing more than a relation between a man and a woman and their offspring.'[10] Only some relations are accepted by society as families, and the constitution of a family involves the individuals within it in particular interactions with society at large and with other persons in society. An adequate concept of the family must take account of its central role in social as well as personal relationships, in societal as well as biological reproduction.

I argue that though most groups recognize marital and reproductive units, they develop a coherent definition of family only when distinctions other than those of gender, age, individual personality, and propinquity begin to be required to organize different kinds of duties and rights in the maintenance and reproduction of society. A family system represents a *subdivision* of relationships set up by kinship or location. It is a way of generating priorities or hierarchies in people's loyalties, obligations, and rights to labor or resources. As such, it is not surprising that the definitions and functions of the family vary as widely as do the obligations, rights, types of labor mobilization, and distribution of resources in different cultures.

Sylvia Yanagisako warns that it is impossible to 'construct a precise, reduced definition for what are inherently complex, multifunctional institutions imbued with a diverse array of cultural principles and meanings.'[11] However, we may be able to identify the kinds of issues and problems that are being addressed when a society does define 'the family.' Despite wide variety in the organization and even the definition of families, all known societies of any significant size or complexity seem to use the concept to institutionalize and legitimize certain special, socially sanctioned relationships among various members of the group. And whatever unit a society or a subgroup within society defines as a family is the unit that determines the rights and obligations of its members in terms of inheritance, use of the prevailing set of resources, and initial 'social placement'[12] into the social configuration of labor and rewards. The determination of rights and obligations may be direct, as when production and distribution are organized through kin networks, or it may be indirect, as when birth into a particular family determines whether one will work for a living or control the labor of others, but in either case it seems to be one of a number of common patterns, rights, obligations, and associations that swirl around families in all societies.

In most non-state family systems, kinship connections to particular families or lineages involve people in sharply defined work and redistribution relationships, giving each individual definite obligations toward other members of society. Sex taboos, gender definitions, and marriage rules create interdependence and exchange, ensuring that all individuals are members of overlapping groups, with mutual and interpenetrating responsibilities and rights. Where classes arise, however, property ownership rather than blood ties increasingly becomes the primary determinant of social rights and obligations to labor, although many societies have gone through a prolonged period of conflict between the two competing systems of labor organization. As the state or the market establishes interactions in work, distribution, and consumption, the role of kinship becomes more constricted, a process that can be traced in the switch from exogamy to endogamy and the narrowing of sex and marriage taboos that once helped to organize social relationships into wider networks of exchange.

But even when property exchange and civil rule have almost totally replaced kinship as the organizational principle in economics and politics, families remain important in at least one key economic sense. If they do not organize or deploy labor directly, they still determine whether or not an individual belongs to a class that has access to labor through its control of political power or its ownership of property. Even today, despite the supposed usurpation of family functions by the market and the state, the family continues to play a critical role in determining one's place in the labor structure. Christopher Jencks, for example, has concluded that family background accounts for from 55 to 85 per cent of the earnings advantage of those who succeed economically in America, while the 1966 Coleman Report found that the 'family resources' children brought to school affected their rates of learning more than the resources at the school itself. Family relations also continue to affect the distribution of work and its rewards; the high divorce rate in contemporary America simply provides one new basis for doing so. Divorce is the greatest single predictor of poverty for children and their mothers, channeling women and youth into the new areas of low-paid, part-time work that comprise the fastest growing sector of the American economy.[13]

Conceptualizing the Family

As one way of negotiating these analytical difficulties, I suggest that we see the family as the concrete expression of a socially sanctioned *relationship* between social and biological reproduction. It is a social institution that embodies a particular pattern of relationships among individuals as biological and social beings. But it is also an ideological concept through which people express their ideals about how biological and social reproduction ought to be coordinated. The family organizes and legitimizes the differential rights and duties associated with those resources and tasks, as well as providing an arena in which people try to cope with their different positions (gender along with class) in the larger social structure.

For most societies, the term 'family' is not just a description but an explanation and a prescription. The concept of family seems to be a way of organizing or symbolizing certain kinds of group interactions in terms of personal relations, while at the same time it explains and enforces an individual's place in group interactions: 'These things happen between unit A and unit B because a member of unit A is from a certain family'; 'Because she occupies a certain position in a certain family, a member of unit A must behave toward unit B in a particular way.' Families create a group of people who are connected in particular ways to other groups, at the same time and as part of the same process as drawing boundaries between groups. The boundaries may be residential, economic, social, political, or psychological, but they always have to do with defining the rights and obligations of their members, not just toward each other *within* the family, but toward the larger social network. A family system is a tool for channeling people into the prevailing structure of obligations and rights, then attaching the tasks and rewards associated with that structure to a definition of self. The family is the physical and the mental place where we link our personal relationships to our social relationships, our reproductive relations to our productive ones.

Both as an institution and as a conception, the family mediates between people's definitions of themselves as individuals and as members of society. It is one of the main tools we use to understand and define ourselves in relation to the overarching social structure. The family regulates and limits the personal activities of its members while its members simultaneously shape, redirect, even dissolve and reconstruct the family to affect their role in the larger social network. The family is thus 'a terrain of struggle,' both as a social unit, working with or against other groups in society, and as a changing set of personal interactions and conflicts over roles. Since the family is an explanatory and legitimizing device, a symbol system that functions as ideology, as well as a concrete constellation of relationships in the larger socioeconomic universe, its very definition is part of that struggle. That is why the family is always as much a political institution as a personal one.[14]

The family provides people with a way of assigning priorities to interpersonal interactions in the process of producing, consuming, and reproducing the necessities of life. As such, it is the key intermediary unit between the obligations and rights of its individual members and those of other social constructs. 'As a social (and not a natural) construction,' Rapp remarks, 'the family's boundaries are always decomposing and recomposing in continuous interaction with larger domains.'[15] Yet people *conceive of* the family as a natural phenomenon, even where the fiction is blatantly obvious. It is thus a socially sanctioned relationship that explicitly rejects its social origins: a relationship whose legitimacy is attributed to biological and/or supernatural 'facts.'

These 'facts' are used to foster conformity to the roles defined by the relationship: families are presented as somehow prior to any social contract, as biologically natural or supernaturally ordained – a point powerfully reinforced by the prohibition of some sexual interactions within the family and the enforcement or strong support of others. All this works to link one's most intimate personal definitions – indeed, one's very sexuality – to social obligations and expectations. (This is not to say that the link is always harmonious or functional: a person's psychological identity or sexuality may become a victim of those rights or obligations, or a way of rejecting them.) The family is thus the place where we conceptualize ourselves in relation to the social structure, where we link a personal identity to our social identity, even if the family is not always the place where our personal identity is actually forged, and even if the link involves ambivalence or outright conflict.

The family is both a place and an idea. It is above all an *idea*, a 'socially necessary illusion' about why the social division of obligations and rights is natural or just. This idea recruits or channels people into the places where social reproduction takes place. In modern America for example, Rapp argues, families recruit people into households.[16] But the idea of 'Family' is also used to share resources beyond households, to deny resources within households, and to label some households illegitimate agents of social reproduction. And the idea has some material base, for the family is also a *place*, distinct from household, from which people derive particular connections to rights, resources, and duties. It assigns individuals their initial position in the network of social reproduction on the basis of their imputed position in the scheme of biological reproduction, while it simultaneously offers an arena in which people can use changes in their social position to renegotiate their personal relations and biological definition.

The family's biological or supernatural legitimation is always loose enough to admit some personal flexibility into the construction or dissolution of families; thus the link between personal and social relations constitutes a feedback loop. As families assign people their initial place in the social order, so changes in people's place in the social order help them to reconstruct their families, while new family relationships help them to further affect their place in the social order. In some kin corporate societies the emergence of quite small differences in surpluses allowed certain patrilocal lineages to accumulate wives and children, whose labor enabled household heads to do the feasting and gift-giving that made them 'big men.' The ability of 'big men' to call in more labor and bride wealth eventually produced sharper socioeconomic stratification and new family arrangements. In modern America, the sons of men who succeeded in their careers partly through the unpaid work of their wives have discovered that the ability to avoid or shed a wife can sometimes greatly increase their financial solvency.

If these considerations have any merit, several conclusions must be drawn by family historians. First, the study of families must always be linked to a study of the whole mode of production of any given society. We should start 'by identifying the important productive, ritual, political, and exchange transactions in a society and only then . . . ask what kinds of kinship or locality-based units engage in these activities.' We must link family changes to transformations in the mode of production and 'social reproduction,' including struggles over political ideologies and religious values. Michael Anderson suggests 'that the student of family history must spend as much time exploring the wider culture and economy of a society as he or she spends investigating its familial behavior.'17

Second, we must understand there is no such thing as 'the' family in any given society. Different subgroups, with different positions in the larger network of social relations, will construct and sanction different kinds of families. Families must be studied, then, in their historical, sociological, cultural, and psychological specificity. Yet because families are socially sanctioned, we cannot dissolve family history into the histories of multitudinous separate families. There is an ideal family type, generally codified in law and religion, and a normative prescription for how individuals should relate within the family. We need to study the interaction between the ideal and the reality, between the pressures of the dominant social institutions or classes and the needs of different subgroups in society. The slave family was not a simple imitation of the slave owner's family nor a helpless victim of the traffic in human beings. Neither, however, was it a self-actuated creation free from the constraints of white owners. Working-class families have preserved special class and ethnic heritages, yet they have also been greatly affected by the economic decisions and ideological pressures of their employers.

The correction to 'history from the top down' is not to deny the impact of the top on the bottom but to admit the two-way nature of the penetration. Slave-owners' families *also* derived from the dialectic of slavery and cannot be understood without reference to the impact of slaves on white relations. Likewise, the organization of bourgeois families in the northern manufacturing centers, the cult of domesticity, and the contradictory tasks assigned to women took shape under the constraints of a society where entrepreneurs and upwardly mobile middle-class families were outnumbered by workers whom they wished to socialize and control yet from whom they also needed to insulate themselves.18

Third, defining the family as a socially sanctioned relationship between social and biological reproduction suggests that the key to understanding any family lies not in its size or structure, but in its articulation and interaction with both the larger social network and the changing roles or demands of its individual members. Household structure, family composition, and demography are useful pieces of data but on their own allow us to draw few significant conclusions about family life. More potentially productive is the study of the life cycle or life course, as proposed by Glen Elder, Tamara Hareven and others, which examines the 'intersection' between individual life histories, family needs, and historical forces. Even this approach, however, tends to conceptualize family needs and historical forces as essentially separate phenomena. The concept of intersecting trajectories or 'linkages' between parts of society reflects a functionalist model of society in which separate things arise independently and then get selected to 'fit' in ways that make the system work. What we really need to do is approach families as organic parts of a total yet ever-changing network of social interactions in which equilibrium is never achieved.[19]

Our analytical tolerance of disequilibrium must also be extended to the internal life of the family. Since the family is a social construct through which individuals are assigned to – or resist assignment to – their position in the larger social network, we need to examine the struggle *within* families over roles, resources, power and autonomy.[20] Because the family's assignments are made on the basis of imputed biological and sexual criteria, we need to pay greater attention to the link between the organization of production and consumption in society at large and the struggles within families over sexuality, reproduction, and gender roles. In Western history the ideology of family has long included a special association of women with domestic affairs. But because this association obscures a wide range of actual behavior, we need to pay particular attention to the impact of different family arrangements on women in their various familial and nonfamilial roles.

Fourth, we should avoid the temptation to label the family as a dependent or independent variable, as a malleable object acted upon by grand historical forces or an amazingly resilient institution that organizes itself to deflect the impact of social change, allowing its members to carve out their own culture. The family cannot be separated from the total network of social relations: when one changes the other changes, and the seeds of change may derive either from the larger structure or from the dynamics of family life within it.

We can recognize the family's impact on the larger structure, however, without elevating the family into a primary historical force. If the family is a socially sanctioned institution that coordinates biological and social reproduction, it follows that the family plays a fundamentally conservative social role, reproducing differences in the position of various groups *vis-à-vis* the system of production and distribution. This is not to say that the family cannot conserve values that challenge the dominant ones in society. Joseph Demartini has found that student activists of the early 1960s were not rebelling against their parents so much as extending or acting on shared values passed down to them by their parents.[21] Ironically, the importance of family values in shaping student activism in this period may well have stemmed from the family's conservative role, for families were probably the one place of refuge for traditions of liberalism and resistance stifled in the 1950s.

To stress the conservative nature of families is also not to say that any individual family does not try to change or resist its position in the system. In order to do so effectively, however, the family normally mobilizes its members to take maximum advantage of their particular relationship to the means of production, which means perpetuating the system even while attempting to change its own place in it. A working-class family trying to earn enough money to buy a farm is not undermining the system of wage labor from which it is trying to escape: quite the contrary. The ghetto kin networks that pool and circulate resources are adapting rationally and effectively to the necessities of a poverty that stems from social rather than family pathologies, but they also hold back any particular individual who might threaten social solidarity for such 'selfish' ends as going on in school. The same family that is an effective locus of resistance to ethnic or class oppression may achieve this by the ruthless suppression of the desires of its individual members, as so many immigrant girls, pulled out of school to work for the family, could testify. Indeed, the role of the family in 'taking up the slack' during hard times, by increasing unpaid work at home to save money, suggests that the very strength of the family for working-class survival is its ability to fall back on the self-exploitation of its members.[22]

In focusing attention on the different ways that families are embedded in the specific social relations of society, we may be able to avoid grand historical pronouncements about the relationship of family history to industrialization or 'modernization.' Thus we can examine how the social relations of an emerging market economy interacted with the ideology of the American Revolution and the demography of the middle class to produce the domestic family, without concluding that the private family with the woman at its domestic center is an inevitable component of any industrialization process. Nor need we postulate unilinear theories of social change whereby some grand historical family transformation begins in one sector of society and trickles down or seeps up to the rest. For the 'modernization' of one sector, at least in a competitive economy or polity, often involves the devolution of another (as with the expansion of non-industrial work for women and the rise of illiteracy during the Industrial Revolution), while the same forces that impel one class to restrict its household size and family interactions may stimulate another to expand its household or extend contacts with kin.[23]

Bearing these considerations in mind, let us turn to a brief examination of some recent studies in Western family history. In tracing the historical evolution of Western families, historians have traditionally focused on two aspects of family life – structures and values – that entail different sources and different questions and, not surprisingly, often yield different answers. Discussing their findings, I will focus on the English case, since it is the evolution of English family forms that provides the most direct backdrop to the institutions and ideas brought to America by the dominant group of colonizers.

Western Family Structures

From the relative silence of traditional European literary sources about the nuclear family, historians and sociologists once posited a shift from extended to nuclear families in American and European history. Their writing produced a widespread impression that the nuclear family was a modern development, a product of industrialization, and that preindustrial populations lived in large extended families. During the 1960s, however, the Cambridge Group for the History of Population and Social Structure, under the leadership of Peter Laslett, carefully quantified all available parish records in England since the sixteenth century. They found that, from the sixteenth through the nineteenth centuries, mean household size remained fairly constant at about 4.75, and that even the larger households contained relatively few kin, servants being the main variable in size differences. After examining other European and Asian countries as well, the researchers concluded: 'It is simply untrue, as far as we can yet tell, that there was ever a time or place when the complex family was the universal background to the ordinary lives of ordinary people.' Even more devastating to the idea that the nuclear family was a result of industrialization was the finding that the proportion of extended families actually *increased* in industrial towns during the mid nineteenth century.[24]

The belief that there has been a historical evolution from an extended to a nuclear family would seem false, but one should not infer from this that family structure is historically invariant. Lutz Berkner, for example, has pointed out that the statistical predominance of nuclear families in any given census, or group of censuses, may conceal a developmental cycle such as that of the patrilocal stem family, common in many peasant societies, in which a young couple marry and spend their early life together in an extended family, living with the man's parents. When the man's parents die, the couple succeed to the house and spend their middle years in a nuclear family, but when one of their sons marries and brings his wife into the household the family becomes extended again. A substantial majority of households may be nuclear at any given time, but nearly all of them will nonetheless pass through an extended stage. Although Berkner did not claim that preindustrial England had a stem family system, he certainly threw doubt on the universality of the nuclear family in European history.[25]

Other authors have pointed to the frequency of patrilocal joint families – involving co-residence of married brothers and their families – in parts of Western Europe prior to 1550 and in Eastern Europe into the nineteenth century. Nuclear families accounted for only about 50 per cent of the households in Southern France during the late seventeenth and early eighteenth centuries, though they were overwhelmingly preponderant in Northern France at the same time. In some serf settlements in Great Russia, extended and multiple families predominated during the late 1800s and early 1900s. David Herlihy argues that in the ancient Mediterranean world households and families 'differed so widely from each other that they could not be encompassed in a single system of social analysis, or utilized as a useful unit of social measurement.' In light of these facts – to say nothing of evidence that many prehistoric Europeans lived in extended families – Laslett has modified his early contention that 'the human family, if not necessarily the household, must always have been small and almost always nuclear.' He now merely calls attention to 'the extent to which the single family household prevails in England, the Low Countries, and northern France,' and has since the sixteenth century.[26]

We should not, however, exaggerate the early 'modernity' of these families. As Jean-Louis Flandrin has commented, averaging households obscures the specific preindustrial pattern of 'dominant large households and dependent small ones.' Laslett's original essay admitted that 'a majority of all persons lived in the larger households in traditional England, those above six persons in size, in spite of the fact that only a third of all households were in this category and that the overall MHS [mean household size] was less than five.' We should also note that Laslett excluded lodgers from the computation of household size, while conceding that their numbers certainly exceeded those of resident kinfolk 'and may have been of the same order as servants.' In light of these considerations we must conclude that seventeenth-century English families were far from 'modern,' despite some quantitative similarities: The poor lived in truncated families, often without even their very young children; the richer elements – and many of the younger lower classes who worked as servants – lived in large households where few distinctions were made between the biological family and the rest of the residents.[27]

From 1650 to 1749 there was a decline in the number of servants in the average English household but a rise in the number of kin, especially offspring. From 1749 to 1821 this trend continued, with a sharper fall in the number of servants. By 1851, however, the incidence of lodging had increased (though the increase was entirely accounted for by the urban areas rather than a change in rural areas). After the 1850s there was a sharp drop-off in both lodgers and number of offspring, resulting in substantially smaller households. In 1947 (an atypical year, however, due to the postwar housing shortage), the co-resident kin group, beyond the nuclear unit, was actually larger than in any of the earlier periods.[28]

These trends impeach the view that England moved from an extended to a nuclear family system. Looked at in one way, however, they do testify to an increased emphasis on the nuclear family. The move from servants to lodgers, who were less likely to be involved in daily family activities, can be combined with data about changes in morality, architecture, and etiquette to suggest a tendency for the nuclear family to close ranks and seek more privacy. And it is worth noting that by 1947, even though the *number* of co-resident kin was greater, the *range* of kin represented in households had narrowed to immediate relatives, from the previous situation in which the wider kin group was more proportionally represented when kin *were* present.[29]

It is difficult to tell whether changes in family structure over time represent a change in family forms among all classes, a change in the distribution of classes (giving greater statistical prominence to groups that might have displayed the same family characteristics in the earlier period), or a switching around of family strategies within a shifting class and regional configuration. In their most recent work, the Cambridge Group identify four general family patterns, which they associate with different regions of Europe: the West, West/central or middle, Mediterranean, and East. The Western pattern involves neolocalism (establishment of a new household upon marriage), households centered on a single family (with extra labor needs met by adding servants or apprentices rather than kin), and a marriage pattern first described by Hajnal in 1965: late marriage and a high proportion of the population never marrying at all. This Western form is closely associated with a high degree of independence in the way that a household head can dispose of land, labor, or other resources and, especially in England, with the relatively weak 'concept of a family plot or even a family house.'[30]

Yet Laslett reports that households of laborers, in *all* the regions surveyed by the Cambridge Group, 'have to be placed under the heading "west" in most relevant particulars,' while in 'every reproductive demographic particular . . . they were inclined to conform to the English model.' This suggests the possibility that some changes in a society's 'family system' may actually be changes in its class system – or in the class origins of the sources we have available. Renate Bridenthal points out that our sources for family life in places such as preindustrial Europe are those left by the literate upper classes, about themselves, whereas in twentieth-century America we have almost no information on the very rich but reams of statistics kept by the middle class on sections of the working class and the poor. Alternatively, however, the same class may employ different family strategies as its relation with other classes, the ecology, or the state changes. Thus R.M. Smith has found that in the thirteenth century, middling villagers had more interdependent and frequent relations with kin and neighbors than did the richest and poorest members of the village, whereas in the twentieth century the middle class has tended to have fewer such relations than the rich or the poor.[31]

It is also difficult to make unilinear statements about the direction of change. David Herlihy has found, for example, that among the upper classes of Italy a *more* extended family evolved in the eleventh and twelfth centuries, a time when some other families were contracting to a supposedly more 'modern' form. A recent study of French wine growers found that the number of extended households in Cruzy increased between 1836 and 1866. After the 1880s there was a 'renuclearization' of the household among the lower classes but this allowed the landowning classes to sustain a further increase in complex households, as they were then better able to mobilize the labor of their lower-class neighbors. Household composition in industrial English and American towns also grew more complex at the very time that socially dominant views of the ideal family stressed its increasingly nuclear character.[32]

Western Family Structures and Productive Relations

Changes in family and household forms are the result of an extremely complex commingling of class dynamics, ecological imperatives, cultural heritage, economic factors, and political relations. Certain broad generalizations can be made about some associations between socioeconomic conditions and family structure. As we shall see below, however, similar structures may have very different meanings for both the individual and the social network, depending upon a host of other factors.

In general, large, stable, co-residential extended families tend to be found where the supply of labor is inelastic and where collective work groups and mutual aid are required in diversified production and distribution. These families may take matrilocal or patrilocal forms, depending upon the sexual division of labor and the advantages of concentrating related males or females in the organization of production.

The forces of production and distribution, the supply of resources, and the concept of territory must be developed enough to support the exploitation of a given area by a relatively large and immobile group that holds a special association with the place or the resources due to descent from a common ancestor. Yet these factors must not be so developed as to offer opportunities and incentive for the conjugal family to exploit them independently or in competition with the rest of the group, or for the family head to alienate the property. Under such circumstances there is every reason for each smaller unit within the extended family to contribute labor or goods to the common store. Such families, then, are most likely to occur as a dominant social type among pre-state and non-market societies where there is corporate control of land or other resources, where land or resources are relatively plentiful, and where there are few pressures to increase productivity. A number of authors have documented an association of co-residential extended families with widely scattered resources or tasks, when the corporate group requires simultaneous labor in many different places or at a variety of tasks. So long as such labor cannot be mobilized through slavery or wage-work, extended family households are the most effective way of allowing the group to engage in complex, simultaneous tasks.[33]

Extended family households may, however, also be found in certain classes or regions of societies with more developed market and state systems where self-generation of labor or capital allows a group to carve out a specialized niche in the mode of production. Elites may be able to protect themselves from rivals connected to a state apparatus by using extended family ties to make political and military alliances; hence the protracted conflict between aristocratic kin groups and monarchs in medieval Europe. Where institutional sources of security and finance are not available, emerging economic groups, such as the medieval merchants of Genoa, can use complex households as a base for developing early forms of diversified trade and manufactures. When income opportunities are irregular but frequent, or uniformly if only occasionally distributed, multiple-family households seem to maximize the possibilities for achieving income and redistributing resources. Such households are frequently found in areas where people exist by a combination of wage-earning and household production. The availability of waged work for some household members combines with the benefits of pooling labor for domestic production to make such arrangements possible; the instability and low wages of the work make them necessary. Thus there seems to be a pattern in which multiple-family households appear in periods of transition from subsistence production to wage-labor, helping people to cope with the uneven and combined development of market and household production. Multiple-family households also seem to have represented an effective form of survival for eighteenth-century Eastern European serfs after the reimposition of servile restrictions in response to agricultural demand from Western Europe. When household production is not a possibility, extended families among the poor may not have the resources for co-residence but may nevertheless rely on pooling networks outside the household.[34]

Joint patrilocal families, with several brothers and their spouses residing together, were common in parts of Italy and France before 1550, as well as in many Eastern European communities up to the nineteenth century. Where output could be increased considerably by adding land, animals, and other investments to an already existing productive unit, the joint family served to concentrate and mobilize the labor of male members. Joint families have been found frequently along frontiers, either internal or external, in areas of extensive plow cultivation where land is more available then labor, and in newly developed commercial sectors where no institutional means of drawing on new capital and labor supplies yet exist.[35]

But the same possibilities of expanding output that call this form into existence also introduce constant strains into the relationship and put an upper limit on the number of conjugal families that will reside together. Robert Wheaton has pointed out that unless there is 'a general equality between the resources of the individual nuclear components' of this family, the wealthier unit or units will have an incentive to secede. In other words, this family type normally thrives only as long as there is a relatively predictable economic situation in which rapid changes in fortune are unlikely for the separate conjugal units involved in the joint family.[36]

Given an abundance of non-family labor or capital, but only a fixed amount of land, the joint family appears less frequently. The same classes that utilize the joint family in the situation described above may in these circumstances prefer the stem family, to prevent the dispersal of land. 'Arranged in order to select and establish a favored heir,' the stem family serves 'the interests of the rather narrow vertical lineage formed by attaching one younger couple to the patriarch's household, while discarding or disfavoring the other offspring.'[37]

The nuclear family has tended to emerge as the residential norm whenever economic or political conditions have encouraged or necessitated production and distribution by relatively smaller groups. 'Small households,' comment Wilk and Rathje, 'have the advantage of mobility, and are well adapted to make intensive use of limited resources through linear scheduling of labor.' Stephen Weinberger has found that in medieval Provence, as peasants gained more control over their land so that individual activity yielded more variable returns, they tended to dissociate themselves from the extended family, which had a high degree of solidarity but lacked flexibility in responding to rapid changes in economic opportunities. The nuclear family is linked to individualistic economic pursuits, especially where accumulation and investment are necessary for economic advancement but the productive process does not require large amounts of capital. It is also found where relatively stable employment consistently favors one category of household member, such as men.[38] States have tended to favor nuclear family households, both for economic reasons (taxation and labor mobilization) and political ones (the greater ease of controlling an individual family unit as opposed to a united extended family).

In Western Europe, the nuclear-family household was historically associated with a high degree of independence for the household head and the connected possibility of rapid economic mobility, either upward or downward. Laslett's figures show that a household head in the West could often be described as a pauper, whereas this was 'never' true in the Mediterranean and Eastern cases, where households were property-owning corporations: 'The family plot in England was to a surprising extent disposable by the man who had control of it.' Alan Macfarlane comments that 'one of the peculiarities of England from at least the thirteenth century [was] that parents could . . . disinherit their children.' The weakness of corporate control, of course, both contributed to and was accelerated by the early development of commerce and wage-labor in England.[39]

It will be noted that these generalizations are hedged with qualifications and restrictions, for bald statements about the necessary association between any mode of production and a particular family structure are suspect. This is true, first, because 'a particular productive enterprise can be accomplished by a variety of productive units,' depending on the technical organization of production, the social and economic relations under which it is conducted, and the political, legal, and ideological systems that have evolved in a culture.[40] Second, any particular mode of production, especially one based on class differences, will produce a number of *different* household structures, whose necessary relationship to the mode of production derives not from their internal forms but from their articulation with each other. Thus the extended households of wealthy families, from sixteenth-century English estates to nineteenth-century Cheyenne Indians and Languedoc winegrowers, could not exist without the small households of poor families.

Used cautiously, however, studies of the relation between productive activities and household structure are certainly a starting point. Recent work on fertility rates reveals the value of such investigation. Traditionally, preindustrial populations were thought to have maintained themselves by balancing high, though fluctuating, death rates with high and fairly constant birth rates. Population growth, in this analysis, occurred when death rates fell and birth rates continued at the previous high level. This was said to explain the population explosion associated with the initial stages of the Industrial Revolution, while the drop in family size in the nineteenth century was thought to result when modern contraception finally allowed birth rates to adjust to low mortality rates.

It now appears, however, that preindustrial birth rates were extraordinarily flexible, ranging from a high of 55 to 60 per 1,000 in eighteenth-century America to a low of 15 per 1,000 in Iceland in the first decade of that century. A fall in the death rate often led to exceedingly rapid homeostatic adjustments in the birth rate, as happened in eighteenth-century France. Where population growth did occur elsewhere in Western Europe, it was achieved by an *increase* in the birth rate as well as a decline in the death rate. In some areas the death rate actually *rose*, so that population growth was wholly attributable to a rising birth rate. Furthermore, the nineteenth-century fall in the birth rate began *before* the spread of modern contraceptive techniques. It therefore seems more logical to connect changes in the rate of population growth to social conditions rather than to death rates or birth control alone.[41]

In England, according to the most recent reconstruction of national demographic trends, population grew from the mid sixteenth to the mid seventeenth century, and then fell off, not regaining its mid-seventeenth-century peak until the early eighteenth century. The primary factor affecting population growth was variation in patterns of marriage formation. The authors argue that marriage formation rates were in turn responsive to changes in the real wage, though only after a significant delay and only prior to the mid-nineteenth century. Their data are valuable in showing the mutual impact of economic trends and family strategies in the preindustrial world, but it may well understate the responsiveness of personal reproduction to changes in social production. Wrigley and Schofield reject the theory that demand for labor affects population rates, except in the very long run, because they define that demand as the aggregate need for labor in society as a whole and fail to find any harmonious regulation between the aggregate demand for labor and marriage or fertility rates.[42]

But the impact of changes in the social demand for labor on personal reproduction rates has to be considered in light of the family's mediating role between them. Under some circumstances the family may experience a national decrease in demand for labor as an *increase* in its own demand, lower wages for the individual worker making it necessary to have more workers per family. Thus there is no necessary contradiction in the fact that the fall in real wages in the late sixteenth century, and possibly in the eighteenth century too, was accompanied by a fall in the age of marriage and a rise in fertility. Much depends on the qualitative demand for labor, which determines what it will cost the family to produce new workers, as well as the quantitative demand. If a fall in aggregate demand for labor is accompanied by a fall in the cost of producing labor, early marriage and high fertility are an understandable response. Conversely, the rise in the age of marriage in the nineteenth century may have been associated with the shift into occupations requiring longer and more expensive periods of training.[43]

David Levine's detailed study of four English villages in the seventeenth and eighteenth centuries demonstrates that different fertility rates among villages, and occupational variations in fertility within villages, can be explained by changes in both the type and the total amount of labor required within different occupations. As eighteenth-century economic developments increased the number of families dependent upon commodity production (both in the industrializing areas and in the centers of rural protoindustrialization), the relationship between people's work and their demography changed. Traditional incentives to delay marriage disappeared, while at the same time children increasingly became an economic asset to their families: in the protoindustrial economy they were a main source of labor for the family enterprise and in the wage economy they could be put out to work early, often reaching their peak earning capacity by the end of their teens. During the Industrial Revolution fertility increased rapidly in industrial centers where there was a high demand for unskilled labor, and even more rapidly in agricultural sectors producing for the urban market or areas of handicraft production supplying industrial centers. These non-mechanized sectors of the economy could respond to the increased demand (and the increased competition) only by increasing labor inputs at the family level.[44]

A high-fertility demographic strategy, of course, involved tremendous risks for protoindustrial and early industrial households, as an economic slump could catch them with more dependants than workers. A rational population strategy for one family, moreover, might exacerbate unemployment in the class as a whole: having numerous children was nevertheless the surest way to maximize the family's productive capacity. Mahmood Mamdani has reported a similar dynamic in population growth in twentieth-century India, and other studies confirm the basic rationality of dependent classes or countries adopting a high-fertility strategy, despite its long-range ecological effects. Only with growing complexity in the job market, a rising wage rate for the household head, and the increasing cost of producing labor as openings occur in more skilled occupations does it make sense for lower-class families to curtail their fertility.[45]

In America, rapid population growth in the seventeenth and eighteenth centuries was clearly connected to demand for labor. Growth rates were greatest in those areas just behind the frontier – still so sparsely settled that land was available, undeveloped enough that the primary labor requirements were for labor that did not entail a long period of non-productive training, but developed enough to be able to market any surplus resulting from more labor inputs. In the nineteenth century, massive immigration filled US labor needs and native fertility declined, following a substitution effect also evident in the eighteenth-century South, where the smallest white families were found in those regions with the largest number of slaves per household. But Richard Easterlin has demonstrated that variations in immigration rates were themselves dependent on changes in the demand for labor.[46]

The Limits of Structural and Demographic Analysis

Although it is important to compare demographic trends and household structures and seek their economic correlates, such procedures yield only limited information about the history of families. Olga Linares points out: 'Qualitative changes in the meaning of interpersonal obligations may be as important in distinguishing among household types as more easily measured changes in size and form.' Indeed, as Barrington Moore Jr has commented, tabulating structural differences 'necessarily involves ignoring all differences except the one being measured.' Changes in social relations and patterns are not 'reducible to any quantitative differences; they are incommensurable. Yet it is precisely such differences that matter most to human beings.'[47]

Similar forms, for example, can encompass very different interpersonal and social relationships. As Hans Medick notes, a woman may have lived with her grandchildren in some nineteenth-century proletarian houses as well as in rural peasant ones, but it made a considerable difference whether this was the home of her own married life, inherited by her children, or the home that her son or daughter had set up upon marriage and to which she moved after her husband's death left her destitute: 'The "extended family" of the proletariat primarily functioned as a private institution to redistribute the poverty of the nuclear family by way of the kinship system. The extended family of the peasant, on the other hand, served as an instrument for the conservation of property' and as a social institution for the care of the elderly. Similarly, modern marriage and divorce practices may remind one of the easily dissolved pairing units of band-level societies, but they play a different social role and have different personal consequences. For one thing, the immediate result of divorce in contemporary America, where a divorced woman experiences a 74 per cent drop in her income while a man's income goes up by 49 per cent, has no analogue in band-level society, where a man generally needs a wife more than a woman needs a husband.[48]

Changes in Family Relationships in English History: The Heritage of Colonial Families

The reduction of family history to those aspects of family life that can be counted and made commensurable, then, gives us a woefully incomplete picture of our past. Reconstructing the past emotional life of the family is essential; it is also an exceptionally tricky enterprise. Many authors, for example, have argued that seventeenth-century families in England and America were characterized by instrumental rather than affective bonds and that the history of the family since has been one of growing affection, intimacy, and egalitarianism. Possibly the strongest statement of this view has been made by Edward Shorter, who attributes the liberation of family life to lower-class rebellion against repressive sexual and sentimental mores during the Industrial Revolution. This rebellion spread throughout the classes, transforming traditional courtship into romantic love and creating steady improvement in the treatment of children. Unfortunately, Shorter's evidence for sexual liberation – new employment for working-class women and a rising illegitimacy rate – can better be read as the breakdown of some traditional securities, while most historians place the 'discovery of childhood' in the middle or upper classes and find that its results were mixed, leading initially to an increase in severity and proceeding to more permissive attitudes that were reversed in the nineteenth century.[49]

A more sophisticated discussion of the evolution of family emotions is provided by Lawrence Stone, who is well aware of class variations in the experience of family and takes note of exceptions or reverses in the trends he proposes. Yet Stone's uncritical use of upper-class sources and his assumptions about the psychological necessity for a particular kind of family life lead him to paint an overly harsh picture of preindustrial personal relations. Family relations before the mid seventeenth century, Stone suggests, 'contributed to a "psychic numbing" which created many adults whose primary responses to others were at best a calculating indifference and at worst a mixture of suspicion and hostility, tyranny and submission, alienation and rage.' The result was that the 'Elizabethan village was a place filled with malice and hatred, its only unifying bond being the occasional episode of mass hysteria, which temporarily bound together the majority in order to harry and prosecute the local witch.'[50]

There are a number of problems with this picture of the European families in which the first American explorers and colonists were raised. As E.P. Thompson and Alan Macfarlane have pointed out, many of Stone's generalizations about the supposedly brutish family life of the preindustrial poor 'reproduce, with comical accuracy, the ideology and sensibility of eighteenth century upper class paternalism.' But even the upper classes are not treated well by a method that deduces states of feelings from entries in account books and uses sensational press accounts and court cases, by definition atypical, to establish the brutality of every-day human relations. In painting a picture of cold familial relations, Stone frequently interprets 'lack of evidence as indicative of lack of feeling,' as well as actually distorting the record: Macfarlane complains that his own study of a seventeenth-century clergyman's reaction to a child's death cited by Stone as evidence of parental indifference, actually reveals 'a controlled sadness . . . far from a "cold-blooded" lack of feeling.'[51] In arguing that intimate relations between spouses were an eighteenth-century development, Stone has to ignore a whole tradition of English love poetry going back to Chaucer's fourteenth-century 'Franklin's Tale.'

It is true, of course, that many – if not most – literate households in preindustrial England held different values about parental relations to children and about the importance of romantic love between spouses than Americans do today but this did not necessarily have a negative impact on other emotional relationships. 'The Wanderer,' an anonymous Anglo-Saxon poem of the eleventh century, reveals the loneliness and despair of a man bereft of a loved one. The emotions expressed in 'The Wanderer' are no less real, intense, or indicative of sensitive interpersonal relations because they are addressed to the loss of a lord and 'gold-giver' than if they had been occasioned by the loss of a wife or child. In many primitive societies, and also among many communities in early medieval Europe, intensity of feeling between parents and children or between marriage partners has been seen as a threat to larger solidarity groups, and a kind of ritualized sexual or age-group hostility has served to cement loyalty to kin groups and peers. Early Christian writers such as St. Augustine feared the selfish effects of a narrow sexual union and advocated celibacy as a means to creating a wider community of love. Indeed, there is some evidence that in both Europe and America the turn toward a more emotionally nurturing family life was associated with a turn *away* from community sociability or wider same-sex friendships.[52]

Obviously, the evaluation of past generations' states of mind is fraught with difficulties, and it would behoove us to avoid value judgments that may simply reflect our inability to understand the richness and complexity of different emotional patterns. Hans Medick and David Sabean point out that different groups use varying linguistic conventions that often mask the actual mix of instrumental and affective motives in their behavior. Peasant and working-class patterns of communication, for example, constructed to reinforce social categories and solidarities, may disguise affective, individualized emotions in the language of custom, interest, and obligation. As Basil Bernstein has observed, 'tender feelings which are personal and highly individual will not only be difficult to express in this linguistic form' but will also be translated into 'tough terms' that help contain the fear of 'social isolation' that such feelings may evoke. In contrast, middle-class individuals tend to fear social solidarities and deny the strength of social categories, so their language creates the illusion that all relationships are personal, voluntary, and individualized. In the middle class, 'claims to rights and the demands that obligations be fulfilled, property relations, material production, and instrumentality' are 'mediated through a language intent on expressing relationships in a context of individuality' and on denying the existence of material interests.[53]

When instrumental considerations do prevail in a family, this still does not tell us much about the quality of family life. Louise Tilly has used individual case histories to show that family strategies based on instrumental calculation and even on child-sacrificing work practices could be extremely loving *or* extremely brutal, while we also know that marriages based on love and altruism can lead to bitter disillusion and violence. As E.P. Thompson has commented, 'for the vast majority throughout history, familial relations have been intermeshed with the structures of work. Feeling may be *more*, rather than less, tender or intense *because* relations are "economic" and critical to mutual survival.'[54]

Even the frequent abandonment of children in preindustrial populations is not always evidence for lack of parental feeling. John Boswell points out that abandonment of children in the ancient or medieval world did not necessarily lead to their deaths, but was a 'putting out' or 'offering' of a child that was an *alternative* to infanticide. In the Middle Ages the church regulated and facilitated the practice of abandonment through such customs as oblation, the donation of a child to a monastery, while many other 'abandoned' children were probably raised as servants among nearby neighbors. Olwen Hufton has shown that abandonment often represented the only chance of survival for illegitimate children in eighteenth-century France. Many parents tried to keep track of – and sometimes to reclaim – their abandoned children, suggesting that the practice reflected social need rather than lack of love. As for the giving-up of children to other households in sixteenth- and seventeenth-century England, this was less a sign of social alienation than a means to establish 'a dense and overlapping network of association' based on solidarity as well as deference.[55]

Certainly, Tudor and Stuart England did witness a striking amount of human misery and social conflict, expressed in neglect of the infirm, emergence of a criminal underworld in the cities, brutal treatment of beggars and vagrants, and outbreaks of witchcraft accusations. But these problems are best comprehended as consequences of economic, social, and demographic disruptions: enclosures, price inflation, rack-renting, dissolution of the monasteries and dispersion of bands of medieval retainers, the growing absolutism of monarchical government, and the destruction of older social networks and interpersonal patterns. Real wages plummeted during the sixteenth and early seventeenth centuries, while life expectancies fell during most of the seventeenth century. Stone himself points out that 'between 1560 and 1620 there was an abrupt rise in a wide variety of indicators of social "anomy" and a breakdown of consensual community methods of dealing with conflict.' This was 'probably brought on by a combination of socially unmanageable demographic growth, a collapse of cultural norms and controls in the wake of the Reformation, the spread of a profit-oriented ideology, and a growing economic fissure between rich and poor,' as well as the demobilization of unemployed soldiers.[56]

It seems plausible to argue that the brutal family incidents Stone cites in *The Family, Sex and Marriage* were more products than cause of these social conditions and that the self-consciously affective family developed as a refuge from these tensions for those fortunate enough to be free of the worst poverty. To say that affectionate families helped to compensate for the conflicts engendered by class stratification is entirely different from suggesting that the family based on affective individualism is the only source of human sociability, cooperation, and happiness.

Both Christopher Lasch and Richard Sennett question whether the evolution of affective individualism has been such a boon to society or families, and each analyzes that evolution differently. Lasch suggests that the trend toward egalitarian relations – Stone's 'affective individualism' – is a twentieth-century development that has had adverse effects on family life. It has destroyed the productive intensity of the nineteenth-century family, which forced young people to develop a superego by working through the Oedipus complex in conflict with a strong father. His view derives from his definition of the nuclear family as the primary unit of socialization, coupled with his assumption that the only route to personal autonomy is through resolution of the Oedipus complex. Richard Sennett, on the other hand, sees the nineteenth-century family as having many characteristics of affective individualism – a growing role for the mother, intense involvement in child-rearing, and so on – but he labels this family dysfunctional, its inherent conservatism interfering with members' social mobility, its role as refuge from the city leading to an erosion of paternal authority, and its intensity threatening 'to destroy the emotional power and the dignity of the people whom it sheltered.'[57]

Both these authors, however, base their assessments on the assumption that an effective family requires a strong father figure. Often ignored in such debates is the experience of minorities and women. Many non-Western cultures and national minorities within Western cultures have created autonomous individuals and workable communities without either the companionate individualism, the sharp Oedipal struggles, or the strong father figures supposedly fostered in various Western families.[58]

Lasch's nostalgia for the benefits of nineteenth-century struggles against the father ignores the effect of the patriarchal family on wives and female children. Indeed, his work implies that the main point of families is to provide for the emotional development of male children, the only ones whose superegos can be sharpened by confrontation with a father/rival. But the celebrants of affective individualism also sometimes neglect the experiences of women within the family. While Stone and Degler are correct to stress that the rights of English and American women within marriage have increased steadily since the eighteenth century, this should not blind us to some of the losses that working women experienced in the same period, nor to the increased emotional dependency and personal isolation that accompanied the new concept of family life even for middle-class women. Barbara Ehrenreich and Deirdre English have further suggested that the triumph of liberal capitalism replaced older patriarchal ideology with a 'masculinist' world-view that did little to liberate women: it substituted a 'scientific' or 'rational' denigration of womanhood for the personal oppression of women within the household, making women not 'inferiors' but 'aliens.'[59]

One attempt to describe changes in family relations without reducing the complexities of class, gender, and region to a single generalization is that of Louise Tilly and Joan Scott, who identify three stages of the family economy in Europe: the preindustrial economy of household production; the wage economy, relying on wages of children to supplement those of the male household head; and the consumer economy, in which parent–child relations focus on reproduction and consumption rather than wages, wives work, and children are kept out of the marketplace. They do not, however, extrapolate linear trends in either work or emotion as consequences of this evolution. They point out, for example, that the initial impact of industrialization had different results for women workers, depending on the type of industry. Textile centers tended to pull women out of the home; mining or metal centers often saw a reduction in women's non-domestic work.[60]

This model is also broadly descriptive of changes in American families. However, it is important to avoid false dichotomies between types of families and to take full account of the coexistence and interdependence of different family types. The family economy of small masters, which used servants and apprentices to supplement the family workforce, was not a stage prior to wage-work but depended upon a wage economy among poorer villagers. The consumer economy of the middle class and skilled workmen depended initially on the wage economy of immigrant families, who provided domestic servants and cheap piece work, relieving the middle-class wife from much former domestic production. Even today, affluent two-earner 'consumer' families re-create wage economy families elsewhere, as growing numbers of youth go to work in fast-food industries that such 'consumer' families sustain and live at home for a longer period of time. Internationally, Immanuel Wallerstein, William Martin, and Torry Dickinson point out that the family consumer economy in the modern industrial core depends upon a worldwide economy in which a majority of households do *not* receive most of their income from wages. They suggest that the 'commodification' of labor power in families of the core zone rests upon the reproduction of non-commodity households on the periphery (or even, I would add, among the poorest households within the core):

> It is in the interests of employers who hire for wages to hire persons who live in households in which the majority of income is *not* from wages. In such cases, the employer can in fact pay wages that are *below* the minimum wage . . . since the employer can count on the household obtaining sufficient income from other sources to compensate for the *below-minimum* wages.[61]

Family Systems in America

The remainder of this book attempts to examine general trends in American family systems without doing violence to the complexity of family forms and contradictory elements present within each system. It is always easier to critique the generalizations of others than to offer one's own, and the heavy reliance of this work on synthesis of secondary sources forces me to anticipate correction as more detailed studies of particular periods emerge. Nevertheless, I suggest that there have been in American history four broad categories of family systems, four family constellations whose shape was determined by a particular articulation of the dominant mode of production with the various classes, regions, and ideologies that comprised it. An ideal family stood at the center of each constellation; but a number of different families always orbited around that ideal. Each family system was part of the larger universe of social reproduction and each brought the genders into characteristic relations, both in and out of the family; but gender relations, like family orbits, varied in different economic and political subgroups.

The first family system in America was that of the native peoples. This was actually a kinship system rather than a family system, for despite the wide variety of residence, marital, and genealogical rules involved in different kin categories, all early Native American cultures subsumed the nuclear family and even the lineage in a much larger network of kin and marital alliances. The second system, established by the European colonists, was a household-family system, in which separate families had property and inheritance rights that set them off from others, but social reproduction was conducted through household and community institutions that did not privilege the family as a place for decision-making or emotional interactions. This system was part of a larger mode of production that found native principles of social organization an intolerable barrier to its expansion, and Native American systems of social reproduction were almost destroyed in the clash between the two, though right up to the present Native Americans have preserved a commitment to extended family and community ties. Ironically, at the same time as colonial society was destroying one kinship system it was importing another, which it also attempted to destroy. African slaves and their descendants, however, strove with considerable success to preserve or re-create kinship networks and obligations.

From about the 1820s a new family system emerged, corresponding to increasing class stratification in the context of weakly developed institutions for reproducing class differences or expressing class interests. This system was characterized by a greatly idealized and abstract notion of the central, almost sacred, place of the sexual division of labor. Despite the fact that women in all classes worked outside the home throughout the period, the system rested on a conceptual separation between female reproductive activities and male productive ones, and is therefore accurately called the domestic family. The domestic family was organized around a clear division of labor between husband and wife and around child-raising strategies that involved explicit socialization to distinct class values and practices. The domestic ideal simultaneously obscured class and ethnic differences in America and testified to the real centrality of families as places where each class or ethnic group reproduced its position and pursued its own goals and interests.

A fourth type of family system emerged in the early 1900s, when the spread of education, mass production, national corporations, political rationalization, and new housing patterns obviated the need for distinctive reproductive strategies and directed attention to patterns of consumption. Now class differences were reproduced by families doing *similar* things. The new family shifted its axis from the parent–child relationship to the couple relationship and put forward the nuclear family unit as a place for qualitatively different relationships than those to be found with kin or friends. It also assumed a different relation to the state, as its privacy came to depend more and more on state support (and, eventually, on the state's invasion of privacy for alternative family forms). I will detail the evolution of this family in a sequel to this book.

Each of these systems entailed a different way of organizing and conceptualizing the rights and obligations of the individual in relation to others in society. Native American kinship systems extended obligations and rights as widely as possible, either through intricate rituals of kinship reciprocity or through supplementary institutions such as ceremonial friendships, games, and hospitality rules. The colonial household system reinforced class obligations and rights through a rigid system of hierarchy. Family relationships were subordinated to the organization of unequal but mutually dependent relationships within that hierarchy, and only at the very top of society could families extricate their own needs and interests from the larger system of deference and patronization. Even then they risked the violent assertion of customary relations over any innovations they might make. The domestic family developed out of the rejection of these hierarchical bonds and obligations. On the one hand it represented new possibilities for personal freedom; on the other it reflected a denial of wider obligations. Reciprocity and duty became gender obligations rather than social or political ones; inevitably, this spawned a re-examination of the gender roles on which the domestic family depended as well as revealing new possibilities for conflict between classes.

Notes

1. Paul Johnson, *A Shopkeeper's Millennium: Society and Revivals in Rochester, New York, 1815–1837* (New York, 1978), p. 43; *The Diary of Samuel Pepys*, H. Wheatlee, ed. (New York, 1946), vol. 2, p. 57; Jean Louis Flandrin, *Families in Former Times* (Cambridge, 1979), pp. 4–17; David Herlihy, 'The Making of the Medieval Family: Symmetry, Structure, and Sentiment,' *Journal of Family History* 8 (1983). On the difficulty of selecting commensurate 'family' units or relations to study, see David Kertzer, 'Anthropology and Family History,' *Journal of Family History* 9 (1984).

2. Kathleen Gough, 'Is the Family Universal: The Nayar Case,' in Bell and Vogel, eds, *A Modern Introduction to the Family* (Glencoe, IL, 1960), pp. 76–92; Evelyn Blackwood, 'Sexuality and Gender in Certain Native American Tribes: The Case of Cross-Gender Females,' *Signs* 10 (1984); Herbert Gutman, *The Black Family in Slavery and Freedom, 1750–1925* (New York, 1976); Carol Stack, *All Our Kin: Strategies for Survival in a Black Community* (New York, 1974); Elliot Liebow, *Tally's Corner* (Boston, 1967).

3. Susan Rogers, 'Woman's Place: A Critical Review of Anthropological Theory,' *Comparative Studies in Society and History* 20 (1982); Lila Leibowitz, *Females, Males, Families: A Biosocial Approach* (North Scituate, MA, 1978), p.8; Russell Middleton,

'Brother-Sister and Father-Daughter Marriage in Ancient Egypt,' in Ruth Laub Coser, ed., *The Family: Its Structures and Functions* (New York, 1974); M.J. Levy and L.A. Fallers, 'The Family: Some Comparative Considerations,' *American Anthropologist* 61 (1959), p. 649.

4. G.P. Murdock, *Social Structure* (New York, 1949), pp. 2–3; Jane Guyer, 'Household and Community in African Studies,' *African Studies Review* 24 (1981); Leibowitz, *Females, Males*, p. 5; Michael Mitterauer, 'Marriage Without Co-Residence: A Special Type of Family Form in Rural Carinthia,' *Journal of Family History* 6 (Summer 1981).

5. Mark Poster, *Critical Theory of the Family* (London, 1978), pp. 143, 155; Ira Reiss, 'The Universality of the Family,' *Journal of Marriage and the Family* 27 (1965); John Boswell, '*Expositio* and *Oblatio*: The Abandonment of Children and the Ancient and Medieval Family,' *American Historical Review* 89 (1984); Olwen Hufton, *The Poor of Eighteenth-Century France* (Oxford, 1974).

6. Donald Bender, 'A Refinement of the Concept of Household: Families, Co-residence, and Domestic Functions,' *American Anthropologist* 69 (1967), pp. 503–4, and 'De Facto Families and De Jure Households in Ondo,' *American Anthropologist* 73 (1973); Sylvia Yanagisako, 'Family and Household: The Analysis of Domestic Groups,' *American Review of Anthropology* 8 (1979), p. 198.

7. 'New Directions,' *Journal of Home Economics* (May l975), p.1.

8. Jane Collier, Michelle Rosaldo, and Sylvia Yanagisako, ' Is There a Family? New Anthropological Views,' in Barrie Thorne with Marilyn Yalom, *Rethinking the Family: Some Feminist Questions* (White Plains, 1982), p. 33.

9. Ibid., p. 28; Leibowitz, *Females, Males*, p.2l.

10. Carl Degler, *At Odds: Women and the Family in America from the Revolution to the Present* (New York, 1981), pp. 472–3.

11. Yanagisako, 'Family and Household,' p. 200.

12. The phrase comes from Kingsley Davis, who modifies Murdock by adding this to reproduction, maintenance, and socialization as universal functions of the family: *Human Society* (New York, 1950), p. 395.

13. Christopher Jencks, *Who Gets Ahead? The Determinants of Economic Success in America* (New York, 1979); James Coleman, 'Towards Open Schools,' *The Public Interest* (Fall 1967); Frederick Mosteller and Daniel Moynihan, eds, *On Equality of Educational Opportunity* (New York, 1972); *Signs*, special issue on 'Women and Poverty,' 10 (1984). For a discussion of the existence of an American ruling elite, entrance to which is based almost exclusively on family background and inheritance, see G. William Domhoff, *Who Rules America?* (Englewood Cliffs, 1967).

14. Rayna Rapp, Ellen Ross, and Renate Bridenthal, 'Examining Family History,' *Feminist Studies* 5 (1979), p.239 and *passim*.

15. Ibid., p. 233.

16. Ibid., p. 177.

17. Yanagisako, 'Family and Household,' pp. 186–7; Renate Bridenthal, 'The Dialectics of Production and Reproduction in History,' *Radical America* 10 (1976); Michael Anderson, 'Family and Class in 19th-Century Cities,' *Journal of Family History* 2 (1977), p. 140.

18. For a discussion of the impact of slavery on white relations see Eugene Genovese, *Roll, Jordan, Roll: The World the Slaves Made* (New York, 1974) and David Brion David's discussion of Hegel's master-slave dialectic in *The Problem of Slavery in the Age of Revolution, 1790–1823* (Ithaca, 1975), pp. 557–564. On pressures from the working class that helped shape the Northern bourgeois family, see Johnson, *Shopkeeper*, pp. 47–55.

19. Glen Elder, Jr., 'Family History and the Life Course,' in Tamara Hareven, ed., *Transitions: The Family and the Life Course in Historical Perspective* (New York, 1978), pp. 17–64. For an example of the use of the 'linkages' concept, see pp. 35–8. The passages seem to imply that the historical experience of each cohort becomes a fixed variable that can be plugged into an analysis, rather than recognizing that historical experience itself is filtered through and subjected to reinterpretation by the ongoing dialectic between individuals and society. See also Tamara Hareven's thoughtful 'Cycles, Courses and Cohorts: Reflections on Theoretical and Methodological Approaches to the History of Family Development,' *Journal of Social History* 12 (1978). On the difficulties with the life-course approach,

including the problems of making commensurable analyses of individual experiences, household experiences, and family experiences, see David Kertzer, 'Future Directions in Historical Household Studies,' *Journal of Family History* 10 (1985).

20. For examples of fruitful, though very different, historical interpretations using this approach, see Daniel Scott Smith, 'Family Limitation, Sexual Control, and Domestic Feminism in Victorian America,' in Nancy Cott and Elizabeth Pleck, eds, *A Heritage of Her Own* (New York, 1979), Laura Owen, 'The Welfare of Women in Laboring Families: England 1860–1950,' *Feminist Studies* 1 (1973), and Heidi Hartman, 'The Family as the Locus of Gender, Class and Political Struggle: The Example of Housework,' *Signs* 6 (1981).

21. Joseph Demartini, 'Change Agents and Generational Relationships: A Reevaluation of Mannheim's Problem of Generations,' *Social Forces* 64 (1985).

22. See, for instance, Leslie Tentler, 'The World of Work for Working Class Daughters, 1900–1930,' in Mel Albin and Dominick Cavallo, *Family Life in America, 1600–2000* (St. James, New York, 1981), pp. 185–202. As Jonathon Prude has put it, the working class family was both 'victimized and resilient, both altered by the conditions in which it lived and capable of helping people cope with those conditions' ('The Family in Context,' *Labor History* 17 [1976], p. 425). 'Helping people cope,' however, is quite literally a conservative role, and the impact of this on wives has been discussed by Ruth Milkman, 'Women's Work and the Economic Crisis,' in Cott and Pleck, *Heritage*, pp. 507–541. Along similar lines, Linda Gordon suggests that the family system has disguised a sharp decline in the standard of living for the working class: the number of work hours per family has risen in the second half of the twentieth century as inflation has lessened the viability of a one-income family (Gordon, *Woman's Body*, p. 412).

23. On the uneven impact of industrialization see E. Anthony Wrigley, 'Reflections on the History of the Family,' in Rossi, Kagan, and Hareven, eds, *The Family* (New York, 1978) and the articles by Richard T. Vann, Mary Lynn McDougall, and Theresa M. McBride in Bridenthal and Koonz, eds, *Becoming Visible: Women in European History* (Boston, 1977). For a good review of the differences over 'the' trends in family history and their originating groups or factors, see Barbara Harris, 'Recent Work on the History of the Family: A Review Article,' *Signs* 4 (1976).

24. Peter Laslett and Richard Wall, eds, *Household and Family in Past Time* (Cambridge, 1972), p. xi; W.A. Armstrong, 'A Note on the Household Structure of Mid-Nineteenth Century York in Comparative Perspective' and Michael Anderson, 'Household Structure and the Industrial Revolution: Mid-Nineteenth-Century Preston in Comparative Perspective,' in Laslett and Wall, *Household and Family*.

25. Lutz Berkner, 'The Stem Family and the Developmental Cycle of the Peasant Household: An Eighteenth Century Austrian Example,' *American Historical Review* 77 (1972).

26. Walter Goldschmidt and Evelyn Kunkel, 'The Structure of the Peasant Family,' *American Anthropologist* 73 (1971); Richard Ring, 'Early Medieval Peasant Households in Central Italy,' *Journal of Family History* 4 (1979); Robert Wheaton, 'Family and Kinship in Western Europe: The Problem of the Joint Family Household,' *Journal of Interdisciplinary History* 4 (1979); Herlihy, 'Medieval Family,' p. 117; Peter Laslett, 'Mean Household Size in England Since the Sixteenth Century,' in Laslett and Wall, *Household and Family*, p. 144; Peter Laslett, 'Characteristics of the Western Family Considered Over Time,' *Journal of Family History* 2 (1977), p. 98.

27. Flandrin, *Families in Former Times*, p. 65; Laslett, 'Mean Household Size,' pp. 134–6, 154.

28. Richard Wall, 'The Household: Demographic and Economic Change in England, 1650–1970,' in Wall, ed. (with Robin and Laslett), *Family Forms in Historic Europe* (New York, 1983), pp. 493–512.

29. Philippe Ariès, *Centuries of Childhood* (New York, 1962); Wall, 'The Household,' pp. 493–512.

30. J. Hajnal, 'Two Kinds of Pre-Industrial Household Formation Systems,' in Richard Wall, ed., with Jean Robin and Peter Laslett, *Family Forms in Historic Europe* (New York, 1983); J. Hajnal, 'European Marriage Patterns in Perspective,' in D.V. Glass and D.E.C. Eversley, eds, *Population in History: Essays in Historical Demography* (London, 1965);

Peter Laslett, 'Family and Household as Work Group and Kin Group: Areas of Traditional Europe Compared,' in Wall, *Family Forms* (1983), p. 555.

31. Laslett, 'Family and Household,' p. 547; Renate Bridenthal, 'The Family: The View From a Room of Her Own,' in Thorne and Yalom, *Rethinking*, p. 230; R.M. Smith, 'Kin and Neighbors in a Thirteenth-Century Suffolk Community,' *Journal of Family History* 4 (1979).

32. David Herlihy, 'Family Solidarity in Medieval Italian History,' in Herlihy, Lopez, and Slessarev, *Economy, Society and Government in Medieval Italy* (Kent, 1969); Michael Anderson, *Family Structure in 19th-Century Lancashire* (Cambridge, 1971); Harvey Smith, 'Family and Class: The Household Economy of Languedoc Winegrowers, 1830–1870,' *Journal of Family History* 9 (1984).

33. H. Befu, 'Ecology, Residence and Authority: The Corporate Household in Central Japan,' *Ethnology* 7 (1968); Murdock, *Social Structure*; Jack Goody, 'The Evolution of the Family,' in Laslett and Wall, *Household and Family*; Richard Wilk and William Rathje, 'Household Archaeology,' *American Behavioral Science* 25 (1982), p. 632; Pasternak, Ember, and Ember, 'On the Conditions Favoring Extended Family Households,' *Journal of Anthropological Research* 32 (1976).

34. Richard Wilk and Robert McC.Netting, 'Households: Changing Forms and Functions,' in Robert McC.Netting, Richard Wilk, and Eric J. Arnould, eds, *Households: Comparative and Historical Studies of the Domestic Group* (Berkeley, 1984), p. 10; A. Gordon Darroch and Michael Ornstein, 'Family and Household in Nineteenth-Century Canada: Regional Patterns and Regional Economics,' *Journal of Family History* 9 (1984); Hans Medick, 'The Proto-Industrial Family Economy,' *Social Theory* 3 (1976); Marc Bloch, *Feudal Society* (Chicago, 1966); Diane Hughes, 'Urban Growth and Family Structure in Medieval Genoa,' *Past and Present* 66 (1975).

35. Goldschmidt and Kunkel, 'Peasant Family'; Ring, 'Early Peasant Households'; Wheaton, 'Joint Family Household'; Jack Goody, *Production and Reproduction* (Cambridge, 1976).

36. Wheaton, 'Joint Family,' p. 618.

37. Harvey Smith, 'Languedoc Winegrowers,' p. 80. See also Lutz Berkner and Franklin Mendels, 'Inheritance Systems, Family Structure and Demographic Patterns in Western Europe (1700–1900),' in Charles Tilly, ed., *Historical Studies in Changing Fertility* (Princeton, 1978), and McC.Netting and Wilk, 'Households,' esp. pp. 11–14.

38. Stephen Weinberger, 'Peasant Households in Provence: Ca. 800–1100,' *Speculum* 48 (1973); Darroch and Ornstein, 'Family in Canada,' p. 173.

39. Laslett, 'Family and Household,' table 17.5, p. 527 and p. 555; Alan Macfarlane, review of Stone, *History and Theory* 18 (1979), pp. 112–13.

40. Yanagisako, 'Family and Household.'

41. J. Bourgeois-Pichat, 'The General Development of the Population of France Since the Eighteenth Century,' in Glass and Eversley, *Population in History*, p. 490; Sydney Coontz, *Population Theories and the Economic Interpretation* (London, 1968); Michael Drake, ed., *Population in Industrialization* (London, 1969); Linda Gordon, *Woman's Body, Woman's Right: A Social History of Birth Control in America* (New York, 1976); David Levine, *Family Formation in an Age of Nascent Capitalism* (New York, 1977); David Levine, 'Proto-Industrialization and Demographic Upheaval,' in Leslie Page Moch and Gary Stark, eds, *Essays on the Family and Historical Change* (College Station, Texas 1983), pp. 9–34; E.A. Wrigley, *Population and History* (New York, 1969), pp. 113–15.

42. E.A. Wrigley and Roger Schofield, *The Population History of England 1541–1871: A Reconstruction* (Cambridge, MA, 1981).

43. Roger Schofield, 'English Marriage Patterns Revisited,' *Journal of Family History* 10 (1985), pp. 16 and 18.

44. Levine, *Family Formation*; Medick, 'Proto-Industrial Family'; D.E.C. Eversley, 'Population, Economy and Society,' in Glass and Eversley, *Population and History*, pp. 48 and 59.

45. Levine, *Family Formation*; Mahmood Mamdani, *The Myth of Population Control: Family, Caste and Class in an Indian Village* (New York, 1973); Robert Hackenberg, Arthur Murphy, and Henry Selby, 'The Urban Household in Dependent Development,' in

McC.Netting, Wilk, and Arnould, *Households*; Wally Secombe, 'Marxism and Demography,' *New Left Review* 137 (1983).

46. Philip Greven, 'The Average Size of Families and Households in the Province of Massachusetts in 1764 and in the United States in 1790,' in Laslett and Wall, *Household and Family*, p. 552; Richard Easterlin, 'Factors in the Decline of Farm Family Fertility in the United States: Some Preliminary Research Results,' in Gordon, *American Family in Social-Historical Perspective*. Easterlin here rejects the demand-for-labor analysis on the basis that fertility rates were high when wage rates were low, but as I have argued the preindustrial family's demand for labor was at its highest when wage rates were low. However, he accepts a demand-for-labor analysis of immigration rates, which did vary directly with wage rates, in *Population, Labor Force, and Long Swings in Economic Growth* (New York, 1968), p. 31.

47. Olga Linares, 'Households Among the Diola of Senegal: Should Norms Enter by the Front or the Back Door?' in McC.Netting, Wilk, and Arnould, *Households*, p. 408; Barrington Moore, Jr., *Social Origins of Dictatorship and Democracy: Lord and Peasant in the Making of the Modern World* (Boston, 1966), pp. 520–1.

48. Medick, 'Proto-Industrial Family,' p. 295; *Women's Economic Agenda Report* (Oakland, 1987), p. 35; Jane Collier and Michelle Rosaldo, 'Politics and Gender in Simple Societies,' in Ortner and Whitehead, *Sexual Meanings* (New York, 1981), pp.283–9.

49. Edward Shorter, *The Making of the Modern Family* (New York, 1975); Joan Scott and Louise Tilly, 'Women's Work and the Family in Nineteenth Century Europe,' *Comparative Studies in Society and History* 17 (1975); Philippe Ariès, *Centuries of Childhood* (New York, 1962); Lawrence Stone, 'The Massacre of the Innocents,' *New York Review of Books*, 14 November, 1974. Other books purporting to find a trend toward emotional liberation and 'better' attitudes toward children (though disagreeing on the class origins of the trend) include: Carl Degler, *At Odds*; Daniel Smith, *Inside the Great House: Planter Family Life in Eighteenth-Century Chesapeake Society* (Ithaca, 1980); Randolph Trumbach, *The Rise of the Equalitarian Family* (New York, 1978); Lloyd deMause, *The History of Childhood*, (New York, 1972).

50. Lawrence Stone, *The Family, Sex and Marriage in England, 1500–1800* (New York, 1977), pp. 80, 93, and 'Massacre.'

51. E.P. Thompson, 'Happy Families,' *New Society*, 8 September, 1977, p. 501; Alan Macfarlane, *The Nation*, p. 116.

52. 'The Wanderer,' in M.H. Abrams, ed., *The Norton Anthology of English Literature*, vol. 1 (New York, 1968) p. 91; Ariès, *Centuries of Childhood*; Aloan Macfarlane, *Witchcraft in Tudor and Stuart England* (New York, 1970); Gordon, *Woman's Body*, p. 194; Nancy Cott, 'Passionless: An Interpretation of Victorian Sexual Ideology, 1790–1850,' and Caroll Smith-Rosenberg, 'The Female World of Love and Ritual,' in Cott and Pleck, eds, *Heritage*.

53. Hans Medick and David Sabean, *Interest and Emotion: Essays on the Study of Family and Kinship* (New York, 1984), pp. 11–13.

54. Louise Tilly, 'Individual Lives and Family Strategies in the French Proletariat,' *Journal of Family History* 4 (1979); Thompson, 'Happy Families,' p. 501.

55. Boswell, '*Expositio* and *Oblatio*'; Hufton, *Poor of 18th-Century France*; Grant McCracken, 'The Exchange of Children in Tudor England,' *Journal of Family History* 8 (1983), p. 309.

56. Lawrence Stone, *The Crisis of the Aristocracy, 1558–1641* (New York, 1974); C.H. George, 'The Making of the Bourgeoisie,' *Science and Society* 4 (1971); John Pound, *Poverty and Vagrancy in Tudor England* (London, 1981); Macfarlane, *Witchcraft*; Wrigley and Schofield, *Population in History*, pp. 439 and 441; Lawrence Stone, 'Interpersonal Violence in English Society, 1390–1980,' *Past and Present* 101 (1983), pp. 31–2.

57. Christopher Lasch, 'The Emotions of Family Life,' *New York Review of Books*, 27 November, 1975, p. 39 and *Haven in a Heartless World*, p. 182 and *passim*; Richard Sennett, *Families Against the City: Middle Class Homes of Industrial Chicago, 1872–1890* (Cambridge, MA, 1970), p. 217. Sennett's approach is, of course, in opposition to the classic sociological formulations about the functional nature of the nuclear family for modern industrial systems. See, for example, Talcott Parsons, Robert Bales, *et al.*, *Family*,

Socialization and Interaction Process (Glencoe, 1955) and Neil J. Smelser, *Social Change in the Industrial Revolution* (Chicago, 1959).

58. James Axtell, *Indian Peoples of Eastern America* (New York, 1980); Carol Stack, *All Our Kin: Strategies for Survival in a Black Community* (New York, 1974); Colin Turnbull, *The Forest People* (New York, 1962); Nancy Tanner, 'Matrifocality in Indonesia and Africa and Among Black Americans,' in Michelle Rosaldo and Louise Lamphere, eds, *Women, Culture and Society* (Stanford, 1974).

59. Barbara Ehrenreich and Deirdre English, 'Reflections on the "Woman Question," ' *Working Papers for a New Society* (Cambridge, MA, 1978) Keith Snell, ed., *Annals of the Laboring Poor: Social Change and Agrarian England, 1600–1900* (Seaman, OH, 1972).

60. Louise Tilly and Joan Scott, *Women, Work and Family* (New York, 1978).

61. Immanuel Wallerstein, William Martin, and Torry Dickinson, 'Household Structures and Production Processes: Preliminary Theses and Findings,' *Review* 3 (1982), p. 440.

2

The Native American Tradition

Successful establishment of families from Europe on the American continent was both consequence and cause of the destruction of an entirely different system of social and biological reproduction. Reconstructing that system presents some difficulties. Aside from the fact that early records of Indian life were penned by Europeans whose ethnocentric prejudices distorted their understanding, many Indian societies had drastically altered their behavior or form in response to the European presence long before Europeans set down their first impressions of 'traditional' Indian life. There were apparently both friendly and hostile contacts between Indians and Vikings as early as the eleventh century, while Bristol fishermen were probably regularly fishing in Newfoundland by 1480. Within only a few years of Columbus's 'discovery,' European explorers, traders, and slavers arrived with new diseases, technologies, and demands for Indian goods. They kidnapped Indians to take back to Europe and introduced new types and methods of conflict into Native American relations.

One immediate impact of Europeans on Indian culture was the introduction of Old World pathogens for which Indians, protected from similar diseases by low population densities, the lack of domesticated animals, and the special conditions of early migration from Eurasia, had no acquired immunities. The results were catastrophic. Early fishing contacts in the fifteenth and sixteenth centuries touched off epidemics even before European exploration and settlement processes were well begun. The first encounters of English colonists with Indians in Delaware and New England included reports of recent massive deaths among the Indians. 'Englishmen, take that land,' offered the Wampanoag chief Massasoit, 'for none is left to occupy it.' In Georgia, De Soto's 1540 expedition found that the population had recently suffered a devastating plague, possibly spread from an earlier one that had depopulated Ayllon's coastal colony in 1526. Squanto, the famous Indian ally of the Pilgrims, had been carried off as a slave in 1614 and then worked his way to England, Newfoundland, and home, only to find all his people destroyed by disease. Individuals or groups struggling to survive after such massive demographic losses surely engaged in behavior quite different from that sustained by traditional kinship ties. Thus even the earliest European accounts are often of new behaviors, composite villages, and changed community institutions and beliefs.[1]

Experience with European militarism also stimulated change in Native American political organization. The brutal Spanish pillage of Florida and New Mexico in the first half of the sixteenth century destroyed many Indian groups and forced others to reorganize. There is debate over whether the Iroquois Confederacy, formed in the second half of the fifteenth century, was a reaction to conflict with the Algonkians or was formed in response to French intrusions into North America. The Powhatan Confederacy in Virginia, however, already established when the Jamestown colony was founded, was certainly a response to European penetration, for it was created when Indians from Florida or the West Indies, fleeing the Spanish, moved into the area and subjected or otherwise unified the original inhabitants into a military federation. By the first decade of the 1630s the Mohawks of the Northeast coast had developed a new and destructive warfare in response to the Micmac alliance with the French, while New England Indians had been drawn into European political and trading networks and embittered by the 'propensities of English visitors . . . toward violence and kidnapping.'[2]

Generalizations about 'traditional' Indian culture are further complicated by the fact that Indian societies were neither static nor unitary even before the coming of the Europeans. The 'Moundbuilders' of the Ohio River Valley, for example, had built elaborate urban cultures while Europeans still lived in nomadic bands, but had gone into decline about 500 AD. At the time of European exploration of North America there were at least 10–12 million Indians living in North America, organized into at least 600 different societies and speaking more than 200 languages. Some lived by horticulture and resided in semi-permanent or permanent villages with complex social structures. The Hopi and Zuni peoples of the Southwest, who lived in huge, apartment-like structures built on steep cliffs or mesas, had practiced agriculture for more than 3,000 years. Other groups, nomadic gatherers and hunters, had not embraced the Neolithic Revolution. Plentiful resources and an efficient fishing technology had produced a high degree of stratification in personal wealth and status in the Northwest, while hunters such as the Shoshone, Micmac, and Naskapi and horticulturalists such as the Iroquois and Algonkian lacked significant differences in rank or wealth.

It is important, then, to use caution in generalizing about the social relations and family arrangements of Indians before European arrival. We are aided, however, by recent anthropological and historical research that attempts to re-create the historical context and development of kinship societies, so that it is now possible to discern some clear patterns in traditional Native American groups. In none of the North American societies was production based on the private ownership and utilization of land, was distribution based on the market, or were politics and justice administered through a territorial state with coercive power over all within its boundaries. This gave rise to distinct forms of social organization and typical relationships between family and society, whether the preferred family form was a simple conjugal unit based on a shallow descent system or a complex kin network tracing its descent far back through either the female or the male line.[3]

Social Relations in Traditional North American Indian Societies

Native American societies lacked the private ownership of land and resources that was the basis of European social organization. Particular groups, individuals, or families were often associated with certain resources or territory, but this association conferred few exclusive rights. 'Owners' had to be approached and their permission sought to use the resources they directed, but it was inconceivable that people would be denied use rights to fill their needs. As one authority has summed up the meaning of such 'title' in unstratified societies, 'individual ownership in these cases does not mean exclusive right of use, but a sort of stewardship, the right to *direct* the exploitation of the economic tract held by the local group.'[4] Thus the concept of free, exclusive, and unfettered title was foreign to Indian societies. Instead, every territory supported a bundle of use rights, often distributed among a wide range of different people.

The inability of any sector of a Native American society to monopolize resources or deny access to others meant that there was no permanent labor force, created because one section of a society had to work for others in order to gain access to food, shelter, and clothing. The fact that no one could hoard resources and deny them to others also removed the motivation for theft. William Penn wrote: 'give them a fine Gun, Coat, or other thing, it may pass twenty hands before it sticks. . . . Wealth circulateth like the Blood, all parts partake; and though none shall want what another hath, yet exact Observers of Property.'[5]

Among the relatively settled East Coast tribes, land that was not used by the group could be loaned or even given in perpetuity to another tribe, but only on condition that the recipients reside there and maintain good relations with the donors. Land 'transfers' were political rather than economic exchanges, defining and coordinating the use rights of different groups so as to avoid conflict. The use rights of the 'donors' were generally reserved, and even the right to settle did not include the right to hoard the resources or deny them to others. As Chief Black Hawk of the Iroquois summed up the system:

> land cannot be sold. The Great Spirit gave it to his children to live upon, and cultivate as far as necessary for their subsistence; and so long as they occupy and cultivate it, they have a right to the soil − but if they voluntarily leave it, then any other people have the right to settle upon it.[6]

The missionary John Heckewelder described the Iroquois concept as follows:

> Whatever liveth upon the land, whatsoever groweth out of the earth, and all that is in the rivers and waters flowing through the same, was given jointly to all, and everyone is entitled to his share. From this the principle of hospitality flows as its source. . . . The stranger has a claim to their hospitality, partly on account of his being at a distance from his family and friends, and partly because he has honored them with his visit and ought to leave them with a good impression on his mind. . . .[7]

In all Indian societies sharing and reciprocity were a simple matter of survival, and hospitality was therefore one of the highest values. In the 1770s, William Bartram noted that the Creeks had a common granary open to all in need of food, and described the rituals of hospitality that prevailed:

> A man . . . calls in at another town, if he wants victuals, rest or social conversations, he confidently approaches the door of the first house he chooses, saying 'I am come'; the good man or woman replies, 'You are; it's well.' Immediately victuals and drink are ready . . . he needs no one to introduce him, any more than the blackbird or thrush, when he repairs to the fruitful groves. . . .[8]

In the 1720s the Jesuit Father Joseph Lafitau reported that among the Iroquois, strangers were fed before they were questioned about their mission, and as late as the nineteenth century George Catlin observed in his travels among the Plains Indians that 'Every man, woman, or child in

Indian communities is allowed to enter any one's lodge, and even that of the chief of the nation, and eat when they are hungry. . . .' A French missionary at the end of the seventeenth century claimed that a Micmac Indian 'would rather die of hunger than eat alone a Teal which he had killed, even though it might be the means of restoring his strength; he would take it to the Wigwam, where he knew others, like himself, were in need of it, & each one would have his share.'[9]

Such principles of production and distribution militated against the emergence of bounded families, set apart from larger networks of cooperation and social intercourse. The pattern of resource use described above required that individuals assert and rely upon their connections with each other. The simplest way to effect such connections is by informal sharing and reciprocity. As we have seen, this was very common in Indian groups: organization of production and distribution was often accomplished at the local level on this basis alone, with little or no regard for kin relations. But such local sharing is limited in both time and space; sometimes broader, more regularized rights and obligations are necessary. Foragers who range widely or locate in different ecological niches during different seasons may need broader connections in *time*: there must be some continuity in storing seed, congregate together only on occasion. Food producers need deeper connections in *time*: There must be some continuity in storing seed, working the land, knowing when it should be burned over or allowed to lie fallow, and so forth. Kinship ties provide a means of formalizing obligations and circulating both goods and services over space or time.

Kinship provided Native Americans with a system of assigning rights and duties on the basis of a commonly accepted criterion – a person's blood relationship (though this might be fictive) to a particular set of relatives. Kinship rules regulated an individual's place in the overall production and distribution of each group's dominant articles of subsistence; they established set patterns in his or her interactions with others. Among many Indian societies people were grouped into different sections, moieties or phratries, and clans; each of which was associated with different territories, resources, skills, or simply personal characteristics. Being related to someone from this section conferred specific rights that could be expected from others in the group and imposed specific obligations toward others. One might expect certain kinds of food or support from one's father's relatives and owe certain kinds of food or labor to one's mother's relatives. Exogamy, the requirement that an individual marry out of his or her natal group into a different clan or section, assured the widest possible social cooperation by making each individual a member of intersecting kin groups, with special obligations and rights toward each category of relatives.

Sections and subsections, found among many California hunting societies, connected people across space: They provided, as Aram Yengoyan has commented of similar arrangements in Australia,

> a means of linking vast numbers of individuals and groups . . . into a network which permits small mobile units to spatially expand and contract under varying environmental conditions . . . [bringing] spatially and socially distant groups together for mutual interaction and mobility.[10]

Unilineal descent groups, on the other hand, found among many of the horticultural groups along the eastern coast, connected people across time: the systematic exclusion of either the maternal or the paternal line permitted less geographically widespread linkages but established continuity among a particular group of people who could pass on certain tasks, material or spiritual skills, or rights of resource use, as well as working together in the same area. In both cases, relatives or potential relatives were categorized in terms of the rights and obligations – not just to food but also to marriage partners – that might be expected from them. This provided a predictable but flexible way of circulating labor and sharing resources while exploiting them effectively.

Kinship relations were not necessarily limited to actual blood relatives. Adoption set up the same kinship rights and obligations, and some groups also had special 'Friend' partnerships organized around relations of mutual aid. The point here is that sharing did not arise out of some mystical attachment to kin ties; on the contrary, kin ties arose out of and in order to extend sharing. Moreover, Indian kinship-based societies were extremely flexible about compensating for any lack of actual blood ties by inventing fictive kinship devices.

The role of the family, then, was to circulate people and resources, ensuring that all individuals would have a call upon the labor or products of specific others. This militated against the development of economic inequalities. It also reinforced an ideology that made sharing or generosity rather than accumulation the main source of prestige.

It is true, of course, that an exceptionally generous family group could gain differential prestige, and even be credited with having a special relationship to the ancestors or spirits who were thought to look after the group's welfare. Such status might attract spouses or even unrelated followers to the kin group, providing more workers to produce goods for redistribution and hence increasing the prestige and rank even more. There was thus some internal basis for the development of rank in Indian kinship societies.[11] This was taken to its highest extreme in such northwest groups as the Tlingits and Kwakiutl, who developed elaborate ranking systems in which leading kin groups used polygyny and slavery to accumulate extra labor. With this labor they hosted huge redistribution ceremonies (potlatches) that gained them political leadership and some economic privilege. Unlike other Native American groups, leading clans could restrict access of non-kin to certain resources while calling upon their labor. Yet even here the ranking system had not hardened into a class society, as rank still depended upon giving away wealth and was lost if a house-group was unable or unwilling to redistribute the products of the labor and obligations it was able to mobilize. Before the epidemics and the new, individually accumulated wealth introduced by the Europeans, an individual could not simply throw a potlatch in order to gain power or prestige: potlatches were limited to important social events and collectively recognized occasions.[12]

In South America, the potential for hierarchy contained in kinship relations and the potential for property contained in redistribution were fertilized by various historical circumstances and grew into the massive, exploitative Aztec and Inca Empires. But throughout North America, up until the extensive and prolonged dislocations provoked by American colonization, leveling mechanisms prevented the disruption of reciprocity and redistribution. Gift-giving, ceremonial feasting, exchange networks among friends and kin, potlatches, adoption, the exogamous circulation of spouses: all these practices circulated both goods and labor, precluding the development of a class and state system. The family arrangements of Native American groups sustained these systems of reciprocity.

Unlike a state system, which makes sharp distinctions between family duties and civil duties, domestic functions and political ones, Native American societies had few institutions that were set up on a basis other than kinship. There was no opposition between domestic or 'private' functions and political or public ones. North American Indians had no institutionalized courts, police, or army. No agencies of taxation or coercion existed to support an official religion, bureaucracy, or forced labor apparatus. The lack of property and the mobility of Indian life prevented the development of the idea that any group could be defined by or limited to a particular territory, much less that it could exercise authority over all persons within its territory.

Just as kinship regularized economic reciprocity, so kin ties also regulated personal relationships. With no courts, jails, or police, kin connections controlled behavior and administered justice. In North

American Indian groups murder was an offense not against the state but against the kin group, and it was therefore the responsibility and right of kin to punish the perpetrator. Since to involve strangers in punishing the offender would have subjected them to the revenge of the perpetrator's kinsmen, this would have been as immoral for Indian society as it is considered wrong today to take such a responsibility on oneself rather than delegating it to the state. Sometimes the revenge involved a painful death for the murderer, but it was also a rather limited revenge, one life being thought sufficient to pay for another.

In 1650 an Iroquois hunter was murdered by five French military men, who were sentenced to die by the commandant of the fort. The commandant's account of the incident points to the very different concepts of justice held by Indians and Europeans:

> They were led out, and all five were bound each to a post. The Iroquois were astonished at the ample justice that was rendered to them, and entreated mercy for four of them; because, as they said, they had lost only one man, it was not just to kill five for him, but one [only ought] to die. They were given to understand the five were equally criminal and, without exception, merited death. The Iroquois . . . redoubled their entreaties to obtain mercy for four, and for this purpose made presents of porcelain collars, but all five men were shot to death.[13]

The Iroquois might well have tortured the one individual to death, but they were clearly not accustomed to such wholesale 'justice.' Death was in fact sometimes avoided altogether by the payment of goods to the murdered person's family: Penn comments that among the Delaware – and this held true for many other Indian groups – the customary price was double for a woman what it was for a man. In many tribes, it was the chief's role to avert retaliation by giving presents to the aggrieved party or inflicting wounds upon himself to fill the requirement that blood be shed.[14]

This was a rather different conception of leadership than the European one, in which state officials *took* presents from offenders or sentenced *others'* blood to be spilled. Among most pre-contact Native American groups, leadership and rank involved at least as many obligations as privileges. Marshall Sahlins has argued: 'In primitive society social inequality is more the organization of economic equality. Often, in fact, high rank is only secured or sustained by o'ercrowing generosity: the material advantage is on the subordinate's side.' An early Dutch missionary observed: 'The chiefs are generally the poorest among them, for instead of their receiving from the common people as among Christians, they are obliged to give to the mob.' William Penn reported that when he gave a 'King' some amount of pay or presents, it would be sent on to another:

> Then that King sub-divideth it in like manner among his Dependents, they hardly leaving themselves an Equal share with one of their Subjects: and be it on such occasions, at Festivals, or at their common Meals, the Kings distribute, and to themselves Last.

Robert Lowie, reviewing the role of leaders among North American Indians, has concluded that the role of chiefs was primarily to resolve disputes peacefully and redistribute goods. Even among the hierarchical northwest societies, rank was achieved by *giving away* goods.[15]

In return for these services, chiefs and leading individuals received very little of the unquestioning obedience that the colonists associated with leadership. Some groups, like the Shoshone, had only a rudimentary system of leadership, much of which was situational and temporary. But even among more highly organized tribes, there was no such thing as a coercive apparatus to compel obedience. Writing in 1774, James Adair commented: 'The power of their chiefs is an empty sound. They can only persuade or dissuade the people.' Among the Navajo, reports John Hurdy, 'No adult was required to obey the wishes of another. Leaders were followed as long as, in the opinion of individual followers, their direction was sound.' George Catlin testified that the Plains Indian chief 'has no control over the life or limbs, or liberty of his subjects, nor other power whatever, excepting that of *influence* which he gains by his virtues, and his exploits in war.'[16]

The combination of personal autonomy and interdependence on which Indian societies rested created a precarious balance that could tip from generosity to hostility or vengeance and quickly back. It sometimes required the sacrifice of individuals to the exigencies of survival, but it also resulted in a collective responsibility for others and a tolerance of personal independence that were totally foreign to most colonists. An example of this balance is found in the role of violence in Indian societies. Scalping and torture were apparently well established among some East Coast groups before contact with Europeans, but they were quite limited. They increased in scope and intensity and spread to other Indian groups, such as those on the Southeast Coast, only after a prolonged period of conflict with the settlers.[17]

The question of torture needs to be seen in the context of the limited nature of Indian war. Few prisoners were taken, and of these only a small number were consigned to torture. George Catlin described the extreme punishment inflicted on a few prisoners among the Plains Indians, but noted that the rest were adopted into the tribes with all the rights of kinsmen. Among the Iroquois and many other groups, the women decided which captives would be tortured to wreak vengeance for a fallen kinsman and which adopted as a replacement for that kin. Henry Timberlake declared that female Cherokee chiefs could, with the 'wave of a swan's wing, deliver a wretch condemned by the council, and already tied to the stake.' Sometimes a captive might be tortured first, in a sort of purgative ritual, and then adopted, henceforth to be treated as a full member of the group. European captives often testified that the beatings which preceded their initiation into Indian society were actually 'administered with great mercy' and that care was taken to avoid life-threatening or permanent injuries. All accounts agree that Indians in the early period of contact did not rape their female captives.[18]

During the early colonial period some white captives chose to become permanent members of Indian groups, resisting attempts at their reincorporation into colonial society. Even those who returned home often noted the humanity with which they had been treated. One former captive, a Mrs Johnson, asked: 'Do [Europeans] ever adopt an enemy and salute him by the tender name of brother?' Mary Rowlandson, captured during one of the bloodiest clashes between colonists and Indians, wrote an account of Indian 'brutishness' in which the Indians compare quite favorably to contemporary reports of how colonists treated captives or social inferiors. Once having survived a bloody raid on her household, she led a life of bartering, bickering, and social interaction that few indentured servants in colonial America would have been allowed. Rowlandson left her 'master and mistress' freely to visit other households, asking for food and drink and occasionally sleeping the night. She ate out of the communal pot (though she was cuffed for uncleanly putting her own dipper into it) and bartered her sewing skills for food and privileges. She records incidents where she was treated roughly but also reports that her son's captor 'told me he loved him and he should not want.'[19]

Indians were as horrified by the mass killings of European war as the Europeans were shocked by Indian torture of captives. In the seventeenth century, Roger Williams noted that Indian battles were 'farre less bloudy and devouring than the cruell Warres of Europe; and seldome twenty slain in a pitch field.' Captain John Underhill reported contemptuously that the Indians would call off a battle after only a few casualties and lacked the stomach for the European kind of war, which, they complained, 'slays too many men.' The trader James Adair commented: 'The Indians are not fond of waging war with each other, unless prompted by some of the traders'; 'they are usually satisfied with two or three scalps and a prisoner.'[20]

Life was precarious in Indian societies and death was seldom sentimentalized, but cooperation rather than conflict was generally the most effective way to ensure survival. A recent authority has concluded that 'the motives for aboriginal war appear to have been few, and the casualties slight.' Indian folk tales and myths do not display the expectation of hostility when new groups meet; more frequently, they speak of encounters in which magical gifts are obtained from friendly strangers. Indian religion also stresses the dependence of humans on their brothers and sisters of the animal world rather than human domination of nature.[21]

Native American Family Arrangements

Two broad types of kinship systems prevailed in North American Indian societies, both based on exogamy, which forced people to marry out of their section or clan and establish larger networks. In the foraging groups of the Northern woods and the Great Basin, descent was bilateral rather than unilineal, being traced through both mother and father, and the descent system was rather shallow. Residence rules were quite flexible, and a young couple tended to establish a new residence upon marriage.

Food-producing groups, on the other hand, or those with plentiful but fluctuating resources to manage, tended to organize families around unilineal descent groups. These descent groups passed on rights, obligations, knowledge, and patterned social relations within a group of people who lived and worked together on a regular basis. The exclusion of one parental line created larger, more geographically concentrated work groups, with greater continuity over time. The historical choice of the male or female line possibly had to do with whose work required the most coordination and continuity of roles. Most of the Great Plains and prairie Indian tribes seem to have been patrilineal. Matrilineal tribes included many East Coast tribes, the Creeks, Choctaws and Seminoles in the South, and the so-called Pueblo tribes of the Southwest, such as the Hopi, Laguna, Acoma, and Zuni. Some groups were patrilineal during the hunting season and matrilineal during the growing season.

In unilineal kinship systems, extended family ties determined the daily organization of work and the self-identification of the individual. These ties were to the natal kin group rather than the conjugal family, and did not set up a necessary identity between residence, marriage, and lines of social interaction. In a matrilineal society, for example, a man might have closer ties to his nephews and nieces than to his sons and daughters (who belonged to a different descent group than his own), while the same might be true for a woman in a patrilineal society.

In none of these groups did the nuclear family stand alone, emotionally or economically. Among many foraging and hunting societies small family groups spent part of the year on their own but coalesced into much larger bands during the summer, at social ceremonies such as dances, courtships, and games, or where there were big concentrations of game or fish. At these times there might be an exchange of members, with the next season's small groups composed of different families, or even reconstituted families, since divorce was easy and child-exchange common. In many northeastern tribes, a nuclear family might live in a small wigwam during one season but join other families in a larger longhouse in another. In the South, densely populated villages formed around areas of crop cultivation during the summer but broke down into smaller hunting units in the fall and might re-form into different collections of individuals in the winter, sometimes establishing large camps of women, elders, and children, while young males went on extended hunting forays. In the North and West, too, the composition of camps, bands, and hunting groups varied from season to season in the distribution of both families and individuals.

This constant flux created a world where the nuclear family was only one of many overlapping ties and had almost no functions that were not shared by other social groupings. As Edward Spicer has commented,

> the nuclear family constituted a group whose existence was more or less submerged in a larger whole through emphasis on descent [or collateral kin] ties. Thus no nuclear family, whether among the close-knit Western Pueblos or the more loosely knit Seris or Western Apaches, had anything approaching an independent existence.[22]

The nuclear family was not a property-holding unit, since resources and land were available to all or were held by the larger kin corporation, while subsistence tools and their products were made and owned by individuals rather than families. Its lack of property meant that the Indian nuclear family had less economic autonomy than the European. The lack of a state, on the other hand, gave the Indian family more political autonomy, since families were not bound to follow a leader for any longer than they cared to. However, this political autonomy did not create isolation or a sense of primary involvement with one's 'own' nuclear family: there was too much reciprocal dependence throughout the group for that; and the lack of a state also meant that there was no sharp division between public life and private life. No nuclear family occupied a private sphere of work, ritual or socializing.

Marriage was an important means of circulating labor and establishing mutual obligations between family groups; the formality of marriage depended on how formal and lasting such obligations had to be. In most band-level societies marriage seems to have been a matter of individual choice, and divorce was easy. Among the Ute and Allen Canyon Paiute, observes Marvin Opler:

> The creeping lover, the flageolet serenade, the women's initiative at dances, grandparental adoptions, and even instruction in abortion techniques freed girls as well as boys for sexual exploration leading to trial marriages. . . . Divorce was effected simply by returning to the parental camp. In the case of adultery either spouse physically accosted the adulterer, and the contest of strength could settle matters.[23]

In more complex kinship systems relatives might be more closely involved in negotiating a marriage or trying to get a couple to stay together. While most groups allowed free sexual experimentation before marriage and recognized the right of a woman to refuse a husband, attitudes toward adultery varied. Among some cultures it seems to have been tolerated; in others the kin group might punish it severely. Some societies blamed the woman or her male seducer; others seem to have applied sanctions equally to men and women. Among the Winnebago it was considered unseemly to search for evidence of adultery, and a man's jealousy was excellent grounds for his wife to leave him. A young man was told: 'Women can never be watched. If you try to watch them you will merely show your jealousy and your female relatives will also be jealous. After a while you will become so jealous of your wife that she will leave you. . . . Everyone will consider you a very bad man.'[24]

Whether or not adultery was punished, full rights of separation or divorce were common for both men and women. Separation was frequent, but normally occurred before children were born. Sometimes the newly married couple abstained from sex for a period while they got to know each other and determined whether they were in fact compatible. Bartram thought that the Creeks married for only a year at a time, renewing or not at their pleasure, though he said they seldom split up after having children. In other tribes, one or the other spouse initiated a divorce by returning to his or her family of origin. Which spouse this was depended upon the residence rules of the group. If the marriage was matrilocal, the man had to leave; if patrilocal, the woman left.[25]

The flexible organization of Indian families facilitated a very direct relationship between personal and social reproduction. A variety of practices allowed a kin group to expand or contract according to environmental necessity. Frequent and prolonged nursing held fertility rates down; as did abstention from sex during specified periods, the access of women to some methods of birth control and abortion, and the ability of any conjugal family to get food or labor through the principles of sharing, without having to literally bear its own labor force.

A kin group facing a shortage of members could borrow a child from relatives, adopt a captive to replace a lost kinsman, or engage in some form of polygyny. Such customs allowed Indians to regulate the total population and its distribution in accord with ecological constraints. The result was generally stable rates of population growth, with the density of population depending on the environment. Foraging Indians in Maine had population densities of perhaps 41 individuals per 100 square miles, while the crop-raising Indians of southern New England sustained about 287 persons on the same amount of land.[26]

The Sexual Division of Labor

Indian kinship systems rested on a clear division of labor by sex and by age. The sexual division of labor was often the central organizing principle of daily work. Men did the hunting and took on any tasks of war that might arise. In eastern horticultural societies women cultivated all the food crops (except tobacco) in cooperative, all-female work groups. In the South men participated with women in the cultivation of communal cornfields, while women took responsibility for household gardens of melons and pumpkins. Both men and women took part in fishing, game drives, shellfish and plant gathering. Among foraging groups, men hunted large animals, while women gathered, processed, manufactured, and caught small game.

The amount and difficulty of the work performed by each sex appears to have been roughly the same, though this was not always obvious to Europeans, among whom only aristocrats hunted and men did the bulk of agricultural labor. Men's work came in intensive bouts: Male hunters might pursue game for days or weeks at a time, after which they would experience equally long periods of leisure. Women's work was more evenly spread out. But under normal circumstances foraging in pre-contact societies seems to have afforded a comfortable subsistence with a shorter workday than our own. Even among crop-producers, reported the eighteenth-century captive, Mary Jemison, 'labor was not severe. . . . In the summer season, we planted, tended and harvested our corn, and generally had all our children with us; but had no master to oversee or drive us, so that we could work as leisurely as we pleased.'[27]

The sexual division of labor varied from group to group. Among many foraging societies, the division was quite minimal; groups that required a greater degree of specialization relied on a stricter demarcation of gender roles. Seldom, however, was the division totally rigid. Even among the Sioux, in other ways a very sex-divided society, 'Bravery among women was equally . . . deserving of recognition as it was among men,' while male hunters 'were not exempt from gathering vegetables.'

Young Apache and Iroquois wives might accompany their husbands on the hunt and actually take part in the chase. When men were in camp for several days at a time, they often did childcare for wives or sisters and helped with women's tasks. Among the Menomini Indians of Wisconsin, women 'could gain respect without censure if they chose also to engage in male activities such as fishing, hunting, dancing in a male fashion, or foot racing.'[28]

Where the division of labor was comparatively strict and was maintained by ridicule of those who casually violated it, Indian cultures frequently had institutionalized means whereby an individual could legitimately take on the activities and characteristics of the other sex. In many societies, including most of the Plains groups, a young man could acceptably take on the dress and the life of a woman. As Father Joseph Lafitau disapprovingly observed:

> Among the Illinois, among the Sioux, in Louisiana, in Florida and in Yucatan, there are young men who assume women's costumes . . . and take it as a mark of honour to lower themselves to womens' occupations . . . and their profession of an extraordinary kind of life makes them pass for people of a superior order above the common run of mankind.[29]

Among the North Piegan there was a socially recognized deviant category of 'manly-hearted women,' who might claim the economic roles and social perquisites of men. A woman could also take on the entire lifestyle of a man and might even marry another woman, assuming the social role of husband. Evelyn Blackwood has found that cross-gender roles for women as well as for men were widespread and socially acceptable among such groups as the Klamath of southern Oregon, the Mohave, Apache, Maricopa, and Cocopa of the Southwest, and the Kaska of the Yukon Territory. Cross-gender women could rear children by marrying a pregnant woman or a divorced woman with children, or by adopting. Lesbian activity was an accepted part of the relationship but was not categorized as such, since social role was a more salient piece of a person's identity than her biological gender.[30]

Marriage effected a literal exchange between male and female products, each spouse being thought to 'own' the products of the other. The essential reciprocity of the exchange can be seen in the fact that the male could do what he liked with the female products and the female could do what she liked with the male products. In some groups women's labor provided the goods that their husbands used in feasting; but the products of a man's individual hunt seem to have been fully and freely disposable by his wife. The missionary David Zeisberger, for example, reported that a husband who presented his wife with a deer 'says nothing, if she even gives the greatest part of it to her friends, which is a very common custom.'[31]

Women who chose to remain single were rare, but there was a place for them too, especially since women had a right to game by virtue of membership in a kin group and did not depend solely on a husband's hunting. The options for single women among Canadian Indians were observed with horror by Baron de LaHontan in the early eighteenth century, when he reported the existence of women who, 'through a principle of Debauchery,' refused to marry:

> That sort of Women are call'd ... *Hunting Women*: for they commonly accompany the Huntsmen in their Diversions. To justify their Conduct, they allege that they find themselves to be of too indifferent a temper to brook the conjugal yoak, to be too careless for the bringing up of Children, and too impatient to bear the passing of the whole Winter in the Villages. Thus it is, that they cover and disguise their Lewdness. Their Parents or Relations dare not censure their Vicious Conduct; on the contrary they seem to approve of it, in declaring ... that their Daughters have the command of their own Bodies and may dispose of their Persons as they think fit; they being at liberty to do what they please.[32]

Children gradually assimilated adult gender roles and knowledge by imitation and through the stories and ceremonies passed down by elders. Child-rearing was generally permissive. Some European observers were horrified by the failure of Indian parents to beat, scold, or even reprimand their young. Jesuits, for example, frequently commented on the 'excessive love the Savages bear [for] their children.' As Nicholas Denys observed:

> Their children are not obstinate, since they give them everything they ask for, without ever letting them cry for that which they want. The greatest persons give way to the little ones. The father and the mother draw the morsel from the mouth if the child asks for it. They love their children greatly.

And this, one missionary commented, 'in spite of the doubt that they are really their own.'[33]

As the missionary noted, love for children extended beyond blood ties. One Naskapi reacted scornfully to a Jesuit who worried about the possibilities for illegitimacy in the free social intercourse between Naskapi men and women: 'Thou hast no sense. You French people love only your own children; but we love all the children of the tribe.' When the Delawares, Shawnees, and Senecas were required by a peace treaty in 1764 to hand over all their 'prisoners,' 'whether adopted in your Tribes, married, or living amongst you, under any Denomination or Pretence whatever,' observers reported that the Indians did so 'with the utmost reluctance, shed torrents of tears over them, recommending them to the care and protection of the commanding officer.' The young 'prisoners' often clung to their Indian families with 'bitter lamentations.'[34]

If indulgence was granted to the young, status and privilege often accrued with age. Grandparents were looked upon with respect and often intervened in family situations. Elizabeth Hanson reported, for example, that though her Indian master ordered his son to beat her son, 'the old squaw, the Indian boy's grandmother, would not suffer him to do it.' Among the Algonkians, old men in a hunting party were often credited with the kill, while old women, reported an observer in 1709, continued to garden, since the Indians had 'their young men plant, reap, and do everything [the women are] not capable or doing. . . .'[35]

The Status of Women in Native American Societies

What was the status of women within such systems? Many authors have asserted that Indian women 'were property and treated as such. . . . They were made beasts of burden and traded like horses.' In 1767 Adam Ferguson declared that Indian women were 'the slaves and helots of their country,' while William Penn believed that 'the Wives are the true Servants of their husbands' (though, he added, 'otherwise the Men are very affectionate to them'). Numerous stories about ill-treatment of women come from the Great Plains region. Among some Great Plains tribes, such as the Blackfoot and the Piegen, a husband might cut off the nose of a wife who was unfaithful, though men were not subjected to punishment for the same offense. One writer declared in 1809:

> Although the squaws are very ill treated by all the Indians, it is said they are treated much worse by the Sioux than any other tribe, whence it follows that mothers frequently destroy their female children, alleging as a reason, that it is better they should die than continue a life so miserable as that to which they are doomed.[36]

Other indications suggest, however, that Indian women had a high degree of autonomy and played a respected role within their societies. There are accounts of women chiefs, medicine workers, shamans, and prophets among many Indian groups. Women took part in all deliberations of the Cherokees, and though they did not serve on the War Councils they advised the war chief (a temporary rank) on strategy. James Adair commented disgustedly that the Cherokees 'have been a considerable while under petticoat-government, and allow their women full liberty to plant their brows with horns as oft as they please, without fear of punishment.' European observers were frequently horrified by the sexual egalitarianism of Indian societies.[37]

The gatherers of the Southwest built their most elaborate ceremonial cycles around a girl's entrance into puberty. Among the Hopi, Zuni, and other western Pueblo tribes, the woman 'owned' the house, which was the center of economic and religious activities, and played a vital role in the religion. The word for wife in Wisconsin Indian dialect meant partner, and Jesuits noted with extreme disapproval that Montagnais-Naskapi Indians involved women prominently in decision-making. A late eighteenth-century English manuscript based on the report of John Norton, who had lived as an adopted member of the Mohawks, expressed surprise at commonly circulated reports about the ill treatment of women: 'the truth is that the Women are treated in a much more respectful manner then [sic] in England and that they possess very superior power. . . .' This was also the view of Bartram, who observed in 1789 that 'the condition of women is as happy, compared to that of the man, as the condition of women in any part of the world.'[38]

We have already seen that a man might gain 'honour' by adopting a woman's role. Indeed, sometimes a whole tribe might be categorized as female. This was not a reduction in status but a socially acceptable use of the division of labor to organize relations among as well as within groups. The Delaware, for example, were given the woman's role in their relations with the Iroquois Confederacy, which meant that they were honorably charged with the preservation of 'the belt of peace and the chain of friendship.'[39]

Many foraging bands fostered a 'personal autonomy . . . that applied as fully to women as to men' and seem to have granted women a sexual freedom equal to men.[40] But more complex societies also accorded women important positions. Indeed, the most well-documented case of an Indian society where women played a central and powerful role in all affairs is that of the Iroquois, the five northeastern tribes that united into a confederacy in the fifteenth century (six after the Tuscarora were admitted in 1722) and controlled an area more than 1200 miles long and 600 miles wide.

The basis of the Iroquois economy was the communal farming of maize, beans, and squash – 'the Three Sisters.' People lived in rectangular longhouses, about 50 to 100 feet long, each occupied by an extended matrilineal kin group composed of eight to ten conjugal families. Domestic chores and horticultural labor were organized by the matrons, who divided the food among the conjugal families once a day, normally using up any leftovers through the law of hospitality. Village headwomen are mentioned in myths, but at least by the time of any written records the sachems were males, chosen by the matrons from among the men belonging to certain matrilineages. The matrons could replace a sachem if, after three warnings, he continued to fail in the performance of his duties. A woman might also act as regent for a sachem too young to rule, and the women were entitled to a speaker in the council. The matrons could 'veto' a declaration of war by simply refusing to provide food when asked to do so by the male war party.

Women were thought to collectively own the land, and the earliest treaties with the whites were signed by the matrons along with the sachems. Women's planting and cultivating activities, as well as their fertility, were the focus of religious celebration, and men and women were equally appointed 'keepers of the faith.' Women also practiced medicine, either in all-female societies or in a group with men. They were conceived of as the cohesive, integrating force in the society.[41]

Father Joseph Lafitau declared in the 1720s: 'Nothing is more real than the women's superiority. It is they who really maintain the tribe. . . .' In 1788 an Oneida chief delivered a message from the women to the colonial officials in Albany: 'Brothers, our ancestors considered it a great offence to reject the counsels of their women, particularly of the female governesses. . . . *Who*, said our forefathers, bring us into being? *Who* cultivate our lands, kindle our fires and boil our pots, but the women?' In 1791 the matrons declared to Colonel Proctor: 'You ought to hear and listen to what we women shall speak, as well as to the sachems, for we are the owners of this land, and it is ours.'[42]

Some of the contradictions in reports about the status of Indian women may be due to actual variations among the multitude of Indian societies, but we should note that in many cases the reports of low status are particularly suspect. Numerous anthropologists have shown that observers have consistently distorted gender relations in stateless societies by imposing their own hierarchies onto native categories and making ethnocentric interpretations of native customs. Statements that women were property, for example, probably stem from a misinterpretation of the custom whereby a prospective husband gave gifts or service to the family of the bride. Anthropologist Harold Driver, however, concludes that the institution of bride price gave the groom no rights over the person of his wife: 'All the husband purchases is the right to share with her the type of sexual and economic life permitted and approved by the society in which he lives.' Alice Schlegal has pointed out that among the matrilocal Hopi there was a comparable 'groom price' and short period of groom service that represented the transfer of the husband to the wife's household.[43]

In evaluating the reliability of reports that Indian women were badly treated, it is also important to take into account the fact that most such observations came after the Indian way of life had experienced profound changes as a result of epidemics, intensified warfare, the fur trade, and displacement. The overall effect of such processes was to remove the nuclear family and its individual components from the protection of the larger community or kin group and to lower the status and autonomy of women in relation to men.

The Impact of Contact on Kinship Systems and Gender Roles

Racial or cultural antagonism between Europeans and Indians was certainly not inevitable. Many contacts were peaceful, and a mutually beneficial dependence seemed possible. European traders brought heavy cloths, metal knives, fish-hooks, needles, awls, and pots that were valued by Indian men and women. The Indians showed the Europeans trails through the wilderness, introduced them to new foods and medicines, taught them survival techniques.

Some Europeans found Indian life more attractive than their own. Virginia found it necessary to impose severe penalties on colonials who ran away to join the Indians, while Michel Guillaume Jean de Crevecoeur raised the question of why 'thousands of Europeans are Indians, and we have no examples of even one of those Aborigines having from choice become European.' James Axtell has documented the large number of women and men who, taken captive by the Indians and adopted, refused to return to white society or, once returned, promptly ran away again. For their part, Indians were generally unwilling to take on the burdens of colonial agriculture and political hierarchy, but they maintained a receptive attitude toward European technology and religious ideas, incorporating some aspects of each into their own way of life without feeling the need to make pronouncements about whose life or beliefs were better.[44]

The good relations achieved by many individual Europeans and Native Americans often extended to intermarriage, which was particularly common among fur traders and Indian women. Such marriages had instrumental motives: traders gained entry into Indian society, and with proper alliances could find their influence much increased. Indians also profited from the alliance, expecting, often correctly, to gain access to European resources at the forts just as the traders gained access to Indian communities. Yet the presence of instrumental motives did not necessarily mean that ties of affection and sentiment were absent. Traders grieved when their Indian wives died, recording their sorrow and respect for the departed. They frequently made careful provision for their wives and children in case of their own death. Some took their families back to Europe; others stayed, largely from loyalty to their Indian families, and settled permanently. Indian wives of white traders often played an equal or leading role in household decisions, and trading company supervisors sometimes complained that the husbands of Indians developed loyalties that cut across their responsibilities to the company.[45]

But growing alongside these interpersonal instances of respect, cooperation, and intimacy was a widening clash between two incompatible modes of production, exchange, and social reproduction. The simple barter of goods that had at first promised mutual benefit brought into conflict two wholly different systems of organizing and conceptualizing exchange. In a money economy all goods are commensurate, and a good is defined not by who made it or who wears it but by its price. But some goods in Indian societies, as in most non-market societies, were made to express particular things about their owners and were often destroyed upon their owner's death. Other goods circulated only in limited channels and could not be exchanged for other types of goods. Thus Indian wampum was originally a symbol of personal prestige and interpersonal deference, given not in return for food or trade items but as part of a gift-exchange *relationship*, or as tribute, bride wealth, or recompense for injury. It was given in amounts that directly expressed and were inextricable from the particular relationship between the giver and the recipient. Wampum was a *sign* of power, prestige, and wealth, not a *means* to establish power or rank. To give or possess too much wampum was to step outside the social order.[46]

Dutch and English traders, however, actively encouraged the production of wampum in amounts in excess of the Indian tradition and sought to convert it to a fixed medium of exchange. They were aided in this task by the spread of diseases that often wiped out as much as 90 per cent of a tribe's population. Plagues decimated kin networks, disrupting social continuity and elevating the role of young male leaders at the expense of elders and women. They discredited traditional religious and medical practices, eroding the commitment to both material and spiritual values of communalism. Disease spread more quickly in the populous villages of sedentary groups, so that smaller, formerly marginal groups moved into new prominence, transforming traditional relations among Indians. Epidemics may also have increased the level of personal violence in many groups, given the widespread custom of raiding to replace lost kinsmen and the general social anomie that naturally accompanied such devastation.[47]

Coupled with this 'biological havoc,' trade with the Europeans had a more profoundly destabilizing effect than it might otherwise have had:

> The political crisis created by the epidemics made wampum a necessary acquisition for any sachem trying to expand – or even retain – his or her power. As greater and greater quantities became available to more and more individuals ... an inflationary cycle in the price of prestige objects fueled trade all the more. Possession of wampum became increasingly common, with widening effects on status systems ...[48]

New possibilities for individual accumulation led to new concepts of private property. The transition is well illustrated among the Naskapi Indians, who developed a hitherto unknown concept of trespass, though they initially defined it only as entering another's territory to obtain furs *for sale*. In Maine, the declining beaver hunt led to increasing competition among families, who began to allocate to themselves fixed hunting territories from which others could be excluded.[49]

Traditional Indian social organization had rested on constant circulation of both goods and labor on the basis of kin and marital relationships. The ability of individuals or nuclear families to acquire goods outside that structure and use them independently undercut the perception that sharing was the most important aspect of a person's life. It gave those receiving the most goods an incentive to free themselves from traditional obligations to kin and other group members. At the same time, ritual exchanges of labor or goods that had once cemented group solidarity could now be the route to individual wealth or power at the expense of the rest of the group. Individuals who were either traditionally influential or had been made so by the colonists could use their kin ties to pull in the labor of others – no longer for redistribution, but for the processing of more products to be funneled out of the system for sale. As they did so they undermined the principles of kinship society: prerogatives of wealth, concentrated within a single family, came to be more important than more extensive ties of blood or reciprocity.

In case after case where historical records of the transition exist, we see the same pattern – the growing independence of the nuclear family *vis-à-vis* the extended household, kinship and community group in which it had traditionally been embedded. Some nuclear families, freed from the obligation to redistribute, found themselves wealthier than before. Most, however, 'freed' from the protection of such redistribution, became poorer. And as the traditional family system was undermined, the way was opened for warriors, raiders, hunters, and trappers to pursue individualistic aims that brought little benefit to elders, women, and children, whose welfare remained intertwined with a disintegrating collectivity. 'The system of trade, and the small pox,' wrote Catlin, 'have been the great and wholesale destroyers of these poor people.' [50]

The two different notions of property underlying the different exchange systems led to other problems as well. When colonists received a commitment from a chief or headman, whom they mistakenly called a king or even an emperor, they did not understand that he could only present his views to the people, all or some of whom might legitimately ignore him. When colonists 'bought' land from an individual or even a group they had no idea that Indians could conceive only of granting use rights – and seldom exclusive ones – to the resources of an area, rights that could be revoked if the original recipients behaved improperly toward the donors or ceased to personally occupy the land. Indians did not recognize the right of colonists to fence or sell the land they had been allowed to use; colonists were furious when Indians failed to honor European terms of sale.

The different concepts of property were tied to two different approaches to survival itself. To the colonists, the new land was unimproved wilderness, free to be claimed by anyone willing to labor upon it. And labor upon it the colonists did. They cleared the land far more thoroughly than the Indians had ever done, plowed more deeply into the soil, built more permanent dwellings, and hauled rocks or felled trees to make sturdy fences around their private cornfields or ricefields and their gardens. They branded animals and expected the Indians to recognize that they were property, even when the cattle munched through Indian communal cornfields or the pigs rooted in their clam beds.

Indians, on the other hand, practiced extensive rather than intensive food production. Crop-growers had developed a sophisticated horticulture that was well adapted to their own needs while making minimal demands upon the soil. They mixed their crops and rotated their fields in ways that modern research shows to be extremely effective in conserving the soil. They also engaged in selective clearing and burning to produce the tender young shoots and small plants that attracted and supported a large supply of wild game, as well as encouraging the growth of the various berry bushes that provided such plentiful harvests from June through September. All this, however, required considerable space. Indians took advantage of seasonal diversity in natural resources by moving with the seasons according to where there were crops, fish runs, concentrations of game. This pattern of subsistence produced a stable ecology, and though it also meant that there were occasional periods of hunger, the Indians seem to have consciously chosen leisure over the intensive work required to produce a surplus sufficient to tide them over lean periods.[51]

They may have been more far-sighted than the colonists realized in making this choice, for intensive monoculture, such as maize in the

North and tobacco or rice in the South, exhausted the soil more quickly than Indian methods. One response of the colonists was to seek new land, violating early agreements with the Indians. Another was to make fertilizer out of the huge fish runs that had represented a mainstay of many Indian groups' existence. Raising livestock was also an expansionary proposition, as the amount of grain required to deliver a pound of meat protein is far more than that required to deliver the same amount of nutrition in bread or cereal. Livestock 'required more land than all other agricultural activities together,' points out William Cronon: 'Regions which had once supported Indian populations considerably larger than those of the early English settlements came to seem inadequate less because of *human* crowding than because of *animal* crowding.'[52]

The pressure of colonists on the land forced Native Americans into the defensive adoption of concepts of ownership, with the disastrous results summed up in a petition by the Mohegan Indians to the Connecticut State Assembly in 1789:

> In times past our Fore-Fathers lived in Peace, Love and great Harmony, and had everything in Great plenty. . . . They had no Contention about their lands, it lay in Common to them all, and they had but one large dish and they Could all eat together in Peace and Love – but alas, it is not so now, all our Fishing, Hunting and Fowling is entirely gone. And we have now begun to Work on our Land, Keep Cattle, Horses and Hogs and we Build Houses and fence in Lots. And now we plainly see that one Dish and one Fire will not do any longer for us – Some few that are Stronger than others and they will keep off the poor, weake, the halt and the Blind, and will take the Dish to themselves . . . poor Widows and Orphans must be pushed to one side and there they must Set a Craying, Starving and die.

The petition ends with the request that at least 'our Dish of Suckuttush may be equally divided amongst us.'[53]

But of course, once the dish was divided, even equally, it was going to shrink, for then needy or indebted individuals and families might be prevailed upon to sell their holdings, while if a family died out its portion no longer reverted to the group as a whole, but could be claimed by the colonial state. Anticipating these results, colonial leaders consciously attempted to break down communal land-ownership by enmeshing the Indians in debt and legislating individual property rights limited to the nuclear family. As Secretary of War Henry Knox wrote to George Washington in 1789: 'Were it possible to introduce among the Indian tribes a love of exclusive property, it would be a happy commencement of the business.'[54]

These changes in property and power relations led to a deterioration in personal relations as well. In fur trading areas, intensified competition for declining game led some traders to coerce Indian groups into giving them women; others made temporary unions and abandoned the women as soon as more expedient alliances presented themselves. White fathers, especially officers, began to try to wean their half-Indian sons and daughters away from Indian society entirely. These children became dependent upon white society. As competition among companies led to mergers and a decline in employment possibilities, the increasing racism of the late eighteenth century provided an excuse for excluding the children of mixed families.

Deterioration in relations was especially marked in areas of colonial settlement, where conflicts over politics and land were added to those over trade. Colonists eyed Indian lands, and increasingly discovered reasons why Indians were not entitled to them. Indians tended to respond piecemeal, depending upon the culture or the circumstances. Some granted more land or even made alliances with colonists against other Indian groups; others fought back by attacking the settlements which had encroached on their territory or enmeshed them in debt. Colonists made no distinction among different Indian groups in retaliating.

The impact of all this was to destroy the symmetry of relations *within* Indian societies as well as the balance between Indians and Europeans. The new importance of war increased the prestige and authority of warriors and often led to the eclipse of traditional governance principles. Among the Cherokees, the war organization increasingly supplanted the clan sections that governed the villages in times of peace. English authorities preferred to deal with this warrior hierarchy rather than the traditional leadership, and did all in their power to build it up. Harold Hickerson argues that the increased warfare between the Chippewa and the Sioux which resulted from the fur trade 'enhance[d] the status of younger men in the village as warriors, often in opposition, especially in the more populous villages, to the older civil leadership,' which had included elders and women. Hickerson suggests that the presence among Indian tribes of strong and well-organized warrior sodalities, which often achieved solidarity by denigrating womanhood, should be seen as an early symptom of the decay of a kinship-based system of social and political organization.[55]

Correlatively, European products were obtained through goods or activities which the males traditionally had directed as their part of the division of labor. Formerly, the labor of men and women, while different, had contributed equally to the subsistence of the group. Now a two-tier economy developed, in which male tasks resulted in the acquisition of new goods by trade or payment from the Europeans while the women continued to work for subsistence or became one-sidedly dependent on male activities.

The qualitative differences that now seemed to divide the labor of males and females led to an ossification of sex roles that had once been flexible and increased the burdens of 'women's work.' T.J.C. Brasser argues of the Algonkians that 'before contact, labor was well divided between the sexes, but after contact the men were seriously diverted from their normal activities to meet the demands of the traders. . . . and the responsibilities of the women increased.' In the case of the Iroquois, hints in the literature suggest that this may have temporarily elevated the authority of women, increasing their decision-making power as males were diverted into trade and warfare. If so, however, the Iroquois were a forlorn exception to the general rule – and even they were to experience a rapid reversal of this with more extensive contact. In most cases, the heightened importance of men in trade and warfare meant an entirely new organization of subsistence in which males acquired the new sources of wealth and women became mere processors of male-owned goods or producers of simple use-values. In either case males now had special access to important new resources, and thus gained in power and prestige.[56]

Conversion to Christianity and incorporation into colonial political units further weakened group cohesion and undermined the position of women. While trade and new forms of warfare gave men access to new sources of power and prestige, white missionaries and government officials attempted to impose their values of patriarchal authority upon the Indians with whom they had contact. The earliest land treaties between the Iroquois and the Europeans were signed by the matrons of the tribes as well as the chiefs, but the whites consistently attempted to deal with the chiefs only. Missionaries remonstrated with Indian men about allowing themselves to be 'henpecked' by women, and attempted to teach Indian children European sex roles. Among the southern Choctaw Indians, missionaries introduced the patrilineal family and tried to break down the extended matrilineal kinship system. Indian converts to Christianity defied custom by imposing greater controls and inflicting corporal punishment on women and children, a practice that divided kin networks and sometimes led to violent confrontations between converts and traditionalists.[57]

The Case of the Plains Indians

We are now in a better position to evaluate the reports of women's degraded status among the Plains Indians. Ironically, the Plains Indian life portrayed in the popular media since the nineteenth century was entirely a result of European influence. It was the rise of the fur trade, the new demand for pemmican, and the decline of farming villages due to disease – all consequences of European contact – that increased the reliance of Indians on the buffalo hunt, while it was the horse and gun – also introduced by Europeans – that made hunting an individualized, male activity. Alan Klein has pointed out that buffalo were originally hunted through 'impounding,' in which all the men and women of the tribe surrounded the animals and drove them into a trap, where they were dispatched with clubs. In this period, he argues, the entire family participated equitably in the distribution of meat and hides. The introduction of the horse, however, led to the exclusion of women, children and old people from the process of acquiring buffalos. As farming declined, these members of society 'became *subjects* of distribution rather than active participants in it.'[58]

When the fur trade stimulated men to kill more buffalo than they needed for subsistence, the wife's traditional role of hide-processing became greatly magnified and the most successful hunters needed to pull in more labor. Both Klein and Oscar Lewis have shown that this was achieved through a fall in the age of marriage for women to preadolescence, a sharp increase in the number of wives per hunter, and a tightening of restrictions upon wives. Writing in the nineteenth century, George Catlin also noted the connection between polygamy and labor needs, observing that it was most common 'Amongst those tribes who trade with the Fur Companies . . . and the women are kept for the greater part of the year, dressing buffalo skins for the market. . . .' (The reported frequency of mutilations of adulterous women in the nineteenth century should be related to this increase in male authority and also, perhaps, to the fact that an unfaithful wife challenged the husband's control over her work as well as her sexuality.[59])

At the same time, the individual nature of the fur trade exacerbated wealth differentials and social fragmentation. The rise of male sodalities 'worked to take up the slack left by the erosion of the collective mode of production and distribution' but also further 'raised the already rising position of men *vis-à-vis* women.' With the beginning of the reservation system, from the 1870s, Plains Indian women lost all remnants of their traditional role in 'supervising the distribution of meat from the collective hunts.'[60]

The image of Indians chasing buffalo, making war on each other, and dominating women, children and elders was obviously an attractive one to nineteenth-century Americans. If traditional Indians lived thus, it was possible to argue that first the colonists and then the expansion of the Republic had brought 'civilization' to the New World, where before there had been hunger, disease, violence, and male dominance. But hunger, disease, widespread violence, and male dominance in Native American populations were largely consequences of appropriation of property, population increase, and successful expansion by the settlers. The history of the establishment and reproduction of settler families in America must be read against this backdrop of destruction of Native American kinship systems.

Notes

1. Jack Forbes, ed., *The Indian in America's Past* (Englewood Cliffs, 1964), p. 89; T.J.C. Brasser, 'The Coastal Algonkians: People of the First Frontier,' in Eleanor Burke Leacock and Nancy Oestreich Lurie, eds, *North American Indians in Historical Perspective* (New York, 1971), p. 66; Cornelius Jaenan, *Friend and Foe: Aspects of French-Amerindian Cultural Contact in the Sixteenth and Seventeenth Centuries* (New York, 1976) p. 97; William Cronon, *Changes in the Land: Indians, Colonists, and the Ecology of New England* (New York, 1983), pp. 85–9; James Axtell, *The European and the Indian* (New York, 1981), pp. 248–9.

2. Forbes, *Indian in America's Past*, pp. 36–38; Jaenan, *Friend and Foe*, pp. 12–17; Francis Parkman, *Pioneers of France in the New World* (Williamstown, MA, 1970), p. 200; John Tebbel and Keith Jennison, *The American Indian Wars* (New York, 1960), pp. 2–9, 14–15; Peter Farb, *Man's Rise to Civilization* (New York, 1969); Neal Salisbury, *Manitou and Providence: Indians, Europeans, and the Making of New England, 1500–1643* (New York, 1982), p. 109.

3. For good examples of how to analyze so-called primitive societies on their own terms, taking account of observer prejudices and the impact of colonization or trade, see Eleanor Leacock and Mona Etienne, eds, *Women and Colonization: Anthropological Perspectives* (New York, 1980); Ruby Rohrlich-Leavitt, 'Peaceable Primates and Gentle People,' in Barbara Bellow Watson, ed., *Women's Studies: The Social Realities* (New York, 1976), pp. 169–202; Marshall Sahlins, *Stone Age Economics* (Chicago, 1972); Eleanor Leacock, *Myths of Male Dominance* (New York, 1981); Eleanor Leacock, 'Women, Power and Authority,' in Leela Dube, Eleanor Leacock, and Shirley Ardener, eds, *Visibility and Power* (New York, 1987).

4. Melville Jean Herskovits, *Economic Anthropology: The Economic Life of Primitive Peoples* (New York, 1965), p. 333.

5. *William Penn's Own Account of the Lenni Lenape or Delaware Indians*, ed. Albert Meyers (Somerset, NJ, [1683] 1970), p. 30.

6. George Snyderman, 'Concepts of Land Ownership Among the Iroquois and their Neighbors,' in William Fenton, ed., *Symposium on Local Diversity in Iroquois Culture* (Washington, D.C., 1951), p. 16. The lay brother Sagard-Theodat wrote in the 1620s that 'all the forests, meadows, and uncleared land are common property, and anyone is allowed to clear and sow as much as he will and can, and according to his needs; and this cleared land remains in his possession for as many years as he continues to cultivate and make use of it.' Charles Johnston, ed., *The Valley of the Six Nations: A Collection of Documents on the Indian Lands of the Grand River* (Toronto, 1964), p. 7. See also James Axtell, ed., *The Indian Peoples of Eastern America* (New York, 1981), p. 110; Cronon, *Changes*, pp. 61, 66–67. Even the relatively stratified northwest groups, who practiced slavery, had large areas of communal property and resource rights and strict limits on inheritance (James Arneson, 'Property Concepts of 19th Century Oregon Indians,' *Oregon Historical Quarterly* 81, 1980).

7. Lewis Henry Morgan, *Houses and House-Life of the American Aborigines* (Chicago, 1965), pp. 49–50.

8. Francis Harper, ed., *The Travels of William Bartram* (New Haven, 1958) pp. 311, 326.

9. Judith Brown, 'Economic Organization and the Position of Women Among the Iroquois,' *Ethnohistory* 17 (1970), p. 161; George Catlin, *Letters and Notes on the Manners, Customs and Conditions of the North American Indians* (New York, [1844]

1973), vol. 1, p. 122; Jaenan, *Friend and Foe*, p. 86.

10. Aram A. Yengoyan, 'Demographic and Ecological Influences on Aboriginal Marriage Sections,' in Richard Lee and Irven DeVore, eds, *Man the Hunter* (Chicago, 1968), p. 199. See also 'Discussions' in Lee and DeVore, p. 284; Coontz and Henderson, eds, *Women's Work, Men's Property: The Origins of Gender and Class* (London, 1986), pp. 116–19; Janet Siskind, 'Kinship and Mode of Production,' *American Anthropologist* 80 (1978).

11. An excellent model for how such transformation can occur in kinship societies is presented in J. Friedman and M. Rowlands, 'Notes Toward an Epigenetic Model of the Evolution of "Civilization" ',in Friedman and Rowland, eds, *The Evolution of Social Systems* (Pittsburgh, 1978). See also J. Friedman, 'Tribes, States, and Transformations', in Maurice Bloch, ed., *Marxist Analyses and Social Anthropology* (New York, 1975), pp. 161–202; Morton Fried, *The Evolution of Political Society* (New York, 1967); Robert McC.Adams, *The Evolution of Urban Society: Early Mesopotamia and Prehispanic Mexico* (Chicago, 1966).

12. Julia Averkieva, 'The Tlingit Indians,' in Leacock and Lurie, pp. 317–42; Helen Codere, *Fighting with Property* (Seattle, 1950); Philip Drucker, 'Rank, Wealth and Kinship in Northwest Coast Society' *American Anthropologist* 41 (1939), and *Cultures of the North Pacific* (San Francisco, 1965); Clellan Ford, *Smoke from Their Fires: The Life of a Kwakiutl Chief* (London, 1941); Ronald Olson, *Social Structure and Social Life of the Tlingit in Alaska* (New York, 1976); Ruth Underhill, *Indians of the Pacific Northwest* (New York, 1945).

13. *I Have Spoken: History through the Voices of Indians*, compiled by Virginia Armstrong (Chicago, 19667), pp. 4–5.

14. Penn, *Lenni Lenape*, p. 39; Robert Lowie, 'Some Aspects of Political Organization Among the American Aborigines,' in Ronald Cohen and John Middleton, eds, *Comparative Political Systems: Studies in the Politics of Pre-Industrial Societies* (Garden City, 1967), p. 73.

15. Sahlins, *Stone Age*, p. 205; Gary Nash, *Red, White and Black: The Peoples of Early America* (Englewood Cliffs, 1973), p. 237; Robert Lowie, 'Aspects of Political Organization,' pp. 74–5; Penn, p. 31; Farb, *Man's Rise*, pp. 186–7.

16. James Adair, *The History of the American Indians* (London, 1925), p. 428; John Hurdy, *American Indian Religions* (Los Angeles, 1970), p. 158; Catlin, *Letters and Notes*, vol. 2, p. 239.

17. Axtell, *The European and the Indian*, pp. 16–35; Jaenan, *Friend and Foe*, pp. 122–7, 138–43; Jennings, *Invasion*, pp. 160, 166.

18. Catlin, *Letters and Notes*, vol. 2, p. 240; Grace Steele Woodward, *The Cherokees* (Norman, 1963), p. 40; James Axtell, 'The White Indians of Colonial America,' *William and Mary Quarterly* 32 (1975), p. 71.

19. Axtell, 'White Indians,' p. 74; Mary Rowlandson, 'The Sovereignty and Goodness of God' [1682], in Alden Vaughan and Edward Clark, eds, *Puritans among the Indians: Accounts of Captivity and Redemption, 1676–1724* (Cambridge, MA, 1981), pp. 33–75. On the brutal treatment of indentured servants in the early colonial period, see Richard Hofstadter, *America at 1750: A Social Portrait* (New York, 1971).

20. Roger Williams, *A Key into the Language of America* (Detroit, 1973), p. 237; Frances Jennings, *The Invasion of America: Indians, Colonialism and the Cant of Conquest* (Chapel Hill, 1975), p. 150; Adair, *History*, pp. 379, 388.

21. Jennings, *Invasion*, p. 159; D'Arcy McNickle, 'Americans Called Indians,' in Leacock and Lurie, *North American Indians*, pp. 57–8; Ruth Underhill, *Red Man's Religion* (Chicago, 1965).

22. Edward H. Spicer, *Cycles of Conquest* (Tuscon, 1962), p. 472.

23. Marvin K. Opler, 'The Ute and Paiute Indians of the Great Basin Southern Rim,' in Leacock and Lurie, *North American Indians*, p. 269.

24. John Gyles, 'Memoirs of Odd Adventures, Strange Deliverances, Etc.,' in Vaughan and Clark, p. 121; Bartram, p. 135; Adair, *History*, p. 144; Opler in Leacock and Lurie, p. 269; Nancy Lurie, ed., *Mountain Wolf Woman, Sister of Crashing Thunder; the Autobiography of a Winnebago Woman* (Ann Arbor, 1966), p. 123, note 5.

25. *Travels of Bartram*, p. 327; John Upton Terrell and Donna M. Terrell, *Indian*

Women of the Western Morning (New York, 1974), p. 115; Axtell, *Indian Peoples*, pp. 71–102.

26. Cronon, *Changes*, p. 42.

27. Axtell, *Indian Peoples*, p. 138. For a discussion of leisure in primitive societies, see Sahlins, *Stone Age*, pp. 1–37.

28. Royal B. Hassrick, *The Sioux: Life and Customs of a Warrior Society* (Norman, 1964), pp. 32, 179; Regina Flannery, 'The Position of Women Among the Mescalero Apache,' *Anthropological Quarterly (Primitive Man)* 5 (1932), p. 29; David Smits, 'The "Squaw Drudge": A Prime Index of Savagism,' *Ethnohistory* 29 (1982), p. 296; Louise and George Spindler, 'Male and Female Adaptations in Cultural Change,' *American Anthropologist* 60 (1950), p. 229.

29. Father Joseph Lafitau, *Customs of the American Indians Compared with the Customs of Primitive Times*, ed. and trans. William Fenton and Elizabeth Moore (Toronto, 1974), vol 1, p. 57. See also Terrell and Terrell, *Indian Women*, pp. 130–31; Donald Forgey, 'The Institution of the Berdache Among the North American Plains Indians' *Journal of Sex Research* 11 (1975), pp. 1–15; Susan Hartmann, 'Women's Work Among the Plains Indians,' *Gateway Heritage* 3 (1983), p. 8.

30. Oscar Lewis, 'Manly Hearted Women Among the North Piegan,' *American Anthropologist* 43 (1941), pp. 173–87; Evelyn Blackwood, 'Sexuality and Gender in Certain Native American Tribes: The Case of Cross-Gender Females,' *Signs* 10 (1984), pp. 22–44.

31. Axtell, *Indian Peoples*, p. 92. See also pp. 87, 107, 137.

32. Baron LaHontan, *New Voyages to North America* [1703] ed. Reuben Thwaites, (New York, 1970), vol. 2, p. 463.

33. Eleanor Leacock, 'Montagnais Women and the Jesuit Program for Colonization,' in Etienne and Leacock, p. 28; Jaenan, *Friend and Foe*, p. 94. See also Axtell, *Indian Peoples*, pp. 6, 15, 18, 24, and 30.

34. Eleanor Leacock, 'Introduction,' in Frederick Engels, *The Origin of the Family, Private Property, and the State* (New York, 1975), p. 38; Axtell, 'White Indians of Colonial America,' pp. 60, 63; Smits, ' "Squaw Drudge",' p. 297.

35. Elizabeth Hanson, 'God's Mercy Surmounting Man's Cruelty,' in Vaughan and Clark, *Puritans Among Indians*, p. 239; Robert Grumet, 'Skunqsquaws, Shamans, and Tradeswomen: Middle Atlantic coastal Algonkian Women during the 17th and 18th Centuries,' in Etienne and Leacock, p. 58; J. Lawson, *A New Voyage to Carolina*, ed. H.T. Lefler (Chapel Hill, [1709] 1967), p. 184. For more on the position of the aged in communal kinship societies, see Leo Simmons, *The Role of the Aged in Primitive Society* (New Haven, 1946) and Donald Cowgill and Lowell Holmes, eds, *Aging and Modernization* (New York, 1972).

36. Winfred Blevins, *Give Your Heart to the Hawks* (New York, 1973), p. 191; Leacock, 'Introduction,' in Leacock and Lurie, *North American Indians*, p. 22; Penn, *Lenni Lenape*, p. 26; Alan Klein, 'The Impersistence of Persistence: A Diachronic Materialist Study of Plains Indians Values,' unpublished paper, Washington, D.C., 1976; Alan Klein, 'Adaptive Strategies and Process on the Plains: The 19th Century Cultural Sink,' Ph.D. dissertation, State University of New York at Buffalo, 1976.

37. Grace Steele Woodward, *The Cherokees* (Norman, 1969), pp. 40, 43; Henry Malone, *Cherokees of the Old South* (Athens, GA, 1956), p. 3; Grumet, 'Sunksquaws, Shamans, and Traders'; Adair, *History*, pp. 141, 145, 165; Carolyn Foreman, *Indian Women Chiefs* (Washington, 1976); Linda Grant de Pauw, *Founding Mothers: Women in the Revolutionary Era* (Boston, 1975); *Reports and Letters of Herbert Beaver, 1836–1838*, ed. Thomas E. Jessett (Portland, Oregon, 1959), p. 40; Terrell and Terrell, *Indian Women*, p. 113; Jennings, *Invasion*, p. 170.

38. Frederick Eggan, *Social Organization of the Western Pueblos* (Chicago, 1969); Shirley Hill Witt, 'Native Women Today,' *Civil Rights Digest* 76 (Spring 1974), p. 30; Leacock, 'Introduction,' in Leacock and Lurie, p. 23; *The Valley of the Six Nations*, p. 31; Carolyn Niethammer, *Daughters of the Earth: The Lives and Legends of American Indian Women* (New York, 1977); Axtell, *Indian Peoples*, p. 138; Nancy Lurie, 'Indian Women: A Legacy of Freedom,' in Charles Jones, ed., *Look to the Mountain Top* (San Jose, 1972).

39. Axtell, *Indian Peoples*, p. 159.

40. Leacock, 'Montagnais Women,' p. 29; de Pauw, *Founding Mothers*; Opler, 'Ute and Paiute Indians,' p. 269, *Reports and Letters of Herbert Beaver*; Adair, *History*, pp. 141, 164; Jennings, *Invasion*, p. 170.

41. B. H. Quain, 'The Iroquois,' in Margaret Mead, ed., *Cooperation and Competition Among Primitive Peoples* (Boston, 1961).

42. Father Joseph Lafitau, *Customs of the American Indians*, vol. 1, p. 69; William Beauchamp, 'Iroquois Women,' *Journal of American Folklore*, 13 (1900), p. 87. See also Judith Brown, 'Iroquois Women: An Ethnohistoric Note,' in *Toward an Anthropology of Women*, ed. Rayna Reiter (New York, 1975), pp. 235–51: William Fenton, *Symposium*; J.N.B. Hewitt, *Status of Women in Iroquois Polity Before 1784*, Bureau of American Ethnology, Smithsonian Institution, 1932; Frank Gouldsmith Speck, 'The Iroquois,' Cranbrook Institute of Science Bulletin no. 23, April 1955.

43. Harold E. Driver, *Indians of North America* (Chicago, 1969), p. 224; Alice Schlegal, *Sexual Stratification: A Cross-Cultural View* (New York, 1977), p.248. On the distortion of gender roles, see Naomi Quinn, 'Anthropological Studies on Women's Status,' *Annual Reviews in Anthropology* 6 (1977), pp. 181–225; Susan Rogers, 'Women's Place: A Critical View of Anthropological Theory,' *Comparative Studies in Society and History* (1982).

44. James Axtell, 'The White Indians of Colonial America,' *William and Mary Quarterly* 32 (1975), pp. 56–88.

45. Sylvia Van Kirk, *Many Tender Ties: Women in Fur Trade Society, 1670–1870* (Norman, 1983); Jennifer S.H. Brown, *Strangers in Blood: Fur Trade Company Families in Indian Country* (Vancouver. B.C., 1980); *Travels of Bartram*, p. 284; *Fur Trade and Empire: George Simpson's Journal, 1824–1825* (Cambridge, MA, 1931), p. 58.

46. See Sahlins, *Stone Age Economics*, pp. 149–275, and also Gene Weltfish's contention that exchange between two Indian groups 'meant bringing to one the uniqueness of the other. It was this implicit value, rather than profit, that was involved' ('The Plains Indians: Their Continuity in History and their Indian Identity,' in Leacock and Lurie, p. 206).

47. Cronon, *Changes*; Salisbury, *Manitou*; Richard White, *The Roots of Dependency: Subsistence, Environment and Social Change Among the Choctaw, Pawnees and Navajos* (Lincoln, NE, 1983).

48. Cronon, *Changes*, pp. 91, 96.

49. Eleanor Leacock, 'The Montagnais "Hunting Territory" and the Fur Trade', *American Anthropologist* 78 (1954); Cronon, *Changes*, p. 105.

50. Catlin, *Letters and Notes*, vol. 2, p. 250. For examples of the emergence of the nuclear family in different contexts, see Charles Hughes, 'The Changing Eskimo World,' in Leacock and Lurie, p. 390, and Claudia Lewis, *Indian Families of the Northwest Coast: The Impact of Change* (Chicago, 1970), esp.pp. 46–53.

51. The best single source on the difference between Indian and colonial land practices, along with their ecological impact, is Cronon, *Changes in the Land*. Sahlins also describes how 'primitive' peoples tend to choose leisure over surplus production, unless forced into more intensive production techniques by the permanent monopolization of resources by an upper class or by the demands of a state for taxes and labor (*Stone Age Economics*).

52. Cronon, *Changes*, pp. 139, 141.

53. Peter Matthieson, *Wildlife in America* (New York, 1959), pp. 70–71; George Novack, 'The Destruction of Indian Democracy,' in Novack, ed., *America's Revolutionary Heritage* (New York, 1976), pp. 40–41.

54. Armstrong, *I Have Spoken*, p. xxi. For colonial attempts to undermine communal land policies among the Iroquois, see Snyderman in Fenton, *Symposium*.

55. David Corkran, *The Cherokee Frontier* (Norman, 1962), p. 15; Harold Hickerson, 'The Chippewa of the Upper Great Lakes: A Study in Sociopolitical Change,' in Leacock and Lurie, pp. 181–2.

56. T.J.C. Brasser, 'The Coastal Algonkians: People of the First Frontiers,' in Leacock and Lurie, p. 71; Judith Brown, 'Iroquois Women,' p. 236.

57. Martha Randle, 'Iroquois Women: Then and Now,' in Fenton, *Symposium*; Axtell, *The Indian Peoples of Eastern America*, pp. 156–7; Eleanor Leacock and Jacqueline Goodman, 'Montagnais Marriage and the Jesuits in the Seventeenth Century,' *Western Canadian*

Journal of Anthropology 6 (1976); Jon Schlenker, 'An Historical Analysis of Family Life of the Choctaw Indians,' *Southern Quarterly* 13 (1975); Leacock, 'Montagnais Women.'

58. Alan Klein, 'Adaptive Strategies on the Plains,' p. 103.

59. Alan Klein, 'Adaptive Strategies' and 'The Political Economy of Gender: A 19th Century Plains Indian Case Study,' in Patricia Albers and Beatrice Medicine, eds, *The Hidden Half: Studies of Plains Indian Women* (Washington, D.C., 1983); Oscar Lewis, 'Effects of White Contact Upon Blackfoot Culture,' *Monographs of the American Ethnological Society* VI (1942); Catlin, *Letters and Notes*, vol. 1, p. 118.

60. Klein, 'Political Economy of Gender,' p. 164; Patricia Albers, 'Sioux Women in Transition: A Study of their Changing Status in Domestic and Capitalist Sectors of Production,' in Albers and Medicine, *The Hidden Half*, p. 188.

3

Households and Communities in Colonial America

The families established by European settlers in America varied according to the type of colonists who arrived and the local conditions these met, but all were far more bounded units than the families that existed as subsets of Indian kinship systems. Europeans brought private property, which was inherited through families, and state institutions, which related to families as units of taxation, conscription, and social control. Families were not only more important economic and political units than among the Indians, but they were also agents for the reproduction of class differences, rather than for the widest possible circulation of goods and labor. The European families that came to America were connected, albeit at different points, to an international mercantile system whose conceptions of wealth, trade, state authority, and national rivalries stood in sharp contrast to the collective subsistence and individual autonomy of Indian life. At the same time, they were also products of rapid social, economic, and political change in this system, change that would eventually produce capitalism.

Some families and individuals came to America to escape the religious and political persecutions of the older system, some to escape the economic dislocations of the newer one. Middle-class families from the textile centers and commercial cities of Holland and England settled in New England and New York. Land-hungry English gentlemen (and a few ladies), ambitious commoners seeking fast wealth, and sugar-planters from Barbados came to the South, along with deported convicts or paupers, part of a growing class created by rack-renting, enclosures, and inflation. Possibly a majority of seventeenth-century immigrants were indentured servants, who bound themselves to work various terms of service in return for their passage. These people were neither feudal dependants nor self-sufficient peasants or farmers: their social interactions, work experiences, and political relations were not organized through aristocratic manors nor through purely local networks of neighbors and kin; every colony was, rather, part of an emerging system of international commerce.

Yet we cannot understand colonial families if we prematurely label as capitalist the organization and aim of colonial settlements or project back onto the colonies a modern division between an impersonal labor market and political arena on one hand and a private family system on the other. Instead economics, politics, and interpersonal relations in the colonies intertwined and overlapped in hierarchical communities of households governed by a patriarchal system of authority. Patriarchy was itself partly private and partly public: government institutions were highly personalized, while personal relations carried political consequences. Private property in land was the ultimate source of patriarchal authority, so the system was oriented toward gains from agrarian production, but the market was too limited, and too dependent on interpersonal relations, to permit a major concentration on profit-maximization or risk-taking. The economy and polity may best be described as a corporate system of agrarian household production sustained by a patriarchal political and ideological structure.[1]

The family, often subordinate to the household, was an inseparable part of this unified system of economic and personal interdependence, political and social hierarchy, and patriarchal control. Its boundaries were permeable and its distinction from churches, political structures, and property-owning households was often blurred. Like these other colonial institutions, the family was a corporate body in which each individual was subject to the hierarchy of the whole.

The Early Colonies

In New England, Puritan colonists established small nucleated villages which, while firmly based on private property, fostered intensive communal cooperation in the clearing of land and the construction of bridges, roads, churches, and court houses. When land was distributed, farm parcels were scattered around the edges of the village 'so that no family should locate on a single tract.'[2] Villages were built around a meeting house and a church with a graveyard or training field nearby. Initially lands for grazing, collecting firewood, or gathering clay and grass were held in common, though by the mid seventeenth century individuals had encroached upon many of these. Throughout that century, however, the notion of collective responsibility for development remained strong. The town might offer land and certain privileges to attract artisans such as millers or blacksmiths; these in turn would have to agree to remain for a certain length of time and to expect to have their work and behavior subject to scrutiny and rebuke by village leaders.

The laws of New England reveal a society in which village and church officials regulated all aspects of life, from sexual conduct to prices of goods to whether a person could build a fence or take up a trade. Town and church determined where people should live, what they should wear, how long they could put up strangers in their homes; neighbors constantly intervened to report departures from the norm.

The communal or corporate character of this system should not be confused with egalitarianism. From the very beginning, even land divisions mirrored the social hierarchy preached by John Winthrop in 1630, aboard the *Arabella*: 'in all times some must be rich, some poor, some high and eminent in power and dignity, others mean and in subjection.' New England town meetings may have striven for consensus, but it was a consensus based on the leadership of the rich, the high, and the eminent. As Richard Bushman writes of early Connecticut:

> In nearly every dimension of life – family, church, the social hierarchy, and religion – a Connecticut subject encountered unanimous reinforcement of governing authority. The total impact was immense, because each institution was part of a monolithic whole. The preacher's exhortation to submit to domestic authority reinforced the father's dominion in his family. Church discipline added new terrors because censures were delivered before the neighbors and the town's most prominent families, and the assignment of pews in the meetinghouse according to social rank reminded everyone . . . of the deference due superiors.[3]

The Middle Colonies were economically, ethnically, and religiously more heterogeneous than New England. Parts of New Jersey and New York quickly developed widespread landlordism and tenant farming, leading to greater class disparities than in New England. Elsewhere, William Penn's offer of religious toleration and inexpensive land attracted moderately prosperous smallholders whose modernizing beliefs and economic practices had been thwarted in absolutist Europe. From the beginning these people engaged in production for a local market: Pennsylvania and Delaware developed on the basis of dispersed homesteads built in a radius around regional market towns.

On the whole, the Middle Colonies were less corporate in character than New England because they were settled by such diverse groups of people and lacked the nucleated villages that made control over daily life comparatively easy. County government was more important, and less intrusive, than local townships. But concentrations of ethnic and religious groups in the Middle Colonies – settlements of Dutch and Baptists in New York and New Jersey, or Quakers and Germans in Pennsylvania – created smaller corporate bodies that organized economic transactions, social and familial interactions, and work patterns. Religious groups acted as mutual aid and credit societies and closely supervised the lives of their members; ethnic and religious settlements provided places for landless individuals to set up as dependent tenant farmers under landlords who might be expected to feel some mutual obligations. The fact that people often chose to become tenants instead of striking out for the frontier indicates a basic acceptance of corporate values even among the seemingly more individualistic settlers of the Middle Colonies. Moreover, the market towns on which farmers converged twice weekly provided centers for face-to-face transactions that greatly limited the possibility of separating economic calculations from personal obligations and community restraints.[4]

Sam Bass Warner argues that although Philadelphia was marked by 'privatism' by the early eighteenth century, with people working in independent shops and pursuing private economic ends, it was not individualistic:

> Graded by wealth and divided by distinctions of class though it was, it functioned as a single community. The community had been created out of a remarkably inclusive network of business and economic relationships and it was maintained by the daily interactions of trade and sociability. . . . [There was a] unity of everyday life, from tavern, to street, to workplace, to housing, which held the town and its leaders together. . . .[5]

The South lacked the nucleated villages or settled towns of the North. Community and family life were quite unstable in the early decades, due to high death rates, skewed sex ratios, and the fact that probably a majority of the settlers came as single servants who could not get married until they had served their period of indenture. Males between the ages of twenty and twenty-nine were the single most populous sector of southern society in 1625. Competition among these males, coupled with higher mortality rates, contributed to a more volatile political and economic climate in the South, with greater extremes of wealth and fewer communal elements to social life.

In Virginia, discovery of the profits to be made from tobacco caused a rapid dispersal of individuals in search of the rich soil required for its cultivation. The speed of soil exhaustion (four to five years) made settlements impermanent: visitors from the North, with its solidly built homes, were always shocked by the ramshackle construction of most southern houses. Yet the very impermanence of settlement and security among the smaller planters gave all the more social weight to plantations that were large enough (1,000–4,000 acres) to become permanent centers. This created its own kind of corporate hierarchy. By the end of the seventeenth century a native elite had effectively sewn up power in Maryland, the Carolinas, and Virginia. In the early 1700s this elite began to make the fateful transition from an indentured labor force to black slavery.

The distance between farms and the self-sufficiency of great estates, located along major waterways from which export crops could be shipped, facilitated less regulation of daily life and a greater development of competitive individualism than in the North. Ironically, however, the seeming modernity of competition among the great planters, when combined with their dependence on English credit and their lack of a free labor force, fostered almost feudal values of display and patronage.

The 'Great Houses' of the major planters soon became large buildings surrounded by kitchens, dairy houses, small mills, smoke-houses, stables, slave quarters, and work-houses for resident or itinerant craftsmen. Travelers often remarked on the resemblance of large plantations to towns or villages. Lesser planters came to the great estates to buy goods and services not available elsewhere (a constant problem in the South was the desertion of crafts by people anxious to become planters themselves) and to sell their own crops. They were in debt to their great neighbors and dependent on them for credit, manufactures, repairs, and so forth. The great neighbors, for their part, were chronically short of cash. They required a network of support and obligations that could be called upon in need. Much of their ability to achieve this rested on success in establishing their person or house as a social magnet, attracting dependants and confirming social rank. Southern gentry impressed their neighbors, attracted clients, credit, and skilled workmen to their households, and cemented their solidarity with other great families through elaborate rituals of hospitality and a jealous balancing of social duties and prerogatives. Competition was channeled into horseracing, gambling for immensely high stakes, and conspicuous consumption. Control over the lower classes was exercised less through incorporating lower-class servants and workers into household relations of authority (as was done in the North) than by larger rituals of cross-class interaction (generally male) such as the 'treating' of lower-class whites at militia musters or elections.[6]

Southern society, then, had some special characteristics: a greater emphasis on male displays of wealth, power, and competition; a peculiar combination of feudal and mercantile values involving conspicuous consumption, profiteering, and hospitality; and, after the seventeenth century, a growing bifurcation between white identity and black. Yet southern society, like northern, was still based on an organic interdependence of households in a tangle of hierarchy, deference, and obligation. Regulation of tobacco monopolies and administration of local justice by the great planters, enforced deference, upper-class scrutiny of the behavior of indentured servants or slaves, and the legal requirement that all persons attend a parish church prevented southern society from developing anything like a modern individualism: 'The parochial organization – maintained at considerable cost, under legal sanctions – expressed a concept of inclusive community in which all members shared in a corporate responsibility to maintain worship and to receive instruction in duties that were at once religious and social.'[7]

Interdependence, Hierarchy, and Patriarchy

Despite regional differences, then, the economic, social, and political interdependence of colonial societies prevented the emergence of sharp boundaries between economic transactions and personal relations, public institutions and familial ones. In small villages, local market towns, and plantations, craftsmen and traders produced not for an impersonal market but for individual clients who generally placed their orders in advance. In commercial ports throughout the colonies, political officers regulated the price and quality of goods. The poor depended upon leading householders for shelter and food; charity or wages were generally paid in kind. City consumers had to establish personal relations with peddlers or nearby farmers to be assured of regular supplies of food or other farm goods that they did not grow in their own gardens; farmers had to have contacts in town to be assured of getting tools or craft goods that they could not make themselves. Journals frequently record frustrating attempts to get goods that could not be bought at any price, since they were already promised to neighbors or relatives.

While agricultural households aimed at diversity of production in order to fill household needs, self-sufficiency was never attained or even aspired to. A constant circulation of goods and services filled gaps in production or shortages of labor. If frequent conflicts broke out over neighborly rights, obligations, and exchanges, these merely testify to the centrality of such relations and to people's dependence upon each other's proper behavior. Only neighbors who do not depend on each other for vital resources or services can maintain relations of detached civility.

With good reason, historians have again and again described colonial life as 'dense.'[8] This density was an essential part of the corporate nature of colonial life, for it established the interpersonal bonds of obligation and dependence, deference and condescension, that held communities together. Social control was exercised through a continual mingling of classes on terms that underlined their unequal weight and the hierarchy of their relations. Seating at church was based on rank and wealth, and political offices were filled by the elite: the top offices were occupied by the wealthiest members of society, the next levels of office-holding were held by men at the next levels of rank, and so on: 'Even surveyors of highways and grand jurors brought an appropriate degree of prominence to their positions. Everyone sensed the ascending order of social power enhancing the ascending order of civil authority.'[9]

The glue that bound individuals to households and households to community was patriarchy. In the church, in politics, and in the household, older males ruled. Patriarchy should not be construed as precisely the same as male dominance. Certainly the authority of the father was paramount. He usually got custody of the children in case of divorce; disobedience to him was conceptualized as a small form of treason; and his centrality in the household is shown by the fact that he was often the person to whom children wrote home, conveying their respects to the mother in a postscript. Still, it was not all fathers who ruled, but only fathers who were property-owners; and their rule was not exclusively or even primarily over women. They ruled also over lower-class males, who were patronized and expected to defer in what would later come to be thought of as feminine ways.

Moreover, the rule of a household head was not at his private discretion. Household authority and community authority were inseparable. In both North and South courts enforced obedience to the household head, even if he had not asked for help. Household heads were frequently punished for failing to exercise authority over wives, servants, or children, while informal shaming rituals were also used to force males to discipline disobedient behavior they had chosen to ignore. In seventeenth-century New England special public officers (tithingmen) were charged with maintaining family order and reporting household heads who were negligent in enforcement of their authority and duties. In the South, household heads might be ducked for inability to control their servants. New England even had laws that made repeated wilful disobedience of children punishable by death. Although this sentence was never imposed, its existence points to the public nature of colonial patriarchy. So does the fact that patriarchy by no means gave husbands a free hand. Edmund Morgan reports:

When Daniel told his wife Elizabeth that 'shee was none of his wife, shee was but his Servantt,' neighbors reported the incident to the authorities, and in spite of the abject Elizabeth's protest 'that I have nothinge Agenst my husband to Charge him with,' the Essex County Court fined him forty shillings.[10]

Courts frequently required erring husbands to post bond to ensure future good behavior.

Patriarchy led to a social acceptance of inequality and rank that extended far beyond relations between father and child or husband and wife. Servants deferred to masters and masters deferred to their social superiors with words that emphasized their humility, their weakness, their unworthiness. Greater men condescended to lesser, with no sense on either side that this was insulting. Colonial economic and social life can best be conceptualized as a series of ascending but overlapping circles rather than as a series of discrete levels. Individuals were dependent upon people both above and below them; vertical ties were as important in a person's daily life as horizontal ones. Indeed, horizontal solidarities were rather difficult to discern or maintain. Classes melded into and influenced each other, even though – or perhaps because – the rate of mobility between classes was extremely low.

My description of classes as forming a gradual continuum is not meant to imply that there were not extremes of rich and poor, but merely to stress that the distance between the two was filled with innumerable gradations, while the conceptual gap was also not so sharp as it was later to become. The rich did not yet see the poor as having caused their own problems, while the poor did not yet see the rich as having become so through theft of another's birthright or exploitation of others' labor. Even in the seaports, where by 1700 the top 10 per cent of the population controlled 40 per cent of the wealth and the bottom 30 per cent only 3 per cent, Gary Nash reports:

> The incidence of poverty, in fact, was extremely low and was confined for the most part to the widowed, disabled, and orphaned, who were decently cared for. . . . Little stigma was attached to being poor . . . and a sense of social responsibility pervaded poor relief measures.

As Laurel Thatcher Ulrich comments: 'In the home and in the neighborhood, inequality colored interdependence, and interdependence tempered inequality.'[11]

Conflict and discontent were by no means absent in this system. We have already noted the fierce jockeying for place among the great planters, and even when lines of hierarchy were clear, they were not always comfortable. Jan Lewis remarks that eighteenth-century journals 'were often little more than social account books in which Virginians calculated their social debts and credits.' The calculation could be painfully precise. Thus Robert Wormeley Carter noted in his diary that

> Col. F. Lightfoot Lee was married this day to Miss Rebecca Taylor. . . . I received a very slight invitation; but went that I might give no offence. . . . Drank no wine, because I was expressly within the Statute made by Mrs. Taylor; who said at her Table that She wondered how Persons who were paying Interest for money & kept no wine of their own; could come to her House & to [illeg.] it in such a manner as they did. . . .[12]

Members of the northern middling classes were close enough in rank and wealth that the proper relationship of deference and condescension, superiority and inferiority, was not always evident: 'When seating the meeting-house by rank, the settlers invariably squabbled over the order of precedence, for the lines that distinguished one man from another were indistinct.'[13] Neighbors frequently slandered and sued each other over real or imagined insults to their standing or departures from appropriate hierarchical behavior.

Relationships between the upper and lower orders were also not always harmonious. When people perceived leaders as departing from their customary obligations of reciprocity or exceeding their traditional prerogatives, the very absence of impersonal channels for political and economic intercourse made 'the mob' a potent force that could prevail upon leaders to retreat from the offending behavior, and even influence upper-class perceptions and values. Tarring and feathering, charivari rituals, and other elements of popular culture served not only to enforce conformity among the lower classes but also to check the excesses of the elite. Up to the mid eighteenth century, riots 'were a tacitly accepted part of the Anglo-American culture, a quasi-legitimate activity . . . in defense of widely accepted community values.'[14]

The seventeenth century saw many cross-class rebellions which reveal a strong imprint of lower-class discontent and initiative: these include Bacon's Rebellion in Virginia, the overthrow of Governor Andros in Massachusetts, the Leisler Rebellion in New York, the anti-proprietary movement in Pennsylvania, and Culpeper's Rebellion in Carolina. Indentured servants and slaves ran away and occasionally used violence against their masters. Urban consumers rioted over food price increases.[15] But the lower classes had nothing in their social experience to allow them to contemplate an alternative to the political and economic dependency relations that governed daily life. Hence the norm in colonial life was the undisputed leadership of colonial elites, reinforced by community sanctions against those (either high or low) who stepped out of the bounds of corporate interdependence and hierarchy.

Households and Families in Colonial America

To understand the impact of colonial patriarchy on the family, we must grasp the essential unity of personal and politicoeconomic relations in colonial life. This unity was expressed most fully in the household, which was the central economic institution in colonial America. Built around a main room, with perhaps a sleeping loft upstairs, the household was the site, almost simultaneously, of cloth production, carpentry, food preparation, and schooling. The day's agricultural work was organized out of the main room and workers returned there for meal breaks. Households supplied most of their own needs, producing for subsistence and bartering the surplus with other households or exchanging services with them. Even the households of great southern estates were not set apart from the process of production on the plantations they ruled. Cloth was spun, butter churned, ale brewed, accounts kept, and customers or suppliers entertained in the home. By the second half of the eighteenth century the mistress of one such plantation reported that her duties included the provisioning of a household that consumed 27,000 pounds of port, 550 bushels of wheat, and 150 gallons of brandy a year.[16]

The mistresses of such households, large or small, could hardly separate their domestic duties from their social obligations. As Ulrich points out:

> Because families in early America were neither socially nor economically self-contained, a good housewife was also of necessity a 'friendly Neighbor'. . . . Herding was as much a community as a family responsibility. Weaving and fulling were skilled crafts limited to a few males [in the South, sometimes females] in the single neighborhood or village. Even carding and spinning, the perennial fireside tasks, might be hired out to a poor neighbor or widow.[17]

The households – if not necessarily the houses – of property owners were large, including servants, apprentices, and numerous children. The fertility rate of early American families was high, the infant mortality rate in most places lower than in Europe, and the frequent (though by no means inevitable) remarriage of widows and widowers also meant that households often consolidated children of different parents. Households did not normally comprise extended families, since children took up separate residence upon marriage, but paternal authority and extended family ties were strong even after marriage. Fathers often settled their sons on nearby land which the father continued to own, thereby exercising considerable economic control over the sons and their families.

Paternal control frequently extended beyond the death of the father, for wills stipulated how the land could be used or gave detailed instructions about the services and facilities to be provided to the widow by the heirs.

Thomas King, for instance, provided that his heirs must furnish his widow with 'five pounds by the year . . . the one half of it in money the other half of it in Corne and other Provision also wood provided for her fire and winter meat and Sumer meat for two Cows.' She was also to have 'the East End of my dwelling house . . . with a liberty to make use of the Cellars and and [sic] leantoos.' Daniel Snydacher reports that a widespread feature of wills in rural Pennsylvania 'was the network of obligations . . . cast out over the family.' Southern planters encouraged cousin marriages and laid out future education plans in order to control the direction of the family after their deaths. And Philip Greven has described families in Andover, Massachusetts, as having a modified extended structure, a patriarchal character, and deep roots in the community.[18]

The household was the center not only of economic production but also of social services, education, socialization, work training, and religious instruction. Household authority was the basis of the political order, just as household production was the basis of the economy. The head of the family was responsible for the entire household's religious instruction and education. In both North and South, servants lived in the families of their employers and under their authority until they had the means and the right to set up their own families. The explanation of the English Puritan William Gouge was one that would have been readily acceptable to American colonists: 'a family is a little Church, and a little Commonwealth . . . whereby triall may be made of such as are fit for any place of authoritie, or of subjection in Church or Commonwealth.' For this reason, colonial authorities tried to ensure that everyone was a member of a family. Puritan laws provided for the placement of single persons in the families of others. Connecticut imposed a fine of one pound for each week a bachelor lived on his own, while in Maryland the taxes imposed on bachelors were almost punitive.[19]

Households and families had the same corporate, interdependent character as did communities. The frequent use of organic analogies, describing the father as the head and the other members as the limbs, speaks to the lack of individual rights and independent identities within the family. So does the tendency to name children after deceased siblings. This was not a sign that people did not value their children, as is sometimes supposed, but an indication that *what* they valued, for themselves and their children, was the child's identification as part of a corporate body. Another indication of the corporate nature of family life was the practice of guaranteeing the widow a third of the property upon her husband's death but not allowing her to sell it.

The colonies' insistence on family membership and authority has led many authors to describe the family as the most important institution of colonial society. Yet we need to distinguish the importance of *families* in

colonial life from the importance of *the* family. The biological family, in
fact, was less sacrosanct and less central to people's lives than it was to
become during the nineteenth century.

Colonial society demanded membership of a *properly ordered* family,
and actual blood or marital family ties were subordinated to that end.
Thus the lower classes had little family life of their own, often living
in the households of their employers, subject to the employers' rule and
even to their corporal punishment. A child might be removed from home
and placed in another family if his or her parents were deemed unworthy
by the community leadership. The families of redemptioners arriving in
the southern colonies were often broken up, with one or more members
bound out to various households to pay for the passage. Redemptioners'
children between the ages of five and ten could be sent to serve another
family until the age of twenty-one. Among all classes in the North it was
common to send out at least one child to learn housework or a trade in
another home by the time he or she was eleven or twelve, occasionally
earlier. Journals reveal the relative fluidity of household composition,
as one or another member lived elsewhere for a while, servants came
and went, and distant relatives spent short stays. In the South there was
another reason for family fluidity in the seventeenth century: almost 20
per cent of Chesapeake children were orphaned before their thirteenth
birthday, and more than 30 per cent were orphaned before the age
of eighteen.[20] Households might combine the children of a previous
marriage for one or both parents plus the children of their own union,
as well as servants and an occasional cousin or niece.

In all areas of the country, there was a tendency for children
to concentrate in the households of property-owning families, since
non-propertied families had fewer children or sent theirs out as servants
and were less likely to remarry. One study of early American families
found that although only 35.9 per cent of the parents had nine children
or more, more than 50 per cent of all children lived in families with
eight or more other children. Conversely, although 10 per cent of the
couples had three or fewer children, these families included only 2.6
per cent of the total children. A study of Middle Colony Quaker
families found that while only 35.9 per cent of the parents had
eight or more children, 60 per cent of the children lived with at least
seven siblings.[21]

Each household was linked by social obligation, economic need, kin or
servant ties, and law to neighboring households and to church activities,
town meetings and courthouse proceedings. The family was but one of
many overlapping groups and institutions that connected individuals to
each other and to the larger society. The organizing basis of those
connections was not the needs of the individual but the requirements of

church or community: 'The corporate whole, not the individual, was the basic conceptual unit.'[22]

In these circumstances, an exclusive orientation to 'the family,' in its biological or conjugal sense, could not characterize colonial life. The household rather than the family was the important institution in people's daily lives, but since household composition changed frequently and no household stood outside the regulation of church and community, identification was with the society of households or the *position* of household members rather than with a unique, individual family.

Within the household, there was little sense of marital privacy or of special intimacy among blood relatives. As John Demos points out, 'the prevalent assumptions about family life made little distinction between a natural child and a servant of about the same age.' The central room or hall was where work, meals, play, religious instruction, schooling, and often even sleep took place. In the South, kitchen and other work spaces were when possible removed from the central hall because of the heat, but otherwise southern houses also lacked divisions into specialized areas. Even genteel families put several beds into a room, and sometimes several people to a bed. Most household members sat together on benches for meals and prayers, rather than in separate chairs. There was thus little concept of a private family set apart from the world of work, servants, and neighbors. Even the birth of a child reinforced the connection between family and community. Distant kin and neighbor women attended the birth, often displacing the husband and sometimes staying three or four weeks to do the mother's chores while she was permitted to 'lie-in.'[23]

Thus, paradoxically, the importance of the whole network of families in colonial life precluded a self-conscious preoccupation with 'the' family. People's identity and activities do not seem to have been particularly bound up with their biological family. The work unit was the immediate family plus servants, most of whom were productive workers rather than domestics; and no sharp distinction was made between the two groups. In many seventeenth- and eighteenth-century churches families did not sit together in conjugal units; instead, the congregation was seated according to sex and age.

In northern villages, authorities or neighbors frequently intervened in the 'private' affairs of families to ensure compliance with community norms: 'The household, as a microcosm of the town, depended on mutual aid to maintain order, but every household order depended on the town for its existence.' The assumption that household affairs were the business of all community members is seen in Nancy Cott's study of divorce records, which show that neighbors nonchalantly entered what modern people would consider the most private areas of life. Mary Angel and Abigail Galloway, for example, testified that they had caught sight through an open window of Adam Air 'in the Act of Copulation' with Pamela Brichford. They walked into the house 'and after observing them some time . . . asked him if he was not Ashamed to act so when he had a Wife at home. . . .'[24]

The primacy of relations with neighbors can be seen in the very tensions that surrounded neighborly interactions and failed to show up in family ones. John Demos has suggested that 'a man cursed his neighbor in order to keep smiling at his parent, spouse, or child,' displacing family hostilities onto the less threatening target of neighbors. Edmund Morgan has attributed the fact that children were sent out to the households of other families, even when there was no economic reason for doing so, to fear by colonial parents that they might spoil their children. I suggest, however, that the problem of too much love or too much hate within the family was not the central concern of colonial Americans. Departures from the norm in family relations could be resolved, or at least suppressed, by the community. Departures from the norm in neighborly relations threatened the very fabric of social and economic life. A man cursed his neighbor because he was locked into an intense relationship of mutual dependence that circumscribed his individual behavior. At the same time, he sent his neighbor offerings – of goodwill, material aid, even children – because he needed to perpetuate that relationship.[25]

In northern cities and in the South families were less interdependent, but they were still subject to rituals of popular culture that involved shaming individuals who departed from accepted norms, or to outright invasion by direct crowd action. They were also caught up in the web of patronage and dependence that comprised the social hierarchy. In Charlestown, Massachusetts, for example, an elite of merchant-planters, comprising with their families less than 25 per cent of the total population but controlling 70 per cent of the land, exerted power through an extensive network of intermarriage, socializing, and child-exchange, while the town's poor lived as boarders, often with their employers, or shared housing. Even married couples among the poor seldom had a separate family dwelling. In almost all areas of colonial America, indeed, families outnumbered households, meaning that many families shared dwellings. In the South, small farm or planter families were dwarfed by the social preeminence of great planter and merchant households. These combined a vigorous concern for the preservation of the 'line' with behavior patterns that subordinated the family to a much larger network of socializing. As Rhys Isaac comments on the Virginia gentry:

The ideal of the home as a center of private domesticity was not familiar to Anglo-Virginians in the mid-eighteenth century. They lived or aspired to live in the constant presence of servants or guests. Their houses were the sacrosanct settings for hospitality and for the open celebration of the major events of life and death. . . . Indeed, most of the dominant values of the culture were fused together in the display of hospitality, which was one of the supreme obligations that society laid upon heads of household.[26]

Personal Relations inside Colonial Families

Not surprisingly, colonists had little sense that emotional interactions among people were qualitatively different within the family than outside it, or that calculating the material as well as the affective benefits of family relations involved any contradiction. Children seem to have been loved, but treated neither as unique individuals nor as important components of a parent's self-identification. While colonial women seldom put their children out to wet nurses, they regularly exchanged breast milk and nursing services on a convenience basis and sent their children to other households at a relatively early age. Colonial parents were far more strict than Indian ones, and required children to help in more productive activities:

As soon as they could pluck goose feathers or dry spoons, children were also servants. Hired servants, at the same time, were children, needing clothes of their own, firm discipline, and instruction in the Bible. Mothering meant generalized responsibility for an assembly of youngsters rather than concentrated devotion to a few.[27]

Anne Bradstreet illustrates the combination of affection and sternness that comprised colonial parenting. She wrote poems about her love for her children and her desire to nurse them until they were strong enough to fly, but also commented that some children, like some pieces of land, are so 'tough and morose . . . that the plough of correction must make long furrows on their back, and the Harrow of discipline goe often over them, before they bee fit soile to sow the seed of morality, much lesse of grace in them.'[28]

Children related to their parents with an unselfconscious mixture of affection and calculation, evidently free from any sense that filial affection must be kept separate from instrumental motives. Frederick Jones wrote from North Carolina to his father in Virginia asking that he be sent a pole chair, the cost of which could be deducted from his inheritance: 'Your complying will be a particular Instance of yours and my Mother[']s Love and Affection to me, as it will be advancing so much toward my Share or Part, which I have no reason to expect 'till your Death to share with the rest.' After not receiving funds for a year, Walter Jones did not think it disingenuous to ask his brother why he was withholding the 'Testimonies of that Kindness & affection, which I have always Experienced & which Love & gratitude have as constantly prompted me to deserve.'[29]

One striking feature of colonial child-rearing is the emphasis on instilling external obedience to parental, church, and political authority rather than fostering independent decision-making. There was no sense that the family needed to teach social behavior that might conflict with that fostered by other institutions, to give children a unique emotional identification with their parents that would enable them to withstand pressures from peers and community, or to provide its members with beliefs and values that they would not find elsewhere.

This lack of attention to defining an exclusive and individual nexus of emotional relationships between parents and children was also characteristic of marriage relations. Although love was an important part of marriage, and reference to romantic ideals increased over the course of the eighteenth century, love was not the main axis of family relations. The family was part of a unified system of social interaction, emotional dependence, and patriarchal control. Family, church, and government all taught roughly the same things and demanded roughly the same commitments, though perhaps in different degrees; relationships in each area did not require qualitatively different ways of behaving and feeling. The family was not viewed as either a refuge from the community or a counterweight to it. The family was a community; the community was a family. There was no sharp division of physical or emotional labor between the two.

The Quakers of the Middle Colonies have often been cited as particularly modern in their attitudes toward family life. They tended to make the family a relatively self-sufficient unit, fostering affective ties within it, avoiding indebtedness even to kin, making children financially independent at marriage, and stressing the Inner Light that put each individual in direct contact with a merciful God. (Quakers were also the first Americans systematically to limit their families, starting from the era of the American Revolution.) But the meeting served many of the same functions for Quakers as did the town for New Englanders. It scrutinized behavior, intruded into personal life, provided material aid and advice, and was – emotionally as well as governmentally – a higher body than the family. If a Quaker child married outside meeting, the parents were supposed to cut off all ties with the child or risk being disowned themselves: 'The Quaker owed his allegiance first to his religious group and only after that to his own family.'[30]

The lack of privacy both within and between households meant that the family in colonial America did not inhabit a privileged or exclusive sphere of life, either physically or emotionally. Neither did sex. Although colonial authorities regulated and controlled sexuality, sex in the colonial world was not relegated to back rooms. Punishment for sex offenses was public and description of these offenses explicit. Children were not protected from knowing about sexual sins; indeed, Cott's study of divorce records shows that children were sometimes present when the offenses took place.[31]

Discussions of sexual issues were conducted with a frankness notably lacking in nineteenth-century society. In 1666, for example, George Alsop published a promotional pamphlet promising women who came to Maryland that they need not fear lest their 'virginity turn moldy,' for they would soon find 'copulative matrimony.' Virginity, noted another author, 'grows useless' if kept too long. Marriage manuals urged partners to meet 'with equal vigor' in the conjugal act. As late as the 1770s Mercy Otis Warren's propaganda play, *The Blockheads*, alluded to sexuality with a frankness that caused some nineteenth-century scholars to doubt that a woman had authored the book.[32]

Unrelated persons of the opposite sex often shared bedrooms, even beds, and also intimacies that would later be banished from mixed gender groups. For instance, reports Cott:

William Haskell told the full details of his affair with Tabitha Lufkin to two women – both of whom disapproved – as well as to several men. . . . Abigail Bradstreet discussed her marital problems in company with her husband and four other men at her mother's house, including her objection that *'her husband would do it for her . . . which, as She was with child, put her to great pain, & almost killed her* the next day.'[33]

All the colonies had laws against fornication, adultery, and illegitimate births, but their primary intent seems to have been less to preserve prudish values than to preserve social stability and prevent the community from having to support the children. A woman could be flogged if she refused to name the father of a child born out of wedlock; if she did name someone, and the court believed her, the man was required to support the child. Premarital sex that led to marriage aroused less concern: in Maryland, one-third of the immigrant women whose marriages are recorded were pregnant before the ceremonies, yet no presentments for bridal pregnancy were made in any Maryland courts.[34]

Afro-American Colonial Families

African and Afro-American families in colonial days were also permeable institutions, with little sense of domestic privacy or exclusiveness. Not all Africans initially brought to the colonies were slaves, and as we shall see in chapter 4, the establishment of a society based on racial divisions came slowly: class was more important than race in the early period. White indentured servants were often treated as harshly as slaves, while free Blacks and even a few privileged slaves had options open to them that were later closed. As two historians of Virginia write, 'economic status rather than race' seems to have determined who would work and interact together and who would come into conflict.[35]

Nevertheless, slavery involved a much more thoroughgoing break with the past for Africans than did servitude for Europeans. Although some African groups did practice slavery, this status was attached to kinship and community relations; and it was originally far less severe and widespread than it became under pressure from the Europeans. When Africans were sold into New World slavery they became commodities and strangers rather than victims of personal power relations: their ties to kin and community were severed, they experienced unprecedented brutality, and they lost even their common language, for slave-owners consciously mixed up groups from different areas in order to hinder the growth of solidarity. Africans therefore had to construct kinship ties and group solidarities in a far more conscious way than whites, while facing more structural obstacles created by their owners. They began this process on board the slave ships, creating fictive or symbolic kin relationships that were further elaborated upon arrival.[36]

Ira Berlin points out that three different patterns emerged for Africans and their descendants in North America. In the North, slaves did not work in gangs but lived and worked in close proximity to their masters, a fact that mediated the brutality of the master–slave relation, allowed the development of certain types of independence, and speeded up acculturation. Increasing reliance on slave labor in the mid eighteenth century, however, led to deteriorating work conditions, an increase in the importation of men relative to women, higher mortality rates, and lower fertility. At the same time, though, 'Newly arrived Africans awakened Afro-Americans to their African past,' and as reliance on slavery again decreased, northern Blacks combined the knowledge of colonial society gained through acculturation with this enriched sense of their African heritage to develop a strong collective life and significant personal autonomy.[37]

In the Carolina and Georgia low country, Blacks were divided by the evolution of slavery. Some of the earliest black immigrants developed a 'sawbuck equality' with masters who worked beside them clearing the land and defending it against Spanish, French, and Indian rivals. Others gained managerial positions because of white dependence on their superior knowledge of subtropical environments, cattle raising, and rice cultivation. Yet the development of export crops stimulated a mass importation of new slaves in the early eighteenth century. These slaves worked in large gangs under an impersonal and harsh labor regime, finding few points of solidarity with the increasingly urban Creole population. At the same time, the very impersonality of their labor discipline allowed them to retain more of their African culture than elsewhere in North America.

A third pattern prevailed in the Chesapeake: in the early years, a significant class of black freeman owned land, held servants, used the court system, and occasionally attained office. Here too the increasing reliance on slave labor in the early eighteenth century led to a deterioration in work conditions and a decline in the proportion and autonomy of the free population. Small plantations with resident owners meant that field workers were subject to closer supervision outside work than Carolina slaves, while those who attained managerial positions had less authority. Although this led to fewer divisions among Blacks, it also hampered the development of an Afro-American culture. Unlike low country plantation Blacks, 'Chesapeake blacks developed no distinct language and rarely utilized African day names for their children.'[38]

Family life varied according to the conditions Blacks faced. Free Blacks obviously had greater possibilities for marital stability than slave families. In the North, some religious groups performed formal marriages for free Blacks and slaves, and owners sometimes agreed to sell married slaves only in the same area as their family lived. In the South, slaves sometimes gained visiting rights to spouses on other plantations. Yet there were no legal guarantees for such practices, and even the youngest children were on occasion sold separately from their mothers. Slaves on large plantations had more opportunity to interact with kin and keep families together, while slaves on small farms were transferred more and their families tended to be broken up when the owner's family divided the inheritance among its children.

In all cases, however, both slaves and free Blacks overcame the disruptions of the early years to construct lasting marriage systems, solidarity associations, and kin networks. These were often fortified by fictive kin ties, ritual co-parenting or godparenting, and adoption. While owners conceived of slave families in nuclear terms (or simply as relations between mothers and young children, often separating fathers and teenagers from the rest of the family), slaves maintained a commitment to far larger kin networks. Slaves' naming patterns contrast with those of white families, who more often named a child after a deceased sibling or tended to use names that emphasized generational 'depth but little breadth.' Slaves used names to establish as many connections as possible with kinsmen, collateral as well as lineal. As time progressed, naming based on a bilateral system of kinship gave way to greater stress on the father's kin. This may have reflected the influence of the Bible, including slave identification with the persecuted Hebrews of the Old Testament, or it may have been an attempt to compensate for the owners' minimization of paternal bonds.[39]

The nuclear family and the conjugal pair obviously could not be sacrosanct among slave families, which existed, ultimately, only at the sufferance of the master, even if the master often permitted them in order to avoid runaways or resistance. But constraints imposed by slave owners were not the only reason why nuclear families did not become the main source of personal reference and social interactions among Blacks: free Blacks as well as slaves consciously constructed larger units of social interaction and community. In early Virginia these included patron–client relations with white planters, transactional networks with lower-class whites and Indians, and peer group associations based on religion, informal rituals of socializing, and exchange of food or services. As racial distinctions mounted in the eighteenth century, such associations were increasingly confined to Blacks, but continued to extend in many different directions.[40]

Consequences for Sex Roles

Black men and women seem to have had a high degree of sexual equality – partly as a result of African tradition, partly due to women's critical role in both the plantation economy and the slave kinship network. Black women worked alongside men in fields, mines, and salt works. Often an older woman would be issued the rations for the slave quarters and charged with dividing them, while women also helped to raise each other's children and maintained links among kin. Autobiographies of slaves reveal tremendous respect for their mothers and grandmothers. Some early writers concluded that this produced a matriarchal system, but more recent work documents the ongoing involvement of men in the black family and the efforts of black women to facilitate such involvement. Eugene Genovese remarks that far from exhibiting a 'debilitating female supremacy,' slave communities had 'a closer approximation to a healthy sexual equality than was possible for whites and perhaps even for many postbellum blacks.'[41]

Considerable debate persists, however, about the status of white women in the colonial period. Many early writers, surprised by the multitude of roles played by colonial women, tended to emphasize their favorable status when compared to Victorian women. They pointed out that the lack of sharp distinction between home and commerce prevented construction of the rigid boundaries between the sexes that developed in the early nineteenth century, and they stressed the vital productive work of colonial women.[42]

The duties of both men and women revolved around the subsistence needs of the household and the constant small exchanges of goods and services among households. Men plowed and planted, built fences, made and repaired tools, cared for animals. Women gathered and preserved food, butchered small animals, brewed ale, churned butter, made candles, wove and dyed cloth. Both males and females engaged in barter with their neighbors and in the personal negotiations required to assure a supply of goods from town or countryside. Even male artisans and merchants producing for sale did so in their homes, where their wives and daughters would learn at least part of the trade, keep the books, and help supervise the apprentices. The sexual division of labor did not pull men out into a separate public sphere, distinct from women's household affairs and rewarded on a different basis.

Richard Morris, in his pathbreaking study of colonial legal documents, found that wives at the end of the seventeenth century demonstrated a good knowledge of their husbands' businesses. Other writers have pointed out that women often took over their deceased husbands' crafts or succeeded to their positions. In 1710, for example, Ariante Dow was appointed to succeed her husband as City Scavenger of New York, a somewhat quaint name for what we would call a sanitation commissioner. Colonial papers abound with notices that the widow of a particular shopkeeper or craftsman would continue to operate the business as usual.[43]

Dutch settlements had a particularly favorable attitude toward the participation of women in business. Dutch women frequently acted as interpreters or traders with the Indians, whose own experience led them to readily accept women in such a role. In 1679 two visitors to New York wrote of such a woman whom they encountered in Albany:

> This woman, although not of openly godless life, is more wise than devout. . . . She is a truly worldly woman, proud and conceited, and sharp in trading with *wild* people as well as *tame* ones. . . . She has a husband, which is her second one. . . . He remains at home quietly, while she travels over the country to carry on the trading. In fine she is one of the Dutch female-traders, who understand the business so well.[44]

English women also had important rights in the colonies. *De jure*, the married woman, as in English law, continued to be a 'feme covert,' subsumed in her husband's identity and without legal status of her own; but *de facto*, American courts increasingly treated women as individuals before the law. Married women sometimes circumvented the law by conducting business as agents of their husbands, or occasionally by gaining special dispensation by courts or legislatures to act as a 'feme sole.' A feme sole could sue and be sued, make contracts, administer estates, dispose of her own property freely, serve as guardian to a minor, and occasionally participate in community meetings of property-owners. Women with property, such as widows who had taken over a husband's business, often made antenuptial agreements that kept them in control of their property after remarriage, while postnuptial agreements, unknown in England, were also upheld by colonial courts. Daughters tended to be endowed with landed property more frequently than in England. Ironically, however, these advantages were most likely to be enjoyed in jurisdictions that relied heavily on English law rather than in those that broke from that tradition: by the end of the eighteenth century colonial revisions of English law were often connected to encouragement of economic development; they therefore treated customary widows' rights as infringements on the rights of heirs and creditors.[45]

Women also had greater rights of separation and divorce in the colonies than in England. In the South, women were often granted maintenance allowances and permitted to live apart from their husbands. In Massachusetts, four times as many women as men brought divorce actions between 1639 and 1692. A majority were successful. Divorced wives were often granted generous settlements by the courts and did not forfeit their dower rights to one-third of the estate.[46]

Improvements in women's legal status were probably connected to the important productive role that women played in the colonies.[47] In 1619 the Virginia House of Burgesses successfully petitioned for equal land grants for wives as well as husbands since 'in a newe plantation it is not knowen whether man or woman be the most necessary.' The courts of Plymouth Colony were quite explicit about the impact of women's productive role upon their legal rights. The laws provided that the courts could overturn a will that did not adequately provide for a widow, 'especially in such a case where the Wife brought with her good part of the Estate in Marriage, or hath by her diligence and industry done her part in the getting of the Estate, and was otherwise well deserving.' In 1663, for example, the courts increased the share of the widow Naomi Solvester because she had been 'a frugall and laborious woman in the procuring of the said estate.'[48]

Colonial authorities were well aware of the wife's importance even in businesses nominally owned by the man. In Plymouth Colony one man's tavern license was revoked since he had recently 'buryed his wife, and in that respect not being soe capeable of keeping a publicke house.' The social image of women reflected their productive economic roles. Women were often called 'meet-helps' or 'yoke-mates,' and preachers stressed their vital role in the family enterprise. In 1692 Cotton Mather wrote *Ornaments for the Daughters of Zion,* in which he praised women's accomplishments and took for granted that a wife needed to know '*Arithmetick* and *Accomptanship* [accounting], perhaps also *Chirurgery* [surgery] and such other Arts relating to Business. . . .'[49]

Community property rights were also recognized by colonial authorities: despite the fact that the husband controlled all family property, he could not alienate real estate without his wife's consent. In Plymouth Colony, for example, a 1646 law required that in all sales of houses and lands 'the wyfe hereafter come in & consent and acknowledg the sale also.' Similarly, southern colonies required that before a wife could relinquish her dower rights she must be examined privately to see if she 'made her acknowledgment willingly and freely, and without being induced thereto by fear of threats of, or ill usage by her husband, or fear of his displeasure.' The opportunities for males to circumvent these laws in a society based on patriarchy and deference are obvious; but the fact remains that some recourse for women did exist. Widows were entitled to a third of their husband's estate, and could not ordinarily be disinherited.[50]

Recently, however, a number of writers have argued that these facts have been misused to postulate the existence of a 'Golden Age' for women in the colonial era, and they have mounted a forceful attack on such an assessment. They point out that under colonial patriarchy the male household head represented his 'family' (including servants and other dependants) to the public world and was held accountable for its behavior. Male property owners, then, were the ones most likely to deal with political authorities or to be involved in larger economic transactions, such as trade with the mother country. They also represented the political and religious authorities *to* their families, a fact which gave them large powers over the person, property, and behavior of their wives and children. That power was exerted legally, socially, politically, and personally.[51]

The corporate patriarchy that ruled in society at large left no room for individual self-expression on the part of women. A woman was to defer to her husband as the subject deferred to the Crown, to count his opinions as her own, to have no higher desire than to carry out her husband's wishes. Women's personal property was subsumed in their husbands', while women themselves were in fact a form of property. Many colonies punished a man who successfully courted a young woman without her father's consent, thereby alienating his proprietary rights in her. Adultery was defined as sex with a married woman rather than with a married man. If both men and women were brought up on sexual offenses, the fact remains that women's sexual offenses were regarded as violations of male property rights, while men's were simply violations of public order.

Although a man could not sell land without his wife's consent, he could appoint a guardian for his children or apprentice them against her will. Adultery alone was not considered sufficient grounds for divorce by female plaintiffs, but it was for males. Punishments too tended to be different: men more often than women had physical punishment commuted by the payment of cash or the promise to finance or organize some community service. Above all, most white women were daughters or wives in households that were expected to mirror the hierarchy of society as a whole. The wife was expected 'to guid the house &c. not guid the husband.' 'A true wife accounts her subjection [as] her honor and freedom,' declared John Winthrop in 1645, 'and would not think her condition safe and free, but in subjection to her husband's authority.' Even such formidable women as Mary and Margaret Brent, who ruled over the courts-leet on their Maryland plantations, faced clear limits on their behavior. When Margaret used her considerable legal and administrative experience to try to win the right to vote in the Maryland Assembly, this was considered 'beyond her sex.'[52]

Mary Beth Norton has led the attack on what she considers to be the romanticization of colonial women's status. In an early influential article she studied records of claims in English courts by Loyalist women for compensation after the Revolutionary War. She found that they were unable to describe accurately their husbands' holdings, suggesting that they had been confined to a woman's sphere separate from the male world of work and property, and that they referred to themselves as weak, helpless, and dependent where male claimants did not. She concluded that colonial women were at least as confined to a domestic sphere as their nineteenth-century counterparts, but lacked the nineteenth-century compensation of the cult of domesticity. Her view is supported by Alison Hirsch, who argues that younger males spent most of their time in all-male groups, while women moved in predominantly female circles of household work, childcare, and visiting.[53]

There are, however, some difficulties with making an equally one-sided case for an all-pervasive denigration of colonial women, with progress only after the American Revolution. First, the status of women in the late eighteenth century is not a good measure of the early colonial situation, because much evidence indicates that the evolution of economic stratification during that century resulted in a sharper differentiation of sex roles and a restriction of upper-class women from public affairs. By Norton's own admission, the most wealthy women were least able to describe their husbands' wealth, and these women should not be taken as representative of the entire colonial experience of gender. Second, pleading in English courts, unable to cite military service as justification for their claims, Loyalist women were especially likely to appeal to ideas about female dependency that were more highly developed in England than in America.

The most balanced assessment comes from Laurel Thatcher Ulrich, who points out that colonial women had very limited economic and social 'opportunity' but very broad economic and social 'responsibility,' and that the very strength of patriarchy in colonial society gave women important roles as 'deputy husbands.' Moreover, Claudia Goldin has recently documented the fact that some of these roles did in fact diminish after the American Revolution, as women's access to atypical work and to proprietorships declined. In rejecting the myth of a Golden Age we should not let the pendulum swing too far in the other direction, denying the interstices in the patriarchal order that conferred on women some responsibilities and options not available in the succeeding period.[54]

The task here is not to evaluate which experience was 'better' for women – whose standards would we use to judge that anyway? – but to note the changing *pattern* of relationships within and outside the family. The signal difference between colonial patriarchy and later male dominance lay in the radically different bases and justifications for each. Colonial society did not soften woman's subordination in any way; it offered no compensations for her exclusion from wealth and power. She was not told that her special duties were in any sense higher or more important than man's. To the contrary, a woman's place was an explicitly subordinate and dependent one in every arena. The very fact that women were involved to some extent in public life while males were heavily involved in home life meant that women had no sphere for retreat nor any domain in which to exercise special authority. Women had no chance to make a virtue of necessity and forge a distinct female culture with its own high valuation of the woman's role. Nor could a woman who might challenge her role find support in a women's community. The organization of women as a sex to protest their exclusion from power had no base in colonial society.

At the same time, though, a colonial woman's subordination was viewed as a social necessity – one of many unequal relations required by society – not as a unique female condition caused by her biology. A woman's dependence was not qualitatively different from that of a lower-class male. Custom backed by force held women in subjection. They did not need to grapple with reasons for their lack of equal status, since equal status was not even a social value for men. There was thus little pressure on women to internalize a whole set of gender-specific values and emotions. Similarly, males derived their sense of authority from their position in the hierarchy of property ownership, political power, and religious practice: being a man was a necessary but not a sufficient condition for domination; the prerequisites for masculine authority lay in an external power structure, not in the internalization of a special set of gender-related traits.

The subordination of women and the dominance of men were based less on ideas about gender than on ideas about the need for hierarchy in all relations. Despite occasional comments about female 'nature,' colonial society was surprisingly free of preconceptions about any unbridgeable gulf between the masculine and the feminine. Just as men and women did not inhabit separate spheres of work and leisure,[55] neither did colonial society assign the sexes qualitatively different character traits or temperaments. Both men and women were expected to be shrewd in business and humble in religion. In all the colonies, authorities held both husbands and wives responsible for the education and control of children and servants in their households. Men were not defined as providers or breadwinners, nor women as dependants. No such descriptions appear in colonial discussions of relations between the sexes. Only southern aristocrats worked out a well-developed sense of proper masculine traits, explicitly opposed to feminine ones, and even there 'masculine' behavior derived from class position. It was not unmasculine for lower-class males to defer to the gentry.

Femininity was often seen as weaker or more prone to evil than masculinity, but it was not yet equated with a qualitatively different set of capacities. Studies of Puritan sermons up to the mid eighteenth century reveal 'that the Puritans had not yet arrived at definitions of sex roles or personality structure that were as fixed or mutually exclusive as those found in the nineteenth century.' The qualities New England ministers praised in women were those they praised in men: 'prayerfulness, industry, charity, modesty, serious reading, and godly writing.' Both sexes were regarded as equally in need of regeneration, and although ministers noted a connection between female reproduction and religiosity, they did not give 'a sexual content to the psyche and soul. They stressed the *experience* of children rather than the *nature* of the childbearer.'[56]

Social Subordination and Practical Flexibility

Legally and religiously sanctioned patriarchy did not necessarily glorify masculinity *per se* and often coexisted with a practical flexibility about female activities. To understand this, we must recognize that submission and inequality had different meanings for colonial society than they do today. Even though all relationships, as Edmund Morgan has pointed out, were thought by the Puritans to have a dominant and a subordinate party, this hierarchy was not determined by nature save in relations between parents and children. All other relations had to be contracted, making subordination a voluntary act that connoted laudable obedience to God's will, not personal inferiority.[57] The great southern planters were extremely jealous of their public marks of domination, yet even southern society took for granted an unevenness among men that meant deference was not confined to women and slaves.

That a wife should 'guid the house &c. not guid the husband' was demanded by law, religion, and public opinion. Yet this subordination did not imply personal inadequacy in a society based on hierarchy and rank for everyone. Wives were subject to their husbands, just as their husbands were subject to community leaders, who were in turn subject to the Crown. And in the gradated society of colonial America, white women married to householders were certainly not at the bottom. They were above apprentices, servants, slaves, and children, and wielded the same kind of authority over them that other 'superiors' exercised over those below. Thus in 1712 Benjamin Wadsworth, describing the reciprocal duties of masters and servants, noted: 'Under the title of *Masters, Mistresses* also may be comprehended; for they are to be *submitted to.* . . . They are to have an hand in *guiding the house* and governing the Family.'[58]

As Mary Ryan has commented, inequality in colonial society 'was not the peculiar stigma of womanhood, but rather a social expectation for both sexes.' All persons in colonial society were 'inferior' to someone else, and all faced prohibitions and restrictions on their activity. As late as the 1770s a Tory propaganda play summed up the relative lack of distinction between the restrictions on women and the restrictions on men in such a society. The vehicle for the author's sentiments is a Loyalist woman, who berates her husband for his participation in rebel politics. Unable to best his wife's political arguments, the husband tells her that her words are unseemly: 'Consider, my Dear, you're a Woman of Fashion, 'Tis really indecent to be in such Passion; Mind thy Household Affairs, teach thy Children to read, and never, Dear, with Politics, trouble thy Head.' The wife does not challenge this evaluation of her proper concerns, but retorts, with the obvious approval of the author: '. . . Dost thou think thyself, Deary, a *Cromwel* or *Monck*? Dost thou think that wise nature meant thy shallow Pate, to digest the important Affairs of a State?'[59]

Hierarchical relations between husband and wife were necessary for maintaining order in the household, the church, and the state. Prohibitions against women's assuming certain roles were based more on this necessity for order than on a consistent belief in female incapacity. John Cotton's frequently quoted contention that 'a woman is more subject to error than a man' was justified by a peculiarly eclectic list of arguments against a woman propounding questions in church: 'For under pretence of questioning for learning sake, she might so propound her question as to teach her teachers; or if not so, yet to open a door to some of her own weak and erroneous apprehensions, or at least soon exceed the bounds of womanly modesty.'[60]

The subordination of women in colonial society, then, was viewed as a social rather than a biological imperative. Benjamin Wadsworth cautioned the wife:

> Yea, though possibly thou hast greater abilities of mind than he has, wast of some high birth, and he of a more mean Extract, or didst bring more Estate at Marriage than he did; yet since he is thy Husband, God has made him thy Head, and set him above thee, and made it thy duty to love and reverence him.

Similarly, Benjamin Colman felt no embarrassment about remarking to his daughter Jane that, were it not for 'the necessary and useful Restraints of your Sex.... I have no reason to think but that your Genious in Writing would have excell'd mine.'[61]

Being female in colonial America involved 'Restraints' rather than incapacities. Women were not expected to 'know' their place; they were expected to *learn* it. The emphasis on learning in colonial writings attests that women's nature was not considered innately subordinate. There is, indeed, little evidence that colonial women *felt* innately subordinate, for their submission frequently had to be imposed by the courts. In 1663, for example, a Virginia jury found it necessary to order both a female servant and her master ducked, she for incorrigible impudence and he for inadequately governing his household. John Demos, examining interventions by the Plymouth Colony court in domestic matters, found equal numbers of males and females charged with abusive behavior toward the opposite sex, and detected 'no evidence at all of habitual patterns of deference in the relations between the sexes.' A similar conclusion must be drawn from Spruill's survey of southern court cases. This is not, of course, to romanticize the imposition of female submission, which precisely because it was not internalized might be achieved through extreme brutality.[62]

The stability of the colonial social order depended upon regular patterns of hierarchy and deference. Woman's subordination was required by her social role as wife and mother in a household which was 'a little Common-wealth,' a model for the hierarchy necessary in society at large. But this meant that a woman who for one reason or another assumed the social role of household head was not prohibited by her sex from exercising the prerogatives of that position. Widowed landholders met with male property-owners to decide community matters, and there are scattered instances of such women 'votting' in various town meetings.[63] Women could serve as proprietors of a colony, with all the rights thereof. Lady Deborah Moody nominated the magistrates for the colony she governed in New Amsterdam, and they were regularly confirmed by higher authorities. In 1702 Elizabeth Muller was one of the proprietors who signed the document recognizing Queen Anne's right to rule New Jersey. Only four colonies specifically disfranchised women during the entire colonial period.

As Ulrich points out, colonial women might exercise considerable authority as 'deputy husbands' in a patriarchal family economy. Female household heads were free to engage in almost any occupation. While only a tiny minority of women actually worked full time in formal trades, the range of occupations open to such women was wider than in the early nineteenth century. Thus we find women blacksmiths, butchers, barbers, hunters, attorneys, physicians, sextons, undertakers, loggers, shipwrights, gunsmiths, pewterers, jailers, retailers, and typesetters. Women in the colonies kept taverns, ran ferries, painted houses, operated sawmills, gristmills, and printing presses, ground eyeglasses, and managed livery stables. In Virginia, women weavers were paid at a rate comparable to that of men in the same profession. In South Carolina, Eliza Lucas (later Pinckney) initiated the commercial production of indigo, the basis of blue dye, and experimented with the cultivation of silkworms: 'Every kind of work done by men was done, at least occasionally, by women.'[64]

To illustrate these general points, we may consider two different examples of women's position in colonial America. The journal of Sarah Kemble Knight, kept during her trip on horseback from Boston to New York in 1704, pointedly demonstrates the independence that at least some colonial women exercised. Knight recorded no expressions of surprise at her travels except from her first hostess at Billings, who annoyed her by fussing about the dangers for a woman 'on the Rode so Dreadfull late' and by asking 'silly questions.' At one inn, Knight shared a room with a number of male travelers and remarked only on the hardness of her bed. She was gone for five months, leaving her child with her mother, but the journal mentions her family only once, noting that she returned to find 'my aged and tender mother and my Dear and only Child in good health with open arms to receive me.'[65]

The case of Anne Hutchinson, on the other hand, demonstrates that such independence could not be exercised outside established channels. Neither women nor men were allowed to challenge the social order, but rebellion by a female evoked especially harsh responses because it threatened the household authority on which larger political hierarchies rested. Yet the Puritan leaders' persecution of Anne Hutchinson should not be read as evidence of colonial contempt for women. Hutchinson attracted to her cause some of the most important men in the colonies, in addition to the women who gathered for classes in her home. At her first examination by the authorities in 1636, she engaged in a skillful battle of wits with her interlocutors and came out the victor. Her femininity was not enough to convict her. In 1637, however, she rashly admitted to a belief in revelation, which allowed the authorities to institute excommunication proceedings against her. Nevertheless her influence over others continued: in 1639 she fomented a rebellion in Rhode Island against the rule of William Coddington.

The Puritans who excommunicated Hutchinson had no doubts about her capabilities. Used in the service of the Puritan order, her spiritual dedication would have been praised, as Cotton Mather had celebrated the 'Tutoresses' of early Christianity. But Hutchinson challenged the hierarchy of all three interlocked pillars of colonial society: household, church, and community. As Hugh Peter charged: 'you have stept out of your place . . . *you have rather bine a Husband than a Wife and a preacher than a Hearer; and a Magistrate than a Subject.*'[66]

Witchcraft, Women, and Social Change

The much-discussed witchcraft prosecutions of colonial times can provide us with further indications about the ways that female subordination coexisted with access to economic and social power. Women were more likely to be accused and found guilty than men, but the majority of accusers were also women – a fact which hardly suggests an attack motivated solely by patriarchy. As John Demos shows in his massive survey of witchcraft in New England (where cases were more common than elsewhere in the colonies), witchcraft accusations revealed tensions over corporate control versus individualism. Witchcraft suspicions did not seem to occur around limited personal conflicts, such as adultery or sexual jealousy, nor around larger areas of community dispute, such as politics or doctrinal disagreements. Instead, witchcraft accusations tended to be linked to the informal but socially vital middle area where formal community controls were replicated or modified in neighborly interactions. They reflected the interpersonal antagonisms spawned by neighborly interdependence: relations between witches and victims 'were typically complex, many-sided, and altogether *dense.*'[67]

Witchcraft accusations swirled around those who had experienced disturbances – or might be thought to have introduced disturbances – in customary patterns of local relationships. A significant minority of accused witches had experienced sharp mobility, either downward or upward, and Demos found that witchcraft accusations against these were taken especially seriously. Although the majority of both accused and accusers were from the lower social ranks, there are intriguing hints that what was involved was a stepping out of place in the local hierarchy. While the poor gossiped about witches in their midst, such suspicions usually came to trial only when a leading person or persons in the community also felt injured or fearful in some way. This often occurred after the 'witch' demanded favors or crossed social boundaries.

Although witch accusations were directed at those who had stepped out of their place in some way, they at the same time legitimized a certain stepping out of place by the accusers – and not just in the obvious sense that 'possession' or affliction by witches offered opportunities for emotional outbursts and self-display that would not normally have been tolerated. As Alan Macfarlane also found in a study of witchcraft in Essex, England, a second aspect of colonial accusations was that they tended to be initiated by people who had *refused* customary neighborly obligations or interactions that might formerly have been expected by the alleged witches.[68]

Suspected witches typically related to their 'victims' by dropping by to borrow things or attempting to assert a neighborly familiarity that was unwelcome to the 'victim' – entering a birthing room, for example, or asking about the neighbor's children. Witches strained neighborly relations by asking or giving a little too much: one accuser complained that the accused witch made 'so many errands to my house for several things' that he 'could not tell how to deny him what he desired.' Another reported that an accused witch 'brought me many things [such] as mault . . . and is very kind to me,' another that the witch offered to prescribe herbs and dropped by to caress a sleeping infant. One victim lent her cap to a witch and was afflicted when she took it back, refusing to sell it to the borrower; another was struck in the back 'as with a clap of fire' when she refused to lend a pound of cotton. The kind of conflict that generally preceded witchcraft, according to Demos, 'was the transfer of goods, services, and information. One party – usually the alleged witch – approached the other in order to obtain some quite specific resource. Typically, the approach was rebuffed. And this, in turn, evoked a "threatening" or "cursing" response. . . .' The angry response was later taken to explain a subsequent misfortune for the person who had turned down the approach. 'But the most common element in this whole range of cases was a simple request – in effect, the asking of a favor.'[69]

Witchcraft accusations tended to arise where economic individualism was undermining the cooperative principles on which the New England communities were supposed to be based. The colonies troubled by witchcraft accusations had

> the ingredients of a newly emergent pattern: land changing hands at a remarkable rate, contracts drawn (and remembered) with great precision, debts recorded in minute detail, inheritances challenged, boundaries rearranged, common fields reduced to private holdings, timberlands despoiled, and through it all men and women maneuvering vigorously for personal advantage.

All this in a colony founded, as John Winthrop had preached aboard the *Arabella*, on the idea that 'We must be knit together as one man . . . make others' condition our own, rejoice together, mourn together, labor and suffer together, always having before our eyes our commission and community in the work.' Demos relates American witchcraft to the conflict between individualism and neighborliness described for England by Alan Macfarlane and Keith Thomas. He argues, however, that the critical factor was guilt about aggression rather than, as they suggest, about the refusal of neighborly aid, since charity was not an issue in the colonies. Yet charity was not the issue in England either; the very poorest members of society were not involved in the England accusations. Instead, the accusations originated with those who had traditional neighborly obligations to others but were no longer inclined to fulfill them, resulting in a sense of guilt at their cutting off of ties with those directly below them, people with whom they would customarily have been engaged in such reciprocal relations as borrowing, lending, and the exchange of favors.[70]

According to Demos, ' "Projection" was everywhere central to witchcraft accusation.' The witch's 'victims were presumably uncomfortable about . . . their own wishes to intrude, to encroach, to dominate, to attack – their whole assertive side.'[71] But colonial people seem to have had few compunctions about intruding and dominating in a wide range of circumstances. They dominated children and servants and intruded on their neighbors all the time. Rather, particular kinds of intrusions were at issue: requests or approaches by people from whom villagers wished to establish distance or to whom they wished to deny connections and obligations. The projection of witchcraft 'victims,' in other words, was possibly guilt not about their antisocial aggression but about their antisocial denial of traditional 'dense' interactions.

The famous outbreak of witchcraft trials in Salem was atypical in its scope, violence, and traumatic after-effects. Here, witchcraft accusations spilled beyond the circumscribed neighborly boundaries within which witch accusations were usually confined and became associated with the differences between Salem Village, a traditional agricultural village, and

Salem Town, which was rapidly being transformed into a commercial center. Accusations ran from the more traditional to the new, and were directed at the lower-class supporters of the powerful men who had opposed the Salem minister, Samuel Parris, as well as those who represented the 'alien and unfamiliar' to the villagers. Unlike most witchcraft outbreaks, the majority of the accused witches were 'outsiders,' with 82 per cent actually living outside Salem Village. Two historians of Salem's trials comment: 'It is striking how many of the accused witches from the Salem Village area had careers which testified to the power of unfamiliar economic forces to alter and reshape a life.' They were economically mobile, many upwardly so, some downwardly: 'All of these people were on the move, socially and economically.'[72]

Perhaps Salem's practice of letting a witch go if she or he confessed had to do with the reassertion of community norms here: by confessing, the witch acknowledged that departure from accepted hierarchies and stability was both criminal and supernatural; by letting the confessed witch live, the villagers affirmed that their motivation was to reestablish the old order, not to refuse some aspects of it. At any rate, in Salem the result of the witch panic was not vindication of those who had refused interactions with certain neighbors but reassertion of corporate or community control over the behavior of others.

The vulnerability of women to witchcraft charges as well as to the excitement of possession and accusation certainly testifies to their repression in colonial society. Yet accusations made by and against women resonated with other social tensions and carried weight because of women's vital role in the local network of household production and neighborly exchange. When Grace Stout of Salem was arraigned for theft in 1682, 'the witnesses against her included thirty-four persons, among them twenty-one housewives who were able to give precise accounts of the value of work performed or goods received.' These included such small but socially important transactions as kneading bread for other women and purchasing someone's knitted stockings. In 1692 one woman charged with witchcraft was successfully defended by a petition signed by 116 town residents, declaring that she was 'allwys, readie & willing' to help her neighbors. Yet when other dynamics among neighbors came to the fore, the same activities could actually confirm witchcraft accusations. Disputes over such transactions were often too informal to make it into court, but they were far from petty. Interpersonal neighborly relations and small, predominantly oral exchanges comprised the very essence of daily existence: borrowing and lending, exchanging services, creating a network of obligations and personal ties were important both to the maintenance of community and to survival itself; they were also the stuff of conflicts about individualism and obligation.[73] It is no wonder these conflicts led to witchcraft accusations during the early phases of social and economic differentiation in colonial society.

Once people came to accept a certain self-sufficiency (or selfishness, depending upon one's point of view) in household behavior, feelings of guilt about refusing neighborly interactions or anger at neighbors who stepped out of place tended to recede. Demos reports that witchcraft conflicts tended to appear a decade or more after a community's founding and to continue within only a circumscribed time, in inverse proportion to other forms of social conflict: 'The growth and dispersion of the local population, a somewhat broadened range of economic activity, an increasingly firm system of social stratification: these interlocking trends seem gradually to have modified the tensions amid which witchcraft had flourished.'[74] Yet precisely these same factors – population growth, mobility, new economic activities, and increased class stratification – created new conflicts among communities or classes even as they moderated tensions among neighbors.

Signs of Change in the Early 1700s: From Possession to Conversion

By the third and fourth decades of the eighteenth century, many forces had begun to undermine the patriarchal, corporate order of the seventeenth century. The old household system had worked as part of a stable economy in which parents passed on land or occupations to children who had few alternatives. In the context of plentiful land and an inelastic supply of labor, the corporate household economy had allowed for rapid population growth, as children could be utilized in agrarian production at an early age or put out to work in a household with higher labor needs. But by the early 1700s the growth of population was putting considerable pressure on the foundations of the traditional household economy. Population expansion and the overuse of the land by grazing and indiscriminate clearing led in the more settled areas to land shortages that could be solved only by migration. A population whose median age was under eighteen put pressure not just on land but on succession to occupations, parental control over marriage, and reward and authority systems within the household. Parental control over children's marriages and work was weakened when children moved away or when parents could not set them up in an occupation; it was actively challenged by the increase in premarital conceptions that seems to have occurred throughout the colonies from about the 1740s through the end of the century. Servants also became less available, less tractable, and less willing to commit for long periods of service. Yet the substitution of slavery for servitude increased, rather than solved, problems of social control.

At the same time, the dispersal of population and the growth of trade eroded community patterns of deference and domination. In the South, planters 'were forced to adopt harsher and purely commercial relationships . . . with fellow planters and the underlying population,' undermining older interpersonal bonds.[75] In New England, corporate patterns of community regulation broke down as the market in land led to circumvention of older controls over settlement patterns, while the spread of commerce introduced long-run, permanent divisions of interest among individuals and groups where once there had been only shifting local conflicts among mutually dependent neighbors. Bitter fights erupted over issues that polarized these different interest groups into competing factions. Expansion of the paper money supply, for example, created sharp divisions between farmers and city-dwellers, established and newer merchants, creditors and debtors, even whole regions with different relations to the trading system and different interests in political and economic development.

By the 1730s the subdivision and overuse of family lands in Massachusetts had combined with the hardening of class lines to create hundreds of new additions each year to the class of migrant poor. The problem of poor relief taxed both public finances and private charity, but attempts to set up workhouses met tremendous resistance, and the almshouses were also woefully inadequate. Elites had become so embroiled in political struggles for advantage and self-interest that the lower classes began to accuse the upper class of fracturing community solidarity. In economics as in politics, policy increasingly emerged from struggle over competing interests, not from the reciprocity of mutual, albeit unequal, bonds of dependence and obligation:

> The pressure . . . proved too great for the corporate ideology of a single harmonious community to withstand. Pursuit of the common good was everywhere seen as a rhetorical cloak employed by those enjoying elevated status and material wealth to hide their covert selfish interests.[76]

New England felt this shift most traumatically, as its corporate character had been most pronounced in the seventeenth century, but other areas experienced changes that added to the cumulative pressure on older norms throughout the colonies. Some of the Middle Colonies had had a greater commercial and individualistic orientation from the beginning, and by the first decades of the eighteenth century a few Pennsylvania shopkeepers and master craftsmen had moved work out of their homes into small workshops, where they employed people who did not live with or even near them. In the South at the same time, the gentry was experiencing a substantial loss of coercive power over poorer neighbors as the consignment system was transformed by the Scottish merchants who had come to dominate trade with the colonies. Where previously great planters had shipped both their own products and those of their lesser neighbors directly to England, now Scottish 'factors' set up stores in the colonies. Here they sold imported goods in return for tobacco, which they then exported, receiving a middleman's mark-up on both ends of the transaction. The planters were increasingly enmeshed in a web of debt while they lost social and economic control over their neighbors.[77]

It would be a gross exaggeration to suggest that old family and community patterns had entirely broken down, or that individualism was running rampant. Yet the old patterns were certainly showing strains that went far beyond the ubiquitous but limited interpersonal tensions of the previous century. The religious revivals of the 1740s seem to have been one response to the growing inadequacies of the corporate patriarchal order. They began in areas of the country and sectors of the population experiencing the sharpest discontinuities between the restraints/protections of the old order and the opportunities/losses of the new. In Massachusetts, Connecticut, and New Hampshire the revivals hit commercial towns to which people had moved from older communities, leaving many older settlements, such as Andover, relatively untouched. Cities that had experienced recent social and economic turmoil – Boston, for example – were especially caught up in the fervor. In both North and South, the movement had strong support among lower classes resentful of the political and economic maneuvers of those to whom they had formerly deferred. Yet the revivals also had elements that helped people explain, channel, and hence rationalize their new behavior. Philip Greven comments that the evangelical temperament tended to be associated with families or households whose traditional ties with kin and neighbors were attenuated.[78]

Revival meetings expressed both the exhilaration of new-found freedom from patriarchal and corporate controls and the terror of facing the world alone, without parental or community supervision. They provided outlets for the guilt people felt in denying their own past obligations but also for the self-righteousness they found in condemning those who had betrayed the ties first. Converts burned symbols of worldly pride, rejecting the selfish materialism that had undermined the old community, but they also repudiated many of the externally imposed standards of behavior that had sustained that social order.

Paul Boyer and Stephen Nissenbaum draw attention to the similarities in the behavior of girls afflicted by witchcraft in the 1690s and 'sinners' experiencing conversion in the 1740s. In 1692 the mood swings and anxiety were interpreted as signs of possession by witches; in the 1740s they were interpreted as signs of possession by God. The difference, of course, was in the social context of the feelings rather than in the feelings themselves. In the 1690s self-preoccupation and individual nonconformity were still new enough to be seen as alien, as coming from *outside* the afflicted individuals. By the 1740s people were more generally drawn into the individuating forces of the age. They 'accused *themselves* of corruption.'[79] Their solution, however, was not to exorcize the spirit of individualism but to bend it to the way of God.

In the one case individualism was denied and antisocial behavior was projected onto someone else who could be expelled from the community or destroyed. In the second, individualism was accepted as a part of people's lives – a part that could be grappled with and controlled. The acceptance of an ongoing *struggle* with individualism (as opposed to a call for its exorcism) legitimated personal initiative, even departure from community norms. The worst effects of untrammeled individualism could be controlled, but since that control was to be exercised not by the community but through a personal relationship with God, people could more readily accept some fragmentation of older community patterns of deference and conformity.

The revivals appealed to people of all classes in their promise to reestablish social order on a new basis of individual responsibility, but the dynamic of revivals was to foster self-organization and self-reliance among the lower classes, women, and youth; hence they tended to be looked upon with ambivalence by the upper classes – occasionally with outright hostility. Evangelism may have begun as a movement of self-purification, but it could as easily serve to condemn others who had broken away from community controls. The converted were encouraged by some ministers to induce visions in which they saw the future state of grace or damnation of individuals, and by implication passed judgment on them in the here and now.

In Boston, reports Gary Nash, the revivals quickly took on an aspect of social leveling that in the minds of the elite far outweighed the benefits of religious revitalization. In 1740, clerics and other establishment figures had welcomed the charismatic revivalist George Whitefield to Boston; on his return in 1744 they attacked him vehemently. Joseph Fish quickly regretted opening his pulpit in Stonington, Connecticut, to James Davenport: Davenport recruited 104 new church members in a single year – a remarkable number for the time – but when Fish attempted to correct the impression of some members that conversion was a sufficient substitute for careful instruction in the faith, the church 'was fill'd with outcries *against* the preacher.' Women would 'sit down in the broad Aisle with their knitting work in order to shew their contempt, and both men & women would cry out calling the minister a hireling – a dumb dog that would not bark &c.'[80]

In the South revivals originally appealed to both slaves and the white lower classes, as they posed a direct challenge to the social order symbolized by the Anglican Church. Even where revivalists did not openly denounce the rich and powerful, both the strict self-discipline in work or expenditure and the uninhibited emotional expressiveness about one's personal relation to God represented an implicit denial of the intermediary, supervisory role of social superiors. Rhys Isaac suggests that in both South and North the nationalism of succeeding years may have been partly an attempt by the upper classes to redirect such local protests and enthusiasm into channels that might serve their own interests; at the very least the presence of such powerful undercurrents of dissent may have pushed the colonial leaderships further toward building a movement for independence than they might otherwise have gone.[81]

In one sense revivals did what crowd action had occasionally done in earlier days, challenging abuses of authority by leaders or departures from social norms by individuals. The definition of those social norms and of what constituted abuse of authority derived from older corporate notions of public responsibility and mutual obligations. But just as those abuses were more and more occurring *outside* the political system, in the daily economic and social behavior of individuals over whom corporate or patriarchal authorities had little power, so the attempt to curb such abuses had to be aimed at the daily behavior of individuals. In aiming their strictures at individual behavior, even if it was for corporate ends, evangelicals undermined many of the cornerstones of traditional community. Submission to God was a far more subjective experience than submission to church leadership, public pressure, or the dictates of a household head, and required considerably more independent interpretation of God's commands.

Most evangelical preachers held out the promise of a society made united and harmonious by righteousness; but the fact that people now thought community must be *constructed* by voluntary actions reveals the depth of economic and social change. And the participation of individuals in the construction of such communities, no matter how conservative their goals, was a transformative act. No man who had shouted down a minister in the meeting house, no woman who had contemptuously turned her back and taken up her knitting during a sermon, no family whose children and women had confronted the household head with his sins or listened to his own anguish at conversion would be quite the same again.

But no adequate alternative to the corporate patriarchal order was yet on the horizon in 1740, either economically or ideologically. Hence the enthusiasm passed over, leaving few long-term institutional changes and no general ideological transformation. Many congregations that had separated in the zeal of the moment moderated their demands and reinstituted halfway membership. Religious emphasis still rested on God the Father rather than Jesus the Son, and most evangelicals still accepted the need to legislate the morality of those who had not seen the light and possibly never would. Social harmony and the public good were still placed above and in opposition to competition and individual self-interest, even if some points of potential convergence were recognized. The development of a political movement in opposition to Britain in the next decades was to reestablish the primacy of many traditional leaders, even if their authority was again to be challenged after Independence over the question of the reorganization of American society. Corporate patriarchal agrarianism would never be the same, but its replacement by a new social form lay many decades in the future.

Notes

1. Some authors call this a 'household mode of production,' while others call it a system of independent commodity production, petty commodity production, or a precapitalist society. Whether the system deserves a separate category as an independent mode of production or should be seen as a transitional formation thrown up during the international decay of feudal absolutism and mercantilism is not at issue here. The point is that despite the existence of absolute private property in land, widespread exchange of products and land, and involvement in international trade, labor had not been abstracted from particularized personal or political relations into a wage-system, local exchange was not separable from concrete use-values, and international exchange still followed power relations, monopolies, and military conquest rather than vice versa. For a brief guide to the literature on the debate over mode of production see Edwin Burrows, 'The Transition Question in Early American History,' *Radical History Review* 18 (1978), pp. 173–90. For a similar debate about England, see Paul Sweezy, Maurice Dobb, *et al.*, *The Transition from Feudalism to Capitalism* (New York, 1978).

2. Sam Bass Warner, *The Urban Wilderness: A History of the American City* (New York, 1972), p. 11.

3. John R. Stilgoe, *Common Landscapes of America, 1580 to 1845* (New Haven, 1982), p. 44; Richard Bushman, *From Puritan to Yankee: Character and Social Order in Connecticut, 1690–1765* (Cambridge, MA, 1967), pp. 16–17. See also Kenneth Lockridge, *A New England Town: The First Hundred Years: Dedham, Massachusetts, 1636–1736* (New York, 1970); Philip J. Greven, *Four Generations: Population, Land, and Family in Colonial Andover, Massachusetts* (Ithaca, 1970); Michael Zuckerman, *Peaceable Kingdoms: New England Towns in the Eighteenth Century* (New York, 1970).

4. Michael Zuckerman, ed., *Friends and Neighbors: Group Life in America's First Plural Society* (Philadelphia, 1982); Daniel Snydacher, 'Kinship and Community in Rural Pennsylvania, 1749–1820,' *Journal of Interdisciplinary History* 13 (1982). For a different interpretation see James T. Lemon, *The Best Poor Man's Country: A Geographical Study of Early Southeastern Pennsylvania* (Baltimore, 1972). A critique of Lemon's contention that early Pennsylvania settlers were individualistic and profit seeking can be found in James Henretta, 'Families and Farms: *Mentalité* in Pre-Industrial America,' *William and Mary Quarterly* 35 (1978).

5. Sam Bass Warner, *The Private City: Philadelphia in Three Periods of its Growth* (Philadelphia, 1968), pp. 5–6, 21.

6. Gerald W. Mullin, 'The Plantation World of William Byrd II,' in T.H. Breen, ed., *Shaping Southern Society: The Colonial Experience* (New York, 1976); T.H. Breen,

'Horses and Gentlemen: The Cultural Significance of Gambling Among the Gentry of Virginia,' in Elizabeth Pleck and Joseph Pleck, *The American Man* (Englewood Cliffs, 1980); Rhys Isaac, *The Transformation of Virginia, 1740–1790* (Chapel Hill, 1982), pp. 11–138; Thad Tate and David Ammerman, eds, *The Chesapeake in the Seventeenth Century* (Chapel Hill, 1979).

7. Isaac, *Transformation*, p. 136.

8. Lyle Koehler, review of John Demos, *American Historical Review* 90 (1985), p. 278; James Russell Perry, quoted in Jon Kukla, 'Order and Chaos in Early America; Political and Social Stability in Pre-Restoration Virginia,' *American Historical Review* 90 (1985), p. 278.

9. Bushman, *Puritan to Yankee*, pp. 11–12.

10. Edmund Morgan, *The Puritan Family: Religion and Domestic Relations in Seventeenth-Century New England* (New York, 1966), p. 45.

11. Gary Nash, *The Urban Crucible: Social Change, Political Consciousness, and the Origins of the American Revolution* (Cambridge, 1979), p. 21; Laurel Thatcher Ulrich, ' "A Friendly Neighbor": Social Dimensions of Daily Work in Northern Colonial New England,' *Feminist Studies* 6 (1980), p. 400.

12. Jan Lewis, *The Pursuit of Happiness: Family and Values in Jefferson's Virginia* (New York, 1983), p. 23.

13. Bushman, *Puritan to Yankee*, p. 11.

14. Paul Gilje, ' "The Mob Begin to Think and Reason": Recent Trends in Studies of American Popular Disorder, 1700–1850,' *Maryland Historian* 12 (1981), p. 33.

15. Nash, *Urban Crucible*, pp. 35–53; Edward Countryman, 'The Problem of the Early American Crowd,' *Journal of American Studies* 7 (1973), pp. 77–90.

16. Julia Cherry Spruill, *Women's Life and Work in the Southern Colonies* (New York, 1972), p. 66.

17. Ulrich, ' "A Friendly Neighbor",' p. 395.

18. John Demos, *A Little Commonwealth: Family Life in Plymouth Colony* (New York, 1970), p. 75; Daniel Snydacher, 'Kinship and Community,' p. 50; Greven, *Four Generations*, p. 73.

19. Demos, *Commonwealth*, p. 1; Lawrence Cremin, *American Education: The Colonial Experience, 1607–1783* (New York, 1970), pp. 124–37; Spruill, *Women's Life*, p. 137.

20. Darret B. Rutman and Anita H. Rutman, 'Now-Wives and Sons-in-Law,' in Tate and Ammerman, *Chesapeake*, p. 162.

21. Robert Wells, *Revolutions in American Lives: A Demographic Perspective on the History of Americans, Their Families, and Their Society* (Westport, 1982), pp. 50–51.

22. Nash, *Urban Crucible*, p. 5.

23. Demos, *Commonwealth*, p. 108; Richard Wertz and Dorothy Wertz, *Lying-In: A History of Childbirth in America* (New York, 1979), pp. 2–5.

24. Stilgoe, *Landscapes*, p. 50; Nancy Cott, '18th-Century Family and Social Life Revealed in Massachusetts Divorce Records,' *Journal of Social History* 10 (1976), p. 32.

25. Demos, *Commonwealth*, pp. 48–51; Morgan, *Family*, pp. 76–8. The contentiousness of neighborly relations in New England by no means indicates that they were a safe place to express emotion: in most societies we can identify the primary relationships precisely because they are the most fraught with conflict.

26. Ralph J. Crandall, 'Family Types, Social Structure, and Mobility in Early America: Charlestown, Massachusetts, A Case Study,' in Tufte and Myerhoff, eds, *Changing Images of the Family* (New Haven, 1979); Isaac, *Transformation*, p. 71.

27. Laurel Thatcher Ulrich, *Good Wives: Image and Reality in the Lives of Women in Northern New England, 1650–1750* (New York, 1983), p. 157.

28. Ulrich, *Good Wives*, p. 187; John Ellis, ed., *The Works of Anne Bradstreet, in Prose and Verse* (Gloucester, MA, 1962).

29. Lewis, *Jefferson's Virginia*, pp. 25, 29.

30. Barry Levy, ' "Tender Plants": Quaker Farmers and Children in the Delaware Valley, 1681–1735,' *Journal of Family History* 3 (1978); Susan Forbes, 'Quaker Tribalism,' in Zuckerman, *Friends and Neighbors*, p. 171.

31. Robert Oaks, ' "Things Fearful to Name": Sodomy and Buggery in 17th-Century New England,' in Pleck and Pleck, *American Man*, pp. 57–76; Cott, '18th-Century Family Life,' pp. 20–43.

32. Kathryn Jacob, 'Women's Lot in Baltimore Town, 1729–97,' *Maryland Historical Magazine* 71 (1976), p. 284; John and Robin M. Haller, *The Physician and Sexuality in Victorian America* (New York, 1977), pp. 92–5; Mercy Otis Warren, 'The Blockheads,' in Norman Philbrick, ed., *Trumpets Sounding: Propaganda Plays of the American Revolution* (New York, 1972), p. 141; Edmund Morgan, 'The Puritans and Sex,' in Friedman and Shade, eds, *Our American Sisters: Women in American Life and Thought* (Boston, 1973), p. 12; Mary Ryan, *Womanhood in America, from Colonial Times to the Present* (New York, 1975), p. 53.

33. Cott, '18th-Century Family Life,' p. 39, note 36.

34. Lois Green Carr and Lorena Walsh, 'The Planter's Wife: The Experience of White Women in Seventeenth-Century Maryland,' in Gary Nash, ed., *The Private Side of American History* (New York, 1975), vol. 2, p. 78; Spruill, *Women's Life*, pp. 314–26, 339.

35. T.H. Breen and Stephen Innes, *'Myne Owne Ground': Race and Freedom on Virginia's Eastern Shore, 1640–1676* (New York, 1980), p. 104; Hofstadter, *America at 1750*.

36. Herbert Foster, 'Partners or Captives in Commerce? The Role of Africans in the Slave Trade,' *Journal of Black Studies* 6 (1976); Herbert Gutman, 'Afro-American Kinship Before and After Emancipation,' in Medick and Sabean, eds, *Interest and Emotion* (Cambridge, 1984), p. 248.

37. Ira Berlin, 'Time, Space, and the Evolution of Afro-American Society,' in Thomas Frazier, ed., *The Underside of American History* (New York, 1982), vol. 1, p. 46.

38. Berlin, 'Evolution,' p. 71.

39. Gutman, 'Afro-American Kinship'; Gutman, *The Black Family in Slavery and Freedom, 1750–1925* (New York, 1976); Alan Kulikoff, 'The Beginnings of the Afro-American Family in Maryland,' in Nash, *The Private Side of American History*; Merle Brouwer, 'Marriage and Family Life Among Blacks in Colonial Pennsylvania,' *Pa. Magazine of History and Biography* 99 (1975), p. 369; Cheryl Ann Cody, 'Naming, Kinship and Estate Dispersal: Notes on Slave Family Life on a South Carolina Plantation,' in Michael Gordon, ed., *The American Family in Social-Historical Perspective* (New York, 1983) and 'Slave-Naming Practices in the South Carolina Low Country,' *American Historical Review* 92 (1987), pp. 575–6; Stephen Gudeman, 'Herbert Gutman's *The Black Family in Slavery and Freedom*: An Anthropologist's View,' *Social Science History* 3 (1979); Joan Gundersen, 'The Double Bonds of Race and Sex: Black and White Women in a Colonial Virginia Parish,' *Journal of Southern History* 52 (1986).

40. Kulikoff, 'Beginnings,' p. 146; Breen and Innes, *Myne Own Ground*, pp. 34–5; Berlin, 'Evolution,' p. 63.

41. Eugene Genovese, *Roll, Jordan, Roll: The World the Slaves Made* (New York, 1974), p. 500; Angela Davis, 'Reflections on the Black Woman's Role in the Community of Slaves,' *The Black Scholar* 3 (1971); Jacqueline Jones, *Labor of Love, Labor of Sorrow* (New York, 1985).

42. Elizabeth Anthony Dexter, *Career Women of America, 1776–1840* (Clifton,1972) and *Colonial Women of Affairs* (Boston, 1931); Linda du Pauw, *Founding Mothers*; Gerda Lerner, 'The Lady and the Mill Girl: Changes in the Status of Women in the Age of Jackson,' *Midcontinent American Studies Journal* 10 (1969); Ryan, *Womanhood in America*; Page Smith, *Daughters of the Promised Land* (Boston, 1970); Julia Spruill, *Women's Life*; Barbara Welter, 'The Cult of True Womanhood, 1820–1860,' *American Quarterly* 18 (1966).

43. Richard Morris, *Studies in the History of American Law* (New York, 1964), pp. 126–200; Sophie Drinker, 'Women Attorneys of Colonial Times,' *Maryland Historical Magazine* 56 (1961); Jean Jordan, 'Women Merchants in Colonial New York,' *New York History* 58 (1977); Spruill, *Women's Life*, p. 276; Linda Speth, 'More Than Her "Thirds": Wives and Widows in Colonial Virginia,' in Speth and Hirsch, pp. 5–41.

44. Jordan, 'Women Merchants,' p. 419.

45. Morris, *American Law*, pp. 126–200; Roger Thompson, *Women in Stuart England and America* (Boston, 1976), pp. 165–6; Spruill, *Women's Life*, pp. 361–2; Marylynn Salmon, *Women and the Law of Property in Early America* (Chapel Hill, 1986).

46. K. Kelly Weisberg, ' "Under Greet Temptations Heer": Women and Divorce in Puritan Massachusetts,' *Feminist Studies* 2 (1975), pp. 183–93; Nancy Cott, 'Divorce and the Changing Status of Women in Eighteenth-Century Massachusetts,' *William and Mary Quarterly* 33 (1976), pp. 586–614; Thompson, *Stuart England and America*, pp. 177, 179; Demos, *Commonwealth*, pp. 95–7.

47. Some have argued they were due to the scarcity of women, but scarcity *per se* does not guarantee women improved status. It may lead to increased sexual exploitation, as it did for Chinese women in nineteenth-century California (Lucie Cheng Hirata, 'Chinese Immigrant Women in Nineteenth Century California,' in Berkin and Norton, eds, *Women of America: A History*, Boston, 1979). A recent survey of women in pre-industrial societies found that 'a shortage of women is not associated with more value being placed on the lives of women' (Martin Whyte, *The Status of Women in Preindustrial Society*, Princeton, 1978, p. 143). Moreover, by the end of the seventeenth century there was a surplus of women in the larger American towns but no corresponding decline in women's rights. I am unconvinced by the suggestion that the initial 'demographic disruption of New World settlements may have given women power which they were able to keep even after sex ratios became balanced' (Carr and Walsh, 'The Planter's Wife', pp. 68–97).

48. Demos, *Commonwealth*, p. 85.

49. Morgan, *Puritan Family*, pp. 25–6; Cotton Mather, *Ornaments for the Daughters of Zion* (Boston, 1978).

50. Demos, *Commonwealth*, p. 88; Spruill, *Women's Life*, pp. 359–60.

51. The attack on the 'Golden Age' hypothesis is summarized in Mary Beth Norton, *Liberty's Daughters: The Revolutionary Experience of American Women, 1750–1800* (Boston, 1980) and Lyle Koehler, *A Search for Power: The 'Weaker Sex' in Seventeenth Century New England* (Chicago, 1980).

52. Morgan, *Puritan Family*, p. 43; Spruill, *Women's Life*, p. 320; Nancy Woloch, *Women and the American Experience* (New York, 1984), p. 20.

53. Norton, '18th-Century American Women in Peace and War: The Case of the Loyalists,' *William And Mary Quarterly* 33 (1976); Hirsch, 'The Thrall Divorce Case: A Family Crisis in Eighteenth-Century Connecticut,' in Linda Speth and Alison Duncan Hirsch, *Women, Family, and Community in Colonial America: Two Perspectives* (New York, 1983), pp. 43–75.

54. Ulrich, *Good Wives*, p. 37; Claudia Goldin, 'The Economic Status of Women in the Early Republic: Quantitative Evidence,' *Journal of Interdisciplinary History* 16 (1986); Joan Hoff Wilson, 'The Illusion of Change: Women and the American Revolution,' in Alfred Young, ed., *The American Revolution* (DeKalb, 1976), pp. 395–7, 416–19.

55. There were certainly areas of same-sex concentration in early colonial days, and young men had more freedom than women to form peer groups around tavern visiting, militia activities, etc. But married men had little access to separate spheres in everyday life, while women had many areas of intersecting responsibilities and social intercourse with men. Age differences among men were as marked as gender differences between men and women, and other evidence suggests a relatively small specialization in daily childcare routines by older married women, who usually relegated such tasks to older daughters or servant girls.

56. Margaret Masson, 'The Typology of the Female as a Model for the Regenerate: Puritan Preaching, 1690–1730,' *Signs* 2 (1977), p. 305; Laurel Ulrich, 'Vertuous Women Found: New England Ministerial Literature, 1668–1735,' in Vaughen and Bremer, eds, *Puritan New England: Essays on Religion, Society, and Culture* (New York, 1977), pp. 223, 226.

57. Morgan, *Puritan Family*, pp. 25–6.

58. Benjamin Wadsworth, 'The Well Ordered Family,' reprinted in *The Colonial American Family: Collected Essays* (New York, 1972), p. 103.

59. Mary Ryan, *Womanhood in America*, p. 41; Mary V.V., 'A Dialogue,' in Philbrick, *Trumpets Sounding*, p. 36.

60. Lyle Koehler, 'The Case of the American Jezebels: Anne Hutchinson and Female Agitation During the Years of Antinomian Turmoil, 1636–1640,' in Friedman and Shade, *American Sisters*, p. 64.

61. Wadsworth, 'Ordered Family,' p. 39; Ulrich, 'Vertuous Women,' p. 226.

62. Louis Wright, *Life in Colonial America* (New York, 1971), p. 105; Demos, *Commonwealth*, p. 95; Spruill, *Women's Life*, pp. 168–84, 333.

63. Sophie Drinker, 'Votes for Women in Eighteenth-Century New Jersey,' *New Jersey Historical Society Proceedings* 53 (1962).

64. Ulrich, *Good Wives*; Goldin, 'Economic Status'; W. Elliot Brownlee and Mary Brownlee, *Women in the American Economy: A Documentary History* (New Haven, 1976), p. 42; de Pauw, *Founding Mothers*, pp. 23–44; Smith, *Promised Land*, pp. 54–5; Barbara Wertheimer, *We Were There: The Story of Working Women in America* (New York, 1977), p. 13; Thompson, *Stuart England and America*, p. 76; Spruill, *Women's Life*, pp. 263–311.

65. Mrs Sarah Kemble Knight, *The Journal of Madam Knight* (New York, 1935), pp. 6, 71–2.

66. Mather, 'Ornaments,' pp. 3, 101; Koehler, 'American Jezebel,' p. 58.

67. John Demos, *Entertaining Satan: Witchcraft and the Culture of Early New England* (New York, 1982), p. 284.

68. Alan Macfarlane, *Witchcraft in Tudor and Stuart England* (New York, 1970).

69. Demos, *Entertaining Satan*, pp. 285, 294, 296.

70. Ibid., pp. 299–300; Macfarlane, *Witchcraft*; Keith Thomas, 'The Relevance of Social Anthropology to The Historical Study of English Witchcraft,'in Mary Douglas, *Witchcraft Confessions and Accusations* (London, 1970).

71. Demos, *Entertaining Satan*, p. 210.

72. Paul Boyer and Stephen Nissenbaum, *Salem Possessed: The Social Origins of Witchcraft* (Cambridge, MA, 1974), pp. 189, 199, 209.

73. Ulrich, *Good Wives*, pp. 39, 45.

74. Demos, *Entertaining Satan*, p. 371.

75. Michael Greenberg, 'Revival, Reform, Revolution: Samuel Davies & the Great Awakening in Virginia,' *Marxist Perspectives* 3 (1980), p. 104.

76. Nash, *Urban Crucible*, p. 156.

77. For an exceptionally commercial, impersonal town economy in the early eighteenth century, see Stephanie Grauman Wolf, *Urban Village: Population, Community, and Family Structure in Germantown, Pennsylvania, 1683–1800* (Princeton, 1976). On early Philadelphia, see Warner, *Private City*.

78. Philip Greven, *The Protestant Temperament: Patterns of Child-Rearing, Religious Experience, and the Self in Early America* (New York, 1977), pp. 26, 152–6.

79. Boyer and Nissenbaum, *Salem Possessed*, p. 215.

80. Nash, *Urban Crucible*, pp. 204–32; Joy Day Buel and Richard Buel, *The Way of Duty: A Woman and Her Family in Revolutionary America* (New York, 1984), pp. 13–14.

81. Isaac, *Transformation*, pp. 243–69; Isaac, 'Order and Growth, Authority and Meaning in Colonial New England,' *American Historical Review* 76 (1971), p. 736.

4

The American Revolution and the Early Republic: Democracy, Inequality and the Family

The period from 1750 to 1815 is a complex one for family history because of the cross-fertilization between the steady evolution of petty commodity production and economic stratification on the one hand and the political democratization of the revolutionary and early republican eras on the other. A major influence on family life was the attenuation of traditional bases of political and personal domination over others; this increased the economic, religious, and political independence of small propertied households. Yet such independence was tempered by other trends: the entrenchment of slavery in the South; a widening gulf between the duties of husbands and wives, with new stereotypes attached to both masculinity and femininity; and the involvement of many households in market relations that were dominated by a new economic elite. The American Revolution engendered ideas about political and economic equality that sometimes clashed with its promotion of property rights. It removed many barriers to economic expansion and accumulation but also revived some older ideals of responsibility to a corporate whole. People who rejected old forms of obligation and inequality found themselves enmeshed in new ones. In adapting their new ideas about the value of independence to their continued reliance on obligation and inequality, they struggled with new definitions of community, family, and self. The republican family became a mediating institution between the diverging trajectories of political and economic equality – the one increasing, the other declining.

Economic and Social Trends in America, 1750–1815

The early expansion of American commerce and manufacturing evolved primarily from the dynamics of the corporate household system of production itself, not from qualitatively new economic forces. Relatively self-sufficient agricultural communities, based on wheat or grain, did not require full-time workers year round, so most northern households cultivated other productive tasks, developing supplementary crafts or trades. The hard work fostered by corporate norms promoted intensive agriculture, while the conveyance of property to individual heirs led to subdivision of the land, eventually creating an excess supply of workers in relation to household landholdings. This made it necessary for many households to adjust their demography or their inheritance strategies to reduce pressure on the land – curtailing fertility, sending some of their members away from the farm, or moving children into non-farm occupations on a full-time basis.

Some children moved to the cities, swelling the ranks of an urban workforce that had already developed to meet the needs of British mercantilism: unloading or repairing ships, provisioning soldiers, and so on. The expansion of urban areas between 1700 and 1770 redistributed wealth to the wealthiest residents, creating a semi- or unskilled labor force that could be used by entrepreneurs in new forms of casual wage labor. But the erosion of older labor patterns was not confined to the cities. By 1800 the average size of farms in New England and the Middle Atlantic states was substantially smaller than fifty years earlier. Such holdings would not support further subdivision and in fact were already yielding declining returns. This meant that even those without an 'acquisitive capitalist ethic' were drawn into the labor market and trading network in order to survive.[1]

Indeed, it was *especially* those without that ethic who were drawn in. Households that had preserved traditional values by giving each child an inheritance and living in close residential proximity were the ones most likely to find themselves in older, declining regions where their landholdings were no longer sufficient to support the entire family. The spread of commerce and manufacturing in these areas was due less to an eager embrace of capitalism than to the closure of other opportunities as the agrarian household economy reached its limits: 'Farmers at the bottom end of the scale were more likely to be dependent on trade than the well-to-do. . . . Debt or lack of resources made small farmers cut back on family production in favor of the market.'[2]

Under these conditions a subtle but significant change in the circulation of goods and labor began to occur, as local households found themselves drawn into regional trading networks. Trade and labor ceased to move in an essentially circular if unevenly rewarded fashion, swirling around and about, up and down, and back and forth within a bounded community; they began to be drawn toward the shopkeepers who supplied new goods from outside the region and sought local products to use in trade for them. These merchants increasingly offered to sell their imported commodities in return for specified farm goods demanded by their outside suppliers. The family that could not meet all of its own needs thus found itself in the position of having to produce *less* of its own needs (and of traditional goods desired by other locals) in order to raise or produce more of the items that were in demand by the shopkeepers' non-local clients.

As Christopher Clark points out, this

> did not necessarily signal an immediate alteration in . . . attitudes toward profit seeking. . . . The merchant who acquired [the farmer's] goods would certainly perceive them as an opportunity for gain, but for the farmer the transaction still retained much of its old aspect of fulfilling a specific need. He was trading with the merchant rather than with his neighbors merely because he had to use his surplus to obtain goods that increasingly had to be found from outside markets.[3]

Nor did this system break down the predominantly local nature of exchange. It did, however, change the configuration of the exchange, from what one might call an acephalous network where goods flowed in many different directions and cross currents, to an economic pyramid where goods flowed up from farmers to merchants (and thence out of the local area) and down from merchants to farmers, while services were increasingly exchanged only between those at the same level on the pyramid.

The aftermath of the American Revolution accelerated the growth of production for trade. Thanks to the vacuum created by the Napoleonic Wars, American exports tripled between 1793 and 1807. Northern farmers increasingly shifted to dairy and livestock production for urban and European markets. While as late as 1820 only 25 per cent of Northern agricultural production was exported, this represented a substantial shift beyond purely local networks. In the South, cotton production rose from 3,000 to 73,000 bales between 1790 and 1800 (soaring to 334,000 in 1820), while northern merchants made a killing – in all senses of the word – supplying the South with slaves to beat the deadline for ending the trade in 1807. This mercantile expansion stimulated shipbuilding, banking, warehousing, and the insurance industry. All of these enterprises then sought internal outlets for their capital and goods when the embargo and war with England cut into the international trade. Samuel Slater's cotton mill in Rhode Island, founded in 1791, cast a longer shadow than its relatively small employment figures might suggest, and other areas of household production were growing into national manufacturing centers. By 1800 Lynn, Massachusetts, was producing one pair of shoes for every five white women in the country, up from one in ten in 1790.

Increasingly, the old system whereby wealthier households drew temporary labor from their immediate neighbors gave way to one in which shopkeepers or enterprising masters put work out to rural families and thereby assured themselves of a steady and expandable supply of goods to trade beyond the local area. Given the limits of outwork in many areas, labor also began to be drawn away from the farm and into the city. Carville Earle and Ronald Hoffman have noted that the productive wheat and corn economy of the industrious rural families around Philadelphia provided cheap labor for entrepreneurs in the agricultural off-season, especially when recession or depression hit the rural communities and the sparse work opportunities between September and March made survival harder. They consider this labor source the major stimulus to urban growth, manufacturing, and eventually the adoption of new technology, whose purpose was not to compensate for a labor shortage but 'to convert cheap unskilled labor into cheap skilled labor.'[4]

At both ends of the economic scale, the growth of commodity production combined with political-religious changes to create increasing freedom (or alienation) from traditional corporate restraints and/or protections. As early as the 1760s – and especially after the dislocations of the revolutionary era – there was a far less stable economy in America, with new industries, new risk-taking attitudes, new opportunities (or necessities) for personal initiative, and fewer compensations for deference and submission to social superiors. By 1770, the top 5 per cent of Boston's taxpayers controlled 49 per cent of the city's taxable assets, up from under 30 per cent in 1687. In Philadelphia, the top 5 per cent of taxpayers increased its share of assets from 33 to 55 per cent between 1693 and 1774. The top 10 per cent of that city's taxpayers owned 89 per cent of the taxable property. By 1800 wealth was even more concentrated at the top. These trends greatly reduced the moral authority of upper-class patriarchy, while other forces reduced lower-class acquiescence. The class of propertyless workers not safely encased in a richer household increased in numbers by a factor of three to four between 1700 and 1800. The lower classes lost much of their deference in the course of this economic polarization, the religious enthusiasm of the First Great Awakening, and the mass agitation against the British.[5]

Yet these developments did not eliminate the need for reciprocity and interdependence. Among the middle ranks of society, the growing distance between rich and poor tended to reduce interaction with those above or below them on the social scale but to heighten the need for such interaction at their own level. Although agriculture had been increasingly commercialized over the past fifty years, most household production in 1800 was still for a local or regional market, with a relatively inelastic demand, and most new industries were dependent upon or subsidiary to agricultural production. While an elite minority of the population had engaged in land speculation and diversified investment strategies since the 1740s and an unfortunate minority had been shorn of its rights to community support, the overwhelming majority of people still produced for local markets that operated partly on barter and through personal networks. Farming households continued to rely on family and neighbors rather than hired labor. They also did not normally specialize in order to maximize total output but followed a conservative strategy of diversifying production so as to meet household needs and facilitate exchange of goods and services. In the absence of a developed internal transportation and communication system and a unified national market, household employment and personal credit links persisted. These ensured the continuation of dependence and obligation, despite the decline of deference.[6]

The Revolutionary War opened the way for a further development of political independence, economic diversification, and social differentiation in the cities, but it also created counterweights to individualism. Military, political, and ideological mobilizations during the revolutionary period tended to rely on members of the elites for leadership, refurbishing cross-class ties in politics that had been frayed or snapped in economics. The need for agricultural community was also strengthened: the hardships of war led to a temporary decline in urbanization and international trade, while decimating the New England fishing industry and the Carolinas's indigo industry. After the American Revolution, the opening up of new lands and the expansion of the frontier re-created the agrarian household economy in many areas, while Shays' Rebellion was only the most dramatic expression of a very widespread agrarian discontent, extending to the middle ranks as well as the poor, with the too-rapid expansion of commerce.[7]

Even within the larger towns, changes in social relations were profound without constituting a decisive break with older forms of social and economic organization. The very wealthiest households tended to move their business interactions out of the home but maintained relations of patronage and condescension with clients, tradesmen, and even a section of the poor. The growing but still numerically small class of transient workers and permanent poor experienced a radical disjuncture between work, home, peer-group relations, and cross-class interactions. Here the household was eclipsed as a center of economic and social life, relations with upper-class households were sharply attenuated, and social interactions with other members of the lower class became based less on household activities than on individual connections made during work and leisure. But these households were still a minority. By 1771, 29 per cent of Boston's adult male population were neither property owners nor dependants of property owners. Clearly, the viability of corporate patriarchal household control over the lower classes was threatened, if not destroyed, by such a significant figure. Yet 71 per cent of adult males *were* property-owners or direct dependants of property owners, still a far cry from a proletarian majority.[8]

Household and Family in the American Economy, 1750–1815

The economic and political trends discussed above subverted the political authority of property-owning households over their neighbors, eroded the old definitions of each household's effective community, and changed relations of authority and labor within households. At the same time they actually reinforced the primacy of the household in economic, political, and religious life, necessitating *new* connections among households and establishing clear limits to the spread of individualism.

The expansion of commerce in its early phases, for example, strengthened some of the economic and social functions of the family and reinforced the corporate nature of the household, even as it allowed that household to escape much community control. Among the upper classes, before the development of formal credit institutions, family alliances became increasingly important for preserving or combining blocs of capital and for constructing partnerships. In the revolutionary period, Quaker grandees used intermarriage and kinship connections to tighten class solidarity among themselves and further their business connections. In Rochester, New York, commercial growth in the early 1800s involved family partnerships in the city bolstered by strong ties to relatives in the agricultural hinterland. In Salem, 42 per cent of merchants were in business with relatives: 'The result of participation in the boom-town business world was not a collapse of kinship but the strengthening of old family ties and the invention of new ones.' Commercial circles in the South also used family ties: cousin marriage was extremely common among southern planters between 1765 and 1815.[9]

Some households grew larger in the early phases of commerce and industrialization, as the growing inability to subsist without cash created a need to increase labor inputs into shops or farms. From 1750 to the 1820s many master workmen and shopkeepers brought in boarders, live-in apprentices, and more distant relatives to work for them or provide extra cash. In Rochester in 1827 non-related adult wage earners lived in the homes of 52 per cent of the master craftsmen and 39 per cent of the merchants and professionals. The common definition of family continued to include such non-relatives.[10]

The period from 1775 to 1815 saw a tremendous increase in household production, as Americans sought local substitutes for British goods and ready sources of cash or trade without heavy capital investment. Another stimulus to household production came when early merchant-capitalists compromised with workers' resistance to wage-labor by fostering the putting-out system. Families involved in the putting-out industries or in independent household manufacture worked together, producing textiles or shoe bindings instead of sending children out to be apprenticed elsewhere. In 1851 Horace Bushnell looked back to this period as 'The Age of Homespun,' when the whole family was 'harnessed, all together, into the producing process, young and old, male and female, from the boy that rode the plough-horse to the grandmother knitting under her spectacles. . . .' Underneath the romanticization was first-hand personal experience: Bushnell was reared in a New England town where everyone wore homespun. His father was a successful weaver-farmer who owned a carding machine and cloth mill. Hired agricultural laborers and workers in the cloth-dressing shop were supervised by both of Bushnell's parents; the entire household took meals together and dressed in the clothes that the household had made.[11]

The effect of market relations on lower-class families varied. Among the growing numbers of transient workers, especially in the cities, household production declined and family forms diverged; nuclear or single-parent households coexisted with boarding houses or multiple family dwellings. The hardships of war and poverty resulted in an increase in the numbers of poor women with no husband to support them and no regular employment. But some of the most recent innovations in work relations – the factory and the sweated trades – actually reinforced family ties for workers, at least in their initial stages. In the sweated trades, competition and wretched working conditions forced the lower class into an intensified self-exploitation of the family workforce, while many factories recruited labor on a family basis.[12]

Thus the early progress of commerce and manufacturing by no means immediately undermined the household system of production and social control. Indeed, there was a complex symbiosis between rural families, still organized on a corporate, patriarchal basis, and the growth of manufacturing. By the early 1800s, 30–40 per cent of the taxable rural residents in many older settlements had come to depend on outside employment or on the proceeds of their craft or trade for preservation of their family farm. In turn, early manufacturers depended on the continued ability of such families to deploy and exercise authoritative control over labor. 'During the crucial first years of industrialization in the United States,' comments Barbara Tucker, 'the family assumed part of the responsibility for teaching self-discipline in hundreds of factory towns scattered throughout RI, CT, and southern MA.' In Massachusetts and Rhode Island, Samuel Slater actually purchased land for male household heads to work, while they in turn provided children, adolescents, and dependent relatives to labor in his mills.[13] Mill workers were often organized into family work groups, and skilled male workmen themselves hired family members to assist them.

America's huge acquisition of new land in 1803, and the subsequent extension of the frontier, also magnified the importance of household production in many people's lives. Most pioneers settled as families, and in the absence of community institutions and a regular labor pool they were *more* dependent on family labor and family relations than residents in older settlements. When pioneers constructed local church and community institutions, as Mary Ryan reports of the frontier community of Utica, New York, they tried to reconstruct older relations of mutual support between these and the household. Yet although the 'tripartite social order composed of church, state, and family seemed to replicate the [Puritan] system,' it in fact 'tilted the balance of social power in the direction of individual households.'[14]

The importance of the household in the early phases of commodity production tended to counteract the market's individuating impact on workers, reinforcing older notions about the indivisibility of the household unit and the subordination of all individual members to the needs of that unit. Even some of the same factors that had begun to limit the coercive power of public patriarchy – the breakdown of elite control over sections of the lower classes and the erosion of community interdependence, for example – simultaneously reinforced the corporate nature of the individual household and the need for authoritative organization of its tasks. Competition from merchants who could pay cash for labor and the rise of geographic mobility decreased the casual access of small propertied households to non-family labor in the form of apprentices, neighbor children regularly available as live-in servants, or community-wide efforts on large projects. But a substitute in the form of a wage-labor supply was not available or affordable. The ability of households to pull in kin or workmen and to generate obligations that could attract extra labor was therefore still critical – in some instances more so than before. This ability continued to rest on the organization of a corporate family under the authority of the household head.

Although patriarchy had been weakened as a political and economic force in the larger society, then, it still had a real material base in the organization of work along household lines. If the community as a whole was less able to exert corporate control over most households and their members, the family and the individual remained under the corporate control of the household and the subsection of the community to which that household was affiliated. Many mills employed whole families but paid the wages for all directly to the male household head, thus reinforcing the patriarchal structure that employment outside the home might otherwise have weakened. Even growth in the employment of young women outside family settings, such as at Lowell, did not represent a decisive break with corporate household authority but a continuation of old expectations that young women would work for the family and contribute to its patrimony before getting married. The expansion of industry complemented the household system of early market capitalism by providing employment opportunities for daughters, who could help the family economy by sending home wages or purchasing their own trousseaus.

Nevertheless, critical changes *were* occurring. As the community was less able to exert control over the houshold head, it was also less able to give him support, in relations either with other households or with household members. The growth of household production and the decline in the power of the community at large to exert control over household heads elevated the independence of the household head *vis-à-vis* other families but reduced traditional supports for his authority. This had the effect of making him more independent in his decisions, but less secure in his position.

The reinforcement of separate family or household units was itself a result of the weakening of the household *system*. Families relied on their internal resources all the more because they could rely so much less on a neighborhood of interdependent and familiar fellow producers and consumers. New patterns of production, exchange, credit, and political power freed the rich from reliance on the labor, or even the goodwill, of their neighbors. The middling classes were freed from the restraints that had formerly been imposed by their obligations to those above and below them, but they were also deprived of the obligations owed *to* them. The poor experienced an increase in social freedom but a decline in patronage. Thus under the seeming continuity of a society still based on household production and exchange lay an important transformation: the maintenance of family corporate organization and behavior went hand in hand with a loosening of the ties that bound all families in a given locale into a mutually dependent (if highly unequal) system of debt, duty, and obligation.

But the immediate result of the erosion of traditional community ties was not the creation of separate nuclear families trying to make their way alone, as is implied in classic accounts of the origins of American individualism. The incomplete development of the market, credit and insurance institutions, transportation, and communication limited the independence of separate families, reinforcing older values and behaviors of cooperation, mutual aid, income pooling, and personalistic ways of attracting or mobilizing labor. Without welfare, government services, easy credit, or a fully developed labor market that could operate independently of regional variations and personal ties, people still needed support networks; now, however, they had to consciously *build* those networks and could limit interactions that did not further their ends. Hence the apparent paradox of the era: at the same time that separate families began to make independent decisions and take greater responsibility for the educational, emotional, spiritual, and material needs of their members, they also reached out beyond the family to voluntary associations and networks for support.

Although the old community of corporate households had been undermined as a total, all-encompassing unit, the lack of a national market in goods, labor, capital, or even values required each household to construct new communities and support networks. Rhys Isaac observes: 'As old connections were broken and distant new settlements formed, a pattern of voluntary association (and dissociation) was transforming the scene.'[15] No longer limited by the resources of their local community, some households began to develop their own social and cultural institutions, breaking even their nominal ties to an all-inclusive local community. These new ties cut through old community networks and spread out horizontally. Rejecting the older spatially bounded communities that had organized all their members along vertical lines, many households sought ties with others of a similar class, religion, or political orientation, elevating those voluntary ties over interactions with people from other classes and subgroups encountered daily in one's own locale. Identification with a particular *type* of household or family (and through that with a network of carefully selected other households) rather than with a geographically bounded neighborhood of households seems to have increased in proportion as community identification and bonds of deference/dependence among the classes of that community broke down. The older vertical ties that bound unequal households together on unequal terms gave way to new horizontal ties among households of similar social status, religion or political orientation.

The proliferation of voluntary associations in early-nineteenth-century America seems to have been initiated by the upper classes, who founded mercantile associations, credit-pooling consortia, professional organizations, and cultural societies. The Massachusetts Historical Society, for example, incorporated in 1794, comprised the thirty 'wealthiest and most influential inhabitants of the state' – all male, one should add. 'In these new associations ... the point of reference was not the entire nation or even the whole community, but rather the interests of specific and well-defined groups within the society.' Medical and legal professions won the right to license their professions and regulate access to the field. Occupational organizations such as chambers of commerce, farmers' societies, and associations of master craftsmen promoted collective activities within a particular occupation while differentiating their members from other groups. As Stuart Blumin comments, 'it is likely that these organizations – political parties, professional societies, militia units, and the like – were critical to the creation and maintenance of what one is tempted to call a regional elite community.'[16]

But the urge to associate with households of one's peers spread to other classes as well. Between 1760 and 1820 more than 1,900 voluntary associations were founded in Massachusetts alone, creating new communities that allowed people to cut loose from many older local ties and to reach beyond others.[17] Such new communities were still based on identification with a larger corporate whole, not on individualism, but each household had more flexibility – or less security, depending on one's point of view – in defining its community and its place in that community. The household had more responsibility in picking, establishing, and maintaining a group of other households with which to be associated.

This increased flexibility – or lack of security – also applied to internal family arrangements. Although the household continued to operate as a corporate whole, lines of authority within the unit became less linear. Just as the economic reinforcement of the individual household required a more conscious construction of ties *among* households, it also required a reconstruction of ties *within* households.

The expansion of opportunities for investment or employment outside the inherited family property meant that for both rich and poor reliance on the extended family or the lineage decreased. The authority of the grandfather, characteristic of an agrarian society, was undercut by the fact that children could establish their own families without waiting for the inheritance of land. Resources did not have to be used in common: each marital unit could take its resources, be they labor or money, and utilize them independently. Thus in all classes the marital unit was strengthened at the expense of the lineage; or, where family cooperation beyond the conjugal unit remained important, it was siblings or cousins rather than parents and children who worked together, pooled resources, or went into partnership.

The contraction of family farms meant that fewer children could expect to succeed to their occupations through the family; hence children's life decisions were less dependent on the age and activity of their parents. Even before the revolution, children had begun to win increasing control over choice of occupations, marriage partners, timing of marriage, and other life decisions. The greater latitude allowed to the young was accelerated by the turmoil of the revolutionary and immediate post-revolutionary period, which saw a great increase in premarital pregnancies and other indicators of youthful pressure on traditional parental prerogatives.

There was also a shift in the traditional division of paternal and maternal responsibilities. Although young women who worked outside the household did not lose their dependence on the family or their subordination to the corporate whole, they were removed from the personal supervision (and protection) of patriarchy. Women wrote to their sisters and mothers, not their fathers, asking advice about how long to work and what to buy for the future. At the same time, their mothers were losing to the mills and shops many of the income-generating duties they had once been assigned. Instead they were increasingly responsible for domestic production, household chores, and childcare, tasks they had once delegated to younger girls or servants.

Even those families that enlarged and consolidated themselves to provide factory labor in family mill towns such as Webster faced a certain tension in the maintenance of traditional lines and justifications of authority: 'Reasons for adopting or taking in charges emanated less from moral or religious considerations and obligations than from economic necessity. In effect this practice represented a step in the undermining of the family's disciplinary role,' a process accelerated in the 1830s when the introduction of shift work and overtime put family members on different schedules.[18]

Meanwhile, patriarchal relations that had once benefited the entire household ceased in many cases to accomplish their original ends. The outwork system depressed the earnings of urban artisans and subtly subverted the intent of families who had taken it on in order to preserve their farms and their rural independence:

> . . . in many instances the labor which had previously been devoted to manufacturing tasks for the benefit of the household was turned to good account by workshop and factory owners. . . . It enabled industrial production to remain in the home, but . . . 'domestic industry' became an agent, first of mercantile, then of industrial capitalism.[19]

These developments posed a problem for families caught up in the new social relations of petty commodity production: how to accommodate the continued need for the household to work as a unit with the kind of changes that had torn asunder the former unity of public and private patriarchy. Even aside from the impetus provided by the revolutionary experience, it is clear that the definition of the family and the question of sex and age roles within it had to be on the agenda; adjustments in expectations and behaviors were being made by the 1760s. The American Revolution, however, vastly complicated the problem, adding new ingredients to the mix of forces that would eventually produce restructured relationships within and between families, communities, and larger economic and political institutions.

The Heritage of the American Revolution

The American Revolution can be seen, somewhat schematically, as the culmination of individualizing political and economic forces in American society and the take-off point for capitalist development. In the long run, the objective role of the revolution was certainly to clear the way for capitalist expansion and competition. It was fought by social groups who wished to throw off mercantile economic restrictions and establish the bases of bourgeois political liberty. It removed precapitalist barriers to economic and social mobility and bolstered ideas about the sanctity of property rights, which it tended to equate with personal liberty. In this sense it was a classic bourgeois revolution.

But as Isaac Deutscher once observed, 'no revolution is ever bourgeois' to the lower classes.[20] Artisans, laborers, petty traders, and debt-ridden small farmers bitterly indicted British 'aristocracy' and wealthy American collaborators with British rule – an indictment that occasionally suggested a general condemnation of the rich and a call for a reassertion of corporate controls over individual behavior, though without traditional relations of deference and condescension. The revolution unleashed a radical dynamic that revived old notions of social responsibility even as it sanctioned individualistic behavior and goals. Vehement demands for equality sometimes clashed with the notions of property rights that were generally expressed in resistance to British taxation. Committees of correspondence and public safety bypassed traditional political institutions and took government into their own hands. Politics ceased to be confined to an elite but was transformed by direct intervention of the masses into decision-making processes. The revolution also favored the growth of small family enterprises that opposed untrammeled commercial and manufacturing development even if they did not support more radical demands for 'leveling.'[21]

Although America had no internal struggle of the order of those in England in the 1640s or France after 1789, its economic and political reorganization was by no means predetermined. A key issue was whether the abolition of political despotism should be accompanied by attempts to establish economic parity. When Congress tried to get price control committees and other associations formed during the revolutionary period to disband, spontaneous groups sprang up to take action against profiteering and monopolies, investigate supplies of goods, and control prices. Popular tribunals distributed Loyalist lands and goods, challenged rulings from state courts, and compelled creditors to accept payment in paper money or in produce. 'In fact,' comments Gordon Wood, 'more such groups sprang up in the dozen years after Independence than in the entire colonial period.'[22]

Throughout the 1780s,

> New England was beset by conventions voicing . . . local grievances and resentments against the import and commutation measures of the Confederation Congress. . . . In the summer of 1787 even counties in Virginia were rising in spontaneous association, burning courthouses and stopping tax collections.

In Pennsylvania, mass action against profiteering led to appeals by the propertied for armed guards. All over America, argues Staughton Lynd, 'the pressure on legislative bodies from the people "out of doors" reached a high point in the winter of 1779–80.'[23]

Many people believed that the overthrow of British rule was just the beginning of a broader social and economic transformation. The first draft of the Pennsylvania Constitution of 1776 held that the state should be able to regulate property rights in the interests of equality. 'Where wealth is hereditary,' warned a Maryland almanac, 'power is hereditary, for wealth is power.' The upper classes were alarmed enough to join Robert Livingston's mother in a prayer for 'Peace and Independence and deliverance from the persecutions of the Lower Class who I foresee will be as despotic as any Prince (if not more so) in Europe.'[24]

The American Revolution, then, was by no means the 'Revolution of Sober Expectations' that some historians have made it out to be.[25] By the 1790s there was a lively radical millennial movement associated with the tradition of the American Revolution, and many people confidently expected the Second Coming to establish 'a fundamentally restructured, just, and harmonious world' through the new American Republic. On a more secular plane, ambitious plans were proposed for economic, racial and sexual equality, and they found sympathetic listeners in every state. The popularity of such plans was great enough to alarm even such former radicals of the revolutionary period as Joseph Warren, who complained to Sam Adams about the increasing lack of respect for civil government and economic prerogatives: 'My greatest wish, therefore, is that we may restrain everything which tends to weaken the principles of right and wrong, more especially with regard to property.' By 1784 Sam Adams was declaring that 'popular committees and county conventions are not only useless but dangerous.' Whatever their value against the British, he urged, now 'we are safe without them.' He feared that the problem now was 'the danger of errors on the side of the people.'[26]

The fears of property-holders and the hopes of religious and secular radicals did not, however, materialize. Almost 50 per cent of free males owned property, enough to impart a strong sense of identification with calls for social and economic stability. As the economic hardships of the post-revolutionary period faded and some measures were passed for the relief of smallholders, agitation for further economic reform receded from its peak in 1779–80: the Constitution represented an affirmation of property rights and a rejection of more egalitarian plans for social reorganization.

The economic expansion during the heyday of domestic manufacture, while exacerbating the extremes of rich and poor, also created thousands of openings for small entrepreneurs or successful craftsmen to gain, not a fortune, but what was often called a 'competence' or an 'independency.' There were only 3 master craftsmen in Lynn in 1750; by 1800 there were 200. The streets of New York, Philadelphia, Boston, Charlestown, and a host of smaller towns filled with new shops and crafts, as well as with peddlers plying the wares of producers from outside the town. These small businessmen and masters should not be considered 'self-made men,' and they did not consider themselves such. Like their elite counterparts, they formed assocations for mutual aid, cultivated networks of relatives and religious or social co-thinkers, and fostered the personal ties that were still so important for the extension of the market and the establishment of credit. But though they did not credit commercial individualism for their success, neither did their social experience give them cause to fear the expansion of commerce or the removal of restraints on individual economic activity.

Not all small property-owners developed into entrepreneurs, of course, and many urban workmen found their economic conditions less than satisfactory. But so long as property-holding remained widespread (and so long as a craft tradition predominated in which a man's skill was as stable a property and as much under his own direction as land), a clearer sense of class resentment against the larger masters and owners did not develop. The continued interdependence of rural farmers and urban craftsmen; the preservation of craft traditions that kept many masters and apprentices working side by side; the commonality of interest in overcoming the vestiges of deference and privilege based on pedigree while resisting demands from below that smacked of 'leveling' – all these factors combined to keep small artisans and farmers from identifying themselves with the propertyless against the propertied.

Also important here was the persistence of older corporate notions of responsibility, even among wealthier levels of society. It was not only the less affluent mechanics who held to an ideology that significantly limited individual ambition and accumulation even as it sanctioned private property and economic expansion: many masters, before they got caught up in the dynamics of an increasingly competitive market, were as reluctant to exercise 'despotism' as they were to submit to it. As late as 1830, a textile worker from England found that his employers were not eager to follow Adam Smith's advice and the English example in subdividing the work: 'This, sir, is a free country,' replied one master to whom the worker suggested this innovation. 'We want no one person over another which would be the case if you divided the labour.'[27]

A serious revolt of the propertyless was also not on the agenda. These were not yet a substantial majority of the free male population, and, even more decisively, they were not in a position to develop an ideological or organizational framework for resistance. Many were still dependants, living at or near the households or estates of the propertied. Neither at work nor at leisure did they associate primarily with others of their own station, thus gaining a sense of collective interests or power. To the middling classes and even to many workers, the poor appeared a breed apart, not independent householders who had been squeezed out by economic expansion but old-style dependants who had failed to establish productive households for themselves.

Extremes of rich and poor, then, could still be seen not as harbingers of the future but as holdovers from the past, so that workers and employers could bury their differences in a hatred of idle 'aristocrats' combined with a contempt for the poor, whom they saw as victims not of expanding capitalism but of old habits of dependence. There was thus only limited support for ongoing social radicalism, particularly after political and social developments in the 1780s and 1790s created a growing concern for order. Shays' Rebellion of 1786, the Whiskey Rebellion of 1794, the disturbances of the French Revolution, and the victorious slave revolution in Santo Domingo convinced many that political ferment was too risky and some stabilization was in order.

The expanding economy, the heritage of the American Revolution, and the growing concern for social order merged to create the paradox of newly self-conscious (though often shifting) interest groups competing aggressively over policies and office under the hegemony of a common republican ideology, vigorously opposed to both 'privilege' or 'monopoly' and to 'leveling'. As a number of authors have recently demonstrated, a large majority of the middling and upper ranks were able to unite around an anti-aristocratic, occasionally even anti-mercantile, but always pro-economic growth program. Their ideology extolled private property, equality of condition, liberty, social responsibility, and virtue (still defined as a political trait, not a sexual one), without recognizing any insurmountable contradictions among these. It was also contemptuous of the dependency or deference that still characterized the life of slaves and poor folk. 'This fusion of independent liberties and personal sovereignty with social and corporate responsibility [was] very akin to what others have called "collective individualism". . . .'[28]

Although it is true that America was imbued with 'privatism' and an 'acquisitive' spirit at an early stage and that the 1790s saw a rejection of economic radicalism, not even by the early nineteenth century should this be confused with acceptance of cut-throat competition and unlimited aggrandizement by the powerful. Americans' long experience with corporate controls over people's behavior was partly reinforced by the collective organization and action of the American Revolution; and the rejection of involuntary dependence on others had not yet been construed as requiring a denial of *all* dependence. As Sean Wilentz describes the ideology of the urban craftsmen, in a way that applies to rural farmers as well:

> Their vision was egalitarian and suffused with the ethic of the small producer – but not 'liberal' or 'petit-bourgeois,' as the twentieth century understands the terms. It was a vision of a democratic society that balanced individual rights with communal responsibilities – of independent, competent citizens and men who would soon win their competence, whose industry in the pursuit of happiness, as in politics, was undertaken not for personal gain alone but for the public good.[29]

America was not unique in developing such an ideology. European thinkers had already tried to grapple with the question of how to reconcile traditional notions of mutuality with the rapid expansion of commerce and they had developed similar notions of hard work, family responsibility, and restrained individualism. But the American experience involved less clear-cut class polarization than comparable revolutions in Europe; hence American ideology had both a more thoroughgoing rejection of deference and a more ambitious attempt to reconcile the pursuit of profit with the establishment of social order and harmony.

The link between the two was found in the newly independent household of the farmer, artisan, or small manufacturer. Colonial society had pictured the household as a small commonwealth, a model of the hierarchical relations that prevailed in the larger polity and economy; post-revolutionary Americans saw the republic as the sum of small households whose independence was the basis of the liberty that prevailed in the larger polity and economy. The transformation of eighteenth-century evangelical thought is illustrative of this change in orientation. By the early 1800s most evangelicals had shifted their attention away from radical social reconstruction and toward individual conversion, stressing 'the importance of families, in particular, as the connecting link between private virtue and public happiness.'[30] On the political virtue of such families, and their refusal to defer to either corrupt privilege or 'factious' leveling, Americans believed they could construct a society where the pursuit of profit and the pursuit of equality could coexist.

The Contradictions of the Republican Household Ideology

Republican ideology obscured the differences between producers and employers by stressing their common opposition to aristocracy and dependence and by identifying people on the basis of their household relations rather than their class. Jeffersonian inattention to the spread of wage labor had some justification, in that neither masters nor workers had quite articulated their economic distinctions. However, two glaring inconsistencies stood out. First, the identity of ownership and work, liberty and property, that republicanism assumed certainly did not apply to slaves. If the independent productive household was the linchpin of republican virtue, what was the role of slave-holding and slave families? If the new society assumed equality among men, how could slavery continue at all? Second, the society of independent, non-deferring households that Jeffersonians lauded required a more specialized female role within the home while allowing the male head of household to represent his wife and children in public just as propertied community leaders had formerly represented less socially powerful males. How could male domination in the home be the basis of rejection of deference in society? Could either the image of subordinate helpmeet or of frivolous ornament, both of which had uneasily coexisted in the eighteenth century, explain the role of woman in a republican home?

Slaves and women were left out of the benefits of an expanding commercial society and excluded from the pursuit of economic or political liberty. To some extent, indeed, the expansion of economic and political opportunities for white males was even built upon the labor of women and slaves. This posed a major challenge to republican ideology, especially to its conception of the links between public and private life. In the case of slaves and women, the contradictions between the new nation's political ideals and its socioeconomic trends, obscured for white males by the growth of an independent farmer/artisan class and the hegemony of republican ideology, threatened to come to the fore. The revolution proclaimed the brotherhood of man, yet the Constitution legalized slavery. Republican theorists celebrated the death of dependence and the responsibility of individuals to make their own moral decisions, yet politically and economically they subsumed the woman and children of the household in the person of the man.

The conflict between the revolution's rejection of hierarchical explanations for inequality and its reinforcement of slavery and female domestic responsibility led to a sea change in the way differences among people were conceptualized. The high tide was not reached until democratic attacks on slavery and patriarchy in the 1840s and 1850s forced opponents of abolition and women's rights into extreme defenses of their position, but a decisive shift occurred in the early republican period. Although specific explanations of inequality differed for women, Blacks, and later the poor, a common approach informed them all: rejection of the social necessity to *impose inequality* and insistence on the *natural* bases of *differences* in role and position. To understand this change, and how it affected domestic relations, we need to review the justifications for racial and sexual inequality in the colonial period, the impact of the revolution on these, and the intersection of new political ideals with the results of economic expansion after the revolution. It will be necessary to spend some time on the growth of slavery and racism in order to establish the special dilemmas that affected the future of both white and black families in America.

The American Revolution and Blacks

The colonial period

Slavery was one of the most brutal aspects of European expansion in the New World. Contrary to some interpretations, however, white racism against Blacks was not initially the most salient factor in European patterns of exploitation, and racism alone does not explain the origins of black slavery. The word 'slave' derived from Slav, but the spread of a sugar industry to the New World shortly after the halt in slave exports from Russia led to the expansion of black slavery from Guinea, thus creating the expectation that Africa was a logical source of slaves and slaves were likely to be black. Even so, the English tradition in the seventeenth and eighteenth centuries did not prefigure later theories of innate biological inferiority or support institutions built primarily on racism.[31] In other words, slavery came first, and its association with and rationalization by color came afterwards. It is the argument of this section that racist ideology, ironically, assumed its most vehement ideological expression only after the spread of democratic ideas.

Brutal as it was, black slavery was not qualitatively different than other forms of servitude in the British Empire. In eighteenth-century England, Blacks were more readily accepted among the lower classes than servants from the Continent, who were feared and hated. As J.H. Plumb points out:

> Racism [not just against Blacks, but against Irish, Scots, etc.] was a rampant feature of the centuries when slavery was being established in America and it was, therefore, easy to make it one of the justifications for the institution. . . . But the idea of white slavery was in no way repellent to the Tudors or limited by them to savages and heathens. . . . Slavery was only the most extreme of all servile conditions – Servant and slave were more than semantically linked. All servants, regardless of race, were viewed as a 'deviant underclass'.[32]

Many of the first Blacks in the colonies came as indentured servants, and were freed after serving their term. Increasing reliance on slavery came after the failure of indentured servitude to adequately meet the labor needs of the colonies. Africans had no contracts, no influential kin in the Old World, no government officials to protect them from permanent enslavement; their language and religion as well as their color provided a means of setting them apart from other groups; and their greater ability to withstand the malaria of the Chesapeake and South Carolina regions was an advantage, as was the knowledge of rice cultivation that many West Africans brought with them.[33]

Yet even as the servitude of Blacks hardened into slavery in the early years, this was a matter of economic need and specific historical circumstance that was seldom supported by strict racial criteria. Black slaves were taught the same skills and given the same responsibilities as white servants. Black and white servants worked together, mingled socially, ran away, even rebelled together on numerous occasions in the seventeenth century. One of the last groups to surrender after Bacon's Rebellion was an interracial band of rebels. Collaboration among black slaves and white Irish apprentices extended even to the blending of African folk music and Irish ballads to produce the Negro spiritual. The fact that slaves were black was explained, if the question came up, by reference to conquest, custom, or African paganism. In fact, seventeenth-century legislators at first equated slavery with non-Christianity rather than color.[34]

After the 1690s, racial lines began to be drawn more sharply. As black slavery grew, the problem of social control over the slaves mounted; and this was posed even more urgently by the interracial rebellions that punctuated the seventeenth century. 'The answer to the problem, obvious if unspoken and only gradually recognized, was racism, to separate dangerous free whites from dangerous slave blacks by a screen of racial contempt,' writes Edmund Morgan. As early as 1680, the Virginia Assembly repealed a number of penalties that had been imposed on white servants for looting during Bacon's Rebellion, but excluded Blacks from the amnesty. In 1705, the legislature provided that the property of slaves should be seized and distributed to poor whites – 'a highly effective device for dissociating the two.' As the number of slaves and the value of their productivity increased, writes T. H. Breen, it was both desirable and possible to grant some concessions to the proportionally smaller free whites. Many acts hence aimed at giving certain rudimentary privileges to poor whites in return for their help in keeping slaves down. In 1727, for example, a slave patrol was established and rank-and-file whites who served in it were given tax exemptions and release from other community obligations.[35]

But George Fredrickson argues that although 'societal racism' can be said to have developed during this period, 'a rationalized racist ideology did not develop' before the nineteenth century. Colonial society did not require full-blown theories about the inferiority of people who were enslaved, for most people still believed that one's position in the social order was determined by birth, fate, or God's will rather than individual merit or demerit. Thus an early attack on slavery by Samuel Sewell prompted John Soffin to retort in 1700:

> God . . . hath ordained different degrees and orders of men, some to be High and Honorable, some to be Low and Despecable, some to be Monarchs Kings, Princes and Governours, Masters and Commanders, others to be subjects and to be commanded; servants of sundry sorts and degrees, bound to obey; yea, some born to be slaves, and so remain during their lives, as hath been proved. Otherwise there would be a meer parity among men.[36]

Acceptance of slavery as a legitimate social institution permitted extreme brutality in the master–slave relationship. Eighteenth-century slave codes were 'unspeakably harsh'; slaves could be dismembered or burned alive. But this acceptance also meant that slaves continued to be defined more by their social role than by their color. Although color was certainly associated with slavery by the beginning of the eighteenth century, it was generally treated as a correlation rather than an automatic identity, and Blacks who were not slaves were often exempted from color laws. In Boston in 1740, a white watchman was rebuked for apprehending a free Black under a curfew that forbade

Negroes from being out alone after nine or ten p.m. Authorities ruled that the act applied only to 'Negro and Molatto Servants, that shall be unseasonably absent from their Masters Families.' Many colonial laws that have been interpreted as prohibiting interracial marriage actually banned marriage only between black slaves and free white women.[37]

Thus the few Blacks who managed to escape their role as slaves had considerable maneuvering room. Right up to the time of the American Revolution free Blacks could still hold property, bear arms, sue and be sued, testify in the courts, travel freely, even purchase slaves and white indentured servants in most states. Blacks were admitted to membership in the Puritan Church in New England. Virginia and North and South Carolina were the only colonies to ban free Blacks from voting in the early eighteenth century. In 1761 Georgia followed suit, but North Carolina revoked its prohibition in the same year.[38]

Independence and inequality

The American Revolution threw the whole institution of slavery into question. If no man or woman had a birthright to rule, why should some men and women be condemned by birth to slavery? Natural rights, the social compact, consent of the governed – these bourgeois principles of liberty, furthered by the American Revolution, were hard to reconcile with the enslavement of fellow human beings.

Shortly after the Stamp Act riots, northern slaves began to sue for their freedom in the courts, and if they could afford to pursue the case, they generally won. In Massachusetts, Elizabeth Freeman won her liberty in 1781 by citing the Massachusetts Bill of Rights. Suits were expensive, so other slaves joined in petitions, quoting from the Declaration of Independence. In 1780 Paul Cuffe, a free black shipbuilder, petitioned the Massachusetts legislature for a tax exemption, raising what must have been an uncomfortably familiar argument – no taxation without representation. Some white voices were also raised in support of civil liberties for Blacks. One reason given by several Massachusetts towns for their rejection of the 1777 state constitution was its disfranchisement of Blacks, Indians, and mulattoes. William Gordon said scornfully that the disfranchising clause was 'blacker than any negro' and proved that the legislators were interested in 'their own rights only and not those of mankind.' In their initial voting laws, most states did not specifically prohibit black suffrage or office-holding.[39]

Manumissions, many prompted explicitly by the egalitarian principles of the revolution, increased dramatically, in the South as well as the

North. Richard Randolph of Virginia freed his slaves by will in 1797 'to make retribution . . . to an unfortunate race of bondmen, over whom my ancestors have usurped and exercised the most lawless and monstrous tyranny . . . in violation . . . of the most inherent, inalienable, and imprescriptible rights of man. . . .'[40]

Southern courts liberalized the rules for manumission, some legislatures granted freedom to slaves who had fought in the revolution, and many states tacitly accepted the freedom of slaves who had run away during the turmoil. Maryland, Virginia, and North Carolina joined northern states in fixing severe penalties for the kidnapping of free Blacks; a North Carolina man was executed for this offense in 1806. Anti-slavery societies were also formed. Even where overt anti-slavery sentiment did not penetrate, 'no one in the South stood up in public to endorse slavery.' Colonial Virginians 'had felt a general complacency about [slavery] . . . rooted in a scarcely conscious assumption that the cosmos consisted of a vast, continuous hierarchy of parts, each in its degree on the scale. Slavery did not pose a problem within such a system,' writes Rhys Isaac. But in a society based on contracts between equal individuals, slavery stood out as a denial of fundamental principles; many people began to be deeply disturbed by the moral dissonance.[41]

Yet at the same time as the ideology of the American Revolution destroyed the consensus that slavery was a legitimate social institution, the economic gains of the revolution reinforced slavery in significant ways. The growth of American trade during and after the American Revolution was largely dependent on the products of slave labor. The invention of the cotton gin in 1793 further enshrined slavery as a central American institution. Cotton soon came to account for more than half the value of all American exports. Demand for slaves rose rapidly, and prohibitions on the slave trade merely stimulated a boom in the slave-supplying states. The number of slaves in the United States increased by 33 per cent in the first decade of the nineteenth century and by another 29 per cent in the 1820s. Fear of slave revolt grew in proportion to the number of slaves and the dependence on slave labor; the revolution in Santo Domingo in 1794 and the Gabriel Prosser Plot in Virginia in 1800 fanned the fear into near panic. Under this pressure, many people's ideals crumbled. Manumissions abruptly ceased in the South and slavery was more firmly consolidated in the law.

Meanwhile, in the North, increased competition and insecurity of tenure among unskilled laborers led to considerable anxiety about economic competition and status maintenance. The fact that freed Blacks were introduced into a society newly based on competition ensured that one response would be to try to exclude Blacks from competition. In economically volatile and competitive settings, writes Robert Cottrol:

> Some ... feel that their rise can occur only if others are prevented from moving upward. Others believe that only by making the distinctions between themselves and those who cannot or will not rise as sharp and as visible as possible will they be permitted to move up the social ladder. These sorts of attitudes have increased tensions even in uniracial social settings where potential candidates for upward mobility have taken pains to disassociate themselves from the attitudes and practices of their original reference groups and instead have adopted, often with a vengeance, the viewpoints of the groups that they have aspired to join. That this sort of attitudinal metamorphosis has created tremendous social tensions in once-homogeneous groups should help us to understand why the children and grandchildren of the eighteenth century slaves and indentured servants, who drew few distinctions among themselves, were on different sides of an increasingly stringent color line in the nineteenth century.[42]

Separation and prejudice were also fostered by the fact that Blacks were unable to take advantage of the new opportunities for independence opening to many white men in nineteenth-century America. Western states, for example, were far more restrictive of Blacks than eastern ones. Workshop and factory employment largely excluded Blacks, leaving them confined to older personal service occupations. Excluded from white working-class associations, Blacks could occasionally be used by employers to break strikes or swing elections, a fact that further exacerbated the competition between Blacks and lower-class whites.

Because of these differences in occupational opportunity, free Blacks tended to have more patron–client ties with aristocratic upper-class whites than did the white lower class, which had been independent longer. Middle- and upper-class whites could 'condescend' to Blacks and expect deference from them in ways no longer possible in many interactions with the white working-class population. Since many lower-class people were now out of these bonds of dependence, the deference and condescension involved began to be explained as a racial rather than a class relation.

Black–white relations also quickly became a political and economic weapon. Because republicans condemned Blacks for 'dependence,' Blacks tended to vote for Federalists and Whigs; in turn the Democrat-Republican Party pushed for Black disenfranchisement. On the other hand, some of the most virulent anti-immigrant groups, such as the Know-Nothings, occasionally supported black rights as a weapon against new immigrants. The resultant political maneuveurs can be seen clearly in Rhode Island, where the elite took away black voting rights in 1822 but restored them in 1845 after Blacks, excluded from

the suffrage demands of the Dorr Rebellion, helped white freeholders to
put down the revolt.

Democracy and racism

With the spread of democratic ideology old justifications of slavery broke
down, leaving men such as Patrick Henry unable to defend the institution
except by 'ye general inconvenience' of doing without slaves.[43] For a man
who reputedly had thundered 'Give me liberty or give me death,' this
was rather uninspiring oratory, and it was unacceptable to many less
adaptable in their moral commitments.

The concept of slavery was morally repugnant to bourgeois ideology.
But the practice of slavery was initally strengthened by bourgeois
expansion, while heightened competition in the urban working classes
led to racial divisions and discrimination in the North as well. The tension
created by the conflict between ideology and practice was to lead to a new
rationale for slavery and exclusion – a rationale that would live on even
after the immediate conflict was resolved.

There was only one way for slave-holders and those who tolerated
slavery to resolve the contradiction between the principles for which
they had fought a war and the property they refused to relinquish. If all
human beings were created equal, but some remained slaves, the slaves
must have some characteristic that rendered them less human. One sprang
immediately to the eye – the color of their skin. The definition of Blacks
was separated from its social basis and redrawn along racial lines. Older
cultural and religious theories about Blacks gave way to a coherent theory
of racism that had been largely absent in early writings on slavery.

The American Revolution, writes Duncan MacLeod, was a watershed,
on one side of which 'racial discrimination was largely implicit and very
largely defined by slavery; on the other it was explicit and existed
independently of slavery.' David Brion Davis, George Fredrickson,
Leon Litwack and Harry Fritz have all commented on the connection
of racism to the spread of Jacksonian democracy, which could deliver
its promise of equality only to a limited number of people and therefore
defined others as unqualified for political and economic rights. Both the
Jeffersonians and the Jacksonians gained concessions for small property-
holders by restricting black and Indian rights, and both therefore recast
the radical egalitarian heritage of the revolution. The revolution, which
had provided the ideological tools to attack slavery, also created new
possibilities and incentives for dividing people on the basis of race.[44]

The link between democratic theory and toleration of slavery was
forged through what Willie Lee Rose has called 'the domestication' of
slavery. She suggests that the term 'domestic' slavery was adopted 'to

avoid the blatant contradiction that property in human beings implied for the natural rights philosophy . . . ; the phrase "domestic institution" came to mean . . . slavery translated into a fundamental and idealized Victorian institution, the family.' Like the family, it was supposed to rest not on force or violence but on a natural division of labor and capacity. Colonial ideology that slavery was a socially necessary convenience gave way to the republican view that it was the natural result of black biology. As democratic opposition to slavery revived after the 1830s, the biological rationale was extended and elaborated. Slavery was eventually put forward as almost a benign solution to the natural incapacities of Blacks. 'The knife of the anatomist has demonstrated,' declared a typical article by 1842, that the physiological nature of Blacks makes 'the yoke of servitude easy, and slavery, which would otherwise be intolerable, *a happy condition.*'[45]

Slave codes were liberalized in significant ways, a somewhat elephantine paternalism came to prevail, and masters were sometimes punished for maltreating slaves. But this liberalization of slavery was attached to more pervasive control over slave life and stricter consignment of Blacks to a separate order of humanity. Slavery became 'tighter as it became softer.'[46] Paternalism also required a vicious repression of free Blacks, whose very existence made a mockery of the claim that Negroes were incapable of surviving without slavery.

The federal government restricted the militia to white men in 1792, and after 1800 the legal and social position of the free black population deteriorated steadily. In 1806 the Virginia legislature effectively halted slave emancipations and began 'a long-term policy of increasing legal debasement' of free Blacks. Rhode Island banned voting by Blacks in 1822. In Pennsylvania Blacks were disenfranchised in 1838. By 1835 free Blacks had lost the right to assembly in most southern states. 'Hardly a session of the legislature passes,' a committee of the Maryland House of Representatives commented in 1843, 'that some law is not enacted restricting them in their rights and privileges.' New legislation limited the mobility of free Blacks and even denied them recourse against reenslavement. In Petersberg, nineteenth-century ordinances required free Blacks to step off the sidewalk to let whites pass. Teaching a Black to read or write was made a criminal offense. Epitomizing the new atmosphere was an 1847 ruling by the State Court of North Carolina – where a man had been executed for kidnapping a free Black as late as 1806 – that 'in this state a black person is presumed to be a slave.'[47]

The American Revolution, then, made old justifications of slavery obsolete without doing away with slavery itself. It further created incentives for employers to divide workers by race and for workers to exclude certain categories of people from training or organization.

Attempts to reconcile the contradiction between the revolution's pro-fession of human rights and the new nation's continuation of slavery and racial discrimination led to a change in rationale. What could no longer be justified as an inequality imposed by man was now seen as a difference imposed by nature. The difference was explained on the grounds of biology.[48] The 'domestication' of slavery was part of a general pattern whereby inequalities once accepted as social necessities upheld by forcible domination came to be defined as presocial and natural in origin. This pattern can also be discerned in post-revolutionary discussions of the white family and women's role within it.

Women and the American Revolution

The colonial subordination of women

Most white women in colonial America were wives and mothers in families expected to mirror the hierarchy and subordination of society as a whole. A typical New England catechism summed up the importance of order in the family:

Q. *What is the fifth commandment?*
A. Honor thy father and thy mother. . . .

Q. *Who are here meant by father and mother?*
A. All our superiors, whether in family, school, church, and commonwealth.

Q. *What is the honor due to them?*
A. Reverence, obedience, and (when I am able) recompence.[49]

The father was the head of the family and the woman owed reverence and obedience to him. The wife's subordination to her husband, however, was considered a social rather than a biological law. Restrictions on women were part of the generally restrictive climate of the time, and did not require special justification. There were also restrictions on servants, children, the lower classes. The legitimacy of male domination was seldom questioned, and this obviated the need for a coherent theory of feminine incapacity. Samuel Willard declared in 1726 that between husband and wife 'there is a Subordination, and they are ranked among unequals.' But Willard specifically highlighted the social nature of the subordination by saying that the word inferior 'is a general word, and signified to be ordered under another, or to keep Order, being a Metaphor from a Band of Souldiers, or an Army.' In fact, the *Oxford English Dictionary* indicates that the word inferior was used to refer to people's position or rank, rather than to their personal qualities, right up to the nineteenth century.[50]

Changing images of women in the pre-revolutionary period

The effects of social and economic change in the late eighteenth century on sex roles were mixed. Growing social stratification and economic individualism had some negative results for the position of women. In the upper reaches of society they created a class of men who moved in predominantly male business circles, removed from the household networks in which their wives and daughters remained. Such men were likely to make wills depriving their wives of custody over their children and management of their estates. Moreover, as the eighteenth century progressed, more and more men made their eldest sons rather than their wives executors of their wills. The spread of a brisk land market led to the view among those with speculative or commercial ambitions that women's dower rights were an encumbrance on the mobility of land and a check on the freedom of private property. Joan Hoff Wilson has found a striking increase in the renunciation of dower rights by women in the late eighteenth century, and has interpreted this as a setback for women.[51]

For the wealthiest groups, especially in the urban areas, the household was less and less a center of production or even important social and political interaction. The elite merchant conducted his business in upper-class taverns or clubs and demonstrated his affluence by the conspicuous non-productivity of his household. The leisure of his wife or daughter was displayed in the fact that she could immobilize her body in corsets, grow long fingernails, indulge her sensibilities, and cultivate her manners in line with the 'ladies' books' that were being imported from England. Laurel Thatcher Ulrich argues that new ideas of domesticity and gentility first grew up among wealthy town-dwellers during the middle of the eighteenth century, and 'that the first specialized "good housewives" in New England were "pretty gentlewomen" of mid-eighteenth-century towns.' For such women, 'this narrowing of roles was accompanied by a heightening of the ceremonial meaning of housekeeping, a phenomenon which historians can glimpse in increased attention to the rituals of the table and the garden, but especially in needlework.' The new emphasis on gender in these families is obvious in the paintings of upper-class women, which drew attention to large bosoms, slender waists, and other exaggerated symbols of secondary sexual distinctions.[52]

Women in such families may have experienced an increase in leisure and socializing time but they also suffered a loss of connectedness to public, especially economic, life. The effect can be seen in Mary Beth Norton's study of the claims of Loyalist women for compensation after the American Revolution. Women whose husbands had worked out of the home were unable to describe precisely their husbands' property; the 'very wealthiest women . . . tended to be the ones most incapable of describing their husbands' business affairs.' Similarly, Julia Spruill notes 'a decline in the vigor and self-reliance of women in wealthier [southern] families and a lessening of their influence in public matters' during the eighteenth century:

> Sarah Drummond, Virlinda Stone, and Margaret Brent stated their requests confidently and boldly, professed no ignorance of politics, and made no attempt to excuse their interference in in matters of public concern. . . .The women of the later period appear disinclined to admit any interest in public policy and anxious lest their private requests be mistaken for unwomanly meddling in politics.[53]

But not all the results of increased stratification and wealth were inimical to women. Among the same upper classes in this period women gained greater choice over marriage partners, greater access to divorce, more educational opportunities, and an expanded role in religious work. Men who did not trust their own wives with financial independence supported measures to protect their daughters' property from unscrupulous husbands or simply from husbands' creditors.[54]

Furthermore, the trend toward increased gentility did not affect all women. Many widows continued to exercise broad discretionary powers, often taking over their husbands' businesses, and many wives continued to work alongside their husbands in household or agricultural production. The surge of domestic manufacture in the last third of the eighteenth century opened up new opportunities for some women inside the household economy. Female workers were vital in the development of cottage industries. In 1798, for example, a twelve-year-old Dedham girl pioneered a new way of making straw braid for bonnets, creating employment for hundreds of women in and around her town.

Nationalist sentiment, moreover, militated against widespread acceptance of gentility and the cult of the lady, both associated with Britain. Thus Mercy Otis Warren's 1776 propaganda play *The Blockheads* poked fun at the aspirations of Loyalists to ornamental womanhood. Mrs. Simple, a caricature of the would-be colonial lady, blithely dismisses her husband's objections that their British allies have left them to starve: 'These delicate gentlemen and ladies would despise us as yankees, to see us maunching bread and cheese, etc. – they would have very nasty ideas about us, for what goes in must come out; – Oh it makes me sick to think of it!'[55]

Reprints of English 'ladies' books' were circulated with caution in the anti-British atmosphere of the revolutionary period, as English notions of male and female spheres were sometimes regarded as smacking of 'Aristocracy.' As late as 1792 the United States edition of *The Lady's Pocket Library* was prefaced with the hope that American readers 'will not be offended if [the author] has occasionally pointed out certain qualities . . . as peculiarly feminine, and hazarded some observations . . . on the different characters which mark the sexes.'[56]

Thus no definitive new pattern of female roles – nor, by implication, of male ones – had triumphed by the American Revolution. Images of women as helpmeets and ornaments existed side by side, and special definitions of women as mothers were still rare. Women were not yet exclusively identified with the 'tender sentiments' nor men by their lack of sentimentality. Being hardheaded and shrewd were still positive traits in women; indulging in tears or emotional displays on some occasions was still appropriate for men. Indeed, some men addressed each other as 'dear' or signed letters to each other with their 'love.'[57] The revolutionary period further complicated the issue, slowing down the progress toward separate spheres and involving women in activities that greatly increased their public roles and sense of involvement in the world.

Women and revolution

The American Revolution mobilized women in unprecedented ways. Women read and discussed authors such as Tom Paine and thought deeply about the political implications as well as the military outcome of the revolution. Mercy Otis Warren was an effective propagandist for the patriots and the only major figure of the revolution to write a history of the struggle. Sybil Luddington, Deborah Sampson Gannett, Margaret Corbin, Mary Hays, and a number of female spies were involved in direct military action; other women tore down the statues of George III and melted them to make ammunition or helped to provision the troops. They also dealt summarily with hoarders and war profiteers. Abigail Adams wrote to her husband on 30 June 1777 that a number of women had besieged the store of Thomas Boylston, demanding that he cease selling coffee at exorbitant prices. When Boylston refused to cooperate, the women 'seized him by the neck, and tossed him into the cart . . . opened the warehouse, hoisted out the coffee themselves, put it into trucks and drove off. . . .'[58]

The disruption of settled hierarchical relationships during the Revolutionary War allowed women to extend and move beyond the roles already available to them as 'deputy husbands' and raised the question as to why they should not continue to play these roles after the war. Eliza Wilkinson reported in 1779 that southern women gathered regularly to talk politics:

> Never were greater politicians than the several knots of ladies, who met together.... I won't have it thought that ... we are capable of nothing more than minding the dairy, visiting the poultryhouse, and all such domestic concerns; our thoughts can soar aloft, we can form conceptions of things of higher nature ... surely we may have sense enough to give our opinions ... without being reminded of our spinning and household affairs as the only matters we are capable of thinking or speaking of with justice or propriety.[59]

The radical climate produced by the revolution led many republicans to question all political and social inequality, including household relations of superordination and subordination. As long as men were expected to leave politics to their betters, there was no real challenge to the idea that women simply occupied the next rung down – not, after all, a very long step. As the Tory propaganda play discussed last chapter had suggested, women should 'mind their household affairs' just as men should tend their own farms and not pretend to be a 'Cromwel or Monck.' But the democratic ideology of the revolution suggested that every man *was* a potential 'Cromwel or Monck.' If the commoner rejected the rule of his social superiors, why should the wife obey her husband?

There was a new fluidity in male–female relations during the immediate post-revolutionary period. Children of both sexes were dressed more simply and given greater freedom of movement. A relaxation of social constraints on women is surely reflected in the marked increase in premarital sex and the easing of divorce requirements. Some women evidently found no more reason to defer to a husband than they did to a king; witness the sharp retort of Sara Cantwell in a South Carolina paper of 1776 to the routine announcement by her husband that he was no longer responsible for her debts:

> John Cantwell has the Impudence to advertise me in the Papers, cautioning all Persons against crediting me; he never had any Credit till he married me: As for his Bed and Board he mentioned, he had neither Bed nor Board when he married me; I never eloped, I went away before his Face when he beat me.

New Jersey admitted women to the vote two days after the Declaration of Independence and confirmed this in 1790 by specifically referring to voters as 'he' and 'she.' Travelers in America during the 1770s, 80s, and

90s were impressed – though not always favorably – by the freedom exhibited by American women.[60]

Ambitious plans were made for the education of females. Ezra Stiles noted in his diary in 1783 that he had examined Lucinda Foote, aged twelve, in Greek and Latin, and found her well qualified to enter Yale. Stiles also recorded the involvement of his wife and daughters in many family educational activities. New schools for women were founded, amidst much discussion of the need for republican women to understand the principles of the new nation.[61]

Explicit statements of feminism even appeared in some circles. As early as 1773 an almanac in Salem, Massachusetts urged:

Then equal Laws let custom find,
and neither Sex oppress:
More Freedom give to Womankind
Or to Mankind give less.[62]

On 31 March 1776, Abigail Adams wrote to her husband John:

I long to hear that you have declared an independency and by the way in the new Code of Laws which I suppose it will be necessary for you to make I desire you would Remember the Ladies, and be more generous and favourable to them than your ancestors. Do not put such unlimited power into the hands of the Husbands. Remember all Men would be tyrants if they could. If particular care and attention is not paid to the Ladies, we are determined to foment a Rebelion, and will not hold ourselves bound by any Laws in which we have no voice, or Representation.[63]

John Adams's response to her proposals, as Abigail complained to Mercy Otis Warren, was 'very saucy,' but other men were more receptive. Thomas Paine wrote two essays criticizing the restraints society put on female development. At Yale a frequent debate topic was 'Whether Women ought to be admitted to partake in civil Gov't Dominion & Sovereignty.'[64]

In 1779 Judith Sargeant Murray wrote two articles that were published in 1790 under the name 'Constantia.' She demanded female education, inquiring: 'Is it reasonable that . . . an intelligent being . . . should be so degraded, as to be allowed no other ideas, than those which are suggested by the mechanism of a pudding?' In a later essay she lauded women patriots in history for whom 'The name of Citizen possessed . . . greater charms than that of Mother.'[65]

Charles Brockden Brown, America's first novelist, argued in 1796 that the differences between men and women were entirely due to different training:

I humbly presume one has a better chance of becoming an astronomer by gazing at the stars through a telescope, than in eternally plying the needle. . . . Women are defective. They are seldom or never metaphysicians, chemists, or law-givers. Why? Because they are sempstresses and cooks. . . . Such is the unalterable constitution of human nature. They cannot read who never saw an alphabet. They who know no tool but the needle, cannot be skillful at the pen.

Yes . . . of all forms of injustice, that is the most egregious which makes the circumstance of sex a reason for excluding one half of mankind from all those paths which lead to usefulness and honour.[66]

Brown went on to advocate a world in which men and women shared work equally and faced no sex-linked restrictions in education, occupation, dress, or conversation.

National independence and domestic dependence

The democratic ideas of the revolutionary period raised the possibility, as Murray suggested, that women might be valued as citizens rather than simply as mothers of citizens, and might go on to partake of the same freedoms as males of the same social status. However, the social and economic developments of the post-revolutionary era, and the heightened concern for the preservation of order after 1790, created some countervailing pressures, leading to a devaluation of women's work, a sharper division of labor between husband and wife, and a new hostility to women who acted as 'deputies' or substitutes for men.

First of all, the progress of commercial agriculture changed the relative value of male and female labor on the farm. Bengt Ankerloo reports that in both early America and precapitalist Sweden, the diversified farming characteristic of subsistence agriculture required important labor contributions from women and youth:

A wide range of activities made it possible for the peasant to keep his children and servants busy the year round; and more activities were culturally defined as women's work. Market farming, on the other hand, provided relatively fewer work opportunities for women. . . . As rural society changed under the impact of capitalism and technology the only place for the mature woman was as a farmer's wife among young children and adult men doing men's work.

Other researchers have found that during the early nineteenth century

the value of domestic production on [American] farms remained almost unchanged, while that for the market increased greatly. Domestic production was largely in the hands of women; men were involved in market production. Thus the relative value of male and female labor altered substantially.[67]

Although the vast majority of the country remained agricultural after the American Revolution, rural areas as well as urban centers were increasingly drawn into the workings of the national market. The household division of labor grew more rigid, as men's crops and animals were exchanged for cash while women's clothes and food goods remained in the household or were directly bartered for other goods. The daily needs of the family for childcare, food, and clothing came to be organized around the demands and schedule of the market rather than vice versa. Once, households had produced first for their own use and then exchanged what was left over. Now many produced first for cash; production for use filled the gaps left by what could not be bought. Once, households had worked on articles for exchange only when there was time between the daily tasks of subsistence. Now the daily tasks of subsistence had to be worked in between labor for exchange. Not surprisingly, the work of family subsistence and reproduction increasingly came to be conceptually opposed to the work of market production and exchange. Whether women's traditional tasks were seen as inconvenient necessities or pleasurable luxuries, they were clearly distinct from the activities that generated cash and economic position. There was a new separation of market rhythms from family rhythms, even when both remained in the same physical spot.

To some extent this tendency was counteracted by the expansion of domestic industry; where such industry remained strong, as in Lynn, male–female cooperation and mutual respect may well have increased. But as even household manufacture became subordinated to the needs of the market and involved in a centrally directed putting-out system, women tended to do the supplementary tasks rather than those that were directly exchanged for cash. Nancy Cott has studied women's diaries in New England between 1780 and 1820 and found a marked change in women's work over that period, as it began to lose its productive character.[68]

The separation of production from reproduction meant that some women, usually daughters, had to leave the farm and pursue their traditional work outside the household. In fact, young women whose labor had become redundant on the farm provided the backbone of the country's first industrial labor force. But married women and mothers were still needed in the home to fill a number of important social roles. As Benjamin Rush pointed out in 1787, American men were being drawn into so many new and time-consuming occupations away from home that women had to take over child-rearing more completely. The scarcity of servants also increased the wife's responsibility for educating children, who were no longer expected to simply ape their 'betters' or be socialized by community patriarchs. With the increased emphasis on class-specific associations and on education for independence it was, moreover, considered dangerous to leave children to the supervision of servants or apprentices, as in the past. Doing so could reproduce patterns of deference and obligation that were inimical to both economic and political liberty. Thus there was growing social pressure on women to devote more attention to childcare and domestic work.[69]

Not all married women remained in the home, of course. Some free women had no choice but to follow their traditional work out of the home and into sweatshops or factories; slave women continued to labor alongside slave men; plantation owners and manufacturers did not hesitate to work these women twelve to fourteen hours a day, six days a week. But black women were simply ignored in the increasingly racist climate, and white women workers were overwhelmingly young and single, so a social perception developed that women retired from the world upon marriage. Most working women were glad enough to do so. Where they were unable to, they sometimes came into conflict with male workers: Christine Stansell argues that the rearrangement of gender and work in the post-revolutionary city initially exacerbated sexual hostility within the working class.[70]

As for married middle-class women who might aspire to work outside the home, legal sanctions, moral pressure, and systematic discrimination prevented any significant exodus from the home into the expanding commercial economy. The professionalization of occupations and the adoption of more stringent educational requirements ended informal arrangements whereby wives and daughters could be taught a skill by their husbands or fathers and succeed to their trades. The emerging medical profession systematically drove women out of midwifery and other health-care occupations, while the traditional access of a few women to atypical occupations declined. Even where, as in Petersburg, more women worked and women entrepreneurs maintained their absolute position, 'the story is one of relative loss, for as professionalization and economic modernization created new positions of authority, women were shunted aside.'[71]

The same relative loss occurred in politics, as new opportunities for political participation and debate opened up for men but not for women. Political relations were now defined on the basis of independence rather than obligation and deference: 'No one who depended on another could fully exercise republican virtue, and thus no dependant – woman, servant, child, or slave – possessed the moral status necessary for citizenship.'[72]

One response to the new political climate would have been to heed the calls for giving women the means to establish their independence. But in the period of social conservatism after 1790, feminism, like abolitionism and 'leveling,' fell into disfavor. Conservative theorists looked to the proper ordering of family and gender relations to provide the security and continuity that seemed lacking in a world of revolution and commercial expansion. Hence the Constitution did not institutionalize the radical ideas and practices set loose by the revolution. New Jersey turned out to be a forlorn exception to the dominant trend: most states adopted the first explicit denials of women's right to vote during the 1790s.

The republican period *did* usher in significant improvements in women's access to education and control over property. Women were given new rights within marriage against husbands who might ill-treat them or squander their money. But these reforms had little meaning for lower-class women, and they were linked to a stricter definition of all women as wives and mothers. As with slavery, the softening was also a tightening. The first Married Women's Property Acts applied only to property brought by the wife to her marriage as inheritance from her father, specifically exempting wages earned by women during marriage. Stansell argues that working women '*lost* ground' in the post-revolutionary decades; at the very least the new emphasis on women's child-rearing roles represented a repudiation of more radical feminism.[73]

Many people were uncomfortably aware of the contradictions in excluding women from public participation in a supposedly democratic society. Charles Brockden Brown pointed out the problems forcefully when he made the female character in *Alcuin* repudiate the title of federalist out of indignation that in a government 'said to be the freest in the world. . . . I see myself, in my relation to society, regarded merely as a beast, or an insect; passed over, in the distribution of public duties, as absolutely nothing, by those who disdain to assign the least apology for their injustice.'[74]

Some apology obviously had to be assigned, and old ones would no longer serve. The democratic ideology of the new nation ruled out any explanation of women's position that was based on the social necessity for, or forcible imposition of, hierarchy and deference. The cult of the 'lady,' popular in English mercantile and aristocratic circles, encountered deep suspicion from republicans. Besides, ladies did not make good wives for up-and-coming businessmen or aspiring workmen. 'Can the tranquil pleasures of retirement, the occupations of housekeeping . . . have any charms for ladies educated in what is called the fashionable style?' asked one writer. 'What, but the most inordinate selfishness and vanity can be the fruit of such training?' More prosaically, other authors pointed out that America's labor shortage deprived housewives of the servant supply that might allow them to devote their attention to the social graces.[75]

Democracy, gender, and family

The problem was to explain women's confinement to domestic life without seeming to violate the new doctrine of Equal Rights. Thus a writer in *The True American* of 18 October 1802 called for a quick correction of the 'defect' in New Jersey's constitution that allowed women to vote, but felt compelled to add:

> Let not our fair conclude that I wish to see them deprived of their rights. Let them rather consider that female reserve and delicacy are incompatible with the duties of a free elector, that a female politician is often subject of ridicule and they will recognize in the writer of this a sincere
> Friend to the Ladies.[76]

For people who did not, like Benjamin Colman, conceive of 'restraints' as 'necessary and useful,' restrictions on women had to be 'for their own good.' Women and men had to understand why, in an equal and democratic society, they still played such different roles. Clearly, the only way to explain women's exclusion from public affairs and economic action in a land where all human beings had an equal right to compete was to define women as naturally non-competitive. Older social explanations of women's absence from political or economic leadership gave way to 'natural' or biological ones. As Elizabeth Fox-Genovese remarks, the ideology of separate spheres became 'the custodian of displaced notions of hierarchy' and 'the gender system . . . came to absorb older notions of . . . dependence.'[77]

The substitution of 'natural' for social explanations of inequality represented neither a subversion nor an oversight of the American Revolution but a logical consequence of its success. American capitalist democracy created new forms of discrimination in the process and *as a result* of destroying old ones. Democratic capitalism removed traditional social barriers to the free pursuit of property, jobs, and status, and to the exercise of political prerogatives; it then had to explain to a population schooled in egalitarian principles why the accumulation of property and political rights was so unequal. Bourgeois expansion created an ideology inimical to hierarchical justifications for inequality, while simultaneously reinforcing unequal property rights and the material base of black and female subordination. The result was a set of new and, paradoxically, more pervasive rationales for inequality even while egalitarian ideals seemed to triumph – rationales with important ramifications for household relations and family life.

In the case of post-revolutionary women the colonial role of mistress of the household gave way to that of mother of republican citizens. Linda Kerber remarks:

In the domesticity of the preindustrial woman there was no sharp disjunction between ideology and practice. But the Revolution was a watershed. It created a public ideology of individual responsibility and virtue just before industrial machinery began to free middle-class women from some of their unremitting toil and to propel lower-class women more fully into the public economy. The terms of domesticity were changed, and pundits could not bring back the past. The best they could do was to assert that properly educated republican women would stay in their homes and, from that vantage point, shape the characters of their sons and husbands in the direction of benevolence. The prescription rang shrill. So long as the literature of domesticity persisted, it would always embody an anti-intellectual connotation, a skepticism about the capacities of women's minds.[78]

A very similar process of redefining women's roles in terms of motherhood took place in France after the French Revolution. There too the first result of the breakdown of old deferential habits was an interest in women's rights. In 1791 Olympe de Gouge published a feminist manifesto calling for universal suffrage, equal rights to public office, and marriage reform. In 1792 Pauline Leon demanded that women be given the right to bear arms and Etta Palm led a delegation to the Assembly to argue that women should share in the benefits of the revolution they had helped to win.

As in America, however, the French Revolution wiped out older political and economic privileges exercised by upper-class women, bourgeois economic development strengthened the need for middle-class women to remain in the home, and the extension of political rights to more men highlighted female exclusion as a unique circumstance requiring special explanation. While reforms took place in women's rights as wives and mothers, women's political clubs formed during the revolution were outlawed and women's rights advocates were berated as insulting nature's order and violating biology itself. The Committee of Public Safety clearly spelled out the bourgeois view of women's role:

Women! Do you want to be Republicans? . . . Be simple in your dress, hard-working in your homes, never go to the popular assemblies wanting to speak there. But let your occasional presence there encourage your children.[79]

The tension between legal and political equality on the one hand and economic inequality on the other has made biological determinism a recurring theme in the history of bourgeois thought. Whenever the democratic ideas of the political and legal realm have threatened to spill over into economic arrangements, biological explanations have been brought forward to prove that further reform would be useless, if not actually counterproductive. In the late nineteenth century Social

Darwinism vied with unionism and internationalism, seeking to explain inequalities among nations or classes as 'survival of the fittest.' Eugenics flourished during the 1920s and 1930s as monopoly capitalism proved unable to erase class distinctions or remove pockets of poverty in America. The first IQ tests were developed to test for the hereditarily unfit – who just happened to be equated with the poor – and a revival of racial IQ theories came after social struggles in the 1960s had achieved significant formal equality that still left Blacks at the bottom of the economic pile. While some people began to wonder if legal, educational, and political reforms were enough, or whether economic changes also needed to be made, Arthur Jensen, William Shockley, and Richard Herrnstein got tremendous publicity for their assertion that *no* changes would work: Blacks were genetically inferior to whites. Similarly, sociobiology, which explains male and female role distinctions as the result of genetic selection, got its greatest funding and publicity in the 1970s, at precisely the point when the women's liberation movement began to question whether complete sexual equality was possible without substantial changes in the social and economic system.

Republicanism and the Family

The American Revolution and the new artisan republic created a new political theory, a reconception of the role and legitimacy of state authority. They also required a new family theory, a reconception of the role of the family and the legitimacy of its authority structures. As the home was released from its obligations to social superiors and economic inferiors, what principles should govern its newly independent operation? Most republicans, like John Locke distinguished between the prerogatives of paternal and governmental power, so that domestic patriarchy lost its anchor in the larger polity and had to depend instead on internal family relations. If a man could continue to exercise sovereign authority over his household on the basis of his hold over inheritance rights, his moral sway, or his organization of the work and workers he directed, well and good; but failings in these regards were no longer automatically overshadowed by analogies to a king. Moreover, the attempt to distinguish paternal from governmental authority led to a stress on the conditional and temporary nature of paternal power that was hard to reconcile with older notions of domestic patriarchy.[80]

Theorists considering the place of the household in a democratic society gave the role of wives and mothers particularly sharp scrutiny both because it was a serious issue in itself and because it served to symbolize the general problem of reconciling corporate responsibilities with individual rights. The consensus in the early republican period was that individual rights did have limits and that the family was the natural place to establish them. Wives and mothers were therefore more sorely needed in the domestic sphere than ever before, since neither government nor community could impose such limits and men were at least occasionally away from home. But the assignment of women to domesticity could be justified in a society that denied the social need for hierarchy only by an ideology that stressed the natural or organic origins of female roles. After the American Revolution there was more attention paid than in the entire preceding 150 years to defining the special characteristics of women, distinguishing these from men's, and explaining how mutual dependence between the two was the basis of social order in a democratic society. Gradually a republican view of womanhood emerged. It confirmed woman's separation from the public world of men but gave her an economic role in supplementing male market activities through domestic production and a 'political role through the raising of a patriotic child.'[81]

What early writers on womanhood were groping for was a new conception of the relation between the state and the household, between public and private life; they sought it in a redefinition of gender relations in the home. Authors and lawyers envisioned the internal operations of the home in the same terms as they understood economic interactions: people who had complementary needs could rationally enter into contracts that would ensure them mutual benefits: 'Marital unions were increasingly defined as private compacts with public ramifications rather than social institutions with roles and duties fixed by the place of the family in a hierarchical social order.'[82]

The private compact relied on mutual needs that were grounded in the different natures of men and women; marriage merely gave social sanction to a presocial division of function between them. The pot was sweetened by the suggestion that the public ramifications of this natural sexual division of labor, organized into a true home, were profound. The new doctrine of republican motherhood, centered in a home free from public interference, promised to reverse the colonial relationship between family and state. Instead of state hierarchies being translated into authority relations within the family, the domestic sphere might translate its harmonious relations of mutual need into the public world.

In their conceptions of both the family and the state, republican theorists tried to accommodate new voluntaristic and contractual views of human relations to old notions about mutual obligations, social responsibility, and necessary limits to the exercise of individual will. Their solutions depended on the preservation of an artisan and farming community and on the elaboration of a strong sexual division of labor. Men could compete in the public sphere without destroying the fabric of society because their domestic holdings were fundamentally equal; republican mothers would make sure that each freehold produced responsible public citizens whose competition would not exceed the bounds of virtue.

But the effort to present economic expansion and competition as an extension of independence, equality, and social responsibility sometimes stretched the republican fabric until it was very thin. Images of the 'producing classes,' harmoniously and mutually benefiting from an expanding economy, could not entirely disguise disturbing alterations in relations between masters and laborers, farmers and merchants, rich and poor. As class lines grew more distinct, Americans held on even tighter to the notion of a unifying national heritage but began to engage in not entirely conscious debates about the meaning of that heritage, each group emphasizing one or another aspect of republicanism over the rest while declaring allegiance to the whole.[83] At the same time, important innovations occurred in the role and image of family life and womanhood, even though the various innovators all claimed to base themselves on the 'traditional' republican family. Those innovations form the subject of the next chapter.

Notes

1. Gary Nash, *The Urban Crucible: Social Change, Political Consciousness, and the Origins of the American Revolution* (Cambridge, MA, 1979); Richard Bushman, 'Family Security in the Transition from Farm to City, 1750–1850,' *Journal of Family History* 6 (1981), p. 239.

2. Bushman, 'Family Security'; Christopher Clark, 'Household Economy, Market Exchange, and the Rise of Capitalism in the Connecticut Valley, 1800–1860,' *Journal of Social History* 13 (1979), pp. 175–7; Kenneth Lockridge, 'Land, Population, and the Evolution of New England Society, 1630–1790,' *Past and Present* 39 (1968).

3. Clark, 'Household Economy,' p. 178.

4. Carville Earle and Ronald Hoffman, 'The Foundation of the Modern Economy: Agriculture and the Costs of Labor in the United States and England, 1800–1860,' *American Historical Review* 85 (1980), p. 1083.

5. James A. Henretta, *The Evolution of American Society, 1700–1815* (Lexington, 1973), pp. 83–118; Gary Nash, 'Social Change and the Growth of Prerevolutionary Urban Radicalism,' in Alfred Young, ed., *The American Revolution* (DeKalb, 1976) and *The Urban Crucible*; Sam Bass Warner, *The Private City: Philadelphia in Three Periods of Its Growth* (Philadelphia, 1968); Edward Pessen, 'We are All Jeffersonians, We Are All Jacksonians: Or a Pox on Stultifying Periodizations,' *Journal of the Early Republic* 1 (1981), pp. 10–11.

6. James Henretta, 'Families and Farms: *Mentalité* in Pre-industrial America,' *William and Mary Quarterly* 35 (1978).

7. Mary Ryan, *Cradle of the Middle Class: The Family in Oneida County, New York, 1790–1865* (New York, 1981), pp. 19–51; David Szatmary, *Shays' Rebellion: The Making of an Agrarian Insurrection* (Amherst, 1980).

8. Henretta, *Evolution of American Society*, p. 96.

9. Frederick Tolles, *Meeting House and Counting House* (Chapel Hill, 1948); Peter Dobkin Hall, 'Family Structure and Economic Organization: Massachusetts Merchants, 1700–1850,' in Tamara Hareven, ed., *Family and Kin in Urban Communities, 1700–1930*

(New York, 1977) and 'Marital Selection and Business in Massachusetts Merchant Families, 1700–1900,' in Gordon, *American Family in Social-Historical Perspective*; Bernard Faber, *Guardians of Virtue: Salem Families in 1800* (New York, 1972); Paul Johnson, *A Shopkeeper's Millennium: Society and Revivals in Rochester, New York, 1815–1837* (New York, 1978), p. 25; Catherine Clinton, *The Plantation Mistress* (New York, 1982), pp. 57–8.

10. Johnson, *Shopkeeper*, p. 46; Faber, *Guardians of Virtue*.

11. Ann Douglas, *The Feminization of American Culture* (New York, 1977), p. 52; Barbara Cross, *Horace Bushnell: Minister to a Changing America* (Chicago, 1958).

12. Stansell, *City of Women: Sex and Class in New York, 1789–1860* (New York 1986), pp. 11–18; Sean Wilentz, *Chants Democratic: New York City and the Rise of the American Working Class, 1788–1850* (New York, 1984), pp. 122–9.

13. Barbara Tucker, 'The Family and Industrial Discipline in Ante-Bellum New England,' *Labor History* 21 (1979–80), p. 56.

14. Jack Ebkin, 'An Analysis of 19th-Century Frontier Populations,' *Demography* 2 (1965); John Modell, 'Family and Fertility on the Indiana Frontier, 1820,' *American Quarterly* 23 (1971); Ryan, *Cradle*, p. 25.

15. Isaac, *Transformation*, p. 312.

16. Henretta, *Evolution*, p. 212; Stuart Blumin, *The Urban Threshold: Growth and Change in a Nineteenth-Century American Community* (Chicago, 1976), p. 46.

17. Richard Brown, 'The Emergence of Urban Society in Rural Massachusetts: 1760–1820,' *Journal of American History* 61 (1974), p. 38.

18. Tucker, 'Family and Industrial Discipline,' p. 69. For examples of changes in the roles of younger and older women, giving productive tasks to young women outside the household and making the wife responsible for domestic maintenance, see Alan Dawley, *Class and Community, the Industrial Revolution in Lynn* (Cambridge, MA, 1976) and Nancy Cott, *Bonds of Womanhood* (New Haven, 1977). For letters that reveal the family's growing reliance on feminine ties of advice and collaboration rather than male fiat, see Thomas Dublin, 'The Hodgdon Family Letters: A View of Women in the Early Textile Mills, 1830–1840,' *Historical New Hampshire* (1966), esp. p. 294.

19. Clark, 'Household Economy,' p. 178. See also Dawley, *Class and Community* and Paul Faler, *Mechanics and Manufacturers in the Early Industrial Revolution: Lynn, Massachusetts, 1780–1860* (Albany, 1981), pp. 20–23, 26–7.

20. Isaac Deutscher, *The Unfinished Revolution* (New York, 1967), p. 87.

21. Patricia Bonomi, *A Factious People: Politics and Society in Colonial New York* (New York, 1971); Richard Brown, *Revolutionary Politics in Massachusetts: The Boston Committee of Correspondence and the Towns, 1772–1774* (Cambridge, MA, 1970); Edward Countryman, *A People in Revolution: The American Revolution and Political Society in New York, 1760–1790* (Baltimore, 1981); Elisha Douglass, *Rebels and Democrats: The Struggle for Equal Political Rights and Majority Rule During the American Revolution* (New York, 1965); Merrill Jensen, *The American Revolution Within the Revolution* (New York, 1979); Merrill Jensen, *The Founding of a Nation: The History of the American Revolution* (New York, 1968); Pauline Maier, *From Resistance to Revolution* (New York, 1974); Arthur M. Schlesinger, *The Colonial Merchants and the American Revolution, 1763–1776* (New York, 1957); Gordon Wood, *The Creation of the American Republic, 1776–1787* (Chapel Hill, 1969); Joyce Appleby, *Capitalism and a New Social Order: The Republican Vision of the 1790s* (New York, 1984).

22. Wood, *Creation*, p. 325.

23. Ibid., pp. 325–6; Staughton Lynd, 'Who Should Rule at Home? Dutchess County, New York, in the American Revolution,' *William and Mary Quarterly* 18 (July 1961), p. 349.

24. Douglass, *Rebels*; Jensen, *American Revolution*; Lynd, 'Who Should Rule?', p. 331.

25. Irving Kristol, 'A Revolution of Sober Expectations,' in *The American Revolution: Three Views* (New York, 1975).

26. Ruth Bloch, *Visionary Republic: Millennial Themes in American Thought, 1756–1800* (New York, 1985), p. 186; Wood, *Creation*, p. 326; Douglass, *Rebels*, p. 18.

27. Wilentz, *Chants Democratic*, p. 62.

28. Faler, *Mechanics and Manufacturers*, p. 50; Appleby, *Capitalism and a New Social*

Order; Robert Shalhope, 'Republicanism and Early American Historiography,' *William and Mary Quarterly* 39 (1982); Roland Berthoff, 'Independence and Attachment, Virtue and Interest: From Republican Citizen to Free Enterpriser, 1787–1837,' and Richard Bushman, ' "This New Man": Dependence and Independence, 1776,' in Bushman, ed., *Uprooted Americans: Essays to Honor Oscar Handlin* (Boston, 1979); Wilentz, *Chants Democratic*, p. 102.

29. Wilentz, *Chants Democratic*, p. 95.

30. Bloch, *Visionary Republic*, p. 224.

31. William Evans, 'From the Land of Canaan to the Land of Guinea: The Strange Odyssey of the Sons of Ham,' *American Historical Review* vol. 85 (1980); Douglas Lorimer, *Colour, Class, and the Victorians: English Attitudes to the Negro in the Mid-Nineteenth Century* (New York, 1978); Anthony Barker, *The African Link: British Attitudes to the Negro in the Era of the Atlantic Slave Trade, 1550–1807* (Totowa, 1978); Alexander Saxton, 'Historical Explanations of Racial Inequality,' *Marxist Perspectives* (1979). Peter Kolchin has demonstrated that Russian noblemen used biological and racial arguments to justify serfdom, even though both were of the same 'racial' stock and had no somatic differences (Kolchin, 'In Defense of Servitude: American Proslavery and Russian Proserfdom Arguments, 1700–1860,' *American Historical Review* vol. 85, 1980).

32. George Fredrickson, 'Toward a Social Interpretation of the Development of American Racism,' in *Key Issues in the Afro-American Experience*, Huggins, Kilson, and Fox, eds (New York, 1971), vol. 1, p. 243; J.H. Plumb, 'On Winthrop D. Jordan's *White Over Black: American Attitudes Toward the Negro, 1550–1812,*' in Allen Weinstein and Frank Otto Gatell, eds, *American Negro Slavery: A Modern Reader* (New York, 1973), pp. 405–6; Robert J. Cottrol, *The Afro-Yankees: Providence's Black Community in the Antebellum Era* (Westport, 1982), p. 20.

33. Edmund Morgan, *American Slavery, American Freedom: The Ordeal of Colonial Virginia* (New York, 1975); Fredrickson, 'Toward a Social Interpretation.'

34. A. Leon Higginbotham, *In the Matter of Color: Race and the American Legal Process* (New York, 1978); Theodore Allen, *Class Struggle and the Origins of Racial Slavery* (Somerville, 1976), p. 11; Morgan, *American Slavery*; Robert Twombly and Robert Moore, 'Black Puritans: The Negro in 17th Century Massachusetts,' in Alden Vaughan and Francis Bremer, eds, *Puritan New England: Essays on Religion, Society, and Culture* (New York, 1977); T.H. Breen, 'A Changing Labor Force and Race Relations in Virginia, 1660–1710,' in Breen, ed., *Shaping Southern Society* (New York, 1976); T.H. Breen and Stephen Innes, *'Myne Owne Ground': Race and Freedom on Virginia's Eastern Shore, 1640–1676* (New York, 1982).

35. Morgan, *American Slavery* pp. 328, 33l, 333; Breen, 'Changing Labor Force,' pp. 116–34. For further discussion of how white supremacy was established to counter labor solidarity, see Lerone Bennett, Jr., 'The Road Not Taken,' *Ebony* 25 (1970), pp. 70–77 and *The Shaping of Black America* (Chicago, 1975).

36. Fredrickson, 'Social Interpretation,' p. 251; Nash, *Urban Crucible*, p. 43.

37. Willie Lee Rose, *Slavery and Freedom*, ed. Willam Freehling (New York, 1982), p. 23; Higginbotham, *Matter of Color*, p. 79; Fredrickson, 'Social Interpretation,' p. 243.

38. Ira Berlin, *Slaves Without Masters: The Free Negro in the Antebellum South* (New York, 1976), pp. 8, 317, 321–2, 364; Clarence L. Ver Steeg, *Origins of a Southern Mosaic – Studies of Early Carolina and Georgia* (Athens, GA, 1975); Morgan, p. 118; Robert Twombly and Robert Moore, 'Black Puritans'; Eugene Genovese, *Roll, Jordan, Roll*, pp. 31–2, 404; Duncan MacLeod, *Slavery, Race, and the American Revolution* (Cambridge, 1974), p. 162; Winthrop Jordan, *White Over Black: American Attitudes Toward the Negro* (New York, 1974), pp. 155–8; Leslie Howard Owens, *This Species of Property: Slave Life and Culture in the Old South* (New York, 1976), p. 15.

39. Benjamin Quarles, *The Negro in the American Revolution* (New York, 1973), p. 45; Cottrol, *The Afro-Yankees*, p. 42.

40. Rose, *Slavery and Freedom*, pp. 9–10.

41. Berlin, *Slaves without Masters*, pp. 30–33, 43–4, 62–8, 74; Jordan, *White Man's Burden*, pp. 121, 155–6; Isaac, *Transformation*, pp. 308–9.

42. Cottrol, *Afro-Yankees*, pp. 158–9.

43. Rose, *Slavery and Freedom*, p. 15.

44. MacLeod, *Slavery and American Revolution*, p.12; David Brion Davis, *The Problem of Slavery in the Age of Revolution, 1770–1823* (Ithaca, 1975); George Fredrickson, *The Black Image in the White Mind: The Debate on Afro-American Character and Destiny, 1817–1914* (New York, 1971); Leon Litwack, *North of Slavery: The Negro in the Free States* (Chicago, 1961); Harry Fritz, 'Racism and Democracy in Tocqueville's America,' *Social Science Journal* 13 (1976).

45. Rose, *Slavery and Freedom*, p. 21; *Southern Quarterly Review* 2 (1842), pp. 327, 330.

46. Rose, *Slavery and Freedom*, p. 25.

47. Genovese, *Roll, Jordan, Roll*, pp. 31–2, 404; MacLeod, *Slavery, Race, American Revolution*, p. 162; Berlin, *Slaves Without Masters*, pp. 317, 321–2, 364; Jordan, *White Over Black*, pp. 155–8; Leslie Howard Owens, *This Species of Property: Slave Life and Culture in the Old South* (New York, 1976), p. 15; Suzanne Lebscock, *The Free Women of Petersburg: Status and Culture in a Southern Town, 1784–1860* (New York, 1984), pp. 7, 91–4.

48. A similar crisis was posed in England by the spread of democratic ideology. A.S. Barker argues that Europeans believed in the cultural inferiority of Africans, but rarely posited a biological basis for this. Only in the 1770s in Britain was there an onslaught of attempts to prove that Blacks were sub-human; this was directly related to the challenge Blacks posed by claiming freedom in an age that supported human rights (A.S. Barker, *The African Link: British Attitudes to the Negro in the Era of the Atlantic Slave Trade, 1550–1807* [London, 1978]; David Brion Davis, *Problem of Slavery*).

49. Robert Bremner, ed., *Children and Youth in America: A Documentary* (Cambridge, MA, 1970), vol. I, p. 32.

50. Ulrich, 'Vertuous Women,' pp. 221–2; *Oxford English Dictionary* (Oxford, 1961) vol. 5, p. 257.

51. Linda Speth, 'More than Her "Thirds": Wives and Widows in Colonial Virginia,' in Speth and Hirsch, *Women, Family, and Community*, pp. 21–4; Joan Hoff Wilson, 'Hidden Riches: Legal Records and Women, 1750–1825,' in Mary Kelly, ed., *Women's Being, Women's Place: Female Identity and Vocation in American History* (Boston, 1979).

52. Ulrich, *Good Wives*, pp. 76–7, 115–17.

53. Norton, '18th-Century American Women,' p. 390; Spruill, *Women's Life and Work*, p. 241. As we saw last chapter, Norton suggests that colonial women were confined to a separate sphere throughout the period. Her data, however, more likely provide 'a measure of increasing specialization in economic life just before the revolution' (Ulrich, *Good Wives*, p. 49). Elsewhere (*Liberty's Daughters: The Revolutionary Experience of American Women, 1750–1800*, Boston, 1980), Norton found that the American Revolution widened patriot women's sphere. Ulrich counters that rather than the American Revolution allowing women to cross a once impenetrable sphere between their work and men's, it simply permitted the resurgence of the role of 'deputy husband,' which had become circumscribed in the late eighteenth century.

54. Peggy Rabkin, *Fathers to Daughters: The Legal Foundations of Female Emancipation* (Westport, 1980); Wilson, 'Illusion of Change.'

55. Warren, 'The Blockheads,' p. 158.

56. Ryan, *Womanhood in America*, p. 107.

57. Pleck and Pleck, *The American Man*, p. 13.

58. Mercy Otis Warren, *History of the Rise, Progress, and Termination of the American Revolution* (New York, 1970); Wendy Martin, 'Women and the American Revolution,' *Early American Literature* 11 (1976), p. 322; John Bakeless, *Turncoats, Traitors, and Heroes* (Philadelphia, 1959); Mary Sumner Benson, *Women in Eighteenth Century America* (New York, 1966); de Pauw, *Founding Mothers*; Elizabeth Ellet, *Women of the Revolution* (New York, 1948); Elizabeth Evans, *Weathering the Storm: Women of the American Revolution* (New York, 1975); Joseph Kelley, Jr and Sol Feinstone, *Courage and Candlelight: The Feminine Spirit of '76* (Harrisburg, 1974); Norton, *Liberty's Daughters*.

59. Linda Kerber, *Women of the Republic: Intellect and Ideology in Revolutionary America* (Chapel Hill, 1980), p. 226.

60. Monica Kiefer, *American Children Through Their Books, 1700–1835* (Philadelphia, 1948), p. 197; Spruill, p. 182; Joan Hoff Wilson, 'Illusion of Change,' pp. 404, 415; Andrew Burnaby, *Travels Through the Middle Settlements in North America* (London, 1791); Marquis de Chastellux, *Travels in North-America in the Years 1780, 1781, and 1782* (Dublin, 1787); Claude Blanchard, *Journal* (Albany, 1776); Ray W. Pettengil, *Letters from America, 1776–1779* (Boston, 1924).

61. Ezra Stiles, *The Literary Diary of Ezra Stiles* (New York, 1901), vol. 3, pp. 102–3, 315, 499, 513, 548, 557; Linda Kerber, 'Daughters of Columbia: Educating Women for the Republic, 1787–1805', in *The Hofstadter Aegis, A Memorial*, ed. Stanley Elkins and Erie McKetrick (New York, 1974).

62. Miriam Schneir, 'Unmanageable Pens: Colonial Diaries, Letters, and Broadsides,' *Ms* July 1976, p. 81. See also Anon., *The Female Advocate* (New Haven, 1801); William Boyd, *Woman: A Poem* (Boston, 1790).

63. L. H. Butterfield, ed., *Adams Family Correspondence* (Cambridge, MA, 1963), vol. 1, p. 370.

64. Stiles, *Literary Diary*, vol. 2, p. 490; vol. 3, pp. 15, 167.

65. Constantia, 'The Equality of the Sexes,' *Massachusetts Magazine* (March–April 1790), p. 134; *Independent Chronicle*, 28 October 1793; 'Observations on Female Abilities,' *The Gleaner* III (Boston, 1798).

66. Charles Brockden Brown, *Alcuin: A Dialogue*, ed. Lee Edwards (New York, 1970), pp. 13–14.

67. Bengt Ankerloo, 'Agriculture and Women's Work: Directions of Change in the West, 1700–1900,' *Journal of Family History* 4 (1979), pp. 115, 119; E.A. Hammel, Sheila Johansson, and Caren Ginsberg, 'The Value of Children During Industrialization: Sex Ratios in Childhood in 19th-Century America,' *Journal of Family History* 8 (1983), pp. 353–4.

68. Cott, *Bonds of Womanhood*, p. 67.

69. Benjamin Rush, *Thoughts Upon Female Education, Accommodated to the Present State of Society, Manners, and Government in the U.S.A.* (Philadelphia, 1787); Bloch, 'Moral Mother,' p. 111.

70. Stansell, *City of Women*, p. 30.

71. Elizabeth Dexter, *Career Women of America, 1776–1840* (Francestown, 1950); Gerda Lerner, 'The Lady and the Mill Girl: Changes in the Status of Women in the Age of Jackson,' *American Studies Journal* 10 (1969); Richard and Dorothy Wertz, *Lying In: A History of Childbirth in America* (New York, 1979); Catherine Scholten, ' "On the Importance of the Obstetrick Art": Changing Customs of Childbirth in America, 1760 to 1825,' *William and Mary Quarterly* 34 (1977); Goldin, 'Economic Status of Women'; Lebscock, *Free Women*, p. 169.

72. Stansell, *City of Women*, p. 21.

73. Ibid., pp. 22, 36; Bloch, 'Moral Mothers,' pp. 115, 118–20.

74. Brown, *Alcuin*, pp. 29–30.

75. *Southern Literary Messenger* I (1835), p. 733; Rush, *Thoughts on Education*.

76. Mary Philbrook, 'Woman's Suffrage in New Jersey Prior to 1807,' *New Jersey Historical Society Proceedings* 97 (1939), p. 96.

77. Elizabeth Fox-Genovese, 'Placing Women's History in History,' *New Left Review* 133 (1982), p. 24.

78. Kerber, *Women of the Republic*, p. 231.

79. Jane Abray, 'Feminism in the French Revolution,' *American Historical Review* 80 (1975), pp. 43–62.

80. See, for example, the rather labored explanation of John Locke, in his *Second Treatise of Government*, ed. C.B. Macpherson (Indianapolis, 1980), pp. 88–91.

81. Bloch, 'Moral Mothers'; Kerber, *Women of the Republic*, p. 282.

82. Michael Grossberg, *Governing the Hearth: Law and the Family in Nineteenth-Century America* (Chapel Hill, 1985), p. 20.

83. There is an excellent body of literature on the contradictions and divisions within republicanism, much of it cited elsewhere in this book. A good review of the literature may be found in Shalhope, 'Republicanism and Early American Historiography.'

5

Work Life and Family Life in an Emerging Capitalist Order, 1815–55

By 1800 southern gentry, northern farmers, and old commercial elites, as well as new manufacturers and rising artisans, were insisting on the sanctity of the home. Their pronouncements reflected the new right (or necessity) of the household to 'vet' its associates, to pick and choose among neighbors, refusing interactions with some while pursuing relations with families and individuals who might live elsewhere. But the republican family, like the system of household commodity production with which it was associated, was a transitional institution. The image of the home as a place of retreat from society was initially linked to rejection of deference or aristocratic corruption rather than to any qualitatively new ideas about the relation between family, work, and state or about the organization of the family itself. Most early writers still assumed that children would succeed to their fathers' occupations, that agriculture was the most respectable as well as the most practical vocation, and that households would continue to establish social order through their incorporation of servants, apprentices, and dependants into the domestic order. The republican family had not yet adopted new productive, reproductive, or emotional patterns that revised lines of authority by gender or elevated the parent–child bond above the exigencies of a working relationship among all household members. Only a small group of lower-middle-class Quakers had adopted new reproductive strategies limiting childbirth. Elsewhere in America the rate of population increase peaked during the last decades of the eighteenth century.[1]

There was a certain lack of clarity about gender and age relations in the republican family. The revolutionary period had weakened hierarchical ideology and directed attention toward a 'natural' division of labor, but there was no unanimity about what that natural division entailed for gender or age roles. Some authors put forward new notions about the centrality of children; most, however, simply worried about how to ensure children's continued obedience under changed conditions. The doctrine of domesticity was first elaborated by conservative New England ministers who assumed male control of the domestic sphere even when they addressed themselves to the mothers who were increasingly responsible for its daily workings. Many theorists elevated the role of the mother in the newly independent household, but for others the independence of the household only strengthened domestic patriarchy, removing former corporate interventions into the father's domain. As late as 1840 the Reverend Herman Humphrey could write: 'Every family is a little state, an empire within itself, bound together by the most endearing emotions, and governed by its patriarchal head, with whose prerogative no power on earth has a right to interfere.'[2] Despite superficial resemblances to colonial notions of patriarchy, there is a qualitative difference here that reveals the difficulty of removing public patriarchy without adjusting private sex roles: the patriarch's power can be exercised not in the service of the commonwealth but almost in rivalry with it.

Even after rejection of the egalitarian feminist ideas raised in the 1790s, early American magazines experimented with a number of different definitions of 'the female character.'[3] The European model of the 'lady' was in vogue among some elite circles, and a number of early magazines emphasized women's ornamental charms; but this sat poorly with committed republicans. Another model of natural dependency might be found in the slave, the Indian, or the child, all of whom were said to have minds and natures incapable of reasoned independence. This did not really square, however, with the responsibilities that republican mothers were supposed to assume in raising citizens. In the early 1800s writers wavered between conceptions that stressed female weakness and those that stressed female morality. Not until the 1830s was a coherent new image of womanhood devised, in the cult of domesticity. That image emerged from a decisive change in patterns of social and personal reproduction following the spread of wage labor and the transformation of the artisan republic.

There was good reason for the persistence of older conceptions of household and gender within republican families from 1790 to 1820. Class relations continued to express themselves partly as household relations between master and apprentice, mistress and maid. Differences between master and journeyman, farm owner and help, seemed more a product of age and experience than of permanent differences in access to resources. As Alan Dawley observes:

> The household structure incorporated class divisions between those who owned property and those who did not, because most propertyless people

were dependents in a propertied household – wives, children, slaves, servants, apprentices, journeymen, hired laborers. Apart from these groups, a smaller number of tenant farmers, common seamen and casual laborers set up independent households without a property owner as the head. But for the most part, inequality between the property owners and the propertyless was a domestic affair.[4]

While mechanisms for social and personal domination were greatly weakened in the post-revolutionary period, the free play of the market was as yet limited by participants' continued reliance on personal interactions and local conditions. At the growing extremes of rich and poor, of course, and in some of the new conflicts between masters and journeymen over the pace of work, it was increasingly clear that differences in wealth and power derived directly from relations to the means of production and the market, not from household relations. For most people, however, relations of inequality and social control were poised between the household and the market.

The religious ideology of the time was likewise poised between the old and the new. In New England and New York, the first revivals of the Second Great Awakening were sponsored by conservatives worried about the spread of rationalism and the hubris of democracy. Such conservatives were quickly disturbed by the enthusiasm with which women and youth rather than household heads responded to their pleas, but that enthusiasm was too short-lived and too other-worldly to raise substantial challenges to the social order. Southern revivals sometimes began as challenges to social and racial hierarchies, but usually turned toward personal issues. In Kentucky, meetings during the early 1800s often attracted thousands of people to week-long gatherings. Participants prayed, yelled, and writhed in an ecstasy of guilt and submission to God. In between these bouts of emotional release they held giant cook-outs, transacted business, arranged marriages and work parties. Although hopes of individual salvation were raised higher than traditional Calvinists liked, no one doubted that the world was divided into the saved and the damned – and always would be. Early revivals did not represent a clear doctrinal break with Calvinism or in any way assert the individualism and perfectionism that would characterize later ones.

The Second Great Awakening, which was to transform American culture and provide the impetus for modernizing movements such as abolitionism, actually began with the least modern groups in society – lower-class Southerners, isolated Westerners and, in New England, youth and women initially called into motion by prominent social conservatives. Converted people lambasted themselves for their individualism, pride, and rebelliousness, seeking to reestablish community rather than assert individual rights. Yet in accepting their social place through direct, individual submission to God rather than to traditional community leadership or paternal dictates, these groups implicitly recognized the breakdown of the corporate patriarchal order and raised urgent new questions about the role of 'dependants' in society. Ultimately, the early revivals unleashed too much individualism and self-organization to be satisfactory to conservative forces, but they also posed no real alternative to the old order. Lower-class, youth, and frontier revivals waxed and waned without creating any ongoing and coordinated organizational campaigns. Only when adopted – and transformed – by the middle class between 1825 and 1837 did they gain organizational coherence.[5]

The Transformation of the Artisan Republic

Essentially, people first believed they could separate the public polity from the household polity without reorganizing both, that they could curtail political patriarchy without disrupting either the social or the domestic order. This assumption was questionable from the beginning. It led to new experiments with biological explanations as well as to ambiguous formulations of family roles and religious doctrines. The accelerating pace of economic, social, and political transformation after 1815 made such halfway measures completely untenable and led to a major redefinition of public and private space, moral and community obligations, and male and female spheres. With this came a new form and image of the family.

The pace of change in America between 1815 and 1840 was arguably greater than after the Civil War, and certainly more dramatic in its confrontation with older patterns. Paul David has calculated that between 1800 and 1840 the proportion of the total free labor force employed outside the farm sector rose from 17 to 37 per cent. By 1840, America was already the second most industrialized nation in the world. Although its full-time employment figures were still relatively small, the factory system 'was then already understood by astute men [and, we shall see, by astute women as well] as the wave of the future.'[6]

America had 89 banks in 1811, 246 in 1816, 788 in 1837. 'The value of notes in circulation, which in 1821 had totaled $3 million, by 1833 had reached $10.2 million and in 1837 had soared to $149.2 million.' Most of this increase represented an actual multiplication of production rather than mere speculation. The GNP was, throughout the era, 'about ten times the stock of money and between 30 to 50 times the value of the country's specie.' By 1840, per capita domestic product 'was probably 60 percent higher' than in 1800, mostly 'as a consequence of an impressively rapid rate of advance achieved after 1820.'[7]

A transportation revolution linked all but the most recent frontiers with a national – indeed, international – economy. While most workers continued to live at or very near their work, a growing number of people, not to mention goods, began regularly coming and going over distances that a few years earlier could be traversed only by making a major investment in time or money. A boom in turnpikes from 1815 to 1825 was succeeded by the revolution in commercial freight transportation (and employment of casual labor) that began with the building of the Erie Canal (1818–25). A 'canal fever' and steamboat boom (1830–50) were accompanied by almost frenetic bridge building and harbor improvement. By the 1840s New York and New England were centers of railway expansion.

The growth of urbanization was equally dramatic: 'From 1790 to 1840, every decade but one saw a rate of urban growth nearly double that for the population as a whole, and greater than *any* post-Civil War decade!' The population of New York City tripled between 1800 and 1825. Cincinnati had 750 people in 1800, 24,831 in 1830, and 161,044 in 1860. While a great majority of Americans continued to live in rural areas and small towns, no one was unaffected by this extraordinary growth rate. Even rural areas began to produce for the cities and to consume urban commodities, both physical and cultural, no matter how suspiciously. By the time of Andrew Jackson's inauguration, one million people lived in towns with more than 2,500 inhabitants, compared to 200,000 who lived in such towns in 1790. And counting the number of city-dwellers at any point in time underestimates the actual number of people who gained some experience with urban life in this period, since there were extremely high mobility rates in and out of the cities. There was hardly a person in the North who did not have a relative or acquaintance to recount the marvels or horrors of the city, no parent who did not worry or hope that a son might find employment there.[8]

Work patterns in rural as well as urban areas were transformed by these developments. In post-revolutionary Massachusetts, reports Jonathon Prude, even doctors and lawyers had combined their trades with farming; 'non-agricultural occupations commonly existed as callings hyphenated to farming and pursued as the demands of husbandry permitted.' After 1810, however, there was a 'thorough restructuring of occupational patterns,' with increased specialization at either agriculture or a trade. By 1826, only 81 of more than 1,700 adult males in Newark named farming as their primary occupation.[9]

The legal system adapted to this economic expansion by changing its conception of property from a 'static agrarian conception entitling an owner to undisturbed enjoyment, to a dynamic, instrumental and more abstract view ... that emphasized the newly paramount virtues of productive use and development,' even where such development conflicted with traditional community rights. While colonial New England statutes had severely limited a property-owner's option to develop without community consent, by 1820 New England mill owners had the right to flood nearby land, even if neighbors objected, by claiming that irrigation would benefit productivity. While colonial courts had voided contracts deemed unfair by community standards, nineteenth-century courts simply accepted the workings of the market in setting the terms of a bargain, and upheld even the most unbalanced contract if both parties had agreed to it. The discretion of juries, traditionally the means of establishing community norms over more formal legal standards, was sharply curtailed. So was the jurisdiction of elected officials. 'The judiciary encouraged the shift of policy making from public officials to private entrepreneurs and individuals,' identifying 'private will with the natural order and state action as artificial intervention.'[10]

The very productivity of the republican household order of petty commodity production rapidly created the conditions for its demise. Successful masters, merchants, and shopkeepers took greater control over production by concentrating workers in central shops. In order, however, to exert such impersonal control over the pace and type of work, it was necessary to relinquish many of the personal ties that facilitated social order but hampered economic flexibility. After 1820 employers steadily reduced the number of employees and boarders in their homes at the same time as they backed away from the putting-out system and forced workers to come to a central place of work. As Sam Bass Warner explains the process of economic development in Philadelphia prior to 1860: 'The technique of rationalizing tasks so they could be performed by groups of men and women working within one shop, rather than by individuals [or families] laboring in a neighborhood of households, was ... the largest component in the first wave of urban industrialization.'[11] For both urban individuals who had previously worked in their employers' households and rural families who had filled specific orders in their own homes, as well as for businessmen who left home to supervise their workers or make financial deals with their peers, home and work drew farther apart, in both function and location. The separation of family and work was furthered among the upper classes by the development of credit institutions and testamentary trusts, which allowed merchants to fund themselves from outside the family. They could thus eschew fundamentally defensive kin marriages or partnerships to forge alliances with unrelated members of upper income groups, developing upper-class solidarities rather than more narrowly based – and potentially competitive – kin groupings.

Within the trades, at a pace that varied from place to place but gathered momentum after 1825, there was increasing differentiation between employer and employee. Through the early 1800s it had been possible to see inequalities of wealth and power as involving a graduated continuum that, except at the extreme ends, had more to do with life cycles than class positions. By the 1820s this was clearly not the case: 'The late eighteenth century pattern of wealth distribution, in which differentials were partly related to age, as sons waited to inherit their fathers' property, was replaced by a new one, in which differences emerged permanently on class lines.' Such class differences 'undercut the household as a buffer between property owners and the propertyless and tended to make those who owned productive property and those who did not into two separate social groups.'[12] Class divisions that used to be expressed *within* households were now expressed as differences *among* households. Relations between rich and poor were no longer mediated through the household or channeled into domestic relations of superiority and subordination but took place in larger social and political arenas.

As opportunities for succession to master status or to a farm diminished, workers who had once been future peers with their masters were now permanent wage-earners, who would have to find another position when their current one ended. Increased competition among both masters and job-seekers tempted many employers to evade apprenticeship regulations and hire temporary or unskilled workers whom they had no intention of training. Where a colonial printer had usually been an editor and a bookseller as well as a typesetter and a proofreader, after 1810 journeymen complained that newspapers were owned by 'speculators on the labor of printers,' while 'hireling editors' dictated what should appear in print. No longer did masters and apprentices discuss and share the work, however unevenly; nor did masters concern themselves with the education and moral supervision of their workmen: the master was increasingly a 'boss' – even the word was new – who was primarily concerned with the cash value of his employees' production.[13]

Entrepreneurs began to consolidate and centralize the production of goods. In Lynn, Massachusetts, merchant capitalists took over production centers and exchange networks for shoes: 'In losing their direct link to the market and in relinquishing ownership of the basic raw materials, the 200 shoemakers with master status in 1800 gradually ceased to operate on the old basis, and no new generation replaced them.' A few rose to take control over the production of others; most lost control over their own production and went out of business or had to work for the few who were finding the capital to set up central workshops and would eventually build factories.[14]

The proportion of workers employed by others grew from 12 per cent in 1800 to 40 per cent in 1860; in many towns and cities wage-workers were a near majority by the 1840s. In New York City, two-fifths to one-half of the labor force worked in the trades, but by 1825 even the smaller shops were introducing work patterns based on subdivision or subcontracting of the work, the substitution of unskilled or semi-skilled temporary labor for skilled, permanent employees, and the placement of foremen between the 'master' and his men. By the 1830s, the growth of 'sweating' had transformed a number of the trades.[15]

In Cincinnati, the transformation of the custom trade into ready-made production after 1826 led to subcontracting, the hiring of cheaper women and child workers, and the erosion of apprenticeship and craft traditions. 'Journeymen . . . dropped the honorific term "master" in favor of the more pejorative and market-oriented term "employer" – a term which also indicated a growing sense of class division within the trade.'[16]

Before 1820, writes Paul Faler of Lynn, Massachusetts, neither master nor mechanic group 'had detached itself from the integrated institutions and activities of the neighborhood to pursue its class interests in alliance with counterparts in other neighborhoods.' After 1820, the masters increasingly did so. For example, they pulled out of the old fire companies, which had been based on neighborhood and had included a cross-section of male residents. After this, the fire companies became centers of working-class sociability (and soon, targets of middle-class reform and professionalization). Class segregation even extended to the graveyard when a new cemetery was formed by a joint-stock company: 'Unlike the old cemeteries in which available space went to any citizen of the town, the Pine Grove Cemetery gave lots only to those who paid for them.'[17]

The rapid growth of wealth and class differentiation led to an equally rapid growth of inequality. While a far higher percentage of free male adults than in Europe continued to own property, the discrepancies in amounts owned were often enormous. In the cities there was a growing class of propertyless, unskilled laborers who were casual, transient workers rather than dependants safely encased in the home of a 'responsible' citizen. Matthew Carey reported in the early 1800s that thousands of Philadelphia's poor traveled 'hundreds of miles in quest of employment on canals . . . leaving families behind, dependent on them for support'; pauperism increased steadily during the succeeding period, in both urban and rural areas. Slums made their appearance in the nation's cities, while between 1825 and 1850 the proportion of national wealth held by the richest one per cent of Americans doubled – from 25 to 50 per cent, reaching up to 80 per cent in America's largest cities.[18]

The nature of poverty also changed, and its former association with visible, organic causes such as infirmity or age disappeared. Poverty in colonial days 'had usually been associated with *inability* to work – with the crippled, the aged and the very young.' In the cities, however, it was now associated with 'the changing structure of work itself' – competition, irregular employment, shifts in demand for labor, and boom-and-bust cycles.[19] This challenged older ways of both explaining and alleviating economic distress.

Class and Household Systems in Flux

The restructuring of productive relations outlined above threw into question customary strategies for social and personal reproduction. Traditional mechanisms of domination and traditional ways of compensating for inequality were both eroded. This was a period of class formation and reconstitution that required individuals of all social strata to reassess their methods of exercising power or influence, both within and outside the household.

The old ruling class, based on landed and mercantile wealth and exercising power through personal, political, and social ties, was challenged by rising sections of a new middle class, whose power was based on the ability to increase productivity and compete in a modern market. Narrow elites that used to control whole towns or villages gave way to specialized mercantile, manufacturing, banking, political, and social elites. The newly competitive economic climate merged with the trend toward political democratization to transform upper-class interactions with each other and with the lower orders. Groups originally formed to supplement older town, church, and household relations increasingly began to rival them. Occupational associations and societies for mutual aid, such as the Masons, began to lobby for their own interests. Many began to hook up with political parties to fight for special issues that transcended local boundaries or conflicted with traditional local concerns: 'By 1810, political sectarianism had become a durable feature of many localities. . . . Loyalty to the party chapter sometimes supplanted devotion to a town meeting that was often a battleground rather than a forum for consensus.'[20]

Rivalries and personal animosities that were an integral and limited (if often unpleasant) part of small communities whose members remained fundamentally interdependent took on a far more disruptive character when they were linked to conflicts, interests, and power relations beyond the local community. The influence of personal connections on credit and investment decisions by banks; competition of local and sectional business interests over where to locate canals; the question of how many banks should be chartered in a region, and on what basis: all these and other issues led to bitter feuding within towns and regions among wealthy families. Militia groups, benevolent societies, secret orders, and religious sects were politicized and factionalized. Kinship ties that used to facilitate elite social hegemony now perpetuated such rivalries.[21]

The introduction of these elite conflicts into politics at the same time that class polarization was occurring created the temptation for elite factions – especially those on the 'outs' – to use the democratization of politics as a lever against each other. As Edward Pessen points out, most political changes during the Jacksonian period resulted from 'the maneuvering of astute men' whose administrations favored the economic interests of the wealthy but whose campaigns revolved around the mobilization of 'common men' against their allegedly 'aristocratic' opponents. This drastically changed the old role of politics as an expression of a settled hierarchy based on clear-cut patterns of deference and patronage. It made politics far less predictable as a means of asserting upper-class control over the lower orders, 'limited the jurisdiction of formal central community authority, . . . [and] blurred the calibrations of local hierarchies.'[22]

Attempts to re-create patronage and dependence outside the household led to vote-buying and drunkenness on election days, or to violent resistance. They added to the problem of rowdiness and social control rather than solving it. Slightly more successful were upper-class efforts to simulate traditional household relations of dependence in relief societies, orphanages, and schools for the poor, especially poor women and youth. These organizations initially put forward no new definitions of social or individual morality but simply sought to 'replicate the moral order of the village' by extending elite women's earlier household role in caring for dependants. Thus the Salem Female Charitable Society, established in 1801, tried to reproduce through voluntary organization old household relations of upper-class condescension and lower-class service. The Society's ladies did not attempt to save souls or transform personalities, but to insert needy girls into households where they could be trained in obedience and serving skills. The Female Missionary Society (1814), which predated other women's associations in Utica, New York, and primarily comprised wives of the area's leading urban merchants and attorneys, pioneered no new social and gender relations. Like their husbands, these women organized from the top down, developing a complex administrative apparatus, directing their spiritual and benevolent activities at those below them in the social scale, and offering patronage and advice to more isolated rural women. Their efforts 'enhanced the elite status of their mates and added cultural and religious reinforcement to the male links in the trading networks.'[23]

But by the 1820s these organizations had begun to feel the contradictions of voluntary public participation, primarily by females, in attempts to impose an involuntary domestic order based on male lines of authority. Conflicts arose over the extent and limits of the social code and over methods for insuring compliance with it. Inevitably, also, new concepts of male and female responsibilities were created. At the same time, traditional charity relations were strained by the collapse of intra-class bonds. The mercantile ladies of Salem were increasingly unable to place their charges in their own homes; they turned to households where older patriarchal and class relations did not prevail. As conflicts over work and privileges grew between mistress and maid, the Society sought wages for the girls and 'ironically . . . found themselves selling the labor power of their objects of charity. Such a fundamental contradiction could not long endure.'[24]

The weakening of traditional mechanisms for asserting social control led the elite to experiment with new methods, both private and public, of exercising class and familial power. The most far-reaching processes of class and household recomposition, however, began in the old middle class – the diverse group of farmers, merchants, shopkeepers, small manufacturers, masters, and professionals that had constituted the backbone of the artisan republic; small property-owners or skilled workers whose control over their work processes had guaranteed them access to an economic as well as a political 'independence.' These middling classes faced an especially urgent need to reorder their social and gender relations in order to take advantage of greater possibilities for personal freedom and economic mobility while simultaneously compensating for the decline in the security of their traditional relations.

Successful masters, many of whom still worked with their hands, could now participate in government, send their children to schools of their choice, buy many of the same luxuries formerly limited to the rich, attain social, business, or religious respectability, and even gain political prominence. In Cincinnati between 1819 and 1834, artisans held 22 per cent of the city council seats (the most powerful position in local government); professionals held 14 per cent. In other big cities, such as New York, the dominance of wealth was clearer, but there were still attractive economic and political openings for the small businessman or master craftsman. In fact, the period between 1820 and 1860 was unparalleled in the opportunities it offered to the old middle class for moving into the new bourgeoisie.

In one case study, Herbert Gutman has discovered that the highest percentage of mobility from artisan to business leaders (13.2 per cent) was found

> among those industrialists, merchants, and financiers born between 1820 and 1849. . . . Only a small number of Paterson apprentices became manufacturers between 1830 and 1880, but most successful Paterson iron, machinery, and locomotive manufacturers started their careers as workers, apprenticed to learn a skill, and then opened small shops or factories of their own.

In some western cities, opportunities for advancement were even better. Almost three-fourths of the top manufacturers in Cincinnati in 1859 whose careers could be traced 'had worked their way up through the ranks, either in the same or in different crafts.'[25]

In 1800, 72 per cent of America's lawyers came from the upper class, with only 16 per cent from the middling ranks of farmers, shopkeepers, and professionals; by 1860, 44 per cent of the lawyers were from those middling ranks. Middling people also gained more access to college and to political or bureaucratic positions in this period. This was not exactly equality of opportunity: In both 1800 and 1860, only 12 per cent of the lawyers came from the lower classes. But the fact remains that a rather small initial advantage could be turned to better account, both economically and socially, than before. Despite the demise of the master shoemaker class, more people became entrepreneurs in Lynn between 1830 and 1860 than before or since. Possibly more than at any other time in American history a little capital, a lot of abstinence and hard work, a pinch of luck, a prudent family strategy, *and* the help of others allowed some lower-middle-class individuals or occasional skilled workmen to carve out an advantageous place in the economy.[26]

However, for those who could not make something new of their old middle-class occupations or habits, there was an increased possibility of failure. Caught between the rise in the percentage of wealth owned by the rich and the growing pressure on jobs and skills from wage-earners, the middle class faced a shrinkage in the proportion of property available to it. In 1800, the second, third, and fourth deciles of Northampton's population controlled 45 per cent of the city's wealth; by 1860 they controlled only 25 per cent. Cincinnati's middle ranks saw a smaller but still significant decline in their share of wealth. The proportion of wealth held by the top 10 per cent of taxpayers rose from 55.4 to 67.1 per cent between 1838 and 1860. The bottom half of the population saw its share of wealth shrink from 9.8 per cent in 1817 to 8.1 per cent in 1838 and 2.4 per cent in 1860. Both absolutely and relatively, the middle class improved *vis-à-vis* the lower class in this period, yet it is still noteworthy that the wealth held by the second, third, and fourth deciles of the population declined from 36.5 in 1838 to 30.5 per cent in 1860.[27]

Meanwhile, the possibility that a middle-class family might sink into the ranks of wage-earners was increasingly great. Downward occupational mobility increased between 1820 and 1860 in most major cities, while in rural areas the security of small farmers and shopkeepers was threatened by the fragmentation of landholdings, the rise of debt, and the expansion of larger merchants and manufacturers. In Philadelphia, the stable occupational order of the 1820s gave way in the 1830s to a 'reshuffling' in which 'craftsmen comprised a larger and larger proportion of those who were both upwardly and downwardly mobile.' Between 1790 and 1810 less than one-fourth of the value of probated property in Massachusetts was tied up in debt; a generation later the proportion had risen to nearly one-third. In 1810 only 19.9 per cent of estates had to be auctioned to pay off debts; by 1830 46.2 per cent of estates had to be so disposed. Notices of farm foreclosures began to appear regularly in the New York newspapers of the 1820s.[28]

There were impressive cases of individuals, born into humble circumstances, who made millions. John Jacob Astor and William E. Dodge were household names by the end of the period. But everyone also knew of comfortable – even affluent – businessmen or farmers who had lost everything in business crises such as the panic of 1819 and the depression of 1837 or simply through unwise business practices. All this heightened the sense of personal responsibility for success or failure. Alan Dawley and Paul Faler both comment on the impact on Lynn masters when Ebeneezer Breed, a socially prominent, affluent entrepreneur who had pioneered in the shoe industry, abandoned business, turned to drink, and ended in the almshouse.[29]

At the bottom ranks of the free labor force was a class of permanent wage-laborers, swelled by the downward mobility of some artisans and farmers, the closure of routes to independence that had been formerly available to journeymen or farmers' sons, the entry of young women into the factories and sweated trades and, especially toward the end of the period, by stepped-up immigration. Working-class people experienced a simultaneous increase in their control over their personal life and decrease in their control over their work life. There were many new areas of independent action for men who did not head propertied households. Participation in politics, attendance at church, relations between men and women, were no longer controlled by the elite. Yet at the same time there were new possibilities for economic dependence, even for household heads.

In the eighteenth century, the main mechanisms of upper-class domination had resided not so much in economic institutions as in social and political ones. Jonathon Prude has suggested that, outside the relations of church and household, 'affluent citizens enjoyed only limited [economic] leverage over the less wealthy,' since due to the exchangeability and interdependence of creditor and debtor, neighbor and servant, 'there was no way – no continuing, established institutional structure – through which wealth was translated into domineering economic power.'[30] There was thus, despite pervasive domination of personal behavior, little control exerted over the pace of work, the methods used, the number of breaks. Typically, both master and workmen did the same tasks and shared pauses for meals or drinks. As employers altered their hiring and work practices after 1820, however, this began to change.

At the very time that political and personal independence seemed to have reached new heights, many workers found themselves losing traditional controls over their work processes. A man could order his own household, vote for his choice of candidates (all of whom claimed to honor and defend his interests), socialize with his own mates, choose his own church (or choose not to attend one at all), and yet work at someone else's pace, at someone else's location, to someone else's specifications. Employers steadily tightened their control over the work process after the 1820s. At the same time, the gap between skilled and unskilled wage rates widened dramatically, presenting workers with the dilemma of whether to rebel against the new controls over their work patterns or to adopt and excel at those patterns in order to rise to a skilled position. Although there was considerable local resistance to employers' new controls, high transiency rates, the uneven pace and impact of industrialization, the persistence of a republican ideology shared with the masters, and divisions by craft, gender, race, and partisan politics militated against workers' acceptance of a common oppositional program.[31]

These transformations in work relations were accompanied by equally important changes in household, age, and gender relations. Already seriously eroded by revolutionary and republican ideology, patriarchy was further weakened by the spread of new commercial opportunities and the decreasing ability of fathers to pass on a viable farm or stable livelihood to their sons. Children gained more independence in job-seeking and marriage decisions as male household heads were less able to provide them directly with work. The authority of the father was no longer reinforced by his exercise of class power over unrelated members of the household. Fathers also lost the moral leverage that had derived from supervision of a unified household system of production, exchange, family relations, and religious education.

The spread of wage work, moreover, lessened 'the probability that age would lead to increased wealth and status' for propertied men; it also increased the demand for younger adult workers. Reproduction of a family's class position increasingly depended not on what the father could pass on but on what the son could go out and get. As young men moved into new occupations and participated in the multiplying peer-group associations, 'the corporate life of youth shifted from involuntary associations (family and village) to voluntary associations such as academies, young men's societies, and political clubs.'[32]

The decline in the power and authority available to older male smallholders was reflected in New England churches, which stopped assigning seats by age. By the early nineteenth century, most of them simply sold seats to the highest bidder. Other signs of the dissociation between age and power multiplied. By 1820, at least nine states had instituted mandatory retirement laws for judges. Children ceased to be named after older relatives. Family portraits no longer highlighted the patriarch, instead presenting all family members more or less equally.[33]

Women also experienced shifts in traditional life cycle patterns. Older women had never been painted as favorably as older men in colonial America, but a free, married, middle-aged woman was then at the height of her power and independence. As youths, such women had been child-minders and servants in their own or another's household. Once mistresses of their own households, with servants or older children to look after the young, they became productive workers with a considerable amount of derived authority over apprentices as well as servants and children.

The transition to a market economy reversed this pattern. In Lynn, 'the factories shifted the burden of industrial employment from working wives to young, single women. . . . Reflecting this trend, the term for a female shoemaker changed from "lady shoemaker" to "machine girl," or just plain "girl." ' Women's household work increasingly came to be seen as peripheral to the family economy, while the decline in servants and apprentices left mothers in a newly constricted domestic arena. Young women experienced new independence during the period when they worked outside the household, but upon marriage they retired from socially recognized and remunerated work.[34]

At the same time, the growing division between male responsibility for cash-generating activities and female responsibility for daily household routines and for childcare opened up new avenues for maternal influence. Women had the opportunity and duty to take over some of the moral, religious, and educational tasks that many men could no longer combine with their work life.

The Problem of Class Reproduction and Specialization of Tasks

These changes in class, age, household, and gender relations posed new tasks in social control, family management, and self-definition for all classes. Their impact was to unravel and separate the formerly intertwined roles of employer, husband, father, worker, political actor, agent of social control, religious authority figure, and household supervisor. People even began to experience conflicts among their different roles. For propertied household heads, as we have seen, there was a growing incompatibility among the various behaviors necessary for social control, family leadership, moral self-definition, political influence, and economic endeavor. Women experienced stresses between the new work roles they often assumed when single and the retiring submission that followed marriage. Transitions between jobs and statuses were no longer as predictable or smooth. Poverty was no longer part of a natural order. Relations among individuals of various classes could no longer be explained or regulated by the organic workings of a local community of households.

Yet there were few new institutions or guides for reassigning and demarcating roles. A very incomplete separation of work and home, public and private spheres, remained typical in this period. Work and home, for example, may have moved apart, but not very far. Many people still worked at home, and most people who did not do so walked only a short distance to work. They could return home for lunch, or have lunch brought by a family member. Indeed, it was a sign of success to live at or near work in the affluent but heterogeneous city core, especially in a profession that was not yet subjugated to someone else's time and space. As we shall see, the group of men and women who did the most to elaborate the cult of the home lived in households in which much productive work still took place. Perhaps it was the very lack of sharp physical boundaries between spheres that forced them to develop such strong emotional ones. Work behavior, political behavior, and personal morality were no longer coterminous, but the lines between them had to be delineated; there were still too many overlaps for people to count on each arena to generate a distinctive, appropriate response.

The private sphere continued to encompass such public issues as education, morality, and charity; virtue in the home was still considered to be the foundation of civic virtue, the reason Americans could dispense with governmental or community interference and regulation. Men's public activities still depended on personal (private) recommendations and relations. Conversely, some 'domestic' relations – slave-owning, for example, or the curtailing of older men's prerogatives – were fought out in the public spheres of politics and law. Other political and economic changes – the closure of farming opportunities, the reorganization of work relations – were initially experienced as domestic problems. Men's market and voting activities may have been separated from women's maternal responsibilities, but that left quite a few social and political tasks suspended in between. In Rochester, writes Nancy Hewitt, 'women activists emerged in a community where the segregation of work and home, public and private life, and men's and women's spheres was incomplete. They emerged at the junction of, rather than bridged a gap between, these spheres.'[35]

The lack of specialized institutional channels for sorting out and reconceptualizing roles was particularly clear in the case of youth. 'On farms and in shops and stores young people of different classes mingled in an atmosphere of informality, although their ultimate destinations would be different. Moreover, urban tradesmen and industrialists often operated farms on which their sons supplied the labor.' In the cities, young men seeking work were even more likely to mingle with people of different classes and different class values:

> Unlike many of today's youth, whose careers are determined by a series of institutional associations, whose abilities can be tested and rated, who can be awarded external badges of achievement like university degrees, young men of the 1840s and 1850s had few objective credentials that could distinguish them from others seeking the same place or recommend them for advancement once places had been secured. With the growing numbers of young men looking for work in the cities and with the pressure these numbers placed on an apprentice system that had evolved from less-demanding circumstances, ordered, institutional channels to opportunity were more reduced than they had been before or would be later.[36]

Rapid geographic mobility, economic expansion, and political change enhanced the desire to make clear distinctions between spheres and activities. New roles and new alliances were required but traditional guides for choosing models, presenting oneself, getting people to recognize one's social origins and probable destination, or being able to evaluate others had vanished. People were made, David Brion Davis argues, 'self-consciously aware of aspects of role-playing which are taken for granted in tradition oriented societies' – and which are less necessary in modern societies that have institutional or 'objective' means for measuring and placing people. Along with the self-consciousness about what it takes to present oneself in such situations came a heightened awareness of the possibility of deceiving and being deceived: 'Both on the popular and the literary levels of culture, we find a virtual obsession with hoaxes, impostors, frauds, confidence men, and double identities.' While 'preindustrial methods for coding the urban stranger on the basis of appearance' – costume, mode of address, body markings – had disappeared, 'modern methods based on the stranger's location in the city' had not yet developed. The reliance on 'surface impressions' created a crisis of confidence in social interactions, and a desperate attempt to evaluate people's 'sincerity.'[37]

The erosion of old guidelines for social intercourse as people attempted to develop new class, family, and personal alliances combined with the simultaneous anxiety and optimism unleashed by rapid economic and political change to produce 'the paranoid style' so common to the time. Aristocrats, Catholics, Masons, banks, Abolitionists, the Slaveocracy, foreigners, 'unnatural' women, or any combination of the above might be singled out as threats to the consolidation of 'the' American value system and work ethic – and as adversaries against which to define that value system. Ironically, however, the counterweight to paranoia – 'sincerity' – was an aspect of personal comportment all too easy to counterfeit.

In all classes, these social tensions directed attention toward the family as the place where personal comportment was regularized, social order might be maintained (or circumvented), alien forces could be resisted, and true identities might be discovered and counted upon. There was a growing perception that inadequate families rather than original sin or irresponsible masters were the cause of youthful misbehavior. Middle- and upper-class households expelled members of alien classes from their ranks; working-class households sought interactions with people of their own class and outlook. Although boarding continued to be prevalent, co-residence was increasingly limited to people of the same class or ethnic background. Newark artisans, New England mill owners, and southern gentry all drew sharper boundaries around their families and sought a predictability in gender roles that could be set against the changes in their social and work relations.[38]

Reorganization of the family became a means of redistributing economic, political, and moral duties. Gender differences and new definitions of sexuality emerged as a major organizing force in society at large and an increasingly salient aspect of self-identification for individuals. 'The canon of domesticity encouraged people to assimilate change by linking it to a specific set of sex-roles,' writes Cott. It 'provided a secure, primary, social classification for a population who refused to admit ascribed statuses, for the most part, but required determinants of social order.'[39] It also provided concrete guides for new behavior.

As workers separated into groups defined by gender, age, or race and the duties of husbands and wives were more sharply divided, young people began to organize their own experiences and feelings on the basis of gender. Barbara Epstein has argued that whereas eighteenth-century conversions involved the same issues for males and females, nineteenth-century ones took on a sex-linked character. For young men, conversion seemed to raise self-esteem and sanction personal initiative by linking it to service to God. Women brought a different set of experiences and tensions to their search for God. Self-esteem and personal initiative were fostered by their new-found independence in youth, but contradicted by their tasks as wives and mothers. Conversion experiences for women seem to have revolved around controlling rebellious impulses connected to the requirement that they abandon youthful independence. Converted women stressed their repudiation of formerly frivolous pursuits, accused themselves of stubbornness and rebelliousness, and turned the act of submission into an emotional triumph.[40]

Since institutional means did not exist to channel people into the new roles and behaviors required for successful adjustment to the spread of wage-labor, subjective, personal mechanisms had to be forged – mechanisms with the emotional weight to substitute for more regularized, 'objective' methods of socialization. In all classes, families had to take responsibility for ordering the relation between public and private space, peer and generational ties, work and leisure activities, social and biological reproduction. And gender was a primary means of defining and imposing that order.

But precisely how was the family to reorganize itself and interact with other households? What were the proper responsibilities of women and men in a society where patriarchy was weakened and yet men were in charge of public life? What kinds of sexual identities and interactions were to be defined as normal? These questions were not just personal but political and economic as well: how to redistribute and prioritize the functions that used to be integrated in the propertied household head with his unified patriarchal, social, religious, and political lines of authority; what standards to use in choosing associates and distinguishing between appearance and reality; how to arrange family life and peer relations to maximize one's position in a newly competitive world while maintaining some larger sense of social responsibility.

If these questions were posed to all classes and both sexes, the answers that became dominant were very largely formulated by one class and one sex. In organizing to rearrange these arenas of life, as Donald Matthews has commented, the leading role seems to have been taken by 'a rising middle class in general and women in particular.'[41]

The decisive change occurred in the 1830s, when revival religions and childcare theorists came to preach a new doctrine of individual responsibility that effectively denied original sin and made each person responsible for his or her personal salvation and economic condition. Revivals were complemented by new forms of association that encouraged people to internalize the values of the industrial order and used mutual aid or peer-group support to circumvent the need for cross-class interactions. The dilemma of how to foster the personal initiative needed to succeed in the new society while discouraging an excess of initiative that could lead to disaster was resolved by new child-rearing techniques. 'Character, once equated with natural physical marks and inborn traits, now came to signify a configuration of moral qualities gradually molded in each person,' remarks Joseph Kett:

> By holding up decision of character as an ideal, youth counselors were, in effect, sanctioning a measure of ambition . . . and assertiveness. But even as they did so, they sensed the need to protect their flanks by pounding home the importance of self-restraint. Intolerance of self-indulgence in youth compensated for tolerance of self-assertion as part of the intricate process of value trading that introduced Victorian morality to America.[42]

In the 1830s, also, republican motherhood became evangelical motherhood, while the republican family was redefined as the site where women imparted virtue to society through their influence upon males. Increasingly, women did the redefining. Early male writers on the republican family were overwhelmed by the output of what Hawthorne was to call 'that damned mob of scribbling women.' Spearheaded by women, revivals, associations, and advice books of the 1830s helped to establish a family strategy based on rejection of alien class values, mobilization of individual initiative, child-rearing practices that required greater parental (especially maternal) involvement in shaping children's character, and a new sexual division of labor which made women responsible for morality and continuity, men for exchange and mobility.

Pioneers of the New Family: Middle-class Men or Classless Women?

Why and how was the reorganization of family and gender relations in America accomplished by the middle class and women? Many recent accounts focus primarily on one of those groups. Some stress the needs of an emerging business class, comprising both manufacturers and middle-class aspirants to economic independence. Paul Johnson, for example, has argued that the new economic prominence of merchants and masters was accompanied by a loss of social and personal authority as work moved out of the home and politics became factionalized: 'while market operations revolutionized the scale and intensity of work, they freed wage earners from the immediate discipline exerted by older, household-centered relations of production.'[43] Both elite men and their middle-class associates began to look for alternative controls over the behavior of workers and youth.

Among the many disciplinary issues facing middle-class employers was one both practical and deeply symbolic: the role of drinking. Until the early 1820s, liquor had been an accepted part of community and workplace interactions. Work breaks at 11 a.m. and 4 p.m. tended to revolve around a glass of whiskey, passed out by the master; political and social occasions saw heavy drinking by both upper-class patrons and lower-class dependants. As employers set up stricter work routines and made the household a more private place, however, they cut down their own drinking and ceased to tolerate workers' drinking on the job. The 200 'most respectable farmers' in Litchfield County who agreed to abandon the customary rations of liquor distributed to farm hands were almost alone in doing so in 1789, but by the 1820s both urban masters and rural farmers were concerned with the necessity for sobriety, personal abstinence, punctuality, steady work habits, and individual effort in an increasingly competitive work environment. Employers bemoaned the fact that many workers and masters still drank on the job and that alcohol consumption, indeed, had reached an all-time high – 7.1 gallons per person over fifteen – in the two decades after 1790; they moved swiftly to remedy this.[44]

As the middle class sought to legislate against alcohol and traditional amusements, workers' drinking and recreation moved to their own neighborhoods and came to express working-class solidarity and defiance of new middle-class norms:

> The liquor question dominated social and political conflict in Rochester from the late 1820s onward. At every step, it pitted a culturally independent working class against entrepreneurs who had dissolved the social relationships through which they had controlled others, but who continued to consider themselves the rightful protectors and governors of their city.

Numerous studies document the anxiety of entrepreneurs, masters, and other middle-class individuals over the growing autonomy of working-class life. Attempts to regulate the working class through politics failed, however, due to upper- and middle-class feuding and lower-class resistance. Employers founded temperance societies and religious organizations, but these divided over the extent of coercion that could or should be used; they were also singularly ineffective in attracting workers.[45]

Middle-class men faced a triple burden: guilt over their abandonment of traditional responsibilities for the moral supervision of the lower classes; concern for how to rebuild middle- and upper-class solidarities; and fear of expanded working-class independence. It is possible to see the revival movement of the 1830s and the emergence of new associations aimed at individual transformation as answering these concerns: evangelical religion offered middle-class men new definitions of morality and social responsibility, more compatible with their actual behaviors. Revivals forged a new unity within the middle and upper classes and constructed new methods for instilling social order.

To understand why the middle class required new ideologies and strategies for both self-control and social control, it is important to remember that the qualitative shift in class and work relations discussed above had not yet produced most of the institutions, practices, or ideologies that mediate, obscure, or regulate the interaction and reproduction of classes and households in modern industrial society. This posed a particular problem for the middle class. Although elite families faced problems of social control over the lower orders, their self-definition was bound up with their wealth and social position, and their children's destinies were clear. Manual workers had to address important questions about how to organize for better conditions and whom to include as workers, but their children's immediate destinies were also set, as the kind of work they could get was limited and their options for postponing entry into work were few. Middle-class families, however, had fewer well-worn paths for their children to follow and less clear-cut boundaries between themselves and other classes.

There were few geographic havens for the middle class. Even in cities with terrible slums, middle-class citizens lived with or very near the poor. In New York, for example, 'respectable' streets were only a few blocks from the intersection where saloons studded each of the 'Five Points' that gave the city's most notorious slum its name. Despite the immigration of Irish and Germans in the 1840s, 'At no time prior to the Civil War did a large ghetto isolate the foreign born from the native Americans.' In Philadelphia, similarly, 'Social and economic heterogeneity was the hallmark of the age. Most areas of the big city [1830–60] were a jumble of occupations, classes, shops, homes, immigrants, and native Americans.'[46]

The widening economic gulf between classes, then, was not reflected in physical distance. This meant that middle-class families had to develop their new strategies for self-definition and social control while in close contact with alternative family patterns and work values. Johnson has described the dilemma facing the middle classes of Rochester:

By 1834 the social geography of Rochester was class-specific: master and wage earner no longer lived in the same households or on the same blocks. But except at the outskirts, no class could claim regions of the city as its own

... residents of the most exclusive streets could look across their back fences or around the corner and see the new working-class neighborhoods. And every night the sounds of quarrels, shouting, and laughter from the poorer quarters invaded their newly secluded domestic worlds.[47]

In big cities, such proximity was reinforced as rising real estate values encouraged landlords or forced middle-class home-owners to sell off back lots. Large square blocks were dissected by alleys along which cheap shacks and tenements were built.

There was also as yet a weak development of institutions to validate and reinforce differential class entry into the world of work. There were clear channels through which the very wealthy and the very poor entered the system, but the middle class had to teach its children to take a different path than either of these other groups. Without a national media, church, bureaucracy, school system, or even national anthem, the middle class had to carve out its own niche against the hostile alternatives of the old elite, determined to defend its privileges, and the lower classes, resistant to the values of business competition.

A major tool in this endeavor was evangelical religion. Revivals relied on group prayer, family and peer pressure, and emotional displays of individual submission to a higher cause to create strong bonds among supporters of the emerging industrial order. As the Reverend Charles Finney described the effect of his methods, the process of helping someone to convert created some of the same bonding as the pain and exhilaration of delivering a child. The revivals healed divisions within the middle class, answered the guilt that men felt as they moved away from traditional responsibilities for lower-class behavior, forged a new set of values that aided the transition into economic individualism, and insulated middle-class families from the competing ideas and behaviors of the working class. Revivalist religion became a substitute for the all-inclusive, involuntary community of traditional society, while simultaneously accommodating new class, sectional, and ideological divisions. By converting to so many different churches and sects, people confirmed their independence from older obligations; by responding to the social pressure of preachers, missionaries, mothers, wives, and feverishly worked-up congregations, by making a public confession at the 'anxious bench' in front of 'people who never again could be strangers,' converts denied that this was a matter of selfish individualism and reaffirmed the primacy of at least some group norms.[48]

The new religious ideology exempted the middle classes of responsibility for social inequality 'by teaching that virtue and order were products not of external authority but of choices made by morally responsible individuals.' It also provided a means of inducing at least some workers to accept a new kind of social control. Protestant sects offered individuals direct contact with spiritual power, just as the franchise offered white males direct contact with political power, as a route to both economic and personal self-improvement. Of the two, religion was arguably more effective. In nineteenth-century America, where every politician claimed to represent the common man but acceded in practice to the businessman, voting was at least as impressive an act of faith as was conversion, and often accomplished far fewer practical results. Conversion at least facilitated entry into the economic community. It established the small businessman's character among his peers and ensured him credit, while workers who showed evidence of religion were hired and promoted in greater numbers than those who spent their Sundays socializing with other workers rather than improving their morals (and their work habits):

> Revivals provided entrepreneurs with a means of imposing new standards of work discipline and personal comportment upon themselves and the men who worked for them ... the belief that every man was spiritually free and self-governing enabled masters to present a relationship that denied human interdependence as the realization of Christian ideals.[49]

New ideas about the moral authority of women arose in reaction to and compensation for the male's abdication of household authority, giving middle-class women new responsibilities in social control. Evangelical doctrines of domesticity absolved men of their responsibility for fostering competition and ambition in society by teaching that these traits could be controlled by women's ability to instill virtue and restraint in the young.

The role of revivals, associations, and new family definitions in the emergence of a new business class seems quite convincing in most accounts of this process, but many versions suffer from two sorts of imprecision. First, some authors tend to lump the entire 'middle class' together, from wealthy capitalists such as the Tappans down to the farmers and small masters or shopkeepers who played the central role in most small town and rural revivals. Accounts that conflate these groups fail to explain the centrality of the lower middle class in the revivals and associations, the force of their condemnations against the rich as well as against the disorderly poor, or the very distinctive concerns of small property owners and professionals.

A good example of the confusion this causes comes in many discussions of the cult of domesticity. Domesticity is often presented as a bourgeois rationalization for the capitalist separation of work and home. Donald Bell, for example, argues that the 'cult of motherhood ... arose as an ideology to reinforce and justify the sexual division of labor and the segregation of roles [between home and work].'[50]

But a problem arises with this interpretation as soon as we look more closely at who was supposedly justifying the split between work and home. Among wealthy families, where productive work had moved out of the home in a majority of instances, women were likely to join the more traditional missionary societies rather than the groups that pioneered new definitions of individual responsibility. Maternal associations, on the other hand, which proposed the sharpest divisions between public and private spheres and showed the greatest commitment to individual transformation, were composed largely of *lower-middle-class* women whose families had experienced a very partial separation of work and home. (There was almost no participation in the first revivals and maternal associations from the working class, who had earliest and most completely found themselves forced to work outside the home.) Sixty-five per cent of the women who belonged to the Maternal Association in Utica, New York, were from households that still combined production and reproduction. Of the forty-six men and women cited by Nancy Cott as major ideologues of the cult of domesticity, 82 per cent came from families in which there was little or no separation of home and work – families of farmers, ministers, lawyers, small-scale shopkeepers, boarding-house keepers, small printers or writers. The large majority of women in whose diaries Cott found evidence of the turn toward domesticity were members of households where much income-generating work took place in a household setting.[51] Why would the cult of domesticity, which allegedly rationalized the new capitalist division between paid work and housework, receive its most complete expression among those who had experienced the *least* separation of work and home?

Second, accounts that emphasize the economic and political interests of the business class cannot fully explain the leading role of women in revivals, associations, and the redefinition of family life. Self-control to compete in the new economy and social control over the lower classes were male needs. Yet this period saw the 'feminization' of American religion; women converted in larger numbers than men and took greater organizational responsibility for benevolent societies, prayer groups, maternal associations, Sunday schools, and missionary work. As the English observer Frances Trollope remarked in 1832:

> Almost every man you meet will tell you, that he is occupied in labours most abundant for the good of his country; and almost every woman will tell you, that besides those things that are within [her house] she has coming upon her daily the care of all the churches.[52]

Barbara Epstein presents evidence that women often came very near to brow-beating their husbands into conversion, and Mary Ryan points out that religious conversions followed matrilineal descent.[53] If revivals legitimated business interests and social control, why were middle-class men initially reluctant to join them and why did wives and mothers play such an important role in cajoling or nagging their menfolk into getting involved?

An alternative approach starts from the special circumstances facing women. This was a period in which their participation in production was curtailed while men gained access to economic and political transactions from which women were excluded. At the same time, however, new opportunities for education and wage-work for young women and new responsibilities in child-rearing raised women's aspirations. Some authors see female leadership in religion and reform as an active attempt to claim a distinctive space in American society. Women sought power and influence in religious associations, new family ideologies, and a rearranged domestic order that gave them control over reproduction and moral ascendancy over men. They even explicitly denigrated male activities in comparison with their own. 'Our men are sufficiently money making,' declared Sarah Josepha Hale. 'Let us keep our women and children from the contagion as long as possible.'[54]

This approach has the merit of treating women as active historical agents. On the other hand, while all women faced these new conditions and presumably desired influence or autonomy, the majority of female activists came from particular classes and regions. Although they often mobilized as women and under the banner of womanhood, their descriptions of and solutions to the problems facing women were class-specific. As Nancy Hewitt points out, women organized as women but generally in defense of same-class men or at least with their support. They parted company with women from different class backgrounds in their organization and ideas.[55]

While both analyses, then, have considerable explanatory power, the problem is to integrate them. As soon as we do so, further questions arise. Why was such a leading role played by the middle class, especially the lower middle class, in a period where the dominant economic trend was the polarization of capital and labor in the process of production? Why did *women*, excluded from capitalist competition and individualism, lead *men* into organizations that sanctioned competition, strengthened individualism, and rejected much of the interdependence and reciprocity traditionally associated with female neighborly relations?

The answers to these questions lie in the economic and political processes that forced small propertied households to develop new family strategies if they wished to escape the descent into wage-labor. The middle class had the most to gain and to lose in the transformation of the artisan republic; women were central to how successfully families negotiated the challenge. Mary Ryan points out that the crisis of family succession caused by the closure of opportunities in farming and the crafts required new strategies of social and personal reproduction. These strategies were forged in the social movements of the 1830s and 1840s, often initiated by women whose class gave them the necessity and whose gender gave them the responsibility to rear their children in a new way.[56]

Why the Middle Class?

Emphasis on the leading role of the middle class rather than the larger capitalists in establishing new conceptions of public and private life needs some justification. The main economic consequence of wage labor was to create a dichotomy between a class that owned the means of production and a class that increasingly had nothing to sell but its own labor power. Michael Katz, Michael Doucet, and Mark Stern have recently argued that the most salient feature of the nineteenth century was the creation of a two-class system. The business class – capitalists and 'their associates, primarily the professionals and business employees who shared their outlook, aspirations, and interests' – was a 'self-confident if internally stratified' group that shared a common cultural outlook, despite political and economic disagreements. The working class, despite big gaps between skilled and unskilled workers, remained qualitatively different from the business class in its working conditions, level of living, and cultural outlook.[57]

There is good reason to emphasize the bipolar nature of these classes in explaining the economic functions – and malfunctions – of the capitalist system. For understanding long term motions of society, furthermore, and the unintended consequences of people's acts, a two-class model has many advantages. In the long run, the intermediary layers or classes of capitalist society, however distinctive their outlook from labor's or capital's, can produce no alternative ways of organizing society. Their special place, indeed, *depends* upon the polarization of labor and capital; their privileges flow from their role as a buffer between the two. Consequently, while they may try to adjust the relationship between the two major classes, they do not try to abolish it. They will often oppose specific acts of the capitalist class, but they tend to even more vigorously oppose working-class organizations or actions that threaten their place between capital and labor. Ultimately, the middle layers have no independent program or basis for structural change. However discontented they may be with big business, their dependence on existing property relations has led them to sanctify the same market forces that favor expansion of large blocs of capital. Most middle-class individuals have ended up siding with the preservation of capitalism; the minority who have rejected capitalism have been drawn to the program and organization of the working class. Leon Trotsky put it most brutally: the middle class, he declared, is 'human dust,' drawn to the magnet of power. Both the reproduction of capitalism and the recurrent challenges to that reproduction come out of the clash between its two main classes, not out of any middle layers.

But in the short run, every clash between the two classes must be studied in its historical specificity; and a leading feature of that clash is often the distinctive response it evokes in a middle class or classes. Thus Karl Marx emphasized the two-class model in his economic and historical analyses, such as *Capital*, but paid scrupulous attention to the role of middle layers in his analyses of concrete political situations, such as 'The Eighteenth Brumaire of Louis Bonaparte'. The clash of capitalists and workers *always* creates an intermediary zone – a safety net for those who fall from the top; a safety valve for the most talented or determined from the bottom; a group of brokers who manage the working class or smooth over the worst excesses of the capitalists but above all maintain their position by mediating between the two. A disparate group held together by its relative success in avoiding the worst insecurities and indignities of wage labor, this middle class has comprised professionals, small farmers or businessmen, managers, writers, ministers and, in the nineteenth century, clerks.

The middle class is constantly created, undermined, and re-created in new form by the dynamics of capitalist competition and the changing relations between capital and labor. It is as necessary to the maintenance of the relations between capital and labor as are the categories of gender and race; like those categories, it takes its meaning from the relations between capital and labor without being reducible to those relations. It is an amorphous group, whose individual members are always moving up or down, but it maintains a distinct identity from the group of wage laborers below and large capitalist employers above.

Arno Mayer argues that in both Europe and America the lower middle class 'has always been a critical mass and, in moments of crisis, a *critical swing group*. Politics may never have been carried on *for* its benefit, and certainly it was never a class *for* itself. Even so, the lower middle class has always been a class *in* itself.'[58] And though this middle class perpetuates capitalist social relations by rationalizing management, providing limited mobility ladders, supporting profit and property rights, and upholding values that encourage one to rise *in* the system rather than *against* the system, it can also raise a powerful opposition to aspects of elite policy that threaten to crush the working class and hence remove the conditions of its existence. For this reason, the upper layer of capitalists is forced to make concessions to the preservation of small businesses and even to adopt middle-class values as its own – or at least to appear to do so.[59]

Precisely because it does not have a collective class interest, the middle class does have a pervasive – and, in the American context, persuasive – class outlook, which denies class solidarity in producing change and elevates the role of individual transformation. It also denies the centrality of productive relations and emphasizes the importance of personal ones. From the moral reform movements of the 1830s to the consumer movements of the 1920s and counter-cultural phenomena of the 1960s, the middle class has tended to organize through personal networks aimed at getting people to change their private decisions and lifestyles.

In the early nineteenth century, this class had a number of special characteristics. First, it imagined itself, with some justice, as representing true republican virtue and continuity with the American Revolution. Its economic needs and personal values were opposed to those of working-class traditionalists, old mercantile and landed elites, and sections of the new bourgeoisie that might be described as 'an aspiring aristocracy.'[60]

Second, this middle class was critically poised in the shift of economic and political relations to a struggle between capital and labor. The basis of its former independence was undermined by the exhaustion of farm land and the closure of traditional middle-class steps to becoming one's own master. Yet an expanding capitalist society offered other ways of avoiding the worst dependence of wage-labor. There was a growing demand for lawyers, educators, cultural workers, social services, and managers. Large sections of the native-born middle class were strategically placed to fill these positions, if they could readjust their family strategies. The Reverend Horace Bushnell, for example, had expected to succeed to his father's profession, but 'Between 1815 and 1820 the expansion of manufacturing cut into the market for homespun woolens, and Bushnell's apprenticeship to his father no longer seemed prudent.' Leaving the home in which he had expected to learn his trade, Bushnell went off to college – dressed for economy's sake in his homespuns – and studied for the ministry (a course financed by his mother's 'household frugality' and sustained by her support and ambition for him).[61]

Finally, if in many later periods the middle class has revealed itself as timid, angry, and small-minded, the antebellum middle class was still optimistic and self-confident – committed to property and order, certainly, but not yet so frightened by the working class that it could not contemplate ambitious change. And though it envisioned that social change as flowing from individual conversions or transformations, it was also not afraid to mobilize its members and allies to effect such conversions. Before turning to the transformations that this middle class created, let us discuss why gender was such an important aspect of the process and why middle-class women played such a leading role.

Why Middle-class Women?

The reason why women played such a vital role in the elaboration and organization of new middle-class values and behavior patterns is that they were specially situated to perceive the problems of reproducing class position in a changing society and to develop family strategies that responded to those problems. First of all, the crisis of authority lay primarily in male relations. The disintegration of organic ties occurred in male roles, as the role of husband and father was set apart from the role of employer or worker, the politician's role came into conflict with the minister's. Men's very immersion in the individualistic economy and polity hampered their ability to provide social solutions to the problems associated with that individualism. In the early nineteenth century men pulled out of the churches that used to keep community order, turned away from conservative household strategies of preserving a farm or an occupation to pass on to their sons (thus forfeiting much of their parental power), and abdicated much household authority as they competed for public power and gain. There was a decline in male church membership in the late eighteenth and early nineteenth centuries, and a significant rise in skepticism.

Women, on the other hand, experienced more unity between their social and personal lives. Their religious commitment was not undermined by immersion in the cash economy, their work roles did not contradict their parental roles, and their goals as private individuals did not conflict with their goals as social actors. They were therefore better placed to move into associations that were still 'poised precariously on the fragile axis between public and private life.'[62] Female networks, unlike male occupational interest groups, could be extended into mutual aid and social control societies without introducing the conflicts of interest that plagued male activities.

Second, male solutions to problems of social order and self control did not work. In politics the problems of individual comportment, self-restraint, and social order were, if anything, magnified. As politics was democratized it was also neatly severed from the economic decisions that affected people's daily lives. The upper classes were no longer able to use politics to impose their standards of personal behavior on the lower orders, but neither was the working class able to use politics to resist the imposition of workplace controls. Political attempts to legislate social order led to more rather than less social strife, heightening conflict between working people and elites and sharpening divisions within the middle and upper classes.[63]

Third, the kinds of changes demanded for the re-creation of a viable middle class were those in which women could play an important, even indispensable, role, because they involved changes in family organization and the sexual division of labor. One immediate response to the crisis of family succession, for example, was to restrict fertility; native-born Americans decreased their fertility by 30 per cent between 1800 and 1860. The exhaustion of the land in key regions of the country combined with the erosion of apprenticeship and the changing labor needs of both commercial farming and capitalist production to raise the emotional and economic investment needed to prepare a child for a middle-class occupation. All women undoubtedly had strong personal reasons for wishing to avoid the pain and risk of constant child-bearing, but in the middle class there were powerful incentives for men to accept an ideology of self-restraint, family limitation, and female purity. As the example of Bushnell reveals, moreover, women's household economies and emotional support could be a critical factor in allowing a son to make the lateral transition into the new middle class.

To understand the challenge facing the middle-class family in the nineteenth century, consider the new requirements for the reproduction of work and social order in a market society where people's labor is no longer deployed for them by social superiors, village constraints, or family inheritance, but is something they have to take out into the world and put up for sale to individual (not corporate) employers. Among the farmers or self-employed artisans of colonial days, children generally were trained for a specific occupation or position, to which they would succeed when the current occupant died or retired. Apprentices would eventually take over a trade; young farmers would inherit land from their parents. Parents had to teach their children obedience to the sometimes frustratingly slow pace of transition, but there was little need to worry about imbuing them with a unique personality and sense of personal initiative. The family did not have a special role in establishing sharply differentiated and class-specific values for its own children. All children were taught obedience to prevailing norms; the family's role in socialization was subsumed in the cross-class ties of the corporate household, the church, and the established social hierarchy.

Personal responsibility, in this system, came as a function of succession to land ownership or mastery of a trade. Becoming an adult, in other words, was not something the child had to achieve on his or her own, never knowing exactly when that momentous transition had occurred. After infancy, young girls and boys began to work under the direction of the parent or household authority of the same sex, doing simpler versions of adult tasks and gradually taking over the full range of those tasks as their mental and physical development permitted. Adulthood corresponded with succession to adult positions in life; it was a social rather than a physical or psychological boundary. Youth referred less to actual chronological age than to the social position of dependency. In colonial days, for example, the term 'young people' had referred primarily to unmarried villagers whose lack of land or a trade made them social and economic dependants. Members of the lower classes, no matter how old, were often referred to as boys or girls. Physical punishment enforced obedience and respect, but general social norms were more or less naturally absorbed, outside the family as well as within it, by close association with role models in a society that lacked significant age grading. Since community norms were largely shared by all classes, parents had less to teach children specific rules than to teach them that the rules, whatever they were, must be obeyed. Hence the emphasis on breaking the child's will but not on molding the child's thoughts: colonial parents did not have to teach their children to internalize specific values to be held against peer pressures.

All this changed in the early nineteenth century, especially for the middle class. Upper-class children could still count on inheritance of a job or business. Lower-class children had to get a job early, while their manual strength was at its peak. But middle-class children had to accept many more discontinuities in their lives as they grew up. They might stay at home longer for education, leave home for training in one area of work, then return for a while again or embark on a different career. In this rapidly changing economic and social milieu, with far higher rates of geographic and occupational mobility than before, middle-class children had to be taught not their parents' skills, rapidly being outmoded, but general values and appearances that would gain them entry to the places where new skills were taught. Increasingly, these values and appearances were class-specific. A youth aspiring to a middle-class occupation had to demonstrate to prospective employers that he was not to be seduced by quick riches or immediate comfort; a working-class youth had to demonstrate his willingness to forgo long-range goals and use his physical strength now.

Middle-class parents were no longer responsible for teaching a well-defined set of skills and a general conformity to common social standards but for imparting a general set of skills and a well-defined social standard that would not be held by many or most of the people the youngster would encounter in the world of work. In a transitional society where there were new class divisions and conflicts but not yet clear residential, cultural, or social barriers between the classes, the middle-class family had to teach the child to internalize the norms appropriate to his or her class ambitions and to reject the norms of other social classes that might be found right across the street. Most middle-class occupations in this period involved small-scale, face-to-face contact in a society no longer regulated by a community of neighbors or a rigid hierarchy. Personal reputation and behavior counted for more than before, when social superiors or neighbors imposed uniform standards on all, or later, when business and government operated through large departments where routine divisions of labor and audits substituted for trust and personal discipline.

The family remained the basis of social order, but in quite a new sense – as a defense against some elements of the community rather than a miniature version of it. The ideal family was no longer a 'little commonwealth'; instead, the ideal commonwealth was a collection of separate little families. Where interpersonal signs of class – such as statutory differences in dress and ability to command deference or obligation to give it – had disappeared, but more 'objective' signals – segregated neighborhoods, conspicuous consumption, schooling badges – were not yet available, family patterns and values, especially the sexual division of labor, took on special importance as indicators and determinants of class. Social hierarchy seemed to derive from family behavior and organization rather than from a larger political or economic authority.

A successful strategy of child-rearing for the middle class did not so much celebrate the distinction between home and work as play them off against each other. While a middle-class man or young woman needed to go outside the home to get an education or accumulate capital, the ultimate measure of success was to escape working-class subordination to market forces. This could best be achieved by avoiding the over-reliance on the market that developed through speculation, living beyond one's means, or accepting initially high-paying but dead-end jobs. Work and market forces were kept from producing dangerous ambition or speculation by the doctrine that the highest good lay in the home; home was kept from becoming an alternative to work by imbuing domestic morality with the values of thrift and accumulation.

The cult of domesticity was a strategy for *resisting* too complete a separation of home and work. A domesticated son neither withdrew from the world of market transactions nor yielded completely to its blandishments. Instead, he attempted to affect the terms on which he entered the market and to maximize the amount of control he could exercise over his work in that market. The worker's mother and, later, his wife provided a counterbalance to influences at work that might lead him to either reject competition altogether or set his sights too high. This is why the cult of domesticity, which does not in fact rationalize an advanced capitalist separation of work and home, was the product of middle-class families.

And within the middle class, it was above all the woman who helped the family steer a middle course through the temptation to either abandon or immerse itself too thoroughly in the market.

Another way that women came to occupy a central place in middle-class life was in providing new forms of motivation and social cement, both in and out of the family. As men lost their coercive powers over children and other adults, a new kind of 'emotional leverage'[64] was required to ensure cooperation and mutual aid. Emotional bonding, between parents and children and within associations, became a particularly feminine contribution to personal and social control. Upper-class women combined such new female bonds with traditional condescension and patronage in their relations with lower-class women, but middle-class women had only the female bonds to rely on. To strengthen those bonds they interlaced them with powerful images of death, separation, and sentimentality, creating a new kind of writing whose middle-class marginality and personalism also spoke to common female experiences in all classes of industrializing, democratizing America.

The Success of the Middle-class Strategy

Disengagement from the obligations and restraints of old community institutions and values paved the way not for social fragmentation but for a recasting of community along new horizontal lines, excluding some local inhabitants while including specific groups or individuals from other communities. Middle-class associations helped people to curtail relations with social inferiors or superiors and support each other in new personal values and behaviors that were extremely class-specific. In order to accomplish these ends, however, public and private interactions were reshaped into divisions by gender within each class, in place of the old divisions by class within each household. Associations, revivals, and the recomposition of domestic life allowed a distinctive class strategy to emerge in the form of a special family strategy. As Ryan points out, this middle-class strategy involved the concentration of 'scarce financial and emotional resources on the care and education of fewer children,' lengthened co-residence of parents and children, the use of peer groups to bind middle-class persons together when outside the family, investment in schooling, and the development of maternal socialization methods designed to inculcate sexual restraint, temperance, family solidarity, conservative business habits, diligence, prolonged education, and delayed marriages – 'that is, the attributes required of the owners of small shops and stores and an increasing number of white-collar workers.' The successful product of this strategy 'was infused not with the spirit of a daring, aggressive entrepreneur but with, rather, that of a cautious, prudent, small-businessman.'[65]

The strategy paid off. Working-class children who had to enter the labor market at a younger age slipped behind the middle-class youths who enjoyed the advantages of parentally subsidized education and training. Middle-class sons were thus able to gain privileged access to the white-collar sector of the economy. Alongside the rapid expansion of unskilled jobs in the cities from the 1830s, many new clerkships opened up there; these were 'entrusted mostly to local sons and fresh arrivals from the American countryside who had contacts among the resident merchants.' The role of associations in cementing those contacts and allowing middle-class youths to find economic sponsorship was well expressed by the wealthy New York merchant Philip Hone in his praise of the Mercantile Library Association:

> An institution of this nature is, to society, like an eddy in one of those rivers of the southern Continent in which gold dust is found. It brings within its vortex, *and concentrating in one spot*, gives a value to the scattered particles of the precious metal; whilst others, beyond the reach of its influence, rendered worthless from the want of the benefits of association, *lie unnoticed* on the shoals, or amid the quick-sands of the stream, or *are swept away, and lost in the undiscriminating ocean.*[66]

The mainly lateral but nevertheless impressive shift in occupations for the middle class can be seen in biographies that have been collected for New Hampshire and Massachusetts lawyers and clergymen. Those born before 1830 had a pattern of late access to the profession, indicating that they had originally been destined for another occupation, usually agricultural, but had managed – probably through prolonged parental co-residence and subsidies – to get the education or make the connections to shift to a new one. These 'delays among northern youth in entering professions reflected the withering of traditions of status and hierarchy in the North'[67] – not to mention the growing importance of a family's ability and willingness to subsidize prolonged education or training periods.

From Middle-class Strategy to Classless Ideal

As the strategy paid off, so the values spread, not only throughout the middle class but upward and downward as well. With business cycles and speculative crashes more common, many upper-class families had cause to remind their children that moderation was an important virtue. Upper-class women, of course, experiencing a loss of former roles within the household, had good reason to seek outlets in religious work and social charity. Allowing them to do so, remarks Nancy Hewitt, was a sound investment by the city's fathers, since the women took pride in the fact that they spent 'female labor rather than male dollars.' In Philadelphia, evangelism appealed to 'rising industrialists who lacked the pedigree and wealth' for immediate acceptance into the upper crust, 'former journeymen who had scratched their way to employer status and middling respectability,' and significant sections of the working class, especially rural–urban migrants who lacked an organized artisan tradition and identified themselves more as Americans and Protestants than as workers.[68]

Bruce Laurie, Paul Faler, and Alan Dawley suggest that the working class divided into two main categories: traditionalists, who maintained old patterns of sociability, continued to drink on the job – or, when that was forbidden, in the taverns of their new neighborhoods – and refused to put punctuality above spontaneity; and modernists, who accepted the new work ethic and family strategies for producing self-control. Modernists, in turn, divided into those who adopted new methods of self-control in order to improve their work or gain promotion from the bosses and those who adopted them in order to resist the bosses more effectively. Both types of modernist, however, took on some of the values and behaviors associated with middle-class revivalism and domesticity, a process that accelerated after the Depression of 1837.[69] Part of this was due to defeat and demoralization, part to recognition of the effectiveness of using domestic ideology to demand a family wage, part to the appeal of the mutual aid component of associations, and part, surely, to the fact that of the various working-class strands of behavior – traditionalism, rebellion, and evangelism – only the evangelist offered a clear explanation for the changing roles of women and children.

By the 1840s the domestic theory of the family was so thoroughly hegemonic that even opponents of its conclusions would thereafter utilize its assumptions about gender differences. As Alexis de Tocqueville observed: 'In no country has such constant care been taken to trace two clearly distinct lines of action for the two sexes. . . .'[70] Other middle-class values prevailed as well. By 1835 a quarter-million people had become teetotalers and two million more had renounced the use of distilled liquor. Consumption of alcohol fell from seven gallons per capita in 1830 to three gallons in 1840.

Belief in the individual's responsibility for his own fate spread to both conservative congregations and working-class organizations and was secularized by men such as Abraham Lincoln, who declared in 1859: 'If any continue through life in the condition of the hired laborer, it is not the fault of the system, but because of either a dependent nature which prefers it, or improvidence, folly, or singular misfortune.'[71]

Yet the very success of middle-class values led to the eventual abandonment of organization by the middle class. As families succeeded in placing their sons in new occupations, tensions within the movement surfaced. The highly individualistic nature of many of the new occupations tended to work against the collectivist and mutual-aid components of associations and revivals. The potential conflict between male peer associations and maternal generational ties was obscured so long as the male ties were confined to boyish identifications that could be controlled by maternal intervention. But as young men moved out of the home, forming groups such as the Odd Fellows and the YMCA, peer ties threatened to supplant maternal ones. Sharp conflicts arose between female moral reform societies, who claimed maternal rights of supervision over youthful morality, and groups of clerks who claimed to be perfectly capable of handling their own morality through their consciences and their friendships with like-minded young men.[72]

Differences arose within the associations over how far to go in seeking individual perfection and what to do when human institutions thwarted that goal. Idealistic youth in the 1810s and 1820s had seen no contradiction between 'doing good' and 'doing well.' By the late 1830s and 1840s, however, new tensions over slavery, wage labor, and women's rights led some people to conclude that the existing leadership and institutions in society were too corrupt to cooperate with. Associations divided over goals and tactics. Working people embraced association for their own ends. Radicals founded communal societies that challenged both property notions and family roles. And conservatives sounded a retreat.[73]

Once having created new routes to self control and social control, then, a majority of middle-class activists pulled out of associations and divided up the tasks once assigned to these groups. The economic and political functions of moral reform societies were taken over by public, male-run institutions; the 'ideological and social functions' became 'the stock-in-trade of private conjugal families.' Middle-class women and children returned to a home that their associations had transformed.[74]

Or, at least, most middle-class women and children did. The next chapter will explore the triumph of the conservative version of the domestic family, discuss its role in industrializing America, and point to the contradictions and tensions inherent in its triumph. But even before the Civil War there were important limits to the hegemony of middle-class values and family practices. One such limit was set by the institution of slavery; another derived from the reality of class stratification.

Families under Slavery

Slaves, of course, had no access to the familial division of labor that signified success for northern whites. The tightening of slavery and hardening of racial prejudice described in the last chapter meant that slaves experienced a steady loss in access to artisanal skills during the nineteenth century. Family strategies designed to pass on such skills, far less those constructed to enable a son or husband to pursue a career, were clearly irrelevant to slaves. Slave children were set to work early by their masters, at any rate, and had little chance for a prolonged childhood. Frederick Douglass noted in his autobiography that he could not remember seeing his mother until he was seven: 'The domestic hearth, with its holy lessons and precious endearments, is abolished in the case of a slave mother and her children.'[75]

Slave women worked in foundries, salt works, and mines. They plowed fields, laid track for railroads, and made up half the labor force that dug South Carolina's Santee Canal. Most slave narratives confirm the 1846 account of Lewis Clarke: 'The bell rings at four o'clock in the morning and they have half an hour to get ready. Men and women start together, and the women must work as steadily as the men and perform the same tasks as the men.' Eugene Genovese reports: 'Not unusually a woman would rate as the most valuable field hand on the place or as the single most powerful individual. Some excelled in such exacting roles as logrollers and even lumberjacks.'[76]

Contrary to contemporary anti-slavery accounts based on the theory of domesticity, the lack of clear sexual spheres was not in itself degrading. Autobiographies of slaves reveal tremendous respect for their mothers and grandmothers, and the relative equality of slave women and men in the plantation economy produced some exceptionally strong, independent women. An outstanding example is Harriet Tubman, who made nineteen journeys down South to lead slaves up through the Underground Railway, despite a price on her head that reached $40,000. Victorian moralists considered slaves licentious and dissolute; more recent research reveals a pattern of sexual egalitarianism in which premarital sex was tolerated for both men and women, but fidelity was expected from both after marriage. As Genovese has remarked, 'What has usually been viewed as a debilitating female supremacy was in fact a closer approximation to a healthy sexual equality than was possible for whites and perhaps even for many postbellum blacks.' Moreover, the lack of domestic privacy and rigid gender distinctions allowed slaves to develop a sophisticated, multilayered symbolic, communal, and religious life.[77]

Slaves also managed to preserve family networks in face of tremendous difficulties. They built extended family ties of real and fictive kin, used complex naming patterns to reinforce connections that might otherwise be weakened by physical distance, and maintained links through visiting, sending messages, passing on oral histories of relationships, or even running off to see each other. Slaves lived within and tended to 'a thicket of family connections that enveloped every member: aunts and uncles, nephews and nieces, cousins, and, occasionally, grandparents.'[78]

The continuity and social centrality of slave kin networks can be seen in the case of the descendants of one black slave and an Irish servant, who were able, nearly a hundred years after the marriage, to support their suit for freedom by citing relationships with more than a hundred kinfolk and drawing on extraordinarily detailed stories that had been passed down to them: 'They recounted the details of the wedding ceremony, the priest's name, and Nell's rebuke of Charles Calvert when the proprietor of Maryland attempted to dissuade her from marrying the slave: "she rather go to bed to Charles than his lordship." '[79]

Embedded in these networks, even the nuclear family was a viable institution among slaves. Most slaves lived in two-parent households that lasted until the death of one spouse. Nuclear families were important sources of cooperation, companionship, sexual satisfaction, self-esteem, socialization, and survival techniques. They were also remarkably resilient, as shown by the widespread and heroic efforts of Blacks during and after the Civil War to find and reconstruct their families.[80]

Yet it will not do to minimize the impact of slavery on black families. The tremendous interregional sale of slaves from the Old to the New South (1830–60) was a brutal forced migration that severed community and kin ties even when nuclear family units were not disrupted, and we have no way of knowing how many consensual unions, recognized by the slaves but not by their owners, were split up. One study of marriages between slaves in Tennessee, Louisiana, and Mississippi during the period 1864 to 1866 suggests that almost one-third were broken up by the masters. Gutman estimates that only one in six or seven was dissolved prior to the war. But even the smaller rate is significant, and all slave families lived with the threat of dissolution as well as with the frequent physical (including sexual) intrusion of masters or foremen into their lives. The fact that many slavemasters did tolerate marriages was testimony only to the persistence of the slaves: breaking up families led to so many runaways that masters sometimes were forced into accepting family ties, particularly those between husband and wife or mother and children; but slave families had no legal rights.[81]

Slavery also affected white family values and behaviors in the South. Its inimical impact can be seen in the tendency for the violence and contempt toward slaves to spill over into owners' relations with their own wives and children, as well as in the insistence of most Southerners on the inseparability and immutability of slavery and patriarchy. In 1836, a resolution of the Mississippi legislature declared: 'We hold discussions upon the subject of slavery as equally impertinent with discussion upon our relations, wives, and children. . . .' One author has even found that the areas of most extensive slave-holding were also the areas where white kin and community ties were weakest: slavery 'isolated [white] Southern males and left them outside the traditional family-kin oriented network of personal relationships.'[82]

As the South grew more and more dependent on slavery and the North increasingly emphasized contracted labor, a vast cultural difference opened up. Southerners revived many precapitalist ideals of organic interdependence, hierarchy, honor, and patriarchy; they retreated from democratic rhetoric in explaining household relations, whether with slaves or with women and children. While Northerners engaged in protracted discussions about the proper ordering of family life and groped after biological justifications for assigning women to the private sphere, Southerners frankly admitted the blatant inequality involved in both slavery and marriage.[83]

Some Southerners, of course, believed in economizing, deferring gratification, and working toward household independence. Many, however, associated such values with Yankee 'meanness,' and admirers of northern middle-class ideals generally saw themselves as a minority in the South. The continuing conservatism of southern class and family strategies can be seen in the fact that there was no pattern of delayed entrance to professions, such as was associated in the North with new middle-class access to such jobs: southern professions were dominated by gentry families whose sons entered early as a consequence of family inheritance; there was little or no room for an emerging middle class to gain a foothold.[84]

Less concerned to reorganize customary patterns of social reproduction, Southerners made fewer innovations in gender and family roles. Indeed, Jean Friedman argues that men and women's spheres separated far more slowly in the South than in the North, so that kin and neighborhood rather than gender remained the primary modes of self-identification and many modernizing reform movements consequently failed to develop.[85]

Poor and Working-class Families

In the North too there were limits to the hegemony of middle-class family practices and values. The working class and the unemployed of the cities, for example, had a very different experience of work and family life.

Increasingly concentrated at the bottom of the urban social order were free Blacks. In Philadelphia, mounting discrimination ensured that the black population experienced a decline in wealth and skill levels between 1838 and 1847, foreshadowing a trend that would spread to other cities after the Civil War. This had striking effects on black families. One in five adult Blacks in Philadelphia, for example, had to live as a servant in a white household, because of the unavailability of other work. There was a steady decline in the viability of two-parent households among the poorest sections of the black population in these years: by mid century, one-third of the poorest half of the black community lived in female-headed households.[86]

In Boston the percentage of skilled Blacks remained stationary, but unskilled and semi-skilled Blacks were displaced by Irish competition. The resultant poverty made separate nuclear families difficult to maintain. Nine to twelve per cent of Boston's black children lived apart from their families of origin and most Blacks lived in multiple family dwellings, often with non-relatives in the household. Again, while the hardships of a poverty-stricken life should not be trivialized, this did not lead to social anomie: urban Blacks built a dense network of religious and mutual aid societies that allowed them to engage in group action and militant opposition to slavery and racism.[87]

More white workers were likely to have the incentive or necessity to adopt middle-class family and gender patterns as a route to maximizing their work opportunities. 'Modernists' might find that such patterns enabled them to retain or gain jobs from small masters; alternatively, adoption of new methods of self-control, family organization, and gender roles might be weapons for labor organization or resistance to the degradation of apprenticeship. But such adoption was neither inevitable nor universal; nor did new working-class family and sex roles have a content identical to those of similar middle-class ones.

For many workers, of course, middle-class elevation of the domestic family to a central focus of life was simply unrealistic. Christine Stansell argues that in urban areas after the revolution, 'disruption of household economies fostered new forms of insecurity: for women, uncertainties about men's support and commitment; for men, the loss of accustomed kinds of authority within their households and workplaces.' Among the working poor, married women seem to have avoided full-time wage labor out of the home whenever they could, less from sexual principle than from necessity: Jeanne Boydston argues that 'wives' labor [in the home] produced as much as half of the family subsistence' and that due to the low wages paid women by employers, 'a wife working without pay at home may have been more valuable to the family maintenance than a wife working for pay – inside or outside the home.' But this strategy did not produce self-sufficient nuclear families. In one New York City district in 1855, 28.1 per cent of male artisans relied on more than one income, 49.4 per cent were boarders, and only 22.5 per cent supported a family solely on their own earnings.[88]

'Domestic' work in lower-class families was vastly different from that of their middle-class counterparts, for it involved women in a dense network of interactions outside the immediate family. Poor women scavenged for clothing, food, and other goods (an activity that 'sometimes shaded into theft'), bartered with neighbors, peddled drink or food out of their kitchens or in the street, visited pawnshops, cooperated (or conflicted) with other women in childcare, garbage disposal, hauling water, and doing laundry, and dealt with male boarders or lodgers.[89]

Periodically, of course, such women had to seek paid work. Competition between these women and male workers may have initially aggravated sexual hostilities, but the involvement of women in wage-work could also lead them to a new consciousness of both class and gender. Occasionally women's militant articulation of these issues might push working-class men into cooperation with women, or at least undercut gender hostility.

The growth of cheap wage-work meant for many women a deterioration in traditional handicrafts. Among the most hard-hit were seamstresses and tailoresses, and they responded with considerable militancy. In 1825, New York seamstresses organized the first all-female strike in America. In 1831, the United Tailoresses' Society of New York was formed and within six months had organized 1,600 women into a strike that lasted more than a month. The needlewomen of Baltimore organized a union in 1833 and won the support of journeymen tailors. In 1835 they formed the United Men's and Women's Trading Society, while in Philadelphia the same year saw a convention of 500 working women who formed a city-wide federation, The Female Improvement Society for the City and County of Philadelphia.

Other women were drawn into newer industries. By the time of the Civil War, one in every four factory workers was female. Many of these worked in the cotton industry. The first mill girls had relatively high wages and lived in a paternalistic setting that at first discouraged militancy. Speed-ups and wage reductions in the 1830s and 1840s, however, brought many women into direct action and self-organization. In 1834, and again in 1836, thousands of female mill workers struck. In 1844, five women workers organized the Lowell Female Labor Reform Association to fight for the ten-hour day. Within a year the Association had more than 600 members in Lowell and branches in all the textile centers. In 1845 the Association presented a petition to the legislature with the signature of more than 2,000 textile workers. This forced the state to set up the first governmental investigating committee on labor conditions in US history. (The committee acknowledged a few 'abuses' in working conditions at the mills but declared that nothing could be done. The Female Labor Reform Association responded with a resolution denouncing 'the cringing servility to corporate monopolies manifested by said committee. . . . May never again the interests of the oppressed, downtrodden laboring classes be committed to their legislation.') At its peak in 1846, the Ten Hour Movement garnered more than 4,000 mill workers' signatures, a number that represented 40 per cent of the Lowell workforce.[90]

Some of these women raised working-class feminist issues. Lavinia Wright, president of the United Tailoresses' Society, demanded the right for women to vote and sit in legislatures. Louise Mitchell, secretary of the Tailoresses, declared that women who wished to rely on men 'would do well to remember who are our *oppressors*. . . . Let us, then, have more confidence in our abilities, and less to the sincerity of men.' In 1834, before the Grimké sisters had started to speak publicly on Abolitionism, kicking off the middle-class women's rights debate, a Boston paper reported that a strike leader of the mill operatives gave 'a flaming Mary Woolstonecraft [*sic*] speech on the rights of women and the iniquities of the "monied aristocracy".' In 1845 Harriet Curtis, co-editor of the *Lowell Offering*, called for equal pay and equal access to jobs for women. And a woman operative declared in 1846:

> Bad as is the condition of so many women, it would be much worse if they had nothing but [men's] boasted protection to rely upon; but they have at last learnt the lesson which a bitter experience teaches, that not to those who style themselves their 'natural protectors' are they to look for the needful help, but to the strong and resolute of their own sex.[91]

Such actions and words 'must have impressed some workingmen that women workers could no longer be simply dismissed.' While some male workers still called for the exclusion of women from the trades, others actively supported striking women as working comrades or at least as specially exploited members of the working class. In areas where male and female work was complementary rather than competitive, a rather egalitarian cooperation in action was sometimes achieved. Elsewhere male workers rephrased their opposition to cheap female labor in terms of protection of women rather than sexual hostility: the 'family wage' demand expressed female as well as male yearning to limit the extent of 'wage slavery.'[92]

But in most cases the hostility was replaced by paternalism rather than feminism. In 'installing the family at the center of their vision of a just social order, the men began a subtle process by which eventually their domestic aspirations for the women would come to override all else.' The Depression of 1837 reinforced the retreat from a radical combination of feminism and class militancy: 'By 1851, working-class paternalism leaned more heavily on genteel formulations of women's nature than on elucidations of women's place in working-class life.'[93]

This development was not simply a result of working-class men's hostility to feminism; it was also due to middle-class women's denial of class. Middle-class support for the relief of working women was often tied to rejection of labor demands and to manipulation of stereotypes about female weakness and virtue. The Seneca Falls convention of 1848 showed no consciousness of the special needs of working women, declaring merely 'that *those who believe* the laboring classes of women are oppressed ought to do all in their power to raise their wages, beginning with their own household servants.'[94] The limits of middle-class sisterhood and the inability of working-class organizations to push past those limits were both cause and consequence of the growing conservatism of the ideal of the domestic family.

Notes

1. J. Potter, 'The Growth of Population in America, 1700–1860,' in Glass and Eversley, eds, *Population in History*; Robert Wells, 'Family Size and Fertility Control in Eighteenth-Century America: A Study of Quaker Families,' *Population Studies* 25 (1971), pp. 73–82.

2. Barbara Epstein, 'Industrialization and Femininity: A Case Study of Nineteenth Century New England,' in Rachel Kahn-Hut, Arlene Kaplan Daniels, and Richard Colvard, eds, *Women and Work: Problems and Perspectives* (New York, 1982), p. 94; Mary Ryan, *The Empire of the Mother: American Writing about Domesticity, 1830–1869* (New York, 1984), pp. 19–27.

3. I am indebted to my research assistant, Kim Buselle, for compiling a collection of magazines from 1790 to 1830 that demonstrate a wide variety of interpretations of womanhood despite seeming unanimity about women's distinctive nature. See also Cott, *Bonds of Womanhood*, pp. 157, 202–3. For a discussion of variations in views of women's 'nature' even after this period, see Ronald Hogeland, ' "The Female Appendage": Feminine Life-Styles in America, 1820–1860,' *Civil War History* 17 (1971).

4. Dawley, *Class and Community*, p. 61.

5. Nancy Cott, 'Young Women in the Second Great Awakening in New England,' *Feminist Studies* 3 (1975); Joseph Kett, *Rites of Passage: Adolescence in America, 1790 to the Present* (New York, 1977), p. 75; William Gerald McLoughlin, *Revivals, Awakenings, and Reform: An Essay on Religion and Social Change in America, 1607–1977* (Chicago, 1978), pp. 106–21; Timothy L. Smith, *Revivalism and Social Reform in Mid-Nineteenth Century America* (New York, 1957); Isaac, *Transformation*.

6. Paul David, 'The Growth of Real Product in the United States Before 1840,' *Journal of Economic History* 27 (1967) p. 165; Edward Pessen, *Jacksonian America: Society, Personality, and Politics* (Homewood, IL, 1978), p. 102.

7. Michael Paul Rogin, *Fathers and Children: Andrew Jackson and the Subjugation of the American Indian* (New York, 1984), p. 253; Pessen, *Jacksonian America*, p. 138; David, 'Growth of Real Product,' p. 155.

8. Paul Boyer, *Urban Masses and Moral Order in America, 1820–1920* (Cambridge, MA, 1978), p. 3; Wilentz, *Chants Democratic*, p. 25; Steven Ross, *Workers on the Edge:*

Work, Leisure, and Politics in Industrializing Cincinnati, 1788–1890 (New York, 1985), p. xvi; David Rothman, *The Discovery of the Asylum* (Boston, 1971), p. 57; Stephen Thernstrom and Peter Knights, 'Men in Motion: Some Data and Speculations about Urban Population Mobility in Nineteenth-Century America,' in Tamara Hareven, ed., *Anonymous Americans* (Englewood Cliffs, 1971), pp. 14–47. Blumin, Warner, and Page Smith suggest that the expansion of voluntary groups must be related to the transiency, in small towns as well as large, that made neighborhood an inadequate basis for entering into enduring relationships: Stuart Blumin, 'Residential Mobility Within the Nineteenth-Century City,' in Allen Davis and Mark Haller, eds, *The Peoples of Philadelphia: A History of Ethnic Groups and Lower-Class Life, 1790–1940* (Philadelphia, 1973), p. 49; Warner, *Private City*, p. 61; Page Smith, *As a City Upon a Hill* (New York, 1966), p. 174; Stuart Blumin, 'Mobility and Change in Ante-Bellum Philadelphia,' in Stephen Thernstrom and Richard Sennett, eds, *Nineteenth Century Cities* (New Haven, 1969).

　　9. Jonathon Prude, *The Coming of the Industrial Order*, pp. 7, 69; Susan Hirsch, *Roots of the American Working Class: The Industrialization of Newark, 1800–1860* (Philadelphia, 1978), p. 4.

　　10. Morton Horwitz, *The Transformation of American Law, 1780–1860* (Cambridge, MA, 1977); Grossberg, *Governing the Hearth*, p. 14.

　　11. Sam Bass Warner, Jr., 'If All the World Were Philadelphia: A Scaffolding for Urban History, 1774–1930,' *American Historical Review* 74 (1968), p. 39. See also Johnson, *Shopkeeper's Millennium* and Dawley, *Class and Community*.

　　12. Clark, 'Household Economy,' p. 183; Dawley, *Class and Community*, p. 61.

　　13. David Montgomery, 'The Working Classes of the Pre-Industrial American City, 1780–1830,' *Labor History* 9 (1968), p. 5; Johnson, *Shopkeeper*, p. 42.

　　14. Dawley, *Class and Community*, p. 25.

　　15. Bushman, 'This New Man,' p. 92; Wilentz, *Chants Democratic*, pp. 31–5, 107–42.

　　16. Ross, *Workers on the Edge*, p. 40.

　　17. Faler, *Mechanics and Manufacturers*, pp. 56, 193–4.

　　18. Dawley, *Class and Community*, p. 11; Lee Soltow, 'Inequality Amidst Abundance: Land Ownership in Early Nineteenth Century Ohio,' *Ohio History* 88 (1979), pp. 133–51; Montgomery, 'Working Classes,' p. 15; Edward Pessen, *Riches, Class and Power Before the Civil War* (Lexington, MA, 1973); Pessen, 'We Are All Jeffersonians, We Are All Jacksonians,' *Journal of the Early Republic* 1 (1981), p. 12.

　　19. Stansell, *City of Women*, p. 3.

　　20. Richard Brown, 'The Emergence of Urban Society in Rural Massachusetts, 1760–1820,' *Journal of American History* 61 (1974), p. 37.

　　21. Johnson, *Shopkeeper*, pp. 62–94; Gary Lawson Browne, *Baltimore in the New Nation, 1789–1861* (Chapel Hill, 1980).

　　22. Pessen, *Jacksonian America*, pp. 155, 155–65; Johnson, *Shopkeeper*, pp. 63–71; Ronald Formisano, 'Deferential Participant Politics: The Early Republic's Political Culture, 1789–1840,' *American Political Science Review* 68 (1974), pp. 480, 486; Blumin, *Urban Threshold*, pp. 141–4; Pessen, 'We Are All Jeffersonians,' p. 21; Prude, *Industrial Order*, pp. 18–25, 29.

　　23. Caroll Smith Rosenberg, *Religion and the Rise of the American City* (New York, 1971), pp. 15–29; Barbara Berg, *The Remembered Gate* (Boston, 1978), pp. 157, 159, 160, 171; Lebscock, *Free Women of Petersburg*, pp. 204–11, 217; Amy Gilman, 'From Widowhood to Wickedness: The Politics of Class and Gender in New York City Private Charity, 1799–1860,' *History of Education Quarterly* 24 (1984), pp. 59–74; Boyer, *Urban Masses*, p. viii; Carol Lasser, 'A "Pleasingly Oppressive" Burden: The Transformation of Domestic Service and Female Charity in Salem, 1800–1840,' *Essex Institute Historical Collections* 116 (1980), pp. 160–62; Ryan, *Cradle of the Middle Class*, p. 84.

　　24. Lasser, 'Burden,' p. 169.

　　25. Herbert Gutman, *Work, Culture, and Society in Industrializing America: Essays in American Working-Class and Social History* (New York, 1976), pp. 212, 221; Ross, *Workers on the Edge*, pp. 78, 79.

26. Pessen, *Jacksonian America*, pp. 89–91; Faler, *Mechanics and Manufacturers*, pp. 62–8, 75.

27. Pessen, 'All Jeffersonians,' p. 15; Ross, *Workers on the Edge*, pp. 43, 75.

28. Davis and Haller, *Peoples of Philadelphia*; Prude, *Industrial Order*; Bushman, 'Family Security'; Blumin, 'Mobility and Change,' pp. 176–80.

29. Dawley, *Class and Community*, pp. 21–3, 77; Faler, *Mechanics*.

30. Prude, *Industrial Order*, p. 13.

31. On the great 'surge' of inequality, both between rich and poor and between skilled and unskilled workers, see Jeffrey Williamson and Peter Lindert, *American Inequality: A Macroeconomic History* (New York, 1980), pp. 42–63, 103. Among recent works that deal sensitively with the failure of the working class to coalesce into a strong social movement prior to the Civil War, without denying the development of class consciousness, militancy, and even an anti-capitalist critique, see: Hirsch, *Roots of American Working Class*; Wilentz, *Chants Democratic*; Alan Dawley and Paul Faler, 'Working-Class Culture and Politics in the Industrial Revolution: Sources of Loyalism and Rebellion,' *Journal of Social History* 9 (1976), pp. 466–78; Howard Rock, *Artisans of the New Republic: The Tradesmen of New York City in the Age of Jefferson* (New York, 1979); and Bruce Laurie, *Working People of Philadelphia, 1800–1850* (Philadelphia, 1980).

32. Hirsch, *Roots*, p. 41; Kett, *Rites of Passage*, pp. 30–31.

33. David Hackett Fischer, *Growing Old in America* (New York, 1978), pp. 78–81, 224.

34. Dawley, *Class and Community*, p. 158; Cott, *Bonds of Womanhood*, pp. 55–8.

35. Nancy Hewitt, *Women's Activism and Social Change: Rochester, New York, 1822–1872* (Ithaca, 1984), p. 22.

36. Kett, *Rites of Passage*, p. 31; Allan Horlick, *Country Boys and Merchant Princes: The Social Control of Young Men in New York* (Lewisburg, 1975), pp. 163–5.

37. David Brion Davis, *The Slave Power Conspiracy and the Paranoid Style* (Baton Rouge, 1970), p. 27; Karen Haltunen, *Confidence Men and Painted Women: A Study of Middle-Class Culture in America, 1830–1870* (New Haven, 1983), pp. 39, 42, 194; Arthur Schlesinger, *Learning How to Behave* (New York, 1946).

38. See, for example, Hirsch, *Roots*; Anthony Wallace, *Rockdale* (New York, 1978); and Lewis, *Pursuit of Happiness*.

39. Cott, *Bonds of Womanhood*, pp. 67, 98.

40. Barbara Epstein, *The Politics of Domesticity: Women, Evangelism, and Temperance in Nineteenth-Century America* (Middletown, 1981).

41. Donald Matthews, 'The Second Great Awakening as an Organizing Process, 1780–1830: An Hypothesis,' *American Quarterly* 21 (1969), p. 42.

42. Kett, *Rites of Passage*, pp. 105–6, 107.

43. Johnson, *Shopkeeper*, p. 38.

44. Mark Lender and James Martin, *Drinking in America: A History* (Glencoe, 1982); W.S. Rorubagh, *The Alcoholic Republic: An American Tradition* (New York, 1979).

45. Johnson, *Shopkeeper*, p. 61; Boyer, *Urban Masses*; Roy Rosenzweig, *Eight Hours for What We Will* (Cambridge, MA, 1983).

46. Paul Weinbaum, *Mobs and Demagogues: The New York Response to Violence in the Early Nineteenth Century* (Ann Arbor, 1979), p. 137; Warner, *Private City*, pp. 50, 53.

47. Johnson, *Shopkeeper*, p. 53.

48. Greven, *Protestant Temperament*, p. 26; Johnson, *Shopkeeper*, p. 101.

49. Johnson, *Shopkeeper*, pp. 106, 138. For a discussion of how revivals helped industrialists to win cultural hegemony, see Wallace, *Rockdale*.

50. Donald Bell, 'Up From Patriarchy,' in Robert Lewis, ed., *Men in Difficult Times* (Englewood Cliffs, 1981), p. 317.

51. Ryan, *Cradle*, p. 91. For the analysis of Cott's figures I am indebted to my teaching assistant, Susan Ann Scott.

52. Barbara Welter, 'The Feminization of American Religion, 1800–1860,' in William L. O'Neill, ed., *Insights and Parallels: Problems and Issues of American Social History* (New York, 1973); Frances Trollope, *Domestic Manners of the Americans*, ed. Donald Smalley (New York, 1949), p. 110.

53. Epstein, *Politics of Domesticity*, pp. 59–61; Mary Ryan, 'A Woman's Awakening: Evangelical Religion and the Families of Utica, New York, 1800–1840,' *American Quarterly* 30 (1978).

54. Nancy Woloch, *Women and the American Experience* (New York, 1984), p. 101. For various accounts of women's motivations and self-organization, though with conflicting evaluations of it, see Ann Douglass, *The Feminization of American Culture* (New York, 1974); Mary Ryan, 'The Power of Women's Networks: A Case Study of Female Moral Reform in Antebellum America,' *Feminist Studies* 5 (1979), pp. 66–85; Daniel Scott Smith, 'Family Limitation, Sexual Control, and Domestic Feminism'; Nancy Cott, 'Passionless: An Interpretation of Victorian Sexual Ideology,' and Carroll Smith Rosenberg, 'Beauty, the Beast, and the Militant Woman,' in Cott and Pleck, *Heritage of Her Own*; Nancy Cott, 'Young Women in the Second Great Awakening,' *Feminist Studies* 3 (1975); Cott, *Bonds of Womanhood*, pp. 140–54; and Welter, 'Feminization of Religion.'

55. Nancy Hewitt, 'Beyond the Search for Sisterhood: American Women's History in the 1980s,' *Social History* 10 (1985) and *Women's Activism and Social Change: Rochester, New York, 1822–1872* (Ithaca, 1984).

56. Ryan, *Cradle*.

57. Michael Katz, Michael Doucet, and Mark Stern, *The Social Organization of Industrial Capitalism* (Cambridge, MA, 1982), pp. 14–63.

58. Arno Mayer, 'The Lower Middle Class as a Historical Problem,' *Journal of Modern History* 47 (1975), p. 418.

59. Peter Stearns goes so far as to argue that 'it was middle-class values that, in many spheres of activity, came to influence the total society most completely.... In fact ... the modern middle class has no clear historical parallel in being capable of dominating any social consensus about proper life style while not wielding power or ... uniformly joining the upper class in defense of the structural status quo.' 'The Middle Class: Toward a Precise Definition,' *Comparative Studies in Society and History* 21 (1979), p. 393.

60. Stuart Blumin, 'The Hypothesis of Middle-Class Formation in Nineteenth-Century America: A Critique and Some Proposals,' *American Historical Review* 90 (1985), p. 304. For more on 'aristocratic' elements, see Pessen, *Riches, Class, and Power* and Frederic Jahler, *The Urban Establishment: Upper Strata in Boston, New York, Charleston, Chicago, and Los Angeles* (Urbana, 1982).

61. Barbara Cross, *Horace Bushnell: Minister to a Changing America* (Chicago, 1958), pp. 3–4.

62. Ryan, *Cradle*, p. 53.

63. Paul Gilje, ' "The Mob Begin to Think and Reason": Recent Trends in Studies of American Popular Disorder, 1700–1850,' *Maryland Historian* 12 (1981), pp. 25–36; Richard Latner and Peter Levine, 'Perspectives on Antebellum Pietistic Politics,' *Reviews in American History* March 1976, pp. 15–24; Sean Wilentz, 'On Class and Politics in Jacksonian America,' in Stanley Kutler and Stanley Katz, eds, *The Promise of American History: Progress and Prospects* (Baltimore, 1982); Michael Leibowitz, 'The Jacksonians: Paradox Lost?' in Barton Bernstein, ed., *Towards a New Past: Dissenting Essays in American History* (New York, 1969); Paula Baker, 'The Domestication of Politics: Women and American Political Society, 1780–1920,' *American Historical Review* 89 (1984), esp. p. 629; Johnson, *Shopkeeper*.

64. The phrase is Paul Boyer's (*Urban Masses*, p. 50).

65. Ryan, *Cradle*, pp. 161, 184–5, 238.

66. Wilentz, *Chants Democratic*, p. 110; Horlick, *Country Boys*, p. 258.

67. Kett, *Rites of Passage*, pp. 35–6.

68. Hewitt, *Women's Activism*, p. 221; Laurie, *Working People*, p. 48.

69. Bruce Laurie, ' "Nothing on Compulsion": Life Styles of Philadelphia Artisans, 1820–1850,' *Labor History* 15 (1974), pp. 335–65 and *Working People of Philadelphia*, pp. 48–9; Alan Dawley and Paul Faler, 'Working-Class Culture and Politics in the Industrial Revolution: Sources of Loyalism and Rebellion,' *Journal of Social History* 9 (1976), pp. 466–80.

70. Alexis de Tocqueville, *Democracy in America* (New York, 1963), vol. 2, p. 212.

71. Rowland Berthoff, *An Unsettled People: Social Order and Disorder in American History* (New York, 1971), p. 198.

72. See Ryan, *Cradle*, p. 154 for a discussion of the change from associational to more privatized concerns and pp. 125–7 for a description of a struggle between clerks and female moral reformers.

73. Lois Banner, 'Religion and Reform in the Early Republic: The Role of Youth,' *American Quarterly* 23 (1971), pp. 676–95; Lawrence Foster, *Religion and Sexuality: Three American Communal Experiments of the Nineteenth Century* (New York, 1981).

74. Ryan, *Cradle*, p. 143.

75. Ira Berlin and Herbert Gutman, 'Natives and Immigrants, Free Men and Slaves,' *American Historical Review* 88 (1983), p. 1192–3; Jones, *Labor of Love*, p. 24; Frederick Douglass, *My Bondage and My Freedom* (New York, 1968), p. 48.

76. Angela Davis, 'Reflections on the Black Woman's Role in the Community of Slaves,' *The Black Scholar* III (1971), p. 7; Eugene Genovese, *Roll, Jordan, Roll: The World the Slaves Made* (New York, 1974), p. 495.

77. Herbert Gutman, *The Black Family in Slavery and Freedom, 1750–1925* (New York, 1976); Genovese, *Roll, Jordan, Roll*, p. 500; Lawrence Levine, *Black Culture and Black Consciousness: Afro-American Folk Thought From Slavery to Freedom* (Charlottesville, 1977).

78. Norton, Gutman, and Berlin, 'The Afro-American Family in the Age of Revolution,' in Berlin and Hoffman, eds, *Slavery and Freedom in the Age of the American Revolution* (Charlottesville, 1983), p. 182.

79. Norton, Gutman, and Berlin, 'Afro-American Family,' p. 191.

80. Gutman, *Black Family* and 'Slave Family and Its Legacies,' *Historical Reflections* 6 (1979), p. 195; John Blassingame, *The Slave Community: Plantation Life in the Ante-Bellum South* (New York, 1972); George Rawick, 'The Black Family Under Slavery,' in Rawick, ed., *The American Slave: A Composite Autobiography*, vol. 1 (Westport, 1972).

81. Blassingame, *Slave Community*, p. 91; Peter Ripley, 'The Black Family in Transition: Louisiana, 1860–1865,' *Journal of Southern History* 41 (1975), p. 371; Gutman, 'Slave Legacies,' p. 195.

82. Catharine Clinton, *The Plantation Mistress* (New York, 1984), pp. 80–81; Genovese, *Roll, Jordan, Roll*, p. 75; William Barney, 'Patterns of Crisis: Alabama White Families and Social Change, 1850–1870,' *Social Science Review* 63 (1979), pp. 525, 530.

83. For examples of a southern version of womanhood that was less concerned with establishing the different biological natures of men and women and more frank about the need for hierarchy and dependence within marriage, see *Southern Ladies' Book* I (1840), p. 325; *Southern Quarterly Review* IV (1842) pp. 287–8; Genovese, *Roll, Jordan, Roll*, p. 75; Hogeland, 'Female Appendage'; *Southern Quarterly Review* I (1842), p. 175; *Southern Quarterly Review* II (1842), p. 271.

84. Kett, *Rites of Passage*, pp. 35–6.

85. Jean Friedman, *The Enclosed Garden: Women and Community in the Evangelical South, 1830–1900* (Chapel Hill, 1985).

86. Theodore Hershberg, 'Free Blacks in Antebellum Philadelphia,' in Hershberg, ed., *Philadelphia: Work, Space, Family, and Group Experience in the 19th Century* (New York, 1981), p. 374.

87. James Horton and Lois Horton, *Black Bostonians: Family Life and Community Struggle in the Antebellum North* (New York, 1979), p. 16 and *passim*.

88. Stansell, *City of Women*, p. 4; Jeanne Boydston, 'To Earn Her Daily Bread: Housework and Antebellum Working-Class Subsistence,' *Radical History Review* 35 (1986), pp. 9, 19; Wilentz, *Chants Democratic*, p. 118.

89. Boydston, 'To Earn Her Bread,' pp. 13–16; Stansell, *City of Women*, pp. 46–52; Susan Strasser, *Never Done: A History of American Housework* (New York, 1982).

90. W. Elliot Brownlee and Mary Brownlee, *Women in the American Economy: A Documentary History, 1675–1929* (New Haven, 1977), p. 42; Philip Foner, ed., *The Factory Girls: A Collection of Writings on Life and Struggle in the New England Factories of the 1840's* (Urbana, 1977), p. 243; Thomas Dublin, *Women at Work:*

The Transformation of Work and Community in Lowell, Massachusetts, 1826–1860 (New York, 1979).

91. Stansell, *City of Women*, p. 133; Archives: 'Making Common Cause: The Needlewomen of New York, 1831–69,' *Signs* 1 (1976), p. 180; Foner, *Factory Girls*, p. 194; Ruth Delzell, *The Early History of Women Trade Unionists of America* (Chicago, no date); Laurie Nisonoff, 'Bread and Roses: The Proletarianisation of Women Workers in New England Textile Mills, 1827–1848,' *Historical Journal of Massachusetts* 9 (1981), pp. 6–7; Lise Vogel, 'Hearts to Feel and Tongues to Speak: New England Mill Women in the Early Nineteenth Century,' in Milton Cantor and Bruce Laurie, eds, *Class, Sex, and the Woman Worker* (Westport, 1977), p. 75; Thomas Dublin, 'Women, Work, and Protest in the Early Lowell Mills: "The Oppressing Hand of Avarice Would Enslave Us," ' in Cantor and Laurie, *Class, Sex*, p. 60.

92. Stansell, *City of Women*, pp. 137–42; Dawley, *Class and Community*.

93. Stansell, *City of Women*, pp. 144, 147–9, 153.

94. Elizabeth Cady Stanton *et al.*, *History of Women's Suffrage* (Salem, 1969), vol. 1, p. 809 (my emphasis).

6

Middle-class Morality in the Mid Nineteenth Century

Antebellum romanticization of the family reflected a real appreciation of the economic and psychic costs of capitalism, both for the small businessman who was thrown into increasing conflict with his employees and for the artisan who faced a loss of control over his work and demotion to the status of hired 'hand.' Insistence on the separation of home and family from market and state represented an attempt to limit the transformation of personal relations into commodity relations, to reserve one arena of life free from the competition, conflicts, and insecurities of an expanding capitalist democracy.

Emotions and personal ties that were now inappropriate in political and business interactions were displaced to the family, and the family was set forth as an alternative to a city that was viewed in increasingly negative terms:

> We go forth into the world, amidst the scenes of business and of pleasure . . . and the heart is sensible to a desolation of feeling; we behold every principle of justice and honor, disregarded, and good sacrificed to the advancement of personal interest; and we turn from such scenes with a painful sensation, almost believing that virtue has deserted the abodes of men; again, we look to the *sanctuary* of *home*; there . . . disinterested love is ready to sacrifice everything at the altar of affection.

The family became the one place where permanent commitments could be nurtured. Thus the family was increasingly described as a 'sanctuary,' an 'oasis,' an 'ivory tower,' a moated 'castle,' or whatever other image expressed its imagined freedom from the corrosion of cash calculations and the clash of interest groups.[1]

This domestic family was often explicitly opposed to fashionable, wealthy society. Domestic writers again and again contrasted the pleasures of home with the 'fashionable gaieties of the City,' the 'vile caricatures of foreign courts, foreign manners, and foreign vices' that prevailed among the *nouveau riche*, and the 'carriages with their liveried servants' that defiled 'our republican streets.'[2]

Within the home, the role assigned to women also revealed discontent with the commercialization of American life. Sarah Josepha Hale believed it necessary 'to remind the dwellers of this "bank-note world" that there are objects more elevated, more worthy of pursuit than wealth,' and that these were under the care of women.[3] Women were put in charge of social and moral obligations that had once been male as well as female concerns, and the sentiment now poured over such obligations implied a critique of competition and economic individualism.

This implicit critique of wage-labor and market relations provided some common ground for the development of working-class and lower-middle-class ideas about women's roles. Both groups contrasted their family and gender values to those of the rich, whose males they portrayed as moral libertines and whose females they portrayed as unnatural mothers. The hostility of the cult of true womanhood toward the upper-class ideal of the lady was not lost upon fashionable observers such as Frances Trollope, who heartily reciprocated the sentiment. Trollope was appalled that in America even wealthy women performed 'the sordid offices of household drudgery'; she complained that American men believed 'that women were made for no other purpose than to fabricate sweetmeats and gingerbread, construct shirts, darn stockings, and become mothers of possible presidents.'[4]

Small town values and settings dominated domestic literature, and the big city was looked upon with fear and mistrust. Ministers such as Horace Mann and Henry Ward Beecher warned against economic ambition and counseled their readers to take a safe middle course in life. Although Beecher would later embrace Social Darwinism, endorse commercial products, and defend big business against the claims of labor, his early writings stressed the perils of commerce, the corruptions of city life, and the preferability of honest work as a farm hand, sailor, or mechanic to that of urban, commercial employment.[5]

Yet the basic tenets of this anti-mercantile or anti-aristocratic domesticity showed little experience or sympathy with the realities of working-class family life. Domestic novelists condemned the 'vice' and 'ignorance' of manual workers or immigrants with at least as much fervor as they deplored the indolence and waste of the irresponsible rich. Their heroes rejected risky mercantile pursuits but always had the possibility of becoming shopkeepers, lawyers, ministers, or teachers. Women writers offered practical advice on how to cook, clothe the family, and furnish the home in order to conserve household resources or minimize economic losses, but none of that advice admitted the possibility that women might have to leave the home to engage in lower-class employment.

In *The American Frugal Housewife: Dedicated to Those Who Are Not Ashamed of Economy* (first published in 1838 and reprinted throughout the period), Lydia Maria Child taught women how to do without servants when economic reverses made that necessary, and claimed that unlike most such books, which were 'written for the wealthy,' hers was 'written for the poor.' But Child's advice, like that of most domestic authors, was aimed at the lower middle class who might face unexpected losses depriving them 'of a few yearly hundreds,' not at working-class families who *regularly* made less than a few hundreds a year. Many of the tips for economizing assumed middle-class lifestyles, education, and basic capital – a range of staple ingredients, spices, cooking aids, kitchen appliances, at least occasional help, and household decorations (to brighten a plain meal) unlikely to be available to a truly poor household. Later in the book, Child more directly addressed herself to the woman 'of moderate fortune' who wasted her husband's money on household furnishings when, had she 'been content with Kidderminster carpets and tasteful vases of her own making,' she might have invested the money at 6 per cent interest and 'saved much domestic disquiet.' And Child's idealization of domesticity was extraordinarily limited by her class biases: she actually suggested in 1843 that the largest problem facing New York's 'squalid little wretches' was the fact that they were not orphans![6]

Despite its anxiety about the economic and political oscillations of American society, the ideology and practice of domesticity provided no way for people to resist or challenge the reorganization of work, the spread of the market, or the constriction of economic and social obligations. The domestic family may have attempted to shield its members from the corruptions and insecurities of capitalist *exchange*, but it never expressed any opposition to the dynamics of capitalist *production*. Domesticity's rejection of market relations among family members was tied to acceptance of such relations among all others; the domestic division of labor between men and women depended on the capitalist division between waged and non-waged work. 'The values of domesticity,' writes Nancy Cott, 'undercut opposition to exploitative pecuniary standards in the work world by upholding a "separate sphere" of comfort and compensation at home.' By 1870, even the sexual radical John Humphrey Noyes accepted the mutual reliance between family and business: 'The two principles as they exist in the world are not antagonistic. Home is the center from which men go forth to business, and business is the field from which they go home with the spoil. Home is the charm and stimulus of business, business provides material for the comfort and health of home.'[7]

Separation of public and private spheres acted to preserve inequities in both. The cult of domesticity validated the economic and political processes that removed law from the private sphere and morality from the public sphere, supposedly giving men 'rights' and women 'virtue.' As Nadine Taub and Elizabeth Schneider point out, this division between public rights and private morality played 'an important role in disguising the very limited nature of the rights afforded people in general,'[8] allowing demands for many reforms to be met with denials of state or market responsibility for such 'private' ends. As for virtue, it increasingly became a personal quality that revealed itself in private interactions rather than public policy. Eventually, indeed, the concept of virtue was totally trivialized by its nearly exclusive association with women's sexual purity.

Domesticity offered the man a temporary escape from competition, a 'sanctuary of domestic love,' 'a quiet refuge from the storms of life,' 'a hallowed place' to 'sweeten his labors.' 'It is at home,' declared one New England pastor, 'where man seeks refuge from the vexations and embarrassments of business.' The family was the place where men could put aside the armor they had donned for the brutal world outside. Men 'become hackneyed by the rough and rude business of the world, our feelings become coarse and less delicate, and less minute'; they must go home to women for refinement and solace. In a world of competition and disappointment, the love of women produced 'the most exquisite and refined happiness which the frail condition of man will allow us in this world.' Woman's love was also presented as a sort of consolation prize to those who could not make the grade – 'For though you're nothing to the world, your'e [sic] ALL THE WORLD TO ME.'[9]

But woman's dependency within the family became justification and incentive for man's absorption in the market. Adam Smith's famous trust in the self-interest of the butcher and baker was based on the assumption that male workers were inspired (or required) to provide for their families: the invisible hand of the marketplace worked because men needed to fill the outstretched hands of their dependants. This function of women in the family was recognized in 1840 by the author of an article entitled 'Get Married': 'If you are in business, get married, for the married man has his mind fixed on his business and his family, and is more likely of success.' Marriage was proof that men were willing to accept the responsibilities of steady work: the unmarried man, warned one women's magazine quite accurately, 'is looked upon with distrust. He has no home, no abiding place, no anchor to hold him fast, but is a mere piece of floatwood, on the great tide of time.'[10]

The thought of the little woman at home was a powerful reproach to the man who slacked off; it also provided a comforting excuse for those troubled by their increasing individualism or competitiveness. Repudiation of traditional responsibilities to community or social inferiors could be seen not as a denial of the pervasive obligation system of precapitalist society, but as a necessary aspect of social responsibility – the need to provide for one's immediate dependants. Dependence that was no longer acceptable in the poor became an admirable, even socially necessary, quality in the wife. Henry Ward Beecher offered this ingenious answer to anyone who might doubt the morality of withdrawing from wider social obligations:

> The family is the digesting organ of the body politic. *The very way to feed the community is to feed the family. This is the point of contact for each man with the society in which he lives.* Through the family chiefly we are to act upon society. *Money contributed there is contributed to the whole.*[11]

Within the family, the wife poured 'healing oil . . . upon the wounds and bruises' that her husband brought home from the workplace, but she did not encourage him to fight for better safety standards on the job. The man's 'refuge' was in fact only a way station where he regained his determination to put up with the strains of the capitalist workplace: 'If all is well at home we need not watch him at the market. One will work cheerfully for small profit if he be rich in the love and society of the home.' An 1834 essay made perfectly explicit this role of the wife in facilitating her husband's adjustment to the market:

> when his proud heart would resent the language of petty tyrants . . . from whom he receives the scanty remuneration for his daily labors, the thought that she perhaps may suffer thereby, will calm the tumult of his passions, and bid him struggle on, and find his reward in her sweet tones. . . .[12]

As mother, too, the domestic woman served the needs of capitalism even while she tried to shield her children from its coarseness. To women fell the task of molding a new personality that could muster the self-discipline necessary for accumulating capital or developing the reputation required for a responsible job while simultaneously shaking off older restraints against individual ambition. Mothers had to teach their sons the class-specific values that would be challenged by some of their associates in the outside world; lest the sons forget, mothers had to teach their daughters how to remind men of those values.

In warning young men about the pitfalls of bad company, mothers trained their sons to distrust everyone outside the family circle – and therefore to feel justified in competing with them. The example of the mother's emotional self-abnegation prepared sons for the self-sacrifice that was required of an aspiring entrepreneur, while consciousness of the emotional debt owed to their mothers often excused the most ruthless behavior in the business world: 'I did it all for you' was generally sufficient to quiet a woman's reproach to her son or husband for uncharitable behavior to neighbors or workers. This role of motherhood can be seen in the life of the industrialist Benjamin Franklin Newell, who in later years recalled how his mother's very fear of the outside world inspired him to succeed in it:

> How well do I remember in the late hours of the night ... she would come to my bedside, and kneeling with overflowing heart pour out her soul in prayer that God would preserve her darling boy from the snares so thick around him. ... How many times I wished that I were older, and had some good work so that I could support her.

Similarly, domestic novelists who condemned money-grubbing also portrayed a son's desire to earn money for his mother as one of the most touching tributes to her sway over his affections.[13]

Mothers used the powerful lever of their self-sacrifice to inspire the filial obedience that had once flowed automatically, if not necessarily lovingly, from the simple fact of parental control over property. Disobedience in colonial days had been restrained by the dependence of each individual on the goodwill, or at least the tolerance, of neighbors and community. As work and community ties unraveled – and before conformity could be inculcated through public education and mass media – it seemed that only emotional ties could restrain deviant or disobedient behavior. Lydia Sigourney proclaimed in 1838 that the mother had an urgent new duty:

> Insubordination is becoming a prominent feature in some of our principal cities. ... Let her come forth with vigour and vigilance, at the call of her country, not like Boadicea in her chariot, but like the mother of Washington, feeling that the first lesson to every incipient ruler should be, 'how to obey.'[14]

In 1856, the Abolitionist Lydia Maria Child commented on why she declined to devote any attention to marriage reform: 'I am so well aware that society stands over a heaving volcano, from which it is separated by the thinnest possible crust of appearances, that I am afraid to speak or to think on the subject.' Women, declared one antebellum newspaper editor, were 'God's own police.'[15]

Female religious activities as well as maternal ties played an important function here. Wives of merchants, master craftsmen, and mill owners often directed religious charities or educational activities that involved them in intimate relations with women of the lower classes. While their intentions may have been quite sincere, these women nevertheless reinforced class differences. The main functions of charitable training and education were to fill lower-class occupations and to teach the moral necessity of acquiring new work habits and repudiating dependence on charity. In Rockdale, for example, the manufacturers relied on the Sunday school both to compensate for the mill's anti-educational atmosphere and to teach the morality of punctuality and obedience. The clergy responded satisfactorily: 'Instead of demanding of the manufacturers that they reform their factories, they demanded of the workers that they recast their own thinking along lines that would render factory reform unnecessary.' Manufacturers' wives and daughters played an indispensable role in imparting this message to the children of mill workers.[16]

Women's work in charity, education, and religion also saved their husbands the private or state expense of funding such needed social services. Modern emphasis on the 'growth' and 'feminization' of the service sector in the twentieth century ignores the fact that women comprised a very large service sector in the nineteenth century, only not for wages.

Another conservative effect of domesticity lay in the way that the image of True Womanhood obscured the growing class distinctions among American families. The definition of women as homebodies allowed contemporaries – and many subsequent historians – to ignore the fact that as home and work separated, large numbers of lower-class women had to follow their traditional work out of the home. If a true woman stayed home, then female workers by definition forfeited all right to consideration because of their sex. 'It is no accident,' suggests Gerda Lerner, 'that the slogan "woman's place is in the home" took on a certain aggressiveness and shrillness precisely at the time when increasing numbers of poorer women *left* their homes to become factory workers'[17] – or, even more frequently, to become domestics in *other* women's homes, a job that accounted for half of all female waged employment as late as 1870.

Faye Dudden argues that such household workers changed from 'help' to 'domestics' in the 1830s. Formerly, the hired girl was usually from another household in a functioning community network. She did productive work as well as personal service and shared most household activities, including meals. But after the 1830s working women whose family background gave them the option to work in shops or factories usually did so, and those who went into service were less likely to share community networks with their employers. At the same time, employers increasingly sought personal services from their servants rather than con-tributions to household production. They demanded longer hours, more work discipline, and a stricter separation of tasks for mistress and maid. Indeed, notes Christine Stansell, 'the cult of domesticity and its attendant notions of the "womanly" became forms of labor discipline.'[18]

The 'separation' of home and economy for middle-class women depended on the market's creation of a class of women available for low-paid and low-status domestic work; middle-class women increasingly used market standards in hiring, training, and paying these women. This exacerbated class differences not only among women but also among children: the prolonged childhood of middle-class youths often depended on the early maturity of young servant girls who worked grueling hours to create the middle-class 'oasis.'

If the construction of a domestic oasis for the middle class depended on a labor force created by competition in the public economy, the hegemony of domestic ideology also required the very market that its proponents claimed to scorn. The domestic sentimentalism of nineteenth-century America, Ann Douglas points out, involved 'the exhibition and commercialization of the self.' It was an escape from the market that had to be bought. Emotion, the supposed counterweight to market relations, became the runaway bestseller in the market. 'It is worth remembering that the sales of all the works by Hawthorne, Melville, Thoreau, and Whitman in the 1850s did not equal the sales of one of the more popular domestic novels.'[19]

The preaching of private domestic virtues became a public, commercial act. Modern movies and television shows that spawn products such as Rambo, He-Man, and She-Ra figurines were anticipated by domestic novels that gave rise to steamboats, cigars, academies, drinks, and lines of clothing named after their heroines and titles. The ladies' friends who advised women to protect their families from the ugliness of ambition and commercial speculation themselves went into business, writing articles, editing magazines, selling their novels, even conducting public classes and lecture tours on the need for (other) women to stay home – though there is evidence that they were quite ambivalent about these activities.[20]

As Christopher Lasch has commented: 'From the moment the conception of the family as a refuge made its historical appearance, the same forces that gave rise to the new privacy began to erode it. . . . The so-called privatization of experience went hand in hand with an unprecedented assault on privacy.'[21] Women were expected to shield the home from the market and impart traditional values, unsullied by commercial life, but increasingly women learned such skills and values from commercial, mass-circulation books and sermons. Women, supposedly protected from the ravages of the marketplace, became particularly susceptible to the influence of mass-produced sentiments. In its very insistence on the separation of work and home, the cult of domesticity brought barter into the realm of private life. Woman had to convince man that her love was sufficient reward for her keep.

The cult of domesticity also played a political role supportive of the emerging capitalist order. The republican ideology of the early national period, especially in the North, had been based on the material reality of a large population of freeholders who owned enough property to guarantee their independence, but not enough to tempt them into idleness or exploitation of others. The cult of domesticity represented a transformation and abstraction of the artisan republic. In the gendered republic, equality came to be seen as residing less in the distribution of property than in the distribution of middle-class domesticity; defense of equality involved not an attack on the power of privileged adults but merely a rejection of 'aristocratic' or 'dependent' notions of child-rearing. The commonality of women's roles *within* different households came to stand for the kind of equality *among* households that male property and work relations no longer pretended to express.

Liberal capitalist theory denied differences among men by redefining property in terms of self-ownership: all men were equal because they owned their own labor; if a man alienated his own labor, he had only himself to blame.[22] The cult of domesticity reinforced this new definition of equality in an interesting way. Women were redefined in terms of their reproductive properties; all men could be equal if they possessed a wife and mother who fulfilled their womanly duties. The cult of domesticity, as Trollope complained, forced the wives of rich men as well as poor to engage in household chores; it thereby suggested that there were no real differences among families in America. The assignment of one behavior pattern and image to all women allowed men to be defined not by their class but by their non-femininity.

Domesticity and Male Dominance

The cult of domesticity did not endorse male dominance any more than it explicitly celebrated capitalist competition. Women used the doctrine of separate spheres to gain moral leverage within the family. Domesticity gave women more control over their reproduction and their sexual relations with their husbands. Domestic ideology was also linked to an expansion of educational opportunities and property rights for women during the first half of the nineteenth century. It has been estimated that in 1780 women's literacy in the Northeast was half that of men's; by 1850 it was essentially the same. New roles for women opened up in religion and popular culture, while older images of women as sexually evil or socially disruptive disappeared from tracts on the nature of woman. European visitors to America invariably remarked on the chivalry exhibited by American men toward women, the care that was taken to protect them from physical discomfort, the thousand courtesies extended them in social situations. 'I have nowhere seen woman occupying a loftier position,' enthused de Tocqueville, and even the acerbic Harriet Martineau admitted that 'marriage is in America more universal, more safe, more tranquil, more fortunate than in England.'[23]

Unlike biological rationalizations for the place of Blacks, theories of woman's separate nature were not simply imposed on women but developed as a dialectic between men and women seeking to explain and come to terms with their new positions in society. The assignment of all women to a special place by virtue of their sex held out the promise of privilege to women who had had no opportunities to be exceptional as individuals. Woman's monopoly of spiritual authority, for example, suggested a reversal of Milton's famous line: she for God only, he for God in her.

Domesticity was no simple gloss for female passivity. In the early period of republican and evangelical womanhood, the 'delicacy of American ideas' did not preclude women from taking a rather tough-minded approach to their side of the division of labor. Moral Reform Societies and Maternal Associations pulled women out of the home to carry on their female labors, and in the 1830s some Moral Reformers adopted an extremely militant tone. Thus the New York Female Moral Reform Society resolved 'that the licentious male is no less guilty than his victims,' and actually printed the names of men suspected of sexual immorality: 'We think it proper even to expose names, for the same reason that the names of thieves and robbers are published, that the public may know them and govern themselves accordingly.'[24]

Frances Trollope was profoundly shocked by the willingness of American women to confront men over such issues. It indicated to her that their 'ultra refinement was not very deep seated.' As example, she related the story of 'a young married lady, of *high standing* and most fastidious delicacy,' who had violated Trollope's ladylike standards of etiquette by stepping outside her home to shame a male acquaintance when he attempted to patronize a nearby brothel.[25]

Even less assertive expressions of female morality were often formulated in ways that emphasized the superiority of women's sphere. 'Our homes — what is their corner-stone but the virtue of a woman, and on what does social well-being rest but in our homes?' asked *Godey's Lady's Book* in 1856:

> Let our temples crumble and capitals of state be levelled with the dust, but spare our homes! Man did not invent, and he cannot improve or abrogate them. A private shelter to cover . . . two hearts dearer to each other than all in the world; high walls to exclude the profane eyes of every human being; seclusion enough for the children to feel that mother is a holy and peculiar name – this is home. . . . Here the church and state must come for their origin and support.[26]

Nevertheless, domesticity posed no serious challenge to male privilege and in certain areas even gave it a new lease on life. If the domestic family was a lower-middle-class creation that served the cause of capital in important ways, it was also a largely female creation that served the needs of men. Certainly, the cult of domesticity allowed a number of women to carve themselves out a special sphere in republican America. But the Victorian view of gender did not challenge female subordination in society, and the emergence of a separate women's culture – however much it was put to use by individual women, or even by radicals – should not be romanticized.

There were important trade-offs for the decline of patriarchal power in the early nineteenth century, and sharply defined limits to the spread of women's influence. One problem was that as men ceded religion to women, they also denied the centrality of religion in public life. Even in 1832 Frances Trollope observed: 'I never saw, or read of any country, where religion had so strong a hold upon the women, or a slighter hold upon the men.'[27] The feminization of American religion was also, despite periodic revival fervor, its marginalization.

Women's privileges, moreover, were often explicitly opposed to their rights. Domestic writers warned women that attempts to exercise 'authority' would lead to loss of 'influence,' with dire consequences. Harriet Martineau complained: 'Indulgence is given her as a substitute for justice. Her case differs from that of the slave . . . just so far as this; that the indulgence is large and universal, instead of petty and capricious.' Even de Tocqueville admitted that American women 'are confined within a narrow circle of domestic life, and their situation is in some respects of extreme dependence.'[28]

Another problem was that the undeniable expansion of woman's rights as wife and mother served a function analogous to that of a dowry: acceptance of those gifts constituted a quitclaim on the rest of the democratic estate. Michael Grossberg comments that women's exclusion from the economy and polity 'helped women gain a foothold in the law in the form of protections for their domestic responsibilities.

Yet that very homebound role imposed severe limitations on the extent of married women's overall legal rights and enhanced judicial power over family life.' Even the new preference for maternal custody of children 'remained a discretionary policy . . . [that] could be easily revoked any time a mother did not meet the standards of maternal conduct decreed by judicial patriarchs.' As Cott remarks, 'In opening certain avenues to women because of their sex, [domesticity] barricaded all others.'[29]

Women's culture developed in the interstices of men's economy and polity. While we may admire the vigor that allowed it to grow and the beauty it created, we should recognize that large sections of the plant were deformed. W.E.B. DuBois saw the essence of slavery as 'the enforced personal feeling of inferiority . . . the submergence below the arbitrary will of any sort of individual.' For all its romanticization of women, the cult of true womanhood was based upon just such a submergence. Thomas Dew explained how woman needed to adapt her personality to the realities of her dependence:

> She must rely upon the strength of others; man must be engaged in her cause. How is he to be drawn over to her side? . . . It must be by conformity to that character which circumstances demand for the sphere in which she moves; by the exhibition of those qualities which delight and fascinate – which are calculated to win over to her side the proud lord of creation, and to make him an humble suppliant at her shrine.[30]

But male worship of such behavior constructed an ideal type that did not admit any of the exceptions or inconsistencies normally allowed a goddess. It was not women in their variety and individuality who were cherished, but the idea of Woman. Writing in 1839, Charles Francis Grund showed an acute perception of just how critical this difference was:

> . . . American ladies are worshipped; but the adoration consists in a species of polytheism, in which no particular goddess has a temple or an altar dedicated to herself. Whenever an American gentleman meets a lady, he looks upon her as a representative of her sex; and it is to her sex, not to her peculiar amiable qualities, that she is indebted for his attentions.[31]

American women were respected and protected only in so far as they represented to society's satisfaction the domestic ideal of womanhood. In personal terms, this meant that a wife who departed from her role could expect little understanding from a husband who loved not her individuality but her ideal image. In social terms, it meant that the needs and demands of women workers, whose numbers were growing at the same time as Woman was being defined exclusively in terms of the home, could be ignored.

Even improvements in education and property rights to some extent benefited middle- and upper-class women at the expense of working ones. The first guarantees of property rights to married women applied only to property brought to the marriage; wages earned after marriage were exempted. Women who achieved contented domesticity or who extended domestic values into the public sphere through moral reform work and writing (even women's rights organizing) depended upon the cheap labor of servant women. And the removal of older disruptive, sexually aggressive images of womanhood from middle-class women resulted in their projection onto lower-class women: 'As propertied women began their ascent into republican motherhood, laboring women became the receptacle for all the unsavory traits traditionally assigned their sex.'[32]

For both the lower-class woman who could not live up to it and the middle-class woman who could not live down to it, the new definition of womanhood bestowed only limited privileges. Fond paternalistic indulgence of women who conformed to domestic ideals was intimately connected with extreme condemnation of those who were outside the bonds of patronage and dependence on which the relations of men and women were based. A good example of the other side of domesticity can be found in a recent study of crime in an early industrial city: although women were arrested less frequently than men, they were sent to jail more often and for longer terms than men convicted of the same crimes. In the eighteenth century, to wear one's blue stockings had meant to go someplace dressed informally for witty conversations; by the nineteenth century the word 'bluestocking' referred to a pedantic woman, usually an old maid, whose activities were ludicrous at best and at worst a mockery of women's most sacred duties. Unconventional women were 'only semi-women, mental hermaphrodites,' declared Henry Harrington in the Ladies' Companion.[33]

Gone were the popular seventeenth- and eighteenth-century farces about physical and verbal marital battles, featuring sharp-tongued scolds who abused their husbands and lewdly offered to give them horns if they showed any 'inability.' Gone was the casual acceptance of male domination, by violence if necessary, to control such behavior. But in their place came woman's domination by her own biology. The medical profession, in fact, helped to establish itself in America by churning out theories about the biological incapacities – and innate domestic urges – of women. By 1847 Dr Charles Meigs was explaining to his male gynecology class that woman 'has a head almost too small for intellect and just big enough for love.'[34]

As the woman's world came to be seen as alien to that of the political and economic marketplace in which men moved, so women also came to be seen as somehow more primitive than men. Tables and graphs were developed to demonstrate the physical inferiority of woman's brain and the weakness of her constitution. If some men attempted to soften the effect of this by stressing the admirable side of woman's primitiveness, the fact remains that woman was seen as closer to and more controlled by nature than man, somewhat like Rousseau's noble savage.

Woman's exclusion from republican politics thus came to be viewed as due to her domination not by men but by her sexual organs. In 1849 Dr Frederick Hollick announced: 'The Uterus, it must be remembered, is the *controlling* organ in the female body, being the most excitable of all, and so intimately connected, by the ramifications of its numerous nerves, with every other part.' As Professor M.L. Holbrook summed up the research between 1820 and 1870, 'It is as if the Almighty, in creating the female sex, *had taken the uterus and built up a woman around it.*'[35]

The equation of womanhood with the womb was so pervasive that American doctors were shocked when a British physician reported in 1864 that sterility could be the fault of the male; this fact had been well known to the Puritans. Ironically, however, the idea that women's nature flowed from their reproductive organs often led to medical interference with those organs. Women who were unable to exhibit the calm sexlessness required of the 'true woman' were subject to the violations of male gynecologists who sought to fight fire with fire by cauterizing women's sexual organs as a treatment for hysteria. Clitoridectomy (removal of the woman's clitoris), initiated in England in 1858 by Dr Isaac Brown, was hailed by many American doctors as a cure for nervous disorders. Ovariotomy, removal of the ovaries, became an accepted form of surgical treatment for female personality disorders: 'Some doctors boasted that they had removed from fifteen hundred to two thousand ovaries apiece.'[36]

And any woman who had no family to protect her, by surgery if necessary, from the biology that defined her was a fair mark for seduction and deceit. The 'dishonored' woman might well feel she had nothing more to lose by becoming a prostitute; and this was, perhaps, as satisfactory a solution as any from society's point of view, for the more 'true women' were created, the more whores were required.

In the long run, not even the 'good' woman could expect all that much from the men around her. By giving women sole responsibility for cleanliness, godliness, culture, and manners, the domestic architects had constructed people that manly men could hardly bear to be around. Frances Trollope expressed the opinion of many observers of nineteenth-century America when she commented that almost 'all the enjoyments of the men are found in the absence of women.'[37]

The role of women in upholding, renewing, and even stimulating the market behavior of men also engendered hostility. Instead of rebelling against the market that dragged them into competition, men often rebelled against the women whom they saw as pushing them there. Much American humor focused on the resistance of male characters such as Huck Finn to female attempts to 'sivilize' them. The popular character Rip Van Winkle was presented as a man who 'would have whistled his life away in perfect contentment; but his wife kept continually dinning in his ears about his idleness, his carelessness, and the ruin he was bringing on his family.'[38]

In 1850 Donald Mitchell's *Reveries of a Bachelor* expressed the ambivalence of men toward domesticity. His bachelor dreams of 'that glow of feeling, which finds its centre, and hope, and joy in HOME,' and imagines the comfort that a wife would bring him. Yet he also fears marriage, in large part because of the financial and emotional responsibilities entailed in taking a wife. His final reverie is of a perfect marriage, but one suspects the real message has been presented earlier: 'I wonder, – thought I, as I dropped asleep, – if a married man with his sentiment made actual, is after all, as happy as we poor fellows, in our dreams?'[39]

The Triumph of Conservative Domesticity

The conservative thrust of mainstream domesticity became especially apparent after 1840, as large sectors of the middle class consolidated their position in the new social order, repudiated the radical implications of perfectionism, withdrew from associations that advocated more far-reaching social changes, and began to count their blessings in comparison to the growing numbers of poor and immigrant workers. The ideology that emerged from these processes compressed the moral enthusiasm and reforming impulse of the gender-based associations of the early years into a family that took less and less responsibility for social issues, devoting itself instead to fine-tuning its own division of labor by age and by sex.

Middle-class family values and sex roles in the 1820s and 1830s, though based on a sharpened division of labor between men and women and a firm exclusion of women from the economic and political world, had not yet defined woman's role as entirely private or personal, and had involved women in associations outside the family. Despite the move toward same-class networks in such associations, moreover, the emerging middle class of the 1820s and early 1830s had too many connections to the emerging working class, which was still primarily native-born, to identify exclusively with the new capitalists against it. However, with the hardening of class lines in the 1830s, the growth of immigration, and the success of the middle-class strategy in securing new positions distinct from the proletariat, a strong conservatizing trend set in.

In the cities, a wave of strikes in 1836 and sporadic outbursts of violent protest throughout the period raised fears about the dangers of lower-class action. These were partly allayed when the Depression of 1837 defeated most early attempts at sustained labor organization. One result was that many demoralized working people seemed to accept the middle-class prescription for individual transformation and self-improvement. For the first time, spontaneous working-class revivals and temperance movements sprang up; yet these movements developed a distinctive working-class approach. They were more secular than their middle-class equivalents, put more emphasis on mutual aid and insurance, and turned a hard edge against reformers who preached from above. Middle-class dominance of social activism was further threatened by the evolution of nativism, whose Protestant and native-born emphasis appealed to the middle class but whose tactics and rhetoric often turned as sharply against employers and evangelists as against immigrants. Meanwhile, a minority wing of the evangelical movement took ideas of individual perfection to the logical extreme of organizing opposition to institutions that stood in the way of human perfection. They pushed beyond moderate anti-slavery to demand immediate emancipation and personal sacrifice in the cause of reform.

All these developments encouraged the majority of the middle class to withdraw from reform activity. After 1845, middle-class spokesmen and spokeswomen projected an increasingly 'negative vision of society at large and ... discouraged involvement in social and political organizations, especially on the part of the fragile female.' Domesticity became more clearly identified with family privacy and the status quo, as 'the increasingly individualized nature of middle-class occupations' combined with middle-class concern about 'foreigners' or lower-class agitation to undermine the former sense that middle-class reformers could improve their own lives while also taking responsibility for social order and collective morality. John Higham has argued that in the 1850s the dominant culture and classes retreated from their dreams of boundless progress and turned toward retrenchment and consolidation.[40]

The social conservatism thus fostered was accelerated by the weakening of middle-class connections to the working class. The earliest factories, it will be recalled, were staffed primarily by daughters of middle-class farmers and artisans. The original mill investors tried to avoid the evils of British industrialization by setting up a paternalistic system that allowed mill work to be a temporary stage of life, preparing women for marriage or more refined jobs such as schoolteaching. But the dynamics of capitalist competition and uneven accumulation overturned these admirable objectives, and in the 1830s and 1840s employers cut wages and increased workloads. Workers responded with turnouts; companies retaliated with blacklists, strikebreakers, even evictions from company housing. Native-born women became less eager to enter the mills; employers sought labor with fewer alternatives to mill work. By 1850 one-third of the mill workers were immigrants. In the 1850s, also, earlier opportunities for job mobility and wage increases for persistent women workers declined; women who remained in the mills came from the most economically marginal families while skilled work was monopolized by native-born males.[41]

The growing association of manual labor with foreigners and skilled work with native-born Americans weakened middle-class identification with a community of fellow republicans. In the cities especially, immigration provided a pool of low-paid workers whose condition could be ascribed to their lack of middle-class values and therefore did not challenge the justice of middle-class privileges.

And there were indeed some real privileges, as the middle-class strategy of the 1820s and 1830s paid off. In the 1850s 'the sons of artisan and shopkeeper fathers shifted to professional and white-collar stations within the American middle class.' The majority of native-born Uticans found middle-class occupations whose working conditions and levels of consumption were qualitatively better than those of the new working class. In Philadelphia, the 'reshuffling' of occupations from 1830 to 1840 ended with the entrenchment of a new and stable middle class, as parents were able to pass on privileged access to work positions to their children. In Poughkeepsie, sons of white-collar workers were six times more likely to attain white-collar jobs than sons of blue-collar workers, and much more likely to regain such employment even after a slip.[42]

At the same time, middle-class pay rates, from public schoolteachers to engineers, rose sharply relative to working-class unskilled occupations, while 'Changes in the relative prices of consumer goods worked to favor the rich, the highly skilled, and the professional' at the expense of the urban poor. By mid century, there were qualitative differences between the housing, furnishings, and recreation patterns of middle-class consumers and those of ordinary artisans or workers.[43]

The 1840s and 1850s, accordingly, saw many middle-class individuals pull back from radical evangelism – though this, of course, only made those who refused to retreat *more* radical as they grew disillusioned with the cowardice, hypocrisy, or even complicity of those they had looked upon as leaders. Mainstream evangelical religion began to stress those elements of faith that supported the economic activities of the prudent small businessman, committed to personal integrity in his contracts with others but unconcerned about the larger implications of his behavior. The old notion of spiritual calling was increasingly conflated with the secular notion of a man's vocation; and success at this vocation, so long as it was achieved without sin, became equated with morality. Horace Bushnell, who had made the personal leap from a corporate household economy to a professional job, also made the ideological leap from revival enthusiasm to Victorian complacency. God, he assured his congregation, had invested in humanity's future like 'a banker whose fund is in.'[44]

Increasingly, moral reformers abandoned their attempts to transform the personality of others and contented themselves with tending to their own souls. When lesser humans proved 'morally unfit' to make the economic and social adjustments required for entry into the new middle class, many reformers turned back to reliance on the state for social control. Although middle-class women tended to be less punitive than middle-class men in the types of state action they supported, most acquiesced in the retreat from social activism. Nancy Hewitt shows that the female middle-class advocates of evangelical reform in Rochester withdrew from associations in the 1840s when the men of their class turned once more to limited political goals. Only a small group of rural, lower-middle-class 'ultraists,' from Quaker backgrounds and with few connections to the secular power structure, continued to organize collectively; they provided the constituency for the women's rights movements of the 1850s.[45]

Institutions run by men began to take over activities formerly conducted by movements of women. 'Women's auxiliaries,' comments Caroll Smith-Rosenberg, 'which at the height of the revivals had assumed innovative and autonomous roles, relinquished leadership to male societies. Formerly iconoclastic and radical women's organizations now began to glorify the home and act in ways that recognized and ultimately reinforced new class patterns.' Women began to be identified by their husbands' first as well as last names, a practice 'almost unheard of' in the 1830s, while men even took over women's ceremonial roles on public occasions. The few times women had formerly spoken to mixed audiences, such as when presenting a flag to a new militia company, were now turned into occasions for addresses on *behalf* of 'the fair sex.'[46]

Finally, motherhood was detached once more from religion and a more secular version of the Christian home appeared. Bushnell, for example, 'upgraded the role of family influence and downgraded that of the revival in shaping character,' substituting 'an ideal of gradual, evenly paced development for that of radical change.' Moral reform societies that had sought total social regeneration in the 1830s moderated their rhetoric, turned inward to the home, and placed their hopes in maternal influence rather than a public assault on vice: 'A view of familial patterns as the preeminent source of poverty moved to the center of the reformers' etiology, displacing the evangelical belief in the defective [but redeemable] moral character of the individual as the fundamental cause.'[47]

All this tended to tame and domesticate women's religious activities. In many cases, indeed, woman's religious commitment came to be explained in almost the same terms as her sewing: 'Religion is just what woman needs. Without it she is ever restless or unhappy.' 'Religion . . . gives her that dignity that best suits her dependence.' By 1867 Henry Ward Beecher could have the protagonist of his novel, Norwood, remark that the family table was 'a kind of altar, a place sacred and so to be made as complete in its furnishings as may be,' an approach that completely collapsed woman's commitment to religion into her domestic duties.[48]

Of course, women were not simply objects of these changes but were among the primary architects of the new conservative values. Catharine Beecher and her father Lyman Beecher were both wary of the radicalism that evangelicism could unleash, in encouraging people to replace community norms by individual conscience in guiding social interactions, but it was the daughter who came up with the clearest way of confining entrepreneurship to the business world and separating it from morality. She conceptualized morality as peculiarly feminine but also as essentially passive. It was not moral fervor but 'submission, purity, and domesticity . . . that placed women closer to the source of moral authority and hence established their social centrality.'[49] This new definition of domesticity did indeed give women elevated authority within the home, but it involved a repudiation of their active role in social reform.

Beecher stripped women's moral quality of its potential radicalism by focusing it on personal comportment, especially the ability to resist temptation, rather than on social relations and reform work. Indeed, her morality allowed economically comfortable Americans to feel self-righteous rather than morally uncomfortable about their success because they had more temptations to overcome than did the poor. 'One could . . . experience a higher level of moral activity,' remarks Kathryn Sklar, 'by choosing, for example, between an untrimmed muslin shirt and a more highly desired lace-trimmed muslin shirt than by giving one's unnecessary clothes away to the poor. It was the temptation overcome that mattered, not the virtue left undone.'[50]

Such morality, divorced from religious enthusiasm, social reality, or even rigorous logic, lacked a firm foundation. If restraint in one's own consumption could substitute for charity, attention to personal comportment could easily shade into preoccupation with personal appearance. A new interest in fashion and beauty grew up alongside – and occasionally even overshadowed – the concern for individual character. Sarah Josepha Hale, for example, had founded the *Ladies Magazine* in 1828 with a powerful vision of woman's moral superiority, urging women to create a 'nobler sphere' than men's, 'purer, more excellent, more spiritual.' In 1837, however, her magazine merged with *Godey's Lady's Book*, and woman's sphere began to be both more sharply limited and somewhat trivialized. By the 1860s, 'fashion plates filled the first 24 pages of the 100-page *Lady's Book*.'[51]

By mid century women such as Hale and Beecher had lined up with the emerging publishing industry to put forward the official, mass-produced version of conservative domesticity. They rejected communal controls over economic behavior or social activism in the cause of morality, but placed woman at the center of the domestic sphere and the family. From that center, they argued, morality could spread forth to encompass the rest of society without the necessity for social activism.

The Middle-class View of Women and the Family at Mid Century

The definition of sex roles and family life that became dominant from the 1850s built upon conceptions of male–female differences and oppositions between home and world that had been formulated in the early nineteenth century. 'The Americans,' remarked de Tocqueville, as early as 1835, 'have applied to the sexes the great principle of political economy which governs the manufactures of our age, by carefully dividing the duties of man from those of woman so that the great work of society may be better carried on.'[52] But the description of women's duties was increasingly tilted away from social engagement and toward romanticization of home and motherhood. The tough-minded female morality that had shocked Frances Trollope tended to subside into sentimentalism and personalism. To man were assigned all the characteristics appropriate for survival in the world of business; to woman were assigned all the emotions and activities that could no longer be admitted into public discourse. Women became the custodians of the 'natural' rhythms and markers of life – birthdays, anniversaries, deaths – and the 'natural' feelings that accompanied these. And almost in proportion as women adopted roles that eschewed social action, so did they redefine their domestic sphere in grandiosely sentimental terms.

As middle-class values and behavior patterns idealizing the independent household lost their real base in a community of relatively homogeneous free producers, the values became more and more artificial. Age and sex roles lost their connection to active class formation and were reduced to abstract stereotypes. Anne MacLeod suggests, on the basis of her examination of children's literature between 1820 and 1860, that by the 1850s the widening gap between the ideal and the real society led authors to turn toward 'melodrama and sentimentality': 'Dramatic illness, fortuitous meetings, unmaskings of villainy – these, rather than the slower workings of time and conscience, were the instruments of moral justice in the late fiction.'[53] Along the same lines, women writers turned to personal evocations of children's suffering or deaths to elicit reactions that broader or more difficult moral and social issues no longer seemed to compel.

Even the physical image of woman was softened and sentimentalized, as the sturdy republican mother of the early nineteenth century was increasingly replaced in the popular imagination by the pale maiden or softly rounded mother of mid-century fiction. Hawthorne had an artist's eye for the change. In *The Scarlet Letter* (1850), he described Puritan women as having 'broad shoulders and well-developed breasts' as well as 'a boldness and rotundity of speech . . . that would startle us at the present day':

> Morally, as well as materially, there was a coarser fibre in those wives and maidens of old English birth and breeding, than in their fair descendants, separated from them by a series of six or seven generations; for, throughout the chain of ancestry, every successive mother has transmitted to her child a fainter bloom, a more delicate and briefer beauty, and a slighter physical frame . . . than her own.[54]

Nevertheless, this weak being somehow managed to produce children and, she was told, here was a source of might that colonial women could never have imagined. Harriet Martineau declared of America: 'Wifely and motherly occupation may be called the sole business of women there. If she has not that, she has nothing.' But if she had that, woman was assured, she had everything. 'Well may we exclaim THE MOTHER!! Oh the significance of the word!' gushed the *Ladies' Repository* in 1842. A contributor to *The Lady's Wreath* declared in 1846: 'On the character of mothers depends, under God, the regeneration of mankind.'[55]

Motherhood was advanced as an unassailable source of power, potentially more far-reaching than man's, as well as woman's most sacred duty. 'How entire and perfect is this dominion,' Lydia Sigourney assured America's mothers, 'over the unformed character of your infant.' Another writer enthused:

> What trust, what confidence, has not God reposed in woman. To man he confides the enterprises of virtue, the labors of government, the conduct of

armies, the mysteries of science, the glorious conquests of eloquence; whilst to woman he trusts man himself.[56]

Barbara Welter has summed up the definition of the middle-class woman in the mid nineteenth century as comprising 'piety, purity, submissiveness and domesticity. Put them all together and they spelled mother, daughter, sister, wife – woman.'[57] This 'cult of True Womanhood' placed women firmly in the home and held up that home as the source of all virtue. Indeed, virtue itself became identified with woman in the home, and the conception of virtue took on private, feminine qualities – qualities that served less as the basis of public behavior than as the antithesis of it.

The secular middle-class family was increasingly cut off from public intercourse, not just conceptually but also physically. Specialized rooms emphasized the separation of family members from tradesmen and casual visitors. The placement of the stairs, for example, 'in an unobtrusive position at the side of the house rather than in a central entrance hall ... clearly implied that visitors were not welcome upstairs.' The titles of articles in women's journals of the 1840s and 1850s reflect a new emphasis on the personal role of the home, in contrast to its former political and social role: 'Woman, a Being to Come Home To'; 'Woman, Man's Best Friend'; or 'The Wife; Source of Comfort and the Spring of Joy.'[58]

The conservative thrust of domesticity was especially apparent in its impact on the working class. Christine Stansell argues that the incorporation of genteel notions of womanhood into working-class paternalism in the 1850s helped to destroy the 'mutualist, egalitarian strains of union thought' that had emerged in the 1830s, undercutting the possibilities for organizing women workers.[59] We have also seen that bonds among middle-class women were often forged on the basis of their repudiation or actual exploitation of working-class women.

Yet the very triumph of conservative domesticity generated an important oppositional movement within the middle class, due both to contradictions within the ideology of true womanhood and to the inadequacies of the conservative middle-class program for grappling with the major issue facing the northern middle class in the 1850s and 1860s – the expansion of slavery and the role of the South in the future development of America. Thus this period of middle-class consolidation also spawned a radical minority movement that pushed liberal ideology to its furthest limits and challenged the fragile balance between the exaltation of female morality and the preservation of male dominance.

The Contradictions of True Womanhood

For one thing, the Victorian image of womanhood contradicted reality at several points. The insistence on the immutability of woman's place, for example, no matter how elevated that place was held to be, stood in sharp contrast to the rapidly expanding opportunities for white men. The doctrine of separate but equal and the undeniable improvement in women's marital rights could not disguise the widening gap between the opportunities for men and women in nineteenth-century America, and this provided an objective basis for feminine discontent.

Neither did the glorification of the home entirely hide the increase in women's employment; as we saw in the last chapter, women workers in the 1830s and 1840s spoke out strongly about the conditions they faced. The women's movement did not spring directly from the labor movement, and the two were not to work together for suffrage until the end of the century, but the employment of women created an atmosphere in which declarations about woman's natural sphere rang a little hollow. So did the enslavement of black women, whose lives contradicted Victorian ideals of womanhood at all levels. Concern over this fact, coupled with shock about the sexual abuse of female slaves, led to a socially acceptable connection between domesticity and moderate anti-slavery.

Women's increased responsibility for family life created other contradictions in the lives of middle-class women. As numerous domestic authors pointed out,

> in a country where a mother is charged with the formation of an infant mind that is to be called in future to judge of the laws and support the liberties of a republic, the mother herself should well understand those laws, and estimate those liberties.

While women were not to utilize those liberties themselves, they had to teach their male children to do so; this made their role in education a vital one, despite discouragement of female learning for its own sake. The Reverend John Gardiner declared that uneducated women were more dangerous than uneducated men, because women exerted the 'most powerful influence on society, as wives, as mistresses of families, and as mothers.'[60]

It was a delicate balance. When women came into contact with new branches of knowledge – all in the name of their educational duty as mothers – they often broadened their conception of that duty. A number of colleges for women were opened in the nineteenth century, beginning with Mount Holyoke in 1837. Oberlin college admitted women in 1834 and graduated its first female in 1841. Although the motivation of administrators appears to have had much to do with providing male students with cultivated wives and preventing them from neglecting their studies in travels to find the company of women, women still benefited greatly from the expansion of educational opportunity. Lucy Stone had spent a few years in a Massachusetts sewing circle, making shirts to finance male students through theological seminary. One day she left the shirt she was working on unfinished and decided to make her own way through college. She entered Oberlin in 1843 and went on to become a leader of the women's rights movement. Another Oberlin graduate was Antoinette Brown, the first woman to earn a theology degree. Elizabeth Blackwell was denied admission to the more prestigious medical schools but received a degree from the Geneva Medical College in upstate New York in 1849 and founded the New York Infirmary for Women and Children in 1857. Maria Mitchell educated herself as an astronomer, winning public recognition after she discovered a comet in 1847. Many of these women became organizers for women's rights.

One of the major justifications for woman's confinement to the home was her moral purity, which must be passed on to her children and should not be contaminated by contact with the rough and ready world of expanding capitalism. Yet the assignment of morality almost exclusively to women fostered a self-righteousness that was not always compatible with the ideal of feminine softness and self-effacement. The President of the Georgia Female College told the members of the 1840 graduating class, 'I would not have you set up for reformers,' but he also defined woman's maternal role in rather aggressive terms:

> No charge of fastidious feeling ought to check her zeal when she utters her rebuke of sin. No indelicacy imputed when she levels her frown on popular vice. No boldness overstepping the limits of prudence should be set down to her account when she disdains the acquaintance and courtesies of the vicious and the dissipated.[61]

Much of Victorian sisterhood stemmed from an internalization of the *oppressive* features of the cult of true womanhood – belief in the innate emotional, moral, and intellectual differences between the sexes and acceptance of the socially assigned division of labor – yet this sisterhood forged an identification with other women and a commitment to mutual protection that was to be a mainstay of the women's rights movement. As Nancy Cott points out: 'Without such consciousness of their definition according to sex, no minority of women would have created the issue of "women's rights" '. (This self-consciousness extended to women workers as well as to middle-class women, and provided a basis for working-class sisterhood. 'We are a band of sisters,' wrote a mill operative in the *Voice of Industry* – 'we must have sympathy for each other's woes.'[62])

Veneration of the sexual division of labor not only led to female solidarity; it could also produce anti-male overtones in even the most staid defenses of domestic womanhood. As we have seen, the reconstitution of family life and gender roles in the early Jacksonian period had often involved the mobilization of militant female reform groups, which targeted male offenders with suspicious zeal. Even solitary religious contemplation may have been used as a release from the constant other-directedness of daily feminine tasks. Many observers of nineteenth-century America commented on an 'epidemic' of illness among middle-class women. Some attributed it to boredom; it is also worth noting that an invalid, by forcing men to minister to *her* physical needs, was engaging in an effective kind of role reversal. Domestic novels reinforced the Victorian ideal of womanhood but often made men the villains of the piece and occasionally, as with the works of Fanny Fern, indulged in satire or critiques of male–female relations. Failed husbands and fathers were stock figures of domestic novels and stories. Temperance societies mobilized women against tavern owners, the liquor industry, and male imbibers, all in the name of preserving the family.[63]

Romanticization of love and marriage also created stresses. New expectations about greater communication in marriage were raised just as men and women had less and less in common. Many women imbued with the cult of true womanhood found that their high ideals for a husband could not be met. In two recent studies of nineteenth-century American women, one of intellectuals and one of domestic proponents, it emerges that more of the 'true women' than the intellectuals remained single. Women who did get married often experienced a 'marriage trauma.'[64]

Even motherhood created tensions. Women, more than ever responsible for socializing children, had less contact than ever with the kind of activities their sons would engage in upon leaving home. The possibilities for overprotection or underpreparation were many, and women tended to express their anxieties in the sentimentalization of childhood deaths. In these tales, a staple of female writing and reading from the 1830s on, mothers grappled with their fears about losing their children but also indulged their fantasies about keeping them: the deaths almost invariably occurred before the child had lost his or her innocence or moved away from the mother's sphere. The temperance tale was even more open in expressing doubts about the effectiveness of motherhood: here the young man ignored his mother's teachings and broke her heart as well as ruining his own life. Tensions over maternal duties also led to numerous conflicts over methods of social and self control between traditional women's moral reform societies and associations of young men, especially clerks.[65]

These contradictions occasionally spawned radical social experiments with new kinds of family arrangements. Followers of Fourier set up more than forty utopian communities, among them Brook Farm, famous for its association with transcendentalist leaders. The Shakers, founded by Ann Lee, preached celibacy and sexual equality and had 6,000 members by 1850, organized in small groups that produced in common and shared their products. The Oneida Community in New York, founded in 1848, banned private property and attempted to break down emotional exclusiveness between man and woman, parent and child. The Mormons recognized private property but also emphasized community priorities, practiced polygamy, and appealed to those frustrated with life in the individualistic East and hostile to its elite. Thousands of people followed Brigham Young across the desert to found a new Zion in Utah.

But such experiments never attracted enough followers to affect mainstream values, and the more widespread symptoms of discontent led to few innovations. Middle-class women tended to experience their tensions as personal crises rather than social problems. Nothing in the social experience of these women, isolated as they were in narrow class and family circles, led them to a social analysis of their conflicts, far less gave them any hope of organizing to end their problems. The contradictions may have raised their stress levels, but they were not sufficient, on their own, to counter the conservative trends in domestic ideology after the 1840s.

Thus moral reform societies tended to lose their excitement and militancy as time went by. Religious and temperance workers projected themselves as prime defenders of the Victorian family, while anti-male attitudes fostered by temperance or purity crusades often became anti-immigrant or anti-working-class attitudes that united middle-class women with men of their own class. Even the most militant temperance vigilante women seldom acted on their own; they were often incited and supported by male reformers who felt that women could get away with more than men could without meeting violent opposition. Most domestic novels portrayed their heroines as triumphing through patience rather than personal initiative. Not until women were mobilized around other social issues connected with early industrialization did they learn both how to analyze their own oppression and how to organize against it. And the women who moved on to feminism did so only by *breaking* with domesticity and orthodox evangelism.[66]

The mobilization that was to cause some women to make this break was that of the anti-slavery movement. Anti-slavery sentiment and organization constituted the most notable exception to the retrenchment of the 1850s, offering some common ground for evangelical radicals and business-minded conservatives who saw the South as an obstacle to prosperity and social peace. But conservative middle-class ideology was simply unequal to the moral commitment and practical efforts necessary to oppose southern expansionism, and this offered new possibilities for the emergence of a radical current within the middle class.

The Anti-slavery Movement and Capitalist Morality

The anti-slavery movement demonstrates both the unprecedented ethical possibilities unleashed by capitalism and the limits that have continually frustrated or distorted those possibilities. The emergence of capitalism, as we have seen, discredited hierarchy and deference, weakening social controls over people's personal behavior. It opened the way toward individual striving, self-expression, and achievement. We often bemoan the decline in interdependence that accompanied the spread of individualism, but in its early form capitalist morality did not deny the need for all social ties and responsibilities, merely the inequalities and compulsions behind so many of them. Indeed, capitalism created the possibility for perceiving some social obligations as extending further than ever before imagined. For one thing, it suggested that there was a common denominator among human beings, extending beyond kin, neighbors, or religious networks. The breakdown of localism and the growth of commodity production made it possible to see ideas and people as well as goods as having a basic commensurability – and some at least came to identify that common denominator as natural rights, not cash value. The triumph of contractual relations excluded personal ties, patronization, and pity from economic behavior, but it also elevated the importance of keeping commitments. While a contract could no longer be broken by appealing to higher moral laws, changed circumstances, community custom, or personal sympathy, it could also not be evaded or weakened by distance in space or time. Capitalism eroded responsibility to non-familial dependants, but it potentially increased responsibility to strangers, because the social contract applied to all. At the same time, the physical productivity of capitalism and the increased rationality of economic decision-making led to a heightened sense that right behavior had long-term consequences and that individuals must use their new-found control over the world to help the cause of progress and enforce the social contract.[67]

All these phenomena led a heroic minority of those who accepted the new capitalist ideology of free labor and individual rights to demand the abolition of the slave trade and the emancipation of the slaves, even when this contradicted their immediate economic interests or cost them physical and social suffering. These people used the ideology of bourgeois democracy and domesticity to create an almost unanswerable argument, for Northerners, against slavery. The argument based its critique on the concept of consent of the governed and the right to one's own labor, and its call to action on the obligation to honor the social contract of republicanism. In 1833, sixty-two people met to form the American Anti-Slavery Society. By 1838 more than 1,350 local societies had been established.

The Abolitionists began as a small minority, even among those opposed to slavery. Their original strength lay among those most favorably inclined toward the new industrial order, but they were a visionary minority within this group. The constituency of the anti-slavery movement also changed over the 1830s, as many wealthy merchants and professionals withdrew, while lower-middle-class artisans and radical labor activists played a larger role.[68] After the annexation of Texas in 1845 the question of the future direction of American expansion – slave or free – became urgent, involving northerners of all classes and most political persuasions. By the end of the 1850s slavery was so unpopular that many people who twenty years earlier had condemned Abolitionist speakers as extremists viewed with approval the attack on Harper's Ferry by John Brown. In 1860, anti-slavery sentiment led to the election of Abraham Lincoln and the Republican Party.

The association between women and anti-slavery was very strong. Women workers were in the forefront of the labor movement on this question. In 1832 Lowell factory women organized a Female Anti-Slavery Society, arguing that labor had to oppose both the northern and the southern magnate – 'the lord of the loom and the lord of the lash' – and mill girls enthusiastically signed and circulated anti-slavery petitions throughout the period. Middle-class women mobilized domestic ideology and female networks to mount especially effective campaigns against slavery. The success of Harriet Beecher Stowe's sentimental anti-slavery novel *Uncle Tom's Cabin* led Abraham Lincoln to greet her with the remark, 'So you're the little woman who wrote the book that made this big war.'[69]

The anti-slavery movement appealed to women because of its connection to family issues and personal morality. But it also influenced women's consciousness by starting them thinking about the sexual degradation and exploitation of female slaves. A number of women saw parallels with slavery in their marriage relations fairly early in the movement's history, especially when Southerners defended slavery as analogous to a husband's power over his wife.[70]

Many black leaders viewed free women, black and white, as fellow victims with slaves. Frederick Douglass, for example, was an early and consistent proponent of women's rights. 'Right is of no sex,' declared the first issue of his paper, the *North Star*, which appeared in December

1847. Black women such as Frances Maria Steward, Susie King Taylor, Sarah Redmond, Anna Douglass, Charlotte Forten, Mary Ann Shadd, and Frances Ellen Watkins Harper were particularly effective Abolitionist leaders, and Stewart made a point of connecting the issues of racial and sexual equality. For their part, white women often took a surprisingly progressive stance relative to their compatriots in opposing racial discrimination. In 1839, for instance, more than 14,000 women signed a petition to the Massachusetts legislature asking for the repeal of state laws that discriminated against Blacks and prohibited interracial marriage. In 1837 the Anti-Slavery Convention of American Women resolved:

> ... that it is ... the duty of abolitionists to identify themselves with these oppressed Americans by sitting with them in places of worship, by appearing with them in our streets, by giving them our countenance in steam-boats and stages, by visiting them in our homes and encouraging them to visit us, receiving them as we do our white fellow citizens.[71]

But most immediately decisive in the emergence of the women's movement from the Abolition movement was the simple fact that women had to fight for their own rights simply in order to fight for the slave's. When Angelina Grimké's future husband suggested that she leave the woman question to others and talk on slavery alone, she wrote back: 'Can you not see that woman *could* do, and *would* do a hundred times more for the slave if she were not fettered?' As the feminist and Abolitionist Abby Kelley wrote: 'We have good cause to be grateful to the slave for the benefits we have received to *ourselves*, in working for *him*. In striving to strike his irons off, we found most surely, that *we* were manacled *ourselves*.'[72]

In 1840 a fight erupted in the American Anti-Slavery Society over the election of Kelley to a business committee. Those opposing women's right to play a public leadership role seceded from the organization and formed their own anti-slavery society. Meanwhile, a worldwide anti-slavery convention had been called in London. The American Anti-Slavery Society sent Charles Remond and Lucretia Mott, along with Wendell Phillips and William Lloyd Garrison. Seven other women were also named as delegates.

Phillips opened the convention proceedings from the floor by proposing that all persons with credentials be seated, and the debate began. Opponents of the motion declared that disorder would reign supreme in the world if God's will were violated by the admission of female delegates. The supporters of women's rights lost and women were admitted as guests only, made to sit in a screened-off visitors' gallery. William Lloyd Garrison, scheduled to be a main speaker, found this situation when he arrived late to the meeting. He refused to participate in the formal sessions of the convention and seated himself with the women in the observers' area as a gesture of solidarity.

Lucretia Mott and Elizabeth Cady Stanton, who met for the first time at this convention, were convinced by the events there that a movement was needed to organize specifically for women's rights. Although Abby Kelley, Lucy Stone, and the Grimké sisters had been speaking for women's rights for some time, the first convention devoted entirely to women's rights came out of this meeting. Sponsored by Mott, Stanton, Ann McClintock, and Martha Wright, it took place at Seneca Falls in 1848. While the meeting was small and largely limited to readers of the *Seneca County Courier*, the only paper in which it was publicized, this was a historic convocation, whose statement of principles was to serve as a base for future organization. The convention was continued two weeks later in Rochester.[73]

Between 1850 and 1860 a national women's rights convention was held every year except 1857. Abolitionist leaders, both black and white, were the best supporters of women's rights. The first National Women's Rights convention was attended by Frederick Douglass, William Lloyd Garrison, Wendell Phillips, S.S. Foster, and Sojourner Truth. Associations of Colored Freemen regularly endorsed woman suffrage from 1848 on. In 1853 Douglass decided against renaming his Abolitionist paper *The Brotherhood* because such a name 'implied the exclusion of the sisterhood.'[74] Also in 1853 Abolitionists supporting women's rights began to be joined by some temperance workers, after the temperance movement experienced a split over the role of women similar to that in the anti-slavery forces. The movement entered the Civil War with a unified stand against slavery and for women's rights.

Reconstruction and the Demise of the Radical Coalition

During the Civil War, women's rights leaders formed the Woman's National Loyal League to fight for an unconditional end to slavery, gathering 400,000 signatures for immediate emancipation. Abolitionists helped organize black military units during the war and opened new schools to serve former slaves during Reconstruction. Southern Blacks flocked to such schools, moved their rich religious and community life out into the open, took an active role in Republican politics, resisted plantation owners' attempts to reimpose gang labor, and sought ways to gain and work their own land.

In 1865, however, President Andrew Johnson ended land redistribution, allowing pardoned Confederate leaders to recover their land. In the same year the Ku Klux Klan and other terrorist groups began to operate throughout the South, assassinating, torturing, or otherwise intimidating both Blacks and whites who did not support the Democrats. Local Republican electoral victories and reforms began to be reversed.

Republicans tried to stem the resurgence of the planters by passing the Civil Rights Act of 1866 and proposing the Fourteenth Amendment, which penalized any state that denied suffrage to its male citizens by reducing its representation proportional to the numbers denied representation. Radicals complained that the amendment still did not guarantee black suffrage in the South and would not even encourage it in the North, where the black population was too small to affect Congressional representation. A few pointed out as well that the slavish respect for property 'rights' of Confederate leaders would allow planters to reassert their power. Women's rights advocates complained that the Fourteenth Amendment also wrote the word 'male' into the Constitution, for the first time giving Constitutional sanction to women's exclusion from the polls.

In 1868 the Republicans proposed the Fifteenth Amendment (passed in 1869), which forbade states from denying suffrage 'on account of race, color, or previous condition of servitude.' Charles Sumner later wrote that he had filled nineteen pages in an attempt to avoid using the word 'male', but that the effort had come to naught. Conservative Republicans were willing to tolerate Blacks voting, which would only minimally affect their northern districts, but not women. The amendment led to a split in the reform movement, with one wing insisting that the amendment should not be supported unless it added the word 'sex,' another arguing that the amendment should be supported as a down payment on the demand for universal suffrage. The second group favored a later amendment on women's suffrage but argued that attempts to link this to the Fifteenth Amendment would only defeat the cause of both Blacks and women.

One problem was that many politicians quite consciously played off the two sides. Thus some Republicans were prepared to tolerate black men voting if this could be used to block woman suffrage, while many Democrats suddenly began to support woman suffrage, but only in so far as it could be used to defeat black suffrage. Democrats gleefully charged the Republicans with hypocrisy in putting aside their former support for woman suffrage. Republicans retorted that the Democrats wished only to embarrass the party in power and defeat all attempts at change. As Carrie Chapman Catt and Nettie Rogers Shuler later remarked: 'Time proved that the diagnoses of motives made by the rival parties against each other were both correct.' Meanwhile, however, supporters of both woman and Negro suffrage had to decide how to approach the Fourteenth and Fifteenth Amendments now that the issues had in fact been separated. Should male Negro suffrage be supported first, as Douglass urged, 'as the culmination of one-half of our demands,' or should reformers take advantage of the need for change to insist that the demands were inseparable?[75]

Many feared that it was a question of practical politics, and that if black men were not first admitted to the vote on their own, then no one would be admitted. Clara Barton later wrote: 'If the door was not wide enough for all at once – and one must, or *all* must wait, then I for one was willing that the old scarred slave limp through before me.' Wendell Philips argued that it was now 'the Negro's hour,' and he should not be held back by others whose time was not yet ripe. Frederick Douglass, declining an invitation to go to Washington to speak for women's rights in 1868, explained his priorities this way:

> The right of woman to vote is as sacred in my judgement as that of man, and I am quite willing at anytime to hold up both my hands in favor of this right. . . . [But] While the Negro is mobbed, beaten, shot, stabbed, hanged, burnt, and is the target of all that is malignant in the North and all that is murderous in the South, his claims may be preferred by me without exposing in any wise myself to the imputation of narrowness or meanness towards the cause of woman.[76]

Others, however, argued that the principle of universal suffrage could and should be won immediately. The Reverend Henry Ward Beecher declared:

> I am not a farmer, but I know that the spring comes but once a year. When the furrow is open is the time to put in your seed, if you would gather a harvest in its season. Now, when the red-hot plowshare of war has opened a furrow in this nation is the time to put in the seed. . . . Now, even if I were to confine – as I by no means do – my expectation to gaining the vote for the black man, I think we should be more likely to gain that by demanding the vote for everybody. . . . The way to get a man to take a position is to take one in advance of it, and then he will drop into the one you want him to take.[77]

Sojourner Truth pointed out that black women needed rights on their own account:

> I come from another field – the country of the slave. They have got their liberty – so much good luck to have slavery partly destroyed; not entirely. I want it root and branch destroyed . . . if colored men get their rights, and not colored women theirs, you see the colored men will be masters over the women, and it will be just as bad as it was before. So I am for keeping the thing going while things are stirring; because if we wait till it is still, it will take a great while to get it going again.[78]

At least two black male leaders also opposed dividing the question. Charles Remond declared: 'All I ask for myself I claim for my wife and sister. . . . No class of citizens in this country can be deprived of the ballot without injuring every other class. . . . Do not moral principles, like water, seek a common level?' And Robert Purvis wrote:

> With what grace could I ask the women of this country to labor for my enfranchisement, and at the same time be unwilling to put forth a hand to remove the tyranny in some respects greater, to which they are subjected?[79]

Yet the compelling tactical arguments on both sides of this question were mixed with prejudices that would seriously hamper future unity. Those who felt it was the Negro's hour often implied that women's demands were of secondary importance, if not actually frivolous. 'As you very well know,' wrote Douglass, 'woman has a thousand ways to attach herself to the governing power of the land and already exerts an honorable influence on the course of legislation.' Stanton reacted strongly against such arguments and deepened the division by making invidious comparisons between the merits of black men and white women. As long as the Black 'was lowest in the scale of being,' she wrote, 'we were willing to press *his* claims; but now . . . it becomes a serious question whether we had better stand aside and see "Sambo" walk into the kingdom first.' Although Susan B. Anthony was usually less inclined to fall back on racist arguments, she nevertheless argued in 1869 that 'if you will not give the whole loaf of suffrage to the entire people, give it to the most intelligent first. . . . If intelligence, justice, and morality are to have precedence in the Government, let the question of woman be brought up first and that of the negro last.'[80]

Perhaps the best example of intransigence on both sides was in the Kansas campaign of 1867, where the Republican legislature submitted to the voters two separate amendments to the state constitution, one for woman suffrage and one for Negro suffrage. As the campaign progressed, however, Republican politicians counterposed the black suffrage amendment to the woman suffrage amendment, and actively worked against the latter. Stanton and Anthony retaliated by accepting the support of a notorious racist, George Francis Train, and publishing his anti-Negro comments in their paper. The result of these divisive tactics was defeat for both measures.

A split in the American Equal Rights Association occurred when Stanton proposed at an 1869 convention that the group focus on getting a woman's suffrage amendment added to the Constitution, no matter what the effect of that activity on the Fifteenth Amendment. Differences over this proposal resulted in the formation of two opposing groups, the American Woman's Suffrage Association and the National Woman's Suffrage Association. The American was supported by the majority, including Lucy Stone and Julia Ward Howe. This group agreed to delay work for a woman's suffrage amendment until the Fifteenth was passed. It confined itself to propaganda work for woman's suffrage on a state level. The National, led by Anthony and Stanton, focused its energies on achieving universal suffrage, actually opposing the Fifteenth Amendment because it did not include women.

Although the National Woman's Suffrage Association is generally considered the more radical of the two groups, this characterization is not entirely accurate. Stanton and Anthony embraced a wider variety of women's causes and tactics than did the American group, which concentrated on state-by-state work for a suffrage amendment. But the National had trouble developing a consistent long-range strategy. Although it at first became actively involved in strike support work for laboring women, it often failed to see beyond the immediate anti-feminist consciousness of male unionists to the long-range congruence of interests between labor and equal rights activists. In consequence, when male unionists did not fully support women's rights, Stanton and Anthony tended to write them off, much to the distress of working women. Thus Anthony began to encourage women to learn skills by acting as strikebreakers, and the National's paper was printed in a non-union office. After this became public knowledge the National Labor Congress refused to readmit Anthony as a delegate to its next convention. Stanton promptly declared that this 'proved what *The Revolution* has said again and again, that the worst enemies of Woman's Suffrage will ever be the laboring classes of men.'[81]

By the late 1870s the leaders of both sides were cooperating again, and the two groups reunited in 1890. But the division revealed the weaknesses of the middle-class reform movement: on the part of women's rights activists, class and racial prejudice; on the Abolitionists' part, the naive assumption that granting suffrage to black men would eradicate the abuses of slavery and the power of the planters. That naiveté sprang from the limitations of the ideology behind bourgeois reform, for if the strengths of Abolitionism were those of capitalism itself, so were its weaknesses.

The Limits of Middle-class Reform

Eric Foner and others have shown that abolitionist arguments against slavery rested partly on an uncritical acceptance, even glorification, of the wage-work system. Abolitionists objected only to 'arbitrary and illegitimate power exercised by one individual over another,' not to structural economic and social inequality. Indeed, their indictment of slavery was attached to a restricted definition of freedom that ruled out traditional objections to other kinds of inequality. Garrison, for example, claimed that only the 'poor and vulger' opposed 'the opulent' simply because they were rich or were employers. Abolitionist dismissal of complaints against the wage-labor system renders quite comprehensible, if short-sighted, many northern workers' rejection of anti-slavery as a diversion from class struggle.[82]

Later, some Abolitionists came to see the need for labor reform, and before that many working people put aside their distrust of Abolitionist leaders to join the anti-slavery crusade and fight in the Civil War. But the result of the Civil War was to reinforce an old ambiguity about the 'republic.' Alan Dawley suggests that Republican-manufacturing leadership of the Civil War sidetracked the political independence of the workers' movement that had begun to develop after 1836, and Eric Foner argues:

> the anti-slavery movement, by glorifying northern society and by isolating slavery as an unacceptable form of labor exploitation, while refusing to condemn the exploitative aspects of 'free' labor relations, served to justify the emerging capitalist order of the North. . . . The choices for America came to be defined as free society versus slave society – the idea of alternatives within a free society was increasingly lost sight of.[83]

Their preoccupation only with arbitrary or illegal power meant that few radicals could conceptualize, much less implement, a program that sufficiently challenged established property relations to provide any hope of combating planter terrorism and federal indifference. Radicals had even less to say about the Depression of 1873–77 in the North and the spreading labor unrest there. The Civil War ushered in a new era of national capitalism, heavy industry, factory production, commercial farming on the basis of credit, and class conflict. By 1870, 67 per cent of Americans engaged in producing goods or services were employed by others rather than self-employed, and more than 27 per cent of these wage-earners were industrial manual workers. Republican ideology, with its dream of a society of small producers, was wholly unequipped to deal with these phenomena. As David Montgomery writes:

> Radicalism was admirably suited for the task of erecting the equality of all citizens before the law, but beyond equality lay the insistence of labor's spokesmen that as the propertyless, as factors of production, wage earners were effectively denied meaningful participation in the Republic. . . .[84]

Just as radicals were unable to go beyond the abolition of slavery to develop a program for economic equality, women's rights activists, who had braved social prejudice to defend black civil rights so long as the issue did not challenge their class privileges, had quite different attitudes toward the immigrants who actually worked for them. Elizabeth Buffum Chace, wife of a wealthy Rhode Island mill owner, had resigned from the Rhode Island Women's Club because it excluded black women; yet in the 1870s, when mill women agitated for a ten-hour day, she denounced them as 'ungrateful' and 'ignorant.' In an interesting reversal of later prejudices, she objected to the marriage of a black abolitionist man to an Irish woman because she was his social inferior.[85]

Unwilling to face the prospect of radically extending their analysis of inequality or risking their new privileges *vis-à-vis* the growing manual workforce, many middle-class people, including former activists, turned their backs on the dislocations and hardship of war and depression to explore the possibilities of the new era for their own class or family. More and more those possibilities revolved around acceptance of the wage-labor system. The capitalist structure, something new and not necessarily taken for granted in the 1830s and 1840s, became the frame of reference for most middle-class people. Towns that had opposed the first factories began to orient their growth and government around industry. Even working people who opposed 'wage-slavery' had to come to terms with the extension and consolidation of capitalist industrialization and there are signs that more workers accepted, however reluctantly, the exigencies of working to a time schedule under capitalists' terms of employment.[86] At the same time, workers' recognition of their permanent enmeshment in the wage system meant that many struggled not so much to recapture a receding artisanal past as to challenge the class relations of capitalism – providing a further incentive for the middle classes to abandon reform.

In this context, the conservative trends of the 1840s and 1850s reasserted themselves over the radical strains in abolitionist organization and agitation. The dominant middle-class ideology of the 1870s increasingly ignored the realities of capitalist expansion, becoming downright hostile to those who tried to call attention to such realities. In literature, the genteel tradition predominated up to the 1890s. Mass production of sentimental scenes by the new engraving industry made art, as Charles Dudley Warner enthused in 1872, 'the help and solace of the many.'[87] Religion turned optimistic, sentimental, and, above all, easy to live with.

In politics, middle-class reformers systematically divested themselves of responsibility for social change, turning charity over to state-run institutions, education to public schools, morality to popular preachers and Sunday schools, and economic development to the captains of industry. Edwin Godkin contrasted the 'reformer of to-day' with that of the past:

His one duty is to find out things. His father was occupied in assailing monstrous and palpable evils, and getting the government into the hands of the many; the son has no such duty. He has no abuse of any magnitude to attack which is maintained by the few for their own comfort. His work is to adjust the relations of the individuals of the great crowd to each other, so that they may be enabled to lead a quiet, and comfortable, and free life.[88]

The next two chapters explore the different 'adjustments' of middle- and working-class families in the search for a 'free life' in the Gilded Age. In chapter 7, I argue that the expansion and consolidation of a full-fledged industrial order involved an elaboration of separate spheres and a heightened reliance on distinctive family strategies for all groups, creating some similarities in ideologies of family and gender. Beneath these similarities, however, class and ethnic differences widened: in work and family organization, childhood experience, fertility rates, and domestic roles. Middle-class families became more isolated from community networks, withdrawing more completely from other classes and from public arenas. Yet these families were not entirely private, nor were they centers of individual fulfillment; they remained extremely conscious of their class functions and ties. The very idea of the family as 'refuge' reflected the limits of middle-class privacy: the family was not yet expected to be an alternative *world*. It is significant that the most vocal proponents of 'private' families were also the strongest supporters of public schools and other such institutions.

Chapter 8 turns to working-class families, which were even more closely enmeshed in class and ethnic ties. This chapter examines patterns of working-class family life, including the special problems and solutions of Black families and the seeming exceptionalism of frontier families. It concludes by discussing the consequences of the labor turmoil of 1885–86, which had far-reaching effects on community and family organization within the working class.

Notes

1. Kirk Jeffrey, 'The Family as Utopian Retreat from the City,' *Soundings* 55 (1972), p. 28; John Todd, *The Moral Influence, Dangers and Duties, Connected with Great Cities* (Northampton, MA, 1841); Cott, *Bonds of Womanhood*, p. 64.

2. Mary Kelley, *Private Woman, Public Stage* (New York, 1984), p. 302.

3. Cott, *Bonds of Womanhood*, p. 68.

4. Trollope, *Domestic Manners*, pp. 157, 280.

5. Henry Ward Beecher, *Lectures to Young Men* (New York, 1850) and *Royal Truths* (New York, 1866).

6. Lydia Maria Child, *The American Frugal Housewife* (Boston, 1833), pp. 6, 89, 90; Stansell, *City of Women*, p. 210.

7. Cott, *Bonds*, p. 69; Ryan, *Empire of the Mother*, pp. 93–4.

8. Nadine Taub and Elizabeth Schneider, 'Perspectives on Women's Subordination and the Role of Law,' in David Kairys, ed., *The Politics of Law: A Progressive Critique* (New York, 1982), p. 135, n.1.

9. Cott, p. 64; 'Essay on Marriage,' *Universalist and Ladies' Repository* (1834), p. 370; *Ladies' Book* 1 (1840), p. 331; *Southern Literary Messenger* I (1835), p. 508; Todd, *Moral Influence*, pp. 18–20.

10. *Ladies' Book*, p. 338; *The Lady's Garland* 4 (1848), p. 132.

11. William Gerald McLoughlin, *The Meaning of Henry Ward Beecher: An Essay on the Shifting Values of Mid-Victorian America, 1840–1870* (New York, 1970), pp. 115–16 (emphasis added).

12. Mary Ryan, 'Femininity and Capitalism in Antebellum America,' in Zillah Eisenstein, ed., *Capitalist Patriarchy and the Case for Socialist Feminism* (New York, 1979), p. 158; 'Essay on Marriage,' p. 371.

13. Dawley, *Class and Community*, p. 34; Louisa May Alcott, *Little Men* (New York, 1962), pp. 295–6.

14. Lydia Sigourney, *Letters to Mothers* (New York, 1838), p. 12.

15. Kirk Jeffrey, 'Marriage, Career, and Feminine Ideology in Nineteenth Century America: Reconstructing the Marital Experience of Lydia Maria Child, 1828–1874,' *Feminist Studies* 2 (1975), p. 123; Ryan, 'Femininity and Capitalism,' p. 155.

16. Wallace, *Rockdale*, pp. 306–34; Johnson, *Shopkeeper*, pp. 116–17; Ryan, 'A Women's Awakening,' p. 618.

17. Lerner, 'Lady and the Mill Girl,' p. 12.

18. Faye Dudden, *Serving Women: Household Service in 19th-Century America* (Middletown, CN, 1983); David Katzman, *Seven Days a Week: Women and Domestic Service in Industrializing America* (New York, 1978); Stansell, *City of Women*, p. 163.

19. Douglas, *Feminization*, pp. 96, 254.

20. Kelly, *Private Woman, Public Stage*.

21. Christopher Lasch, 'The Emotions of Family Life,' *New York Review of Books*, 27 November 1975, p. 40.

22. For an extended discussion of this point, see C.B. Macpherson, *The Political Theory of Possessive Individualism* (New York, 1962).

23. Daniel Smith, 'Family Limitation'; Degler, *At Odds*; Robert Griswold, *Family and Divorce*, pp. 1–17, 39–43; Kerber, *Women of the Republic*, p. 193; de Tocqueville, *Democracy in America*, vol. 2, p. 225; Harriet Martineau, *Society in America*, ed. Seymour Martin Lipset (Gloucester, MA, 1968), p. 296.

24. Carroll Smith-Rosenberg, 'Beauty, the Beast, and the Militant Woman: A Case Study in Sex Roles and Social Stress in Jacksonian America,' *American Quarterly* 23 (1971).

25. Trollope, *Domestic Manners*, pp. 137–8.

26. Woloch, *Experience*, p. 117.

27. Trollope, *Domestic Manners*, p. 75.

28. Martineau, *Society in America*, p. 292; de Tocqueville, *Democracy*, vol. 2, p. 225.

29. Michael Grossberg, 'Who Gets the Child? Custody, Guardianship, and the Rise of a Judicial Patriarchy in Nineteenth-Century America,' *Feminist Studies* 9 (1983), pp. 247, 250; Cott, *Bonds of Womanhood*, p. 201.

30. W.E.B. DuBois, *Black Reconstruction* (New York, 1956), p. 9; *Southern Literary Messenger* I (1835), p. 495.

31. Charles Francis Grund, *Aristocracy in America* (New York, 1968), p. 40.

32. Stansell, *City of Women*, p. 36.

33. Katz et al, *Social Organization*, p. 240; Susan Phinney Conrad, *Perish the Thought: Intellectual Women in Romantic America, 1830–1860* (New York, 1976), pp. 17–20; *Ladies' Companion* 9 (1838), p. 293.

34. Carroll Smith-Rosenberg and Charles Rosenberg, 'The Female Animal: Medical and Biological Views of Woman and Her Role in Nineteenth Century America,' *Journal of American History* 60 (1973), p. 334; Wertz and Wertz, *Lying-In*, p. 58.

35. Barbara Ehrenreich and Deirdre English, *For Her Own Good: 150 Years of the Experts' Advice to Women* (Garden City, 1978), p. 108; William and Robin Haller, *The Physician and Sexuality in Victorian America* (Chicago, 1974), pp. 49–50.

36. G.J. Barker-Benfield, *The Horrors of the Half-Known Life* (New York, 1976), pp. 117, 120; Ehrenreich and English, *Her Own Good*, p. 111.

37. Trollope, *Domestic Manners*. p. 156.

38. Washington Irving, *The Sketch Book* (New York, 1954), pp. 31–2.

39. Donald Mitchell, *Reveries of A Bachelor: Or, a Book of the Heart* (Philadelphia, 1893), pp. 90, 97.

40. Ryan, *Empire*, p. 39 and *Cradle*, p. 153; John Higham, *From Boundlessness to Consolidation: The Transformation of American Culture, 1848–1860* (Ann Arbor, 1969).

41. Thomas Dublin, *Women at Work: The Transformation of Work and Community in Lowell, Massachusetts, 1826–1860* (New York, 1979); Nisonoff, 'Bread and Roses'; Thomas Dublin, 'Women Workers and the Study of Social Mobility,' *Journal of Interdisciplinary History* 9 (1979).

42. Ryan, *Cradle*, p. 178; Stuart Blumin, 'Mobility and Change in Ante-Bellum Philadelphia,' in Stephan Thernstrom and Richard Sennett, eds, *Nineteenth Century Cities: Essays in the New Urban History* (New Haven, 1969), pp. 176–80; Clyde and Sally Griffen, *Natives and Newcomers*, pp. 66–83.

43. Williamson and Lindert, *American Inequality*, pp. 68, 103; Warner, *Private City*, p. 66.

44. Rowland Berthoff, *An Unsettled People: Social Order and Disorder in American History* (New York, 1971), pp. 236–7.

45. Hewitt, *Women's Activism*; Ryan, *Cradle*, pp. 145–242.

46. Smith-Rosenberg, *Disorderly Conduct*, pp. 133–4; Lebsock, *Free Women of Petersburg*, pp. xvi, 231.

47. Kett, *Rites of Passage*, p. 84; Kathryn Sklar, *Catharine Beecher: A Study of Domesticity* (New Haven, 1973); Bertha Monica Stearns, 'Reform Periodicals and Female Reformers, 1830–1860,' *American Historical Review* 37 (1962), pp. 681–4; Ryan, *Empire*, pp. 78–9, 94; Stansell, *City of Women*, p. 202.

48. Barbara Welter, 'The Cult of True Womanhood, 1820–1860,' *American Quarterly* 18 (1966), p. 153; McLoughlin, *Henry Ward Beecher*, p. 176.

49. Sklar, *Catharine Beecher*, p. 83.

50. Ibid., p. 128.

51. Lois Banner, *American Beauty* (New York, 1983); Haltunen, *Confidence Men and Painted Women*; Nancy Woloch, *Women and the American Experience* (New York, 1984), pp. 100–9.

52. De Tocqueville, *Democracy*, vol. 2, pp. 211–12.

53. Anne MacLeod, *A Moral Tale: Children's Fiction and American Culture, 1820–1860* (Hamden, CN, 1975), pp. 156, 157.

54. Nathaniel Hawthorne, *The Scarlet Letter* (New York, 1968), pp. 44–5.

55. Martineau, *Society in America*, p. 301; the *Ladies' Repository* 2 (1842), p. 63; *The Lady's Wreath* 2 (1846), p. 2.

56. Sigourney, *Letters to Mothers*, p. 10; *Southern Ladies' Book* I (June 1840), p. 322; Ryan, *Empire*, p. 50.

57. Welter, 'Cult of True Womanhood,' p. 152.

58. Clifford Clark, 'Domestic Architecture as an Index to Social History: The Romantic Revival and the Cult of Domesticity in America, 1840–1870,' *Journal of Interdisciplinary History* 7 (1976), p. 51; Welter, 'Cult of True Womanhood,' p. 163.

59. Stansell, *City of Women*, pp. 149–53.

60. *The Lady's Garland* II (1825), p. 63; Cott, *Bonds*, p. 118.

61. *Southern Ladies' Book* II (1840), pp. 66, 68.

62. Cott, *Bonds*, p. 201; Foner, *Factory Girls*, p. 90. See also Carroll Smith-Rosenberg, 'Female World of Love and Ritual.'

63. See Ehrenreich and English, *Her Own Good*, pp. 93–7, for the 'epidemic' of female illness, and Griswold *Divorce*, pp. 51–62, on women's use of invalidism as a weapon to get their way. For women's magazines that combined the cult of domesticity with occasional pleas for women's rights, see *The Rosebud* and *The Southern Ladies' Book*. On domestic novels, see Helen Waite Papashvily, *All the Happy Endings* (New York, 1956); Ann Douglas Wood, ' "The Scribbling Women" and Fanny Fern: Why Women Wrote,' *American*

Quarterly 23 (1971). An 1855 novel that broke with domestic traditions and inspired the praise of Nathaniel Hawthorne can be found in Fanny Fern, *Ruth Hall and Other Writings*, ed. Joyce Warren (New Brunswick, NJ, 1985). On the radical potential of moral reform societies, see Carroll Smith-Rosenberg, 'Beauty, the Beast, and the Militant Woman.'

64. Douglas, *Feminization of American Culture* and Conrad, *Perish the Thought*; Cott, *Bonds*, pp.76–7, 80.

65. See Ryan, *Empire*, pp. 58–70, and *Cradle*.

66. Bertha Monica Sterns, 'Reform Periodicals and Female Reformers, 1830–1860,' *American Historical Review* 37 (1962), pp. 684–5; Ian Tyrell, 'Women and Temperance in Antebellum America: 1830–1860,' p. 144; Douglas, *Feminization*, p. 157; Andrew Sinclair, *The Emancipation of the American Woman* (New York, 1965), p. 40; Blanche Hersh, *The Slavery of Sex: Feminist-Abolitionists in America* (Urbana, 1978).

67. There are many excellent discussions of the relationship between capitalist ideology and anti-slavery morality. My thinking on this question has been especially influenced by David Brion Davis, *The Problem of Slavery in the Age of Revolution* (Ithaca, 1966), and the debates over his position on the self-deception of the Abolitionists. See Thomas Haskell, 'Capitalism and the Origins of the Humanitarian Sensibility,' parts 1 and 2, *American Historical Review* 90 and 91 (1985); Howard Temperley, 'Capitalism, Slavery, and Ideology,' *Past and Present* 75 (1977); and AHR forum, with Davis, Haskell, and John Ashworth, *American Historical Review* 92 (1987). Though I accept Haskell's position about the moral progress fostered at some levels by capitalism, I do not think this invalidates the points made by Davis about self-deception or by Ashworth about class blinders (though Ashworth also criticizes the concept of self-deception).

68. John Jentz, 'The Antislavery Constituency in Jacksonian New York City,' *Civil War History* 27 (1982).

69. Karen Sacks, 'Class Roots of Feminism,' *Monthly Review* 27 (1976), p. 34; Gerda Lerner, *The Majority Finds its Past: Placing Women in History* (New York, 1979), p. 112; Ryan, *Empire*, p. 147.

70. Anne Firor Scott, 'Women's Perspective on the Patriarchy in the 1850s,' in Jean Friedman and William Shade, *Our American Sisters* (Boston, 1973), p. 151; Anne Firor Scott, *The Southern Lady: From Pedestal to Politics, 1830–1930* (Chicago, 1970); Linda Brent, *Incidents in the Life of a Slave Girl* (New York, 1973). For a southern woman's horror at the sexual aspects of slavery see Mary Boykin Chesnut, *A Diary From Dixie*, ed. Ben Ames Williams (Cambridge, MA, 1980).

71. Lerner, *Majority*, pp. 98, 124.

72. Hersh, *Slavery*, p. 22; Sinclair, *Emancipation*, p. 37.

73. The best single source for the woman suffrage movement, though it primarily reflects the view of what became the Stanton-Anthony wing of the movement, is *The History of Woman Suffrage*, ed. Elizabeth Cady Stanton, Susan B. Anthony, and Matilda Joslyn Gage (New York, 1881–1922), 6 vols. See also Carrie Chapman Catt and Nettie Rogers Shuler, *Woman Suffrage and Politics* (Seattle, 1969), Eleanor Flexner, *Century of Struggle: The Woman's Rights Movement in the U.S.* (Cambridge, MA, 1959) and Mari Jo and Paul Buhle, eds, *The Concise History of Woman Suffrage* (Urbana, 1978).

74. Benjamin Quarles, 'Frederick Douglass and the Woman's Rights Movement,' *Journal of Negro History* 25 (1940), p. 37, n. 9.

75. Catt and Shuler, *Suffrage and Politics*, p. 48.

76. Sinclair, *Emancipation*, p. 48; Frederick Douglass to Mrs Josephine White Griffing, September 25 1868 in 'Griffing Papers,' published by Joseph Borome in the *Journal of Negro History* 33 (1948), pp. 469–70.

77. Buhle, *Concise History of Woman Suffrage*, p. 241.

78. Ibid., p. 235.

79. Ibid., p. 244; *Life and Work of Susan B. Anthony*, pp. 257–8.

80. 'Griffing Papers,' pp. 469–70; Stanton, 26 December 1865, *History of Woman Suffrage*; Buhle, *Concise History*, p. 259. See also Stanton's protest against giving 'ignorant' immigrants and Blacks legislative priority over 'proud Saxon women': *The Revolution*, 23 April 1868, p. 249.

81. *The Revolution*, March 10 1870. But see the support for unions and strikes in the November 18 1969, issue.

82. Foner, *Politics and Ideology in the Age of the Civil War*, pp. 62–5. See also Sean Wilentz, *Chants Democratic*, pp. 263–4, 330–334; Davis, *Problem of Slavery*; Ashworth, 'Capitalism and Humanitarianism,' AHR Forum; David Lightner, 'Abolitionism, Women's Rights, Labor Reform and Evangelicalism: The Search for Connections,' *Canadian Review of American Studies* 12 (1981).

83. Dawley, *Class and Community*; Foner, *Politics and Ideology*, p. 24.

84. David Montgomery, *Beyond Equality: Labor and the Radical Republicans, 1862–1872* (New York, 1967), pp. 30, 446–7. For an excellent account of Blacks during Reconstruction, see Leon Litwak, *Been in the Storm So Long: The Aftermath of Slavery* (New York, 1979).

85. Hersh, *Slavery of Sex*, pp. 124, 128.

86. For discussion of the growing hegemony of industrial behavior, if not of industrial values, see Jonathon Prude, *Coming of the Industrial Order*, pp. 230–55.

87. Charles Dudley Warner, 'What is Your Culture to Me?' reprinted in Alan Trachtenberg, ed., *Democratic Vistas: 1860–1880* (New York, 1970), p. 343.

88. Montgomery, *Beyond Equality*, p. 382.

7

The Apex of Private Spheres, 1870–90

Middle-class reform, the major driving force of the preceding period, lost steam after Reconstruction, and the middle class increasingly acted as the bulwark of an emerging industrial economy. The new complacency of middle-class thought after the Civil War is perhaps best illustrated in the career of the immensely popular preacher Henry Ward Beecher. Beecher had come to maturity during the earlier reform period and he maintained many of his formative commitments to legal equality, supporting equal rights for both Blacks and women. But though in the 1840s he had advised young men to shun the corruption of city employment and criticized businessmen who wished to be preached a religion that 'soothes their hearts, and makes them feel pleasant,' by the 1870s Beecher's pronouncements were as soothing and pleasant as his affluent Brooklyn congregation could possibly have wished. In 1877, during the great railroad strike, Beecher justified the 10–20 per cent wage cuts decreed by the railroad companies on grounds that $1.00 a day should allow any man to support his family if he did not drink alcohol or smoke. After all, a dollar could buy plenty of bread, and water was free: 'the man who cannot live on good bread or water is not fit to live.' A few years later, Beecher was selling soap endorsements and accepting thousands of dollars in stocks and cash to write favorable editorials about the railroad companies.[1]

The pronouncements of such preachers had small appeal to working people, who acted militantly against the industrial order and, as we shall see, had a vibrant, visible alternative culture. Yet until the end of the period, the middle-class vision of America took almost no account of working-class conditions or culture. Denying their *own* experience as well as that of the poor, middle-class people enveloped themselves in a myth-ical world where success or failure was a matter of personal character in settings that almost never included a factory. The class structure consisted of decadent rich people, dissolute poor, and conscientious businessmen, clerks, or mechanics (as well as occasional bootblacks) who built decent lives by successfully combining private virtue and public competition. A central prop of this mythical world was the concept of the formative role of a nuclear family built upon universal gender roles and emotional commitments to home life.

Proper family life and gender roles, in this myth, both explained and epitomized success or failure in America. Poverty was the result of parental failure to impart good values and work habits; even infant mortality was a result of the 'ignorance and false pride' of individual mothers, equally likely to be caused by middle-class women who did not know how to dress their children as by poor women who did not know how to feed them.[2] Families, however, were not just cause of success; they were the only proper receptacle for its rewards. By the 1860s Beecher had developed the theory that spending money on the family was not only legitimate but even a form of charity, allowing 'little children, the poor, laborers, common people of all kinds' to see the kind of home that could inspire them to improve their lot:

> Whatever expenditure refines the family and lifts it into a larger sphere of living is really spent upon the whole community as well. If no man lives better than the poorest man, there will be no leader in material things.

> Fine grounds not only confer pleasure directly on all who visit or pass by, but they excite every man of any spirit to improve his own grounds.[3]

Such emphasis on the social role of the private family was the main justification for middle-class disengagement from reform during the Gilded Age. Not coincidentally, this age was also the apex of the doctrine of separate spheres – between morality and business, politics and economics, men and women. Connections between laissez-faire justifications of capitalism and the cult of domesticity were made explicit in this period, both in practice and in ideology. As is often the case, the most succinct summary of that connection came at the tail end of the period, when both laissez-faire and domesticity were under attack. As William Graham Sumner put the Social Darwinist defense against calls for government intervention to end social injustice, 'the property of men and the honor of women' were the joint bases of American society and the sole business of government was to defend both 'against the vices and passions of human nature.'[4]

The working class, though it possessed a more distinctive working-class culture than either before or since, was as yet unable to crack these middle-class myths about the nature of American society. Although working people mounted impressive local campaigns that had a strong impact on particular situations or regions, they were unable to generate sustained organizations that transcended local boundaries or challenged the fundamental assumptions of laissez-faire liberalism. Perhaps the key to the seeming hegemony of bourgeois ideology in this period, despite considerable resistance from below, lies in the coexistence of capitalist economic nationalization and centralization with extreme local, regional, and cultural differentiation. Such differentiation required families to play a very specific role by class, locality, and ethnic group, while paradoxically heightening the perception that adoption of universally valid family forms and gender roles might solve or at least alleviate much distress. The unevenness of industrialization, especially its creation of seemingly non-industrial pockets in the West, the South, immigrant communities, and slums, sometimes left the impression that problems derived not from the system itself but from local aberrations or from alien elements interfering with the system. Indeed, Alan Trachtenberg has commented that the period was characterized by a 'perception . . . that America was in the grip of alien forces,' though 'exactly who were the aliens became a bone of considerable contention.'[5]

National Expansion and Local Variation

By 1870 a core industrial area in the Northeast dominated American production and trade, and between 1870 and 1885 a complementary industrial core was built in the Midwest. Between 1870 and 1882 the railroads doubled in size and became a national system linking western and southern raw materials to eastern finance and international markets. Electricity came into use by the end of the 1870s. Mass-circulation catalogue stores such as Sears and Montgomery Ward brought urban products to rural areas, while major department stores began to change the nature of production and consumption in the big cities. Advertising remained mainly local until the 1890s, but grew in volume and importance within local markets.

The GNP increased sixfold between 1869 and 1899 and real wages grew by about 50 per cent, as this was a deflationary period in which wholesale prices fell by about 30 per cent. There was also, however, a tremendous increase in economic insecurity. Major depressions hit in 1873–88 and 1893–97, with smaller panics in 1884 and 1888. Even in good years workers faced seasonal layoffs, housing shortages, new urban diseases, and sudden unemployment. Upward occupational mobility for individuals seems to have increased, but so did downward slide. At the same time economic *rank* became more rigid, while the share of wealth held by the richest one per cent held steady or increased. The decline in opportunity for workmen to rise to a proprietorship destroyed 'a previously important form of long-distance mobility within a career . . . [while] prospects lessened for men to rise . . . in their communities when they did not begin their careers at white-collar employments.' In other words, though individuals experienced more occupational change, even improvement, this was a result of the consolidation of class structure and depended upon more clear-cut acceptance of capitalist work relations and technology.[6]

Perhaps the decisive take-off point for this consolidation was 1877. In that year federal troops were withdrawn from the South and radical reconstruction was effectively abandoned. Six years later the Supreme Court voided the Civil Rights Act of 1875, ruling that the Fourteenth Amendment did not prohibit discrimination by individuals. The great railroad strike in the North and the St Louis General Strike led the government to abandon all pretense of neutrality toward the industrial system: the unreliability of state and local militias in these struggles, due to their members' local ties with striking workers, led to the reorganization of militias on more 'professional' (less community-based) terms, and to a clear commitment from the government to provide troops against strikers. In big cities, the middle and upper classes united around programs to increase both the specialization and the efficiency of the police at repressive functions.[7]

Yet the extension of industrial capitalism, even as it affected every American, did not uniformly 'modernize' the country. The new productivity of mechanized industries created an unprecedented demand for parts and raw materials, the production of which was often not yet mechanized. Employment and exploitation of preindustrial labor in these sectors increased under the demand and pressure of industrialization. Further, workers displaced by mechanization in one area crowded into non-mechanized fields. The plentiful cheap labor created by their competition with each other actually retarded industrialization in many cases. Thus preindustrial and industrial centers of production existed side by side in many cities, turning out the same products.

At the same time, America recruited much of its labor force for heavy industry from preindustrial populations. Most immigrants were of peasant or artisan origin, and America gained a new set of preindustrial or sometimes anti-industrial traditions, values, and skills with each boatload. In the 1850s the Germans and the Irish, followed by the English, were the most numerous immigrant groups. After the Civil War the numbers of Scandinavians began to mount as well. By the end of the nineteenth century the major new immigrants were Italians,

Jews, and Slavs, along with black migrants from the rural South to the industrial cities of the North. In cities like Chicago and New York, immigrants were a majority of the population by 1900. Successive waves of immigrants formed the lowest strata of industrial work, and each group had to adjust preindustrial work habits and values to the new demands of industrial wage-work. The association of national origin with different rungs of the occupational ladder had a divisive effect within the working class.[8]

The uneven pace and contradictory character of industrialization meant that new areas of the country and new sections of the population confronted the transition to industrial work patterns and values at different times and in different ways. In the words of one authority, the effects of industrialization were felt, 'not as a shock . . . but as a series of shivers,' re-creating the tensions and insecurities of the transition over and over again.[9]

In 1870 only 25 per cent of America's population lived in big cities, and although this had grown to 40 per cent by the 1890s, the majority of Americans continued to live in small towns during the Gilded Age. Although Robert Wiebe's description of 'island communities' is surely exaggerated, since transience rates seem to have been as great in most small communities as in big cities, these areas did maintain distinctive values from the big cities and also from each other. They were often highly specialized in economics and politics.[10]

Small towns were far from reactionary in this period. Many important reform movements were based in them; leaders of organized labor often found a place in local government; and minor parties regularly made significant showings. Herbert Gutman has pointed out that workers in small, one-industry settings sometimes had more influence over local affairs than did their urban counterparts, and they remained part of a community that might well join them in resisting absentee bosses and out-of-town troops.[11] However, the solidarity of such areas against the excesses of capital was often based on an ethnic homogeneity and local parochialism that disguised class or national problems as struggles with particular 'aliens.'

Also hindering the development of structural or systemic critiques of industrialization was the fact that many political institutions were being democratized even as most economic ones were becoming more stratified. This trend tended to obscure the fact that political institutions were losing jurisdiction over economic and social areas of life and that the rich were exerting growing control over police, militias, and other non-elective repressive agencies.[12]

The growth of the workforce in the nineteenth century took place primarily among married men and unmarried women, groups with very different needs and outlooks. As opportunities for youthful employment in middle-class and skilled trades decreased, middle-class boys stayed out of the labor market for a longer period of time. Where opportunities for youthful work remained or increased, as in the working class, so did incentives for early marriage. Meanwhile, the number of women workers increased by more than 60 per cent between 1870 and 1890, but fewer than 4 per cent of married women worked outside the home in 1890. Although whole families had at first worked together in some of the early factories, working-class families tended to withdraw the wife from paid employment as soon as possible. In Massachusetts, for example, 'the state census of 1875 counted only 600 married women among the total of 3167 female employees.' By 1900, only 3.2 per cent of the married white women in the entire nation worked outside the home.[13] This led to a gap between the work experiences of men and women which may have been as significant in its own way as the ethnic and racial divisions among American workers.

Industrialization provided more women than ever before with employment outside the home, but many were channeled into non-industrial areas of work. In 1870, half of all women wage-earners in America were domestic servants. Other common areas of employment were sewing, laundering and, to a lesser extent, teaching. Mechanization of a field often meant unemployment for women, pushing them into non-mechanized areas of the economy where their cheap labor could compete with machines. As steam laundries and sewing machines increased output, competition among hand laundresses and sewers led to a fall in rates. Women who had formerly stitched shirts for 16 cents each in desperation dropped their price to 10 cents, even 6½ cents.[14]

Domestic work was both a consequence of industrialization and an explicitly non-industrial job, created by the transfer of productive work out of the home. The servant did not work a set number of hours but instead owed her employer broadly defined personal services. There was no boundary to the working day; domestic servants were at the beck and call of their employers practically twenty-four hours a day. In fact, the employment of domestics was a substitute for the mechanization and rationalization of the home, yet service was an agent of assimilation into industrial society. For immigrant women in particular, it was a lesson in the values, habits, and even the language of the American middle class. At the same time, domestic service reinforced and perpetuated ethnic stereotyping and class patterns of deference and patronization.

Women who found work in the factories earned $1.25 to $2.50 a week, working sixteen hours a day, but they were a minority.

They also faced a different set of problems, as their substitution for more expensive skilled factory laborers could foment increased gender hostility and competition among workers. In Cincinnati, for example, factory workers

> found their daily work lives, and occasionally their jobs, further threatened by the increased reliance upon female and child labor. Between 1870 and 1890, the number of women and children employed in the manufacturing sector mushroomed from 8,894 to 22,912. In 1860, women formed a majority of the workforce only in the clothing industry: by 1890 they constituted more than half of the laborers in the city's clothing, fur textile, regalia and society banner, box, bag, and canned foods establishments.[15]

All these factors worked to prevent the emergence of a unified working-class challenge to, or middle-class modification of, the hegemony of business in the Gilded Age, in spite of – or perhaps also because of – the fact that in many local situations the power of the capitalists was limited by the presence of alternative community values or institutions. Other aspects of uneven industrialization that hindered the growth of a working-class alternative to bourgeois laissez-faire included the replacement of workers' parties by ethnic machines, the revival of divisive struggles over control of personal life through government or legal action, conflict over child labor restrictions and compulsory education among different sectors of the labor movement, the use of female and black labor to break strikes or undercut skilled wages, and the continued geographic mobility of the period, including the much-exaggerated but significant role of westward movement.

Thus America in the Gilded Age lacked an institutional or programmatic alternative to the bourgeois work ethic or the ideology of individual mobility. Even though in practice many communities and groups operated on principles very different from American individualism, they seldom formulated their practices or beliefs in explicit opposition to that individualism or to the structure that created it. Resistance to industrialism was as uncoordinated as the local time systems that prevailed until 1883: 'Bells and clocks struck noon . . . when the sun stood directly overhead: never exactly the same moment from place to place or week to week.'[16]

The institution that mediated between such local variation and the national expansion of industrial capitalism was the family. In every class and community, the family was as important a link between personal life and the wage-labor structure as noon. Like the noon hour break, however, even as the family became an ever more important and universally held abstract ideal it continued to demonstrate extreme local variations.

The Industrial Family

Family strategies, household arrangements, kin networks, the division of labor by gender, and the maintenance of home life became more important aspects of survival, adaptation, and innovation for *all* classes, ethnic groups, and regions between 1850 and 1900. The ability of a middle-class family to finance a son's schooling or the ability of a working-class family to send its children out to work meant the difference between improving class position or slipping down the economic and social ladder. Kin networks assumed heightened importance for immigrants struggling to survive in the big cities, while parental support was crucial to the ability of middle-class newlyweds to establish their eventual independence. The family life cycle became the prime determinant of boarding and lodging for urban dwellers, and the ability to adjust family/household arrangements was critical in successful adaptation to urban life and work. The family, in other words, assumed greater salience in people's lives as older networks of sponsorship and interdependence eroded, and changing job opportunities, housing markets, and educational requirements demanded flexible responses.

The period from 1870 to 1890, I would argue, represented the apex of the family's role in reproducing or improving class position through conscious or at least very specifically tailored and differentiated strategies. Before the 1860s many Americans shared a sufficiently broad range of experiences for much socialization and work training to occur outside the family. For most, no hard and fast lines divided rural and urban experiences, working for others or supervising others. Education was informal, irregular, and frequently interrupted for all classes. Political and cultural divisions had fairly simple cleavages – pro- or anti-slavery, Protestant or Catholic, temperance or non-temperance – that brought people together in associations that seemed to unite all fellow believers.

By the 1860s, however, political, cultural, and religious solidarities were cross-cut by class conflicts; yet class identification was refracted through increasingly variegated immigrant experiences, work settings, and living conditions. Few new institutions or cultural values had developed to help ensure the smooth reproduction of class differences. The public school system was incomplete and unstandardized. National magazines and advertising images had not yet established a new ethic of consumerism to replace the shattered unity of 'producers' or a consumer-debt system to substitute for older compulsions to work. Welfare and credit were largely unavailable through formal institutions. Residential segregation had not reached the point at which it provided a reliable peer group of neighbors to reinforce each other's values and socialize children through group pressure.

The erosion of older extra-familial mechanisms for assigning people to classes and work roles, combined with the inadequate development of new ones, meant that the family moved to center stage. Family networks became the main source of mutual aid, while age and sexual divisions of labor within the family became the primary means of inculcating (or resisting) class values. Family strategy was the principal tool for manipulating one's standing within the class and the primary form of expression for class differences in daily life. A working-class family with many sons could overcome the vulnerable years after the father's earnings had peaked, buy a house, and even achieve significant occupational mobility. A middle-class family whose woman economized sufficiently to send the boy to college and inspired him with the commitment to forgo immediate wages in the interests of establishing his respectability could avoid the downward mobility that less 'effective' families suffered.

In adapting family life to the new centrality of these decisions and behaviors, Americans behaved in ways that created some average trends. It was during this period that American families took on many of the characteristics associated with 'the modern family': they became smaller, with lower fertility rates; they revolved more tightly around the nuclear core, putting greater distance between themselves and servants or boarders; parents became more emotionally involved in child-rearing and for a longer period; couples oriented more toward companionate marriage; and the separation between home and work, both physically and conceptually, was sharpened. Yet most pronouncements about the relationship of industrialization to 'the modern family' remain suspect, for they elide important local, chronological, and class variations.

Despite growing agreement about the proper form of 'the family,' family organization and lifestyles reflected and were limited by class differences more obviously and immediately than either before or since. Susan Strasser has shown that class distinctions in home furnishings, food, and household labor *widened* in the second half of the nineteenth century. In all classes life course was an important determinant of occupational position, but life course itself intersected with class so as to make qualitative differences out of quantitative similarities. Both middle-class and working-class single women, for example, tended to enter the labor force upon the death of a father; but working-class families, being larger, tended to have younger children in the household as the parents aged, while working-class men died much earlier than middle-class men. (At age twenty, male laborers had a life expectancy eleven years shorter than other American men.) Women who entered the workforce at an earlier age, in turn, found less secure and desirable positions than those who entered at a later age.[17]

Family differences were translated into class differences and class differences into family differences at every stage of life. Personal reproduction was not yet harnessed to a national, unified sequence of customs and institutions directing social reproduction. There was, for instance, much more variation in family sequencing and form than was to emerge in the twentieth century. Young people in the nineteenth century exhibited fewer uniformities in the age of leaving school and home, marrying, and setting up households than they do today. Even at ages under eight, nearly 10 per cent of the children studied by John Modell, Theodore Hershberg, and Frank Furstenberg were not living in their parents' households. No close integration between marriage and workforce entry existed: young people's status as children rather than marriage partners determined when and where they would start work. Family decisions were far more variable and less tightly coordinated throughout the society than they would become in the twentieth century.[18]

American fertility, it is true, fell by nearly 40 per cent between 1855 and 1915, but this average obscures some differences that cannot simply be attributed to the 'cultural lag' of immigrants. Thus, for example, a detailed study of New York reveals that the fertility of unskilled workers actually *increased* during this period, while a Massachusetts research project found that native-born semi-skilled workers had higher fertility in 1880 than in 1850. In Southern Michigan, rural areas led in the 'modern' reduction of fertility while industrial Detroit pioneered the adoption of close spacing of children.[19]

Just as the average decline in fertility seems to have masked a temporary increase in fertility among unskilled or semi-skilled workers, other family changes in the industrial period were also not unilinear precursors of 'modernization.' The long-term trend toward nuclearity was slowed down between 1870 and 1890 for a number of groups: these experienced an *increase* in boarding or temporary co-residence with other kin. Rudy Seward's review of national statistics found that 'the number of extended families, families with subfamilies, and number of marital pairs per family ... show their most significant increases between 1870 and 1880.' The Northeast, 'most urban and industrialized' region, 'has the highest percentage of "extended" families, and the percentage actually increases with each decade. This seems to add even more support to [Michael] Anderson's (1971) contention that there was an increase in the incidence of extended families during the industrialization period.' Similarly, Frank Furstenberg and his co-researchers found that in all four ethnic groups they studied in Philadelphia, the number of extended families increased between 1850 and 1880.[20]

In the regional industrial center of Worcester, Massachusetts, the proportion of newlyweds living in their own households declined from 84.5 per cent in 1860 to 63.5 per cent in 1880, though more than 90 per cent of couples with children lived independently in both periods. In Providence as well, 'newlyweds increasingly lived with other people, kin and non-kin, between 1860 and 1880.' The proportion of newlyweds who boarded increased by 500 per cent between 1860 and 1870. The general incidence of boarding and lodging remained at about 25 per cent through the period, with boarding primarily a native phenomenon and lodging a less familial practice correlated with lower economic status. Although boarding seems to have increased for newlyweds of all classes in these areas it came at very different ages, for the age of marriage for middle-class individuals rose while for manual workers it fell. Tamara Hareven estimates that by 1880 'one-half to two-thirds of all urban residents . . . resorted to boarding as a transitory state between their departure from their parents' households and their setting up households of their own'; but she adds that race, ethnicity, and occupation were 'crucial variables' in 'points of transition from one family type to another and [in] the nature of the transition.'[21]

One trend that characterized all classes in the late nineteenth century but ran counter to twentieth-century developments was the increasing length of time that young people lived at home. 'A new phase had entered the life cycle: a prolonged period of time spent with parents between puberty and marriage.' Again, though, this meant different things by class and by gender. Working-class youth tended to get jobs while living at home; middle-class youth tended to go to school. But in the middle class, boys tended to stay in school longer than girls and girls to get jobs at a younger age, while working-class daughters stayed in school longer than working-class sons.[22]

Another common but, it appears, less than 'modern' trend was toward the expulsion of wives from productive labor. Among all classes and ethnic groups, with the notable exception of Blacks, there was a tendency to increase the paid-labor-force participation of young single women but to decrease that of wives. Although first-generation immigrant wives often worked outside the home, second-generation ones tended not to do so. Women's domestic tasks were thus more clearly demarcated from their market activities in this period, just as wives' duties were more sharply divided from their husbands'.

While industrialization and modernity are often thought to be associated with geographical mobility, the trends between 1850 and 1880 went in the opposite direction. In 1850, 47 per cent of native-born household heads resided in states that were not adjacent to their state of birth; by 1880 this had fallen to 35 per cent, while 50.1 per cent now lived in the same state where they were born.[23]

The changes that helped produce more 'modern' family forms, then, started in different classes, meant different things to families occupying different positions in the industrial order, and did not proceed unilinearly. Family 'modernization' was less the result of some functional evolution of 'the' family than the dialectical outcome of *diverging* responses that occurred in different areas and classes at various times, eventually interacting to produce the trends we now associate with industrialization. As Katz, Stern, and Doucet point out:

> The five great changes in family organization that have occurred are: the separation of home and work place; the increased nuclearity of household structure; the decline in marital fertility; the prolonged residence of children in the home of their parents; and the lengthened period in which husbands and wives live together after their children have left home. The first two began among the working class and among the wage-earning segment of the business class (clerks and kindred workers). The third started among the business class, particularly among its least affluent, most specialized, and most mobile sectors. The fourth began at about the same time in both the working and business class, though the children of the former usually went to work and the latter to school.[24] [The fifth did not occur until the twentieth century, and represented a reversal of nineteenth century trends.]

Yet for all these opposing trends and differences by class, the importance of the family unit in directly manipulating entry into the work world and class hierarchy led to certain common themes and perceptions as well. Both middle-class and working-class families, albeit for different reasons and with different emphases, adopted a view of the family that recognized its centrality in determining their future. Security began to be seen not in terms of the community in which one lived, one's potential political influence, or even one's income, but in terms of home ownership, the one thing that guaranteed the future and self-sufficiency of a family. The tendency to hold up the family as a stable haven in a world of flux accelerated, spreading to all classes and to people of all political persuasions. Even the suffragists began to demand voting rights less on the basis of equality than on grounds that this would create better families. There was well-nigh universal agreement that the world depended upon the correct actions and self-sufficiency of independent families, and that such families depended upon a male breadwinner and a female homemaker. Elizabeth Pleck comments: 'What has been described as the "cult of domesticity" might be better understood as the family response to the emergence of a male career,'[25] or, in the case of its working-class version, as the family response to the exigencies of lifetime wage-labor, where earnings peaked at an early age and then fell off sharply.

However, the fact that a family was now considered solely responsible for the success or failure of its members and was increasingly seen as self-sufficient, divorced from the market and the promiscuous crowd, did not in and of itself create the possibilities for family autonomy that were to develop in the twentieth century. Precisely because the family was the principal agent of social reproduction, it had severe constraints on its behavior. These were not all internally imposed. Particularly striking, especially in the smaller towns that still dominated the landscape, was the continuation, even acceleration, of movements claiming the right to scrutinize and regulate family life. Temperance and Prohibition activists tried to intervene into people's at-home behavior; anti-feminists pushed for laws prohibiting abortion and birth control; feminists tried to raise the age of consent and combined their support for birth control with endorsement of population control and personal abstinence; working-class and ethnic associations often paid close attention to the family habits of their members.

The late-nineteenth-century family, then, varied in its organization by class, occupation, ethnic group, and region. But these variations were not the result of private decisions or individual whim; they were conditioned by the specific job opportunities and class relations in any given locale, in interaction with the family's continued role as the primary agent of social reproduction. Not surprisingly, therefore, all classes and ethnic groups recognized the centrality of family organization to their social position and all used the familial division of labor to affect that social position. They thus celebrated the sanctity of the family not because it was independent but because of its critical role in class formation. With these commonalities in mind, let us turn now to the different family values and strategies of the middle and working classes.

The Middle-class Family in the Gilded Age

The middle-class family continued its withdrawal from community and associational life in this period. Families of this class experienced the sharpest drop in fertility rates and increase in the age at which children left home, leading to a growing intensity in the familial experience of childhood. The stress on maternal responsibility for character deepened, while the sexual division of labor was defined ever more strictly as involving a mutually exclusive set of character traits, capacities, and values. Increasing reliance on the family combined with the privatization of economic and political decisions to steadily constrict older republican notions of social morality and public duty. One of the ways in which the separation of spheres evolved in the late nineteenth century was as a substitute for other forms of moral striving. Morality and social responsibility sometimes became equated with being 'manly' or 'womanly.' 'Virtue' lost all political connotations and became a feminine word, referring to a woman's sexual behavior. 'Responsibility,' on the other hand, became a predominantly masculine word, referring as much if not more to a man's duty in supporting his family as to his wider social obligations. The family that had once been seen as an instrument for the moral regeneration of the world came to be the shelter from which people viewed the world in horror or titillation: 'families cuddle the joys of the fireside,' Crane wrote, 'when spurred by tales of dire lone agony.'[26]

The tales that families read as they cuddled together were seldom very realistic. Although the 'discovery of poverty' in the 1890s gave adult middle-class readers a window onto working-class life, most middle-class families resolutely protected their children from such knowledge. Anne Macleod points out that while antebellum children's books dealt out dire consequences to children who disobeyed adult authority, they did not try to protect them from adult reality.

> Death and poverty, for instance, were a commonplace in the children's literature of antebellum America. . . . By contrast, the young heroes of later books, from *Tom Sawyer* to *Peter Rabbit* and beyond, flout adult restriction and survive – but there has been little mention . . . until very recently, of death and social hardship.[27]

Whenever possible, middle-class families moved away from the realities of city life into the suburbs. In cities such as Boston, New York, Omaha, Los Angeles, and Chicago suburbs mushroomed after 1870, often leaving the central city primarily to the foreign-born. The people who moved to these areas were not upper class – only about one-quarter of the residents of many city suburbs owned their own homes in 1890, even through a mortgage – but moderately successful members of the urban middle class. 'American architects recognized that this escape to suburbia sundered the friendships and neighborly ties of the urban family: "But mark what compensation! You gain a home . . . A HOME!" '[28]

There is some evidence that lower-middle-class families which stayed behind in the cities, especially in declining neighborhoods, turned even more inward to the family, in growing fear of the working-class and immigrant populations surrounding them. Richard Sennett's study of middle-class families in Union Park, Chicago, found that there were few clubs, bars, restaurants, or intimate church circles that involved people in groups beyond the nuclear family. Parents supervised their children protectively, escorting them to school and denying them free access to the park. Sennett suggests that nuclear families here no longer even provided for successful adaptation to work. Comparing them to the 10 per cent of the neighborhood's families that were extended, Sennett found that the fathers and sons of the small nuclear (two to four kin present) families were *less* upwardly mobile than the fathers and sons of families that were extended or had five to six kin members present. Although sons of two-to-four-person families managed to avoid unemployment and to have greater residential stability, they also seemed less able to take advantage of new opportunities to move upward in occupation.[29]

Sennett's conclusion that nuclear families were generally dysfunctional for the middle class should be taken with a grain of salt – in light of long-range national figures, one might ask if the sons of extended families did not pursue their occupational improvement within nuclear families of their own. But his study does suggest that the cautious middle-class strategy that had been innovative in the 1840s and 1850s took an increasingly defensive form in the booming industrial city. The family strategies designed by the antebellum middle class were evidently revealing some of their internal contradictions as early as the 1880s. Instead of producing innovators who could flexibly respond to a rapidly changing urban environment, the fearful nuclear families of Union Park produced people whose capacity for initiating new social contacts and taking risks was stunted.

It was against such families, of course, that many late-nineteenth-century writers rebelled. Ironically, though, even self-criticisms of bourgeois culture turned on the centrality of gender roles and family life rather than broader structural or moral issues. Where conservatives saw society's ills as stemming from women who had stepped out of their sphere, critics of middle-class values accused women of being too effective within their sphere and of feminizing men. When men of the 1880s and 1890s denounced the stultification of bourgeois society they blamed it on women and 'rebelled' by asserting their masculinity.

The physical evolution of middle-class society reflected the eclipse of other centers of social reproduction and organization. Suburbs grew haphazardly, on the basis of cost and profit considerations rather than rational planning. Cities were laid out in grid patterns that reduced the land to separate, uncoordinated pieces of real estate, to be used as the purchaser saw fit. Gone was the supervision of colonial authorities over who could build what and where; zoning laws and social regulation of construction did not reappear until the early twentieth century. Private uses were not organized and built around communal or public spaces, as in Europe or Latin America; public spaces were built in the wake of private ones and subordinated to their needs. Thus early park designers sought to build buffers between business sections and residences, consciously highlighting the distinction between the two and tightly restricting public use of such space. Where working-class advocates of public parks desired space for participatory sports, middle-class leaders tried to prohibit such use, desiring instead designs that 'cause us to receive pleasure without exertion' and favoring spectatorship over active use.[30]

But if public space made limited claims to represent historical continuity, civic unity, or social significance, private homes increasingly pretended to such representation. In the 1870s the early preference of middle-class home buyers for 'honest,' 'republican,' and functional homes gave way to an admiration for an eclectic mix of structures and ornamentation that made the house a blend of public building styles from Italian towers to Turkish domes to Queen Anne mansions – a *reductio ad absurdum* of Beecher's dictum that building a fine house was a contribution to the public good. Once, the ideal middle-class home had demonstrated the equality and homogeneity of the American republic by its similarity to neighboring structures; now it was decorated and landscaped to be its own little republic. Once, the middle-class home's simplicity had displayed the piety and humility of its inhabitants; now owners labored to make their homes stand for 'larger visions of morality, aesthetics, class, and civilization . . . a mediating and unifying sacred symbol.'[31]

Such homes, ideally located in the suburbs, displayed on the outside, as a *Cosmopolitan* author put it in 1875, 'stateliness enough to comport with the general dignity and breadth of the American landscape.' Inside, their parlors sought to reveal the 'dignity and breadth' of the inhabitants' families, a task that subordinated personal comfort to obsessive display. Another author asserted in 1877 that 'Provided there is space to move about, without knocking over the furniture, there is hardly likely to be too much in the room.'[32]

These homes were monuments to what Sam Bass Warner has called the 'privatism' of American life, the denial that there is something higher or more transcendent than individual property rights. Like the middle-class family, the middle-class home disclaimed any responsibility to coordinate with community or neighbors, professing its self-sufficiency and ambition for upward mobility. After the Civil War, writes a recent social historian of American architecture, home designs and decorations were justified on the basis of their contribution to the redemption of the family rather than, as formerly, to the redemption of the nation.[33]

Yet these homes were not monuments to privacy, at least in its modern sense. For despite its seeming insularity, the middle-class family was tightly connected to the world of industrial work relations, strongly supportive of those relations, and hence limited in its privacy and its toleration for individuality. The family was still central *as a unit* to forming the work values and fostering the personal behaviors required to maintain or improve class standing. Contrary to many accounts, then, the family was not a refuge from or alternative to the world of work, whatever the wishful imaginings of some middle-class men and women.

Middle-class reformers, remarks Alan Trachtenberg, saw 'the slum as the antithesis of the home' because the home represented the 'transcendence of labor; a place and a time free of the demands of the regulating clock.'[34] But that description actually applies more forcefully to the slum. The middle-class home, like the factory, was based on private property, individual responsibility, the work ethic, regularity, and punctuality. Like the factory, too, the family strictly limited the promiscuous social interactions that might occur in a mobile, expanding, class-stratified society, though unlike the factory it achieved this through a mother's loving guidance and a father's ability to provide a decent home, rather than through the harsh supervision of the foreman or the setting of different employment terms. The slum, on the other hand, lacked respect for private property, denigrated the bourgeois work ethic, denied the desirability of individual advancement, disregarded regularity and punctuality, and imposed few barriers to the free mixing of people and possessions.

The Gilded Age middle-class family had no values that were opposed to the industrial ones of thrift, production, duty, self-control, and punctuality. It was put forward as an alternative to the work world only to the extent that *other* people in the work world did not share or uphold bourgeois values about work, or as an antidote to cases where the clash of interest in actual bourgeois relations undermined the ideal values. In fact, the family was not so much a refuge from the work world as a sanitized ideal of it, where the exigencies of capitalist competition did not lead to instability, conflict, or corruption. Although the nineteenth-century middle class valued the family for its divorce from the *excesses* of capitalist work, it also lauded the family as the primary means by which people were trained to enter and succeed in such work, internalizing its norms and accepting its distribution of rewards and failures. The nineteenth-century family was not a place for people to celebrate spontaneity or indulge in such non-industrial behaviors as sleeping in, puttering around, or doing frivolous things. It was the shallow pool in which mothers first taught their children to swim in the waters of capitalist production – warning them to beware of sharks but still encouraging them to get their feet wet.

The middle-class home, then, did not transcend industrial labor or divorce itself from the imperatives of the capitalist work ethic. Although the home reconciled work and leisure by making 'domestic consumerism' acceptable, it did so only within strict limits. A wife, editorialized one newspaper in 1859, 'is the very best savings bank yet established.'[35] Only later would advertisements label her a 'purchasing agent.'

The family also remained a place for expressing *class* aspirations rather than individual ones. Even the new emphasis on using home decorations, windows, and furnishings to signify a particular family's identity generally boiled down to depicting its economic and social status through mass-produced ornamentation advertised as appropriate to one's occupation. Hence an archetype rather than an individual family emerged: a doctor's home; a supervisor's front yard; a respectable clerk's parlor. The 'individuality' of Victorian middle-class homes was tied to conventional notions of occupational and familial propriety; 'certain patterns were necessary so that other people could clearly read the symbolism of social status and contented family life in the details.'[36]

Homes were built with large porches and elaborately furnished front parlors to receive visitors who were not intimates or kin. The etiquette of visiting was complex and formal, suggesting its continued importance in people's lives. The fact that it took place with social peers but not close friends is demonstrated by the care taken to separate the public part of the house from the private: kitchens were hidden in the back or the basement; stairs to the bedrooms were moved from the central hall to the side of the house; the gentleman's library often had its own entrance; evidence of the family's efforts to maintain its status – cleaning implements, servants, sewing machines – were hidden from view. Diaries and remembrances of Victorian women record their compulsion to receive visitors who might in fact be roundly disliked. And many readers may remember the front parlors of their grandmothers' houses, perpetually reserved for the formal visitors who by this time so seldom came. Only in the twentieth century, with the decline of obligatory visits, could a family assume that visitors would be close enough friends that kitchens and workplaces might be visible and accessible.

Perhaps what has misled some into seeing Victorian homes and families as more personal, individualized structures than they actually were is the peculiarity that the expression of class differences was now channeled through the division of labor by age and gender. In the seventeenth and eighteenth centuries, the sexual division of labor in the household was less important in socializing youth to adult work roles than the property relations. The male household head *and* his wife had more authority over the youths in their home than did the youths' parents; household heads were in turn supervised by church officials and social superiors. In the twentieth century, husbands and wives have separate relations to the workplace, and in consequence there has developed considerable pressure for men to construct their own relations to childhood socialization. But in the nineteenth century, the sexual division of labor within the family was the main source of the class-specific values so necessary for the social reproduction of capitalism. The sexual division of labor rather than the social hierarchy now seemed to govern work assignments and the disposition of political and moral questions. Society was no longer seen as a collection of households divided by hierarchy and united by mutual obligations but as a series of gender relations, divided by function yet united by mutual need. Men's economic and political patterns determined the class status of the family; women's socialization reproduced the values and behaviors necessary for the male child to step into and maximize his position in the social order.

In consequence, there were strict limits on the individuality or privacy of age and gender relations. Separate rooms or, more frequently, separate beds and nooks within a room gave children a limited amount of personal space; but dinner table rules and other formalized interactions emphasized the subordination of each individual's desires to the unit as a whole, the necessity of accepting the work ethic, respecting private property, and taking responsibility for filling one's proper gender role. 'Privacy for the Victorian family was still associated with short periods of time alone, in a special place within the house: a window seat, a cubbyhole under the stairs, a man's library, or "growlery," ' rather than with the entire home experience or organization. Not until the professional home economics movement at the turn of the century was privacy or self-expression for family members claimed as a right.[37]

Even the couple relationship was not as individualized as the emphasis on love and marriage might lead us to believe. On the one hand, the rising divorce rate after 1870 *was* connected to higher expectations about married life and reflected the greater importance attached to having a compatible mate. On the other hand, definitions of compatibility and companionship were still quite conventional, even stereotyped. There was general agreement on what constituted the proper support a man owed his wife and what sort of behavior he could expect in return, unlike the early twentieth century, when disputes over levels of consumption and definitions of support began to mount. Men were judged by their adherence to the work ethic, women by the quality of their domesticity. 'Love' was said to be increasingly important but it was still considered to be something that could be objectively ascertained and measured.[38]

The couple relationship, moreover, was not the central axis of the middle-class family. Victorian Americans did not anticipate the modern family's emphasis on a romantic – far less erotic – relationship between the couple; both same-sex and intra-generational ties often cut across the couple's privacy. A recent study by Marilyn Motz confirms Nina Baym's suggestion that to nineteenth-century women home meant 'not a space but a system of human relations' and commitments extending well beyond the parlor. Kin networks helped women to fulfill their marital and maternal duties but were also, as a last resort, a source of support against the husband: 'When women defined their place in society as the home and family, they referred not to the confines of the house ... but also to networks of female kin.' Married middle-class women often had unmarried women, children, and elder relatives live with them for extended periods of time.[39]

The doctrine of separate spheres venerated not the marital relationship but the sexual division of labor. For many women, this meant that bonds among women were the emotional center of life. In 1839 Fanny Kemble, traveling from England to join her husband at his Georgia plantation, had been horrified to find that the assumption of common bonds among American women even extended to sleeping arrangements. She was surprised by the division of inns into the ladies' part of the house and the gentlemen's, but even more so by the innkeeper's assumption that she would sleep in the same bed as another woman. When she refused, he responded, ' "Oh! he didn't know that the ladies were not acquainted" (as if, forsooth, one went to bed with all one's acquaintances).'[40]

Even after the decline of association, 'female bonds ... formed a denser social and emotional network than ties between the sexes.' The 'womanless' novels of the nineteenth century, reflecting men's desire to escape from their duties toward women, were paralleled by the manless diaries of Victorian women, in which a marriage proposal might rate only a line while page after page was devoted to rhapsodies about a close female friend. The husband might next appear only in the record of his banishment to the parlor when a female friend came to stay and the two women shared confidences and embraces in the marital bed. Letters and diaries of Victorian women reveal an intense, often passionate, glorification of female love. Although these friendships seldom repudiated heterosexuality, they certainly denigrated its significance in women's lives.[41]

Middle-class men also formed new social and 'service' clubs on the basis of gender in this period. These included the Elks (1868), the Eagles (1898), and the Sons of the American Revolution (1889). Secret fraternal organizations, often explicitly extrafamilial, were tremendously popular in the last third of the century: the Masons and Oddfellows had a million members each by 1900. Another limitation on the intensity of marital bonds was the development of a male youth culture. Bachelors joined temperance societies, organizations such as the YMCA, and self-improvement groups in increasing numbers from the 1850s. There also developed a whole literature glorifying a boys' culture, in whose mythology women tolerantly or helplessly looked on while males played at rejecting female influence and escaping domestic ties. The link between the bachelors' culture and women's kin networks was made not through marriage but through 'the tight, indeed controlling, bond between mother and male child [that] was at the very core of the cult of domesticity.'[42]

This highlights another way in which the nineteenth-century family failed to privilege the adult couple relationship: the greatest flights of sentiment in Victorian domestic literature were reserved for the relation between mother and child. Henry Ward Beecher declared that a mother's love was 'brighter than the morning sun, fairer than the evening star, and more constant than either . . . the only [love] that glows with any considerable resemblance to that great central fire from which it flows, for it is a revelation of the love of God. . . .'[43] It is difficult to read women's descriptions of babies' limbs and soft skin – especially dying babies – without feeling an almost erotic intensity to the sentimentalization of motherhood.

But mother and son were not sufficient to each other; thus the mother–son tie was continually supplemented (and rivaled) by non-familial interactions. Women dreamed of incorporating orphans, neglected children, and their husbands into the home; young men dreamed of escaping to an all-male frontier, and in fact they often left their mothers to board with each other or in private homes. Louisa May Alcott took her heroine through rebellious youth to become the mistress (Mama Bhaer) of the enlarged family of Plumfield School, where work and home life were fully integrated and even redeemed street children (though not domestic employees) took part in family celebrations. Female love and self-sacrifice tamed these children and were the basis of their successful adjustment to the middle-class world. Horatio Alger, on the other hand, made his heroes orphans whose rugged individualism (and exceptional good luck) was not at all dependent on female self-sacrifice.[44]

Few nineteenth-century novels revolved around nuclear families that could actually shelter their members from the outside world. Male authors hardly portrayed the family at all; female ones saw it either as a fragile entity that could be torn apart by drink, desertion, or disaster, or as an enlarged sphere whose strength came from its incorporation of elements that might otherwise rival the home. Catharine Beecher, her biographer reminds us, did not envision the ideal home as a haven apart from society but as 'an integral part of a national system, reflecting and promoting [and in the absence of community controls or national culture, being the source of] mainstream American values.'[45] The family was an interlocking system of well-defined age and gender roles that enmeshed the individual in tightly ordered relationships with the larger economy.

Instead of being an arena for personal fulfillment, then, the family was carefully organized along age and sex lines to maximize or at least jealously guard its class position. This organization prevented the middle-class family from completely withdrawing into a private sphere, though it did encourage the family to sharply restrict its contacts with other classes. Parks, suburbs, porches, parlors, and genteel associations of women or men continued to make many family interactions public, and to encourage regulated but vital bonds between the nuclear family and kin or class networks. These bonds continued to be more important than larger institutions or processes in setting the conditions of class reproduction.[46]

Families, Schools, and Asylums

These considerations help to explain an apparent paradox of the age – the fact that the increasing emphasis on the family as sole source of personal support and class identity was accompanied by a growth of public institutions that took over many traditional family functions. Unlike today, when those who preach the sanctity of the private family most vehemently are also those most deeply suspicious of public institutions such as schools and government agencies, it was the middle class *supporters* of domesticity who most enthusiastically embraced the construction of specialized extra-familial institutions to deal with education, crime, mental illness, and poverty. We can understand this only if we bear in mind the limited definition of privacy within the middle class. The privacy demanded by the middle class was social, not personal – the right to non-interference by the rich or the poor, and most especially the right to reject claims put forward by the lower classes. In the nineteenth century, many public institutions could be seen as means to extend this right rather than as threats to it.

The association of institutional growth with the establishment of the self-sufficient family is not accidental. State-run institutions are the necessary accompaniment to an economic system that places full responsibility for self-support upon independent, separate families. Such a system has no intermediary groups or value systems that allow informal, community support of a family whose 'breadwinner' is unable to provide for it. The more the nuclear family is required to fend for itself, the more likely it is that families which are not economically, physically, or emotionally self-supporting, even for a short period of time, will require formal intervention or support. The nineteenth-century family charged the wife and mother with taking care of inevitable biological dependencies – infants, elders, the ill – but social dependencies were difficult to absorb within a single family. In addition, the more the mother was expected to inculcate social control on her own, the more necessary it became for her to rely on institutional guidance in formulating the principles and methods of socialization. Alternatively, the more necessary it was to remove from the home anyone whose mother was not able or willing to inculcate such control or provide the social services necessary for dependants.

The other side of economic and political individualism, then, was social bureaucracy. To the extent that social control over property, political control over persons, and community control over families became unacceptable, there had to be other means of dealing with the excesses of economic competition and political democracy or the failures of familial strategies. The expansion of state intervention in America stemmed not from creeping socialism but from unfettered capitalism; protection of private property and economic individualism required a whole complex of legal and regulatory agencies to ensure that those lacking property or suffering from competition would not disrupt the free play of market forces.[47]

Far from being opposed to the self-supporting family, these institutions arose to buttress it, refusing to let its casualties throw the concept into question or modify its internal arrangements. Just as the American state has never challenged private enterprise or the market but has followed along in their tracks, cleaning up or repairing the rails when necessary, so did American institutions foster the family by inculcating its values, taking care of its rejects or failures and, where necessary, enforcing its separation from other families. Eli Zaretsky points out that the *same* institutions both 'valorized family life in general' and 'threatened the parental authority of the poor' – or anyone else who did not support the social values of the middle class. Institutions emerged as the ultimate guarantors of the self-supporting family, organizing themselves in opposition to traditions or practices that did not make family self-sufficiency their primary goal. The new welfare agencies, for example, explicitly rejected older traditions that implied a social interdependence among families. Charity was decried because it taught people that they might rely on others. 'Let me have one cord of wood to do it with,' declared one philanthropist in 1887, 'and I can ruin the best family in Boston.' Josephine Shaw Howell declared that 'no man can receive as a gift what he should earn by his own labor without a moral deterioration.'[48] The pejorative use of the word 'gift' is particularly telling here, given the historical role of gift-giving not as a one-way act of charity but as a means of establishing mutual obligations and reciprocity.

Domesticity and public social institutions were two sides of the same coin: the price paid for the economic self-sufficiency of the American household. The inevitable dependencies attached to participation in a market economy – infancy, childhood, illness, periods of physical and psychological stress, the need to economize to fill gaps between wages and cost of living – all these were pushed onto mothers. But then institutions grew up to support mothers in these tasks, as surrogate husbands, in lieu of recognition that individuals might need any other support than a nuclear family. America pioneered many methods for using state action to help mothers without a breadwinner, but linked this to an equally striking refusal to admit that a family with a 'normal' breadwinner could not make do on its own. 'No other major industrial nation had such a special concern for its children and such a fear of providing assistance to indigent men. Thus the United States was the world leader in mothers' pensions and a world laggard in social insurance.'[49]

The domestic role of women helped to absorb and disguise the shortfalls of the self-supporting family; in consequence support to domesticity was the one socially acceptable type of aid to individuals: a broken family could be recognized as being unable to compete in the market. Yet when an intact family failed or refused to compete on the terms laid out for it, reverence for domesticity went out the window. Michael Grossberg comments:

> Family law placed restrictions on the right of the state to intervene in what the society considered normally functioning families; and yet, conversely, it augmented state power to intervene in homes labeled troubled or abnormal.[50]

Throughout the nineteenth century, the middle class showed itself most willing to pull lower-class individuals out of the family and place them in institutions. The reasons considered sufficient and the means available for doing so multiplied in the second half of the century, as reformers ' "invented" new categories of youthful deviance,' denied that Constitutional protections applied to children who needed saving, and won the right to impose indeterminate sentences on children bound over to reformatories.[51]

Not until the twentieth century was there a strong concern for keeping underprivileged or deviant children in the home, and then only for non-delinquents. Many institutions discouraged visits from family members until just before discharge. The same middle-class reformers who tried to legislate the building of small apartments for the poor, so they could not sully their nuclear families with boarders and lodgers, sometimes envisioned taking boys out of these private apartments and putting them in a communal room where their sexuality might be better controlled.[52]

The family, evidently, was not so sacred as to be allowed self-determination: either a self-supporting, conforming family or none at all. As Anthony Platt observes:

> Although the child savers affirmed the values of the home and family as the basic institutions of American society, they facilitated the removal of children from 'a home which fails to fulfill its proper function.' The child savers set such high standards of family propriety that almost any parent could be accused of not fulfilling his 'proper function.' In effect, only lower-class families were evaluated as to their competence, whereas the propriety of middle-class families was exempt from investigation and recrimination.[53]

In America, as in Europe, support for schools also rose in tandem with support for domesticity. Unlike the asylum, the school took middle-class as well as working-class children out of the home, and for a longer period of time. David Rothman suggests that once 'parents devoted particular attention to the child they also provided neutral institutions to transmit necessary skills.' Hierarchy could be taught at an impersonal level, seemingly divorced from the maternal love that prevailed at home. British travelers who were shocked by the independence and precocity of American children at home, but delighted by the strict exercise of authority and insistence on punctuality in the schools, did not seem to realize they were seeing two sides of the same system.[54]

Public education was in the long run an important social reform for working people, but the goals of its proponents, often leading manufacturers and merchants, were inextricably linked to their vision of stable class and property relations. Even the structure of the school day was set up to reinforce the industrial system. Emphasis on punctuality and division of the day into set periods helped to inculcate the factory discipline of the clock; obedience and subordination were stressed as antidotes to worker militancy. Such hidden curricula were and remain important aspects of social and ideological control in the schools: 'For example, age grading . . . has taught children that they are members of categories. . . . As another instance, consider the fact that it is in school that youngsters learn that helping their friends is called cheating.'[55]

Schooling served less to teach specific job-related skills than to confirm class origin and assure employers that prospective workers possessed general character traits desired of employees. For one thing, school attendance varied greatly by class throughout the nineteenth century, because even compulsory attendance laws were very lenient. The average American attended school for only four years in 1880, a figure that had risen by just one year in 1890. As late as 1922 less than 20 per cent of the population was graduating from high school, so a high school diploma marked a youth as having a middle-class background. Persistence at school, Howard Gitelman observes, 'could be taken as fair proxy for other characteristics . . . such as perseverance, discipline, and reliability' – not to mention a family well off enough not to require child labor.[56]

Education served to mark out those who were *already* differentiated from most workers rather than providing a route to such differentiation. This is confirmed by the fact that all groups that have experienced long-term mobility in America won economic success first and only subsequently managed to achieve educational success. Indeed, most working-class and immigrant groups obtained their modest economic improvements by 'sacrificing the education of the younger generation' and improving family finances through child labor.[57]

Schools, then, supplemented the family and reinforced its class position. Asylums, on the other hand, substituted for or replaced families. Even here, though, the congruence of family and institution in reproducing the industrial class structure is apparent. The asylum, like the cult of domesticity, developed as a way of separating individuals from the excesses of the public world. The penitentiary, like the mother, had the duty 'to insulate the offender from *all* contact with corruption. . . . Isolation and steady habits, the right organization and routine, would yield unprecedented benefits.' The parallels between family and prison here are obvious, and can be carried further. In seeking to re-create a balance they believed had existed in the eighteenth century, without challenging the transition to the wage-system, founders of the asylums created a peculiarly nineteenth-century, industrial work pattern, just as mothers who inculcated 'old-fashioned' values created new kinds of entrepreneurs and salaried employees.[58]

But deny working-class reality as they might, middle-class families and institutions could not ignore working-class militancy. The rise of working-class organizations, the pressures of immigration, and the insecurities of industrial employment cycles created new issues for both middle-class families and middle-class institutions. They were no longer concerned to transform their world so much as to preserve it. Accordingly, both family morality and institutional activity shifted in the late nineteenth century from self-control and self-organization to social control and repression. In the institutions, moral regeneration had by the 1870s given way 'to custodial care'[59] (as, it might be argued, it had also done in the middle-class families described by Sennett).

Barbara Brenzel, for example, has traced the development of one institution, originally established in 1856 to rehabilitate girls in need and place them as domestic servants. Within fifteen years, 'the concern shifted from saving children to classifying types of depravity'; older girls were now 'treated as cases, rather than souls to be redeemed. . . . The loving family circle was a forgotten dream.'[60] Elsewhere, there was a growing willingness to sanction force where once persuasion had been thought sufficient. Middle-class men professionalized the police and militias, small-town middle-class women turned from exhortation to physical attacks on saloons (often, ironically, relying on their femininity to avoid being prosecuted for their destruction of property), and reform movements tried more and more consciously to impose their will on others through legislation.

Yet all these developments testified to the growing restrictiveness and inadequacy of middle-class family, class, and gender strategies. To the extent that the middle class supported attacks on organized labor, this augmented the ability of larger capitalists to drive out family businesses, impose new controls over white-collar workers, and undermine the independence and social influence of formerly privileged sectors of the middle class. Family strategies that had been bold and effective innovations in the 1840s became inflexible, defensive, even stultifying in the 1880s, seemingly hampering the ability of men to establish new social contacts and recognize new opportunities. Restricting births and turning inward helped a family's sons to avoid unemployment and achieve residential stability, but may have limited risk-taking and upward mobility. The very success of the early middle-class family strategy created both new kinds of dependency within the family and new incentives for youth to pursue private ends outside the family.

Sexual Tensions within the Middle Class

The middle-class family strategy forged in the period of expanding commercial and small-scale manufacturing capitalism was challenged from above by the spread of industrial concentration and from below by the emergence of alternative labor and ethnic strategies. It also, however, was threatened from within. The contradictions of Victorian domesticity and the exposure of many women to Abolitionist radicalism had by this time produced a growing women's rights movement, primarily oriented toward winning suffrage, which challenged certain aspects of the middle-class division of labor by gender and elicited as much hostility as if it challenged even more than it did.

By now it is well established that the women's rights movement shared the main interests and biases of the mainstream middle class. By the 1880s, some of the primary support for woman suffrage came from the temperance movement, but temperance organizations 'turned a sharp edge . . . against an immigrant working-class culture that these middle-class women regarded as epitomizing a vulgar masculinity.' Temperance vigilante activity by females may have destroyed men's property, but only that of men who could be seen as traitors to their class; most middle-class men supported vigilante women and saw their actions as 'essentially domestic in nature.' Temperance leaders expressed feminine sympathy with the wives of drunkards but few 'helped working-class women organize on their own behalf or supported divorce as an option for abused wives'; their remedies tended to increase 'the powers of the dominant class in shaping the most intimate aspects of working-class women's lives.'[61]

Aileen Kraditor argues that in the late nineteenth century suffragists based their case on 'expediency,' using elitist, racist, nativist, and anti-working-class arguments for suffrage where they believed these would strengthen their case. Susan B. Anthony did organize a Workingwoman's Association of New York in September 1868, and female workers at first responded favorably, but they quickly seem to have begun to feel alienated and out of place. 'Although working women were active in the association in the first weeks, by July 1869 the members were all prosperous middle-class women.' Union women were unimpressed by the group, which was able to raise only $30 for the laundresses' strike when bona fide workers' organizations in New York raised over $4,500. Augusta Lewis commented: 'As a society, either the want of knowledge, or the want of sense, renders them, as a working-women's association very inefficient.'[62]

There was also, as we have seen, considerable racism within the movement. Suffragists often argued their case in very reactionary terms, claiming that woman suffrage would increase the white and native-born vote. In the South and Midwest many women proposed poll qualifications that would have excluded black and Mexican-American women from the vote. Some state suffrage organizations supported bills that limited voting rights to the propertied or the 'educated.' But this is not the whole story. The reunited national organization, the National American Woman Suffrage Association, never endorsed the limited suffrage bills proposed in some states, and sometimes led battles against such actions on the part of its affiliates. When the evolution of the suffrage movement is put into historical perspective, we can see that while it adapted to the racist and anti-working-class prejudices of its small-town and middle-class constituency, it did not initiate such conservativism and occasionally resisted it. Thus suffrage leaders could also be found espousing such liberal causes as anti-imperialism, pacifism, labor reform, and unionization. They were supportive of the Women's National Indian Association, formed in 1883 after the publication of Helen Hunt Jackson's *A Century of Dishonor*. By 1886 there were eighty-three branches of this group campaigning for Indian rights in twenty-three states and territories.

The suffrage movement, moreover, continued to provide a platform for radical attacks on patriarchal religion and the sexual double standard, both taboo subjects in Victorian America. In 1896, for example, Susan B. Anthony refused to endorse a new political reform party on grounds that it was too conservative in its approach to civil government. Pointing out that she did not want to be identified with any particular political party, she added that 'least of all could I join yours, which makes "God the author of civil government." If such civil government as we have was made by God, what reason is there to expect any improvement in the future?'[63]

Ellen Dubois has pointed out that suffragists may have accepted women's sphere and fostered bourgeois aims, but they also challenged the male monopoly of public affairs and demanded a civic role for women that was explicitly non-familial. In doing so they made a radical break with evangelism, temperance, and other domestic reforms. They directly challenged a central pillar of the bourgeois organization of social reproduction, and only this makes intelligible the near hysteria of some of their opponents.[64]

For near hysteria it was. James Weir warned in *The American Naturalist*:

> The simple right to vote carries with it no immediate danger, the danger comes afterward . . . , when woman, owing to her increased degeneration, gives free rein to her atavistic tendencies, and hurries ever backward toward the savage state of her barbarian ancestors. I see, in the establishment of equal rights, the first step toward that abyss of immoral horrors so repugnant to our cultivated ethical tastes – the matriarchate. Sunk as low as this, civilized man will sink still lower – to the communal *kachims* of the Aleutian Islanders.[65]

He was not alone in his sentiments. Opposition to female suffrage mounted rather than diminished in the late nineteenth century, and was linked to a growing sense of crisis about gender and sexuality. As Weir's comments reveal, fears about 'the honor of women' were not unconnected to fears about 'the property of men.' The integral but fragile link between separate sexual spheres and class reproduction in nineteenth-century America helps to explain not only the tremendous concern with defining and limiting sexuality but also the particular evolution of that concern.

Many societies have used control over sexuality as a metaphor or measure for other types of personal discipline.[66] In Western Europe and America, concerns for establishing personal discipline were connected to the early spread of banking and manufacture, and were first directed primarily at middle-class men. The needs of capital accumulation and prudent business management required that an aspiring entrepreneur develop a capacity for self-denial and discipline, as well as a sense of self-righteousness in departing from traditional community norms – hence the appeal of demanding religious ideologies to the emerging middle class. The middle classes prided themselves on their restraint, contrasting their well-regulated lives to the debauchery and self-indulgence of both the aristocracy and the poor. This restraint initially applied to all the passions, and sex was not singled out as the central drive to be controlled. But the further progress of industrialization and class stratification seems to have redirected the concern more exclusively toward sexuality.

In both England and America, the spread of commodity production correlated with a veritable phobia about masturbation. Strictures against masturbation were put in terms of a need to husband energy for the struggle to survive in a competitive environment. In fact, most doctors' prescriptions about the need to save sperm sounded very much like society's general exhortations about the importance of thrift: 'Reserve is the great secret of power everywhere.' Phrases such as 'too great indulgence' and 'careless waste' were used in reference to sleep, romantic novels, procrastination, play – anything that drew energy and resources away from work – but they were applied with particular intensity to masturbation: 'The fancies, once turned in this direction, wear a channel, down which dash the thoughts, gathering force like a river as they move away from the fountain-head.' To avoid such a diversion from man's proper course, neither time, money, nor semen should be wasted. The wise man 'saves with the utmost care, and spends with the greatest caution.' Two shifts of emphasis occurred in the course of the nineteenth century. First, worry about female sexuality and masturbation began to overwhelm the earlier preoccupation with male self-restraint. Second, the emphasis changed from self-control to social control and repression.[67]

From the very beginning, of course, contradictions over sexuality characterized the cult of domesticity. Women were defined entirely by their biology; yet their biology was not a subject for polite conversation. Motherhood was a woman's crowning glory; yet pregnancy was an unmentionable disability. The very essence of woman's being was her uterus; yet the effect of the uterus on women's health and even her femininity was pathological. 'It is almost a pity,' mused Dr William Byford, 'that a woman has a womb.' The sharp nineteenth-century decline in fertility also posed the problem of how to deal with a sexuality that was potentially separable from procreation, and it raised uncomfortable issues of individual choice.[68]

The nineteenth-century woman had become the custodian of natural rhythms and biological cycles in a society that was increasingly ruled by industrial rhythms and market cycles. As such, woman was the object of considerable ambivalence. She was scorned but idealized – patronized, but also envied and feared: 'She was seen . . . as a being both higher and lower, both innocent and animal, pure yet quintessentially sexual.' And ultimately she was transformed by industrial society into a carefully domesticated symbol of nature, much as middle-class homes brought nature into their back yard and carefully pruned it of its wildness. As industrialization spread, men's view of women increasingly reflected Victorian ambivalence toward nature: women, like the stylized gardens and parks of the bourgeoisie, were to be untouched by the urgency and uncertainty of industrial life but amenable to its control; no elemental forces prevailed in this pallid imitation of the preindustrial world. Women, for their part, embraced the ideology of female asexuality at least partly as an assertion of their own autonomy and self-control in the one arena left to them. Although many physicians feared that tight corsets interfered with healthy child-bearing, women continued to lace themselves into contraptions that proclaimed their sex yet repelled any assault upon it. 'The corset,' declared one fashion magazine, 'is an ever present monitor, indirectly bidding its wearer to express self-restraint, and it is evident of a well disciplined mind and regulated values.'[69]

But as the century progressed fewer men were prepared to rely on women's self-restraint – perhaps because they feared it would not be enough, perhaps because they feared the self-assertion that accompanied it – and a more repressive, narrow definition of female sexuality was adopted by popular writers. In the 1830s and 1840s the majority of writers had stressed the need for moderation in conjugal sex. In the late nineteenth century, moderation grew into prudery. By the 1870s, some popular marriage manuals advocated female frigidity 'as a virtue to be cultivated, and sexual coldness as a condition to be desired.' Increasingly, one authority comments, 'the term nymphomania was applied to degrees of sexual expression which would be considered quite normal today.' One doctor even referred to a 'virgin nymphomaniac.' Ellen Rothman argues that the range of sexual behaviors that couples felt comfortable with 'narrowed' over the century, while the 'petting' allowed in the early 1800s became unacceptable.[70]

Connected to this narrowing of sexual options was an increased willingness to countenance sexual repression. The campaign against excessive sexuality increasingly moved from an instrument for individual self-control for the middle class to one of social control, both against lower-class and against deviant middle-class women. In the 1870s, emphasis 'shifted from the level of individual exhortation to that of organized efforts to enforce chastity upon the unwilling.' At the same time, a strong movement developed to restrict access to birth control and abortion. Laws and attitudes toward birth control and abortion had been relatively permissive prior to 1860. Between 1860 and 1880 this permissiveness ended. The Comstock Law of 1873 banned any

medicine or article to be used for contraception or abortion, as well as
the advertisement of such devices. By the early 1880s the right of abortion
had been practically repealed.[71]

The conflicts over sexuality in this period reveal gender and class issues
intersecting in interesting ways. On the one hand, moral distinctions often
followed class lines, uniting middle-class men and women against the
lower classes. The Pale Maiden and the Dark Lady, concepts that had
existed in literature 'for purely decorative purposes' before the nineteenth
century, now became symbols of the rejection of sexuality in the good
woman and its resurrection in the bad woman. This moral polarity was
closely connected to class and ethnic stratification. The working-class
woman, the immigrant, and the black woman were assigned a sexuality
that could not be admitted in the middle-class white woman.[72] Men
turned to prostitutes for the sex they could not enjoy with women of
their own station, and the class polarity of sexuality was reinforced by
the pay discrepancies that forced many working women to supplement
their low wages by sale of their bodies.

Middle-class writers in this period also evinced increasing hysteria
about the sexuality of their servants, and the supposed threat this
represented to their young. One physician warned that servants 'took
special delight in poisoning the minds of the young and innocent and
initiating them into the habits of vice'; another blamed servants for any
problems of precocious sexuality that might be found in children.[73]
(This panic, of course, flowed as much from the servants' alternative
approach to social reproduction as from their alleged habits of personal
reproduction.)

On the other hand, at the same time as the middle class worried
about how to control the poor's sexuality, they also divided over issues
of gender; some middle-class men expressed equal fears about the sexual
independence of their own women. Many attacks on abortion were based
explicitly on the ground that a woman should not be allowed to develop
her own goals and agendas, but must take the consequences of marriage.
As racism and national chauvinism mounted in the 1880s and 1890s, a
new charge was leveled at middle-class women: they were contributing
to race suicide. In some circles, the bourgeois woman who had an
abortion replaced the 'fallen' woman or the lower-class outcast as the
main symbol of sexual and social vice: 'the well-dressed and unnatural
female aborter [became] . . . a metaphor for the commercialized city
itself. She was urbane, she was affluent. She rejected God's and
nature's command that she bear and multiply.' 'When men fear work
or . . . righteous war, when women fear motherhood,' Theodore
Roosevelt was thundering by 1902, 'they tremble on the brink of
doom. . . .'[74]

Significantly, however, the women against whom these complaints were made almost never claimed that sexuality and birth control were matters of personal choice; nor did they accept lower-class sexual mores as legitimate. Middle-class feminists and anti-feminists alike emphasized the social, public consequences of sexual behavior, advocated abstinence and self-restraint, and organized movements claiming the right to scrutinize and regulate family life. Aside from the Free Lovers, both sides also relied on state intervention to implement their ideas of proper sexual relations; not even the Free Lovers questioned the centrality of motherhood. When two women died of botched abortions in Boston, the male medical establishment reacted by trying to make abortion a criminal offense, the women's movement by trying to make seduction a criminal offense.[75]

Middle-class proponents and critics of domesticity, then, shared pivotal assumptions, goals, and methods, despite the import of their differences. Discussions of domesticity and sexuality in the working class took place in a qualitatively different framework of material conditions and cultural values. It is to that framework and the families inhabiting it that we now turn.

Notes

1. McLoughlin, *Beecher*, p. 99; Barton Bledstein, *The Culture of Professionalism: The Middle Class and the Development of Higher Education in America* (New York, 1976), p. 52.

2. Nancy Dye and Daniel Smith, 'Mother Love and Infant Death, 1750–1920,' *Journal of American History* 73 (1986), p. 314.

3. McLoughlin, *Beecher*, pp. 113, 147.

4. 'The Forgotten Man,' in William Graham Sumner, *Social Darwinism: Selected Essays* (Englewood Cliffs, 1963), p. 129.

5. Trachtenberg, *The Incorporation of America*, p. 71.

6. Clyde and Sally Griffen, *Natives and Newcomers: The Ordering of Opportunity in Mid-Nineteenth-Century Poughkeepsie* (Cambridge, MA, 1978), p. 261. See also Katz, *Social Organization* and Lindert and Williamson, *Inequality*.

7. Sidney Harring, *Policing a Class Society: The Experience of American Cities, 1865–1915* (New York, 1983).

8. For an overview of immigration, see Leonard Dinnerstein, Roger L. Nichols, and David Reimers, *Natives and Strangers: Ethnic Groups and the Building of America* (New York, 1979); on the problems of adjustment, see Herbert Gutman, *Work, Culture, and Society in Industrializing America* (New York, 1976).

9. Daniel Rodgers, *The Work Ethic in Industrial America, 1850–1920* (Chicago, 1978), p. 22. See also Sam Bass Warner, *The Private City: Philadelphia in Three Periods of Its Growth* (Philadelphia, 1968), p. 71.

10. Robert Wiebe, *The Search for Order, 1877–1920* (New York, 1967). On distinctive small-town values, see Lewis Atherton, *Main Street on the Middle Border* (Bloomington, 1984).

11. Herbet Gutman, 'Industrial Workers Struggle for Power,' in H. Wayne Morgan, ed., *The Gilded Age* (Syracuse, 1970).

12. Horwitz, *Transformation of Law*; Harring, *Policing Class Society*; Donald

Parkerson, 'The Structure of New York Society: Basic Themes in Nineteenth-Century Social History,' New York History 65 (1984).

13. Dawley, Class and Community, p. 158; Elizabeth Pleck, 'A Mother's Wages: Income Earning Among Married Italian and Black Women, 1896–1911,' in Michael Gordon, American Family, p. 490.

14. David Katzman, Seven Days a Week: Women and Domestic Service in Industrializing America (New York, 1978), p. 53; Barbara Mayer Wertheimer, We Were There: The Story of Working Women in America (New York, 1977), pp. 86, 101.

15. Ross, Workers on the Edge, p. 231.

16. Trachtenberg, Incorporation of America, p. 59.

17. Susan Strasser, 'An Enlarged Human Existence? Technology and Household Work in Nineteenth-Century America,' in Sarah Berk, Women and Household Labor (Beverly Hills, 1980), pp. 29–51 and Never Done; Carole Srole, 'Beyond One's Control: Life Course and the Tragedy of Class, Boston, 1800 to 1900,' Journal of Family History 11 (1986), pp. 43–54; Judith McGaw, ' "A Good Place to Work." Industrial Workers and Occupational Choice: The Case of Berkshire Women,' Journal of Interdisciplinary History 10 (1979), pp. 227–48.

18. Modell, Hershberg, Furstenberg, 'Social Change and Transitions to Adulthood,' pp. 319, 322.

19. Michael Katz and Mark Stern, 'Fertility, Class, and Industrial Capitalism: Erie County, New York, 1855–1915,' American Quarterly 33 (1981), pp. 75–6; Jerry Wilcox and Hilda Golden, 'Prolific Immigrants and Dwindling Natives?: Fertility Patterns in Western Massachusetts, 1850 and 1880,' Journal of Family History 7 (1982), p. 277; Susan Bloomberg, Mary Fox, Robert Warner, and Sam Warner, Jr., 'A Census Probe into Nineteenth-Century Family History: Southern Michigan, 1850–1880,' Journal of Family History 5 (1971), pp. 26–45.

20. Rudy Ray Seward, The American Family: A Demographic History (Beverly Hills, 1978), pp. 105, 131; Frank Furstenberg, 'Industrialization and the American Family: A Look Backward,' American Sociological Review 31 (1973), pp. 9–10.

21. Howard Chudacoff, 'New Branches on the Family Tree: Household Structure in Early Stages of the Family Cycle in Worcester, MA, 1860–1880,' in Tamara Hareven, ed., Themes in the History of the Family (Worcester, MA, 1978), pp. 55–72; John Modell and Tamara Hareven, 'Urbanization and the Malleable Household,' Journal of Marriage and the Family (1973); Tamara Hareven, 'The Family as Process: the Historical Study of the Family Cycle,' Journal of Social History 7 (1974), p. 324; Katz et al., Social Organization, pp. 251, 278–80; Mark Peel, 'On the Margins: Lodgers and Boarders in Boston, 1860–1900,' Journal of American History 72 (1986), pp. 813–34.

22. Katz, Social Organization, pp. 251, 272.

23. Seward, American Family, pp. 108–9

24. Katz, Social Organization, p. 347.

25. Elizabeth Pleck, 'Two Worlds in One: Work and Family,' Journal of Social History 10 (1976), p. 187.

26. Trachtenberg, Incorporation, p. 127.

27. Anne Scott MacLeod, A Moral Tale: Children's Fiction and American Culture, 1820–1860 (Hamden, CN, 1975), p. 10.

28. Gwendolyn Wright, Building the Dream: A Social History of Housing in America (New York, 1981), p. 99; Ryan, Empire of the Mother, p. 109.

29. Richard Sennett, Families Against the City: Middle Class Homes of Industrial Chicago, 1872–1890 (Cambridge, MA, 1984).

30. Frederick Law Olmstead, quoted in Trachtenberg, Incorporation, pp. 146–7. See also Warner, Private City, and Rosenzweig, Eight Hours for What We Will.

31. Colleen McDannell, The Christian Home in Victorian America, 1840–1900 (Bloomington, 1986), p. 45.

32. Clifford Clark, Jr, 'Domestic Architecture as Social History: The Romantic Revival and the Cult of Domesticity in America, 1840–1870,' Journal of Interdisciplinary History 7 (1976), pp. 33–56; Wright, Building the Dream, pp. 106, 111.

33. Sam Bass Warner, 'Philadelphia in the Era of the Revolution,' in Gutman and Kealey, eds, Many Pasts (Englewood Cliffs, 1973), vol. 1, p. 164; Wright, Building the Dream, p. 96.

34. Trachtenberg, *Incorporation*, p. 129.

35. McDannell, *Christian Home*, p. 50; Ryan, *Cradle*, p. 201. (McDannell argues that the home did *not* mediate work and leisure but conceptually opposed them as well as public and private spheres; reasons for my dissent are found in the above discussion.)

36. Wright, *Building the Dream*, p. 113; McDannell, *Christian Home*, p. 27.

37. Wright, *Building the Dream*, p. 112.

38. Elaine Tyler May, *Great Expectations: Marriage and Divorce in Post-Victorian America* (Chicago, 1980); Robert Griswold, *Family and Divorce in California, 1850–1890: Victorian Illusions and Everyday Realities* (Albany, 1982). Griswold emphasizes the affective individualism of families, but I believe his evidence will also support an argument for affective gender stereotyping.

39. Nina Baym, *Women's Fiction: A Guide to Novels by and about Women in America* (Ithaca, 1980), p. 49; Marilyn Ferris Motz, *True Sisterhood: Michigan Women and Their Kin, 1820–1920* (Albany, 1983), p. 128; Deborah Fink, 'Rural Women and Family in Iowa,' *International Journal of Women's Studies* 7 (1982), pp. 57–69.

40. Frances Anne Kemble, *Journal of a Residence on A Georgian Plantation in 1830–1839*, ed. John Scott (New York, 1961), p. 34.

41. Mary Ann Clawson, 'Nineteenth-century Women's Auxiliaries and Fraternal Orders,' *Signs* 12 (1986), and *Constructing Brotherhood: Ritual, Class and Masculinity in Europe and America* (Princeton, forthcoming). Ryan, *Cradle*, p. 196; Lilian Faderman, *Surpassing the Love of Men* (New York, 1981), pp. 157–77; Carroll Smith-Rosenberg, 'The Female World of Love and Ritual: Relations Between Women in Nineteenth-Century America,' *Signs* 1 (1975).

42. Ryan, *Cradle*, pp. 163–5, 177 and *Empire of the Mother*, pp. 58–9.

43. McLoughlin, *Henry Ward Beecher*, p. 88.

44. For examples of women novelists' attempts to bring the world into the home, see Catharine Sedgwick's *Home* (1837) and Louisa May Alcott's *Little Men* (New York, 1962 [1871]), especially pp. 20, 59, 313. On boarding see Stuart Blumin, 'Rip Van Winkle's Grandchildren: Family and Household in the Hudson Valley, 1800–1860,' *Journal of Urban History* 3 (1975), p. 309; Katz, *Social Organization*; Modell and Hareven, 'Malleable Household.'

45. Sklar, *Catharine Beecher*, p. 136.

46. Barbara Laslett, 'The Family as a Public and Private Institution: An Historical Perspective,' *Journal of Marriage and the Family* 35 (1973), pp. 486–7.

47. See David Rothman, *The Discovery of the Asylum: Social Order and Disorder in the New Republic* (Boston, 1971). Sidney Harring argues that police not only increased their 'specialization in repression' over the period, thus requiring other agencies to take over some of their earlier civic functions, but even enforced tramp ordinances in ways that helped regulate labor supplies (*Policing a Class Society*, pp. 47 and passim).

48. Zaretsky, 'Place of the Family,' pp. 203, 205.

49. Mark Leff, 'Consensus for Reform: The Mothers' Pension Movement in the Progressive Era,' *Social Service Review* 47 (1973), p. 415; Mike Davis, *Prisoners of the American Dream* (London, 1986), pp. 102–53.

50. Grossberg, 'Who Gets the Child?' pp. 254–5.

51. Anthony Platt, *The Child Savers: The Invention of Delinquency* (Chicago, 1969), p. 145 and *passim*; Stansell, *City of Women*, pp. 209–11; Michael Katz, *In the Shadow of the Poorhouse: A Social History of Welfare in America* (New York, 1986).

52. Wright, *Building the Dream*, p. 128.

53. Platt, *Child Savers*, p. 135.

54. David Rothman, 'A Note on the Study of the Colonial Family,' *William and Mary Quarterly* 23 (1966), p. 631; Richard Rapson, 'The American Child as Seen by British Travellers, 1845–1935,' *American Quarterly* 35 (1965).

55. Katz, *Social Organization*, p. 389. See also Michael Katz, *Class, Bureaucracy, and the Schools* (New York, 1971) and *The Irony of Early School Reform* (Cambridge, MA, 1968); Marvin Lazerson, *Origins of the Urban School* (Cambridge, MA, 1971).

56. Arthur Schlesinger, *The Rise of the City* (New York, 1933), pp. 171–2; Howard Gitelman, *Workingmen of Waltham: Mobility in American Industrial Development, 1850–1890* (Baltimore, 1974), p. 171.

57. Colin Greer, *The Great School Legend* (New York, 1972); Stephen Thernstrom, *Poverty and Progress* (Cambridge, MA, 1964).

58. Rothman, *Discovery*, pp. 83, l08.

59. Ibid., p. 237.

60. Barbara Brenzel, 'Domestication as Reform: A Study of the Socialization of Wayward Girls, 1856–1905,' *Harvard Educational Review* 50 (1980), pp. 205, 208.

61. Epstein, *Politics of Domesticity*, p. 90; Jed Dannenbaum, 'The Origins of Temperance Activism and Militancy Among American Women,' *Journal of Social History* 15 (1980), p. 243, and *Drink and Disorder: Temperance Reform in Cincinnati from the Washingtonian Revival to the WCTU* (Urbana, 1984); Hewitt, 'Beyond the Search for Sisterhood,' p. 313.

62. Aileen Kraditor, *The Ideas of the Woman Suffrage Movement* (New York, 1971); Carole Turbin, 'And We Are Nothing but Women: Irish Working Women in Troy,' in Carol Ruth Berkin and Mary Beth Norton, *Women of America: A History* (Boston, 1979), pp. 214–15.

63. *Life and Work of Susan B. Anthony*, p. 898.

64. Ellen Dubois, 'The Radicalism of the Woman Suffrage Movement,' *Feminist Studies* 3 (1975), 'Politics and Culture in Women's History,' *Feminist Studies* 6 (1980), and *Feminism and Suffrage: The Emergence of an Independent Women's Movement in America, 1848–1869* (Ithaca, 1978).

65. James Weir, Jr., 'The Effect of Female Suffrage on Posterity,' *The American Naturalist* 29 (1895), p. 825.

66. For a fascinating cross-cultural discussion of gender roles and sexual relations as 'scripts' for larger social interactions, see Peggy Sanday, *Female Power and Male Dominance* (Cambridge, 1981).

67. Charles Rosenberg, 'Sexuality, Class and Role in Nineteenth-Century America,' *American Quarterly* 25 (1973), p. 139 and *passim*; Haller and Haller, *Physician and Sexuality*, p. 203; Barker-Benfield, *Half-Known Life*, p. 159.

68. Estelle Freedman, 'Sexuality in Nineteenth-Century America,' in Stanley Kutler and Stanley Katz, eds, *The Promise of American History* (Baltimore, 1982); Ann Douglas Wood, ' "The Fashionable Diseases": Women's Complaints and Their Treatment in Nineteenth-Century America,' *Journal of Interdisciplinary History* 4 (1973), p. 29.

69. Carroll Smith-Rosenberg, 'Puberty to Menopause: The Cycle of Femininity in Nineteenth-Century America,' *Feminist Studies* 1 (1973), p. 59; Haller and Haller, *Physician and Sexuality*, p. 100. See also Nancy Cott, 'Passionless: An Interpretation of Victorian Sexual Ideology, 1790–1850,' in Cott and Pleck, *Heritage of Her Own*, and Howard Gadlin, 'Private Lives and Public Order: A Critical View of the History of Intimate Relations in the U.S.,' *Massachusetts Review* 17 (1976). Smith-Rosenberg takes issue with Cott's point that the ideology of sexual repression was heaviest in the early nineteenth century, pointing to evidence that such repression mounted steadily as the nineteenth century progressed: Carroll Smith-Rosenberg, 'Sex as Symbol in Victorian Purity: An Ethnohistorical Analysis of Jacksonian America,' *American Journal of Sociology* 84 (1978).

70. Smith-Rosenberg, *Disorderly Conduct*, p. 23, n. 23; Rosenberg, 'Sexuality, Class, and Role' p. 139; Ellen Rothman, 'Sex and Self-Control: Middle-Class Courtship in America, 1770–1870', in Gordon, *Family in Social-Historical Perspective*, 3rd edn, pp. 398, 407.

71. Rosenberg, 'Sexuality, Class and Role,' p. 134; Linda Gordon, *Woman's Body, Woman's Right*.

72. Leslie Fiedler, *Love and Death in the American Novel* (New York, 1966), pp. 296–302.

73. Rosenberg, 'Sexuality, Class and Role,' p. 143.

74. Smith-Rosenberg, *Disorderly Conduct*, p. 227; Theodore Roosevelt, *The Strenuous Life: Essays and Addresses* (St. Clair, MI, 1970), p. 4.

75. Freedman, 'Sexuality in 19th Century America,' p. 209; Smith-Rosenberg, *Disorderly Conduct*, pp. 227–8; Linda Gordon, 'Voluntary Motherhood: The Beginnings of Feminist Birth Control in the United States,' *Feminist Studies* 1 (1973).

8

Working-class Families, 1870–90

One of the most striking features of working-class history from the 1870s to the 1890s is the presence of a vibrant, cohesive, even 'universal' working-class culture, paradoxically distributed in separate, localized, occasionally competing forms of social organizations and customs. The gulf between working-class and middle-class values, behaviors, and everyday life was perhaps greater than at any time before or since; and it occasionally surfaced in dramatic confrontations with the industrial order. Yet due to the uneven development of the country, the recruitment of different immigrant groups to different industries at various points in the evolution of work relations and housing stock, divisions between skilled and unskilled workers, and other cleavages, the working-class ethic assumed divergent cultural and political forms. The middle class confronted – and workers operated within – a multiplicity of working-class cultures. These comprised a clear-cut alternative to bourgeois individualism and work patterns without coalescing into a unified national movement that could sustain a political and economic challenge to the emerging industrial order. 'This moral universality amid the particularities of the workers' daily sectoral struggles' was the peculiar characteristic of late-nineteenth-century labor.[1]

The absence of a unified ideological or structural challenge to American capitalism should not be confused with lack of militancy. As Steven Ross points out: 'In the two decades after the Centennial Exhibition of 1876, with its grand celebration of American industry and progress, there were more strikes and more people killed or wounded in labor demonstrations in the United States than in any other country in the world.' Over the course of the period, as we shall see, a greater sense of class solidarity was forged, culminating in the Great Upheaval of 1886. But while this upsurge changed the terms of debate and struggle within American industry, labor was unable to maintain its organizational and ideological gains after 1886. (Ironically, by the end of the 1890s more effective national organizations and campaigns were being built, but many of the values and institutions that had challenged bourgeois cultural hegemony steadily eroded, and the 'moral universality' was 'ruptured.')[2]

To understand the role of the family in the working class during the Gilded Age, it is necessary to grasp both the specificity – even fragmentation – of working-class experience and organization *and* the universality of working-class values. There was tremendous variety in the work experiences of the wage-earning population. In industrial cities such as Philadelphia and Detroit, marked variation was the norm in the scale of firms, rates of pay, application of mechanical power, the proportions and relationships of skilled and unskilled labor in any industry, and the organization of production and authority within various work settings. American industries tended to have far greater pay differentials between skilled and unskilled workers than prevailed in Europe, while other aspects of industrial employment also varied. Textile mills in Massachusetts regulated the work pace and even the personal lives of their employees in strict detail, but they also put up with high employee turnover and rehired workers who had left without proper notice. European observers were amazed by the extent to which speed-ups and sobriety had been imposed on American textile workers: cotton workers in the 1870s operated four looms instead of the two worked by their English contemporaries. Yet as late as 1904 managers gave in to workers' tendency to vote with their feet by closing down the mill on the day the circus came to town. The Winchester Repeating Arms factory in New Haven, Connecticut, began to require on-time attendance only in the 1890s, while skilled iron- and steelworkers set their own hours and hired their own help.[3]

These differences hampered the emergence of movements that could raise demands or coordinate actions extending beyond a craft or local community. Although local communities, especially in smaller, one-industry towns, often provided some support for workers' demands against absentee capitalists, this usually occurred on the basis of older, ambiguous republican slogans or on a new consciousness of ethnic homogeneity. It thereby imposed limits on the growth of workers' organization and class consciousness. While the petty bourgeoisie sometimes aided workers by blocking elite projects, 'the ideological and programmatic influence of such a political force on the workers was certainly at least as pervasive as the obstacles it raised to the wishes of the industrialists.'[4]

David Roediger has shown that the St Louis General Strike of 1877 failed in part because its unrepresentative leadership – disproportionately composed of skilled workers, small proprietors, professionals, and white-collar workers – refused to mobilize unskilled workers or to sanction the widespread cooperation of Blacks and whites that occurred at the rank-and-file level. Identification with local institutions, he argues, encouraged some labor reform but also 'limited the tactical flexibility of labor organizations by committing them to a local boosterism shared with the upper and middle classes.' This divided skilled workers from the 'underclasses' and accentuated racism 'as a means of expressing those workers' inclusion in the community by dwelling on the otherness of Black workers. . . .'[5]

The tremendous divisions between big cities and small towns also impeded solidarity. In places such as Rochester, even the Knights of Labor 'desired social harmony and wished to preserve the sense of individual moral accountability possible in a small town.' Despite the radicalism of full-time organizers, local groups were likely to join Knights of Labor head Terence Powderly in condemning militant actions in the big cities.[6]

Even the strongest protest movements in small towns rarely mounted a supra-local challenge to business interests or to the two-party system; and working-class political alignments were often cross-cut by conflicts over cultural or local issues, especially as immigration mounted. In the big cities, politics was based on the ward system and its patronage apparatus. Machines filled the gaps left between the private sector and government, and bosses parleyed local constituencies and favors into particularistic power bases. Labor often found itself unable to compete with these machines. In addition, the waves of immigrants that poured into the larger cities entered the workforce at different places and with a different set of experiences: factors that initially prevented their collective identification, as well as setting them apart from small-town workers. These conditions are reflected in the way contemporaries, both pro- and anti-labor, usually talked about the working or producing *classes*.

Immigration and Ethnicity

Over the course of the century, America recruited the bulk of its working class through immigration. While the majority of manual workers in America were native-born, many came from recently immigrated families, and first-generation immigrants – one-seventh of the population – were more than two-fifths of the workers in manufacturing and extractive industries. Immigrants made up a majority of the workforce in some of the larger cities, and their ethnic characteristics often seemed to determine their lives and values more than their occupational experience. This has led some historians to elevate ethnicity above class in discussing American family history.

Certainly each group of immigrants drew on its own heritage to develop distinctive work and family patterns, and ethnic divisions frequently cut across class solidarities. But ethnicity cannot be readily or rationally disentangled from class in American history. Ethnicity was fundamental to the making of the American working class, not a historically separate feature laid on top of or opposed to class formation. Most ethnic sub-cultures evolved out of the working-class experience of immigrants, 'and people did not divide ethnic and class feelings into separate components in their minds.'[7]

True, there were important variations in family and gender patterns by ethnic group. While many differences between immigrants and native-born Americans – and among different immigrant groups – are explicable by economic and demographic factors, important cultural differences are equally evident, especially for females. One study, for example, found that non-ethnic variables accounted for all the so-called ethnic differences in labor-force participation for boys, but not for girls. Girls from immigrant families started work and left home earlier than girls from native-born families, but there were also variations among immigrant groups. Irish women tended to withdraw more completely from paid employment after marriage than did Germans. German immigrants tended to socialize in family groups, while Southern Italians maintained stricter sex segregation. Polish families tolerated children's peer groups far less than did Irish, Italian, or black families. Italian mothers who had to work outside the home chose cannery and field work over factory work because it permitted them to work alongside their children. Polish women preferred domestic work to factory work after marriage, while Jewish women avoided domestic work and sought industrial employment, whether at home or in the factory. Immigrant groups had different propensities to purchase their own homes, in part because of different experiences of proprietorship in Europe. Immigrant families consistently had higher fertility rates, higher rates of child labor, and lower percentages of non-kin living with them than did natives. Multivariant analyses of such patterns generally find that ethnic differences 'remain significant even after allowing for the varying occupational distribution.'[8]

But the same study that judged ethnic differences more significant than occupational ones also found that only 8 per cent of the Irish and 6 per cent of the Canadian household heads examined, as opposed to 34 per cent of the native-born, were non-manual workers. Immigrants were so overwhelmingly working-class that their tiny 'middle class' was not in any way comparable to the native-born middle class. Most immigrants who rose to middle-class status did so through manipulating their working-class environments, becoming petty landlords, shopkeepers, or ethnic power brokers. This led them, regardless of occupation, to share the class and cultural characteristics of their neighborhoods, giving an impression of independence to "ethnic" factors that actually reflected a particular group's location in the larger industrial system. Another study purporting to show the impact of ethnicity after 'controlling' for occupation found that *literal* location in the city greatly modified even supposedly ethnic patterns in fertility. Micaela di Leonardo points out that 'the households that immigrants formed, while labeled by themselves and others as "ethnic," varied greatly depending on region, era, and economic circumstance' rather than flowing from some constant cultural 'tradition.'[9]

Differing ethnic patterns, moreover, should be related not just to premigration values but to separate times of arrival, conditions of leaving the old country, and points of entry into American industry, all of which fit groups into the labor market and housing system in distinctive ways. Different nationalities arrived with dissimilar skill levels and age or gender distributions, as well as disparate values, and these interacted with the particular state of the housing stock, the configuration of the labor market, and the reaction of previous arrivals to forge ethnicity and class *together*. Immigrants drew on older cultural patterns in adapting to their new conditions, but they drew selectively, often recasting their old values considerably or highlighting characteristics that had not been predominant in the old world.[10]

If ethnicity and class cannot be disentangled in their origins they also served overlapping functions, as sources of mutual aid, joint action, and collective identification against bourgeois individualism. Nevertheless, unions and cultural/ethnic institutions were often *alternative* ways of responding to the pressures on workers in America and of organizing to meet their needs. Sometimes ethnic ties could facilitate labor solidarity. German bakers in Chicago, for example, first organized successfully because they could count on local support from fellow Germans in their neighborhoods for boycott and label campaigns. Such successful organization in turn allowed the bakers to recognize that the growth of larger bread manufactories required supra-local and intra-ethnic institutions. Jewish solidarity provided a powerful radical base for organizing in the New York garment industry. Sometimes, however, even groups that built a common cultural community outside of work competed with each other on the job market, while in other areas workers called united job actions but failed to build solidarity outside the workplace.[11]

Up until 1880, many ethnic areas were merely small enclaves – perhaps a block or two – that maintained their links to the larger working-class communities of which they were a part. In Philadelphia, industrial affiliation rather than ethnicity remained the 'primary organizing factor' in white residential patterns. In Lynn and Pittsburgh, a centralized working-class district helped overcome differences among the waves of ethnic groups that poured into various levels of the factory, allowing ethnicity to complement rather than compete with class organization. At Fall River and Worcester, on the other hand, scattered mills and housing concentrations reinforced the divisions introduced by segregated hiring practices and led to deep divisions within the working class. In many areas ethnic divisions deepened in the late nineteenth century, as 'increasing class segregation of housing was overlaid by simultaneously expanding ethnic differentiation.'[12]

Immigrant families, then, faced special circumstances and created varied strategies for coping with them, while the working class often divided along ethnic lines. But in analyzing the changing patterns of family life in the nineteenth century, it is possible – perhaps even necessary – to discuss immigrant families as part of a general working-class configuration, remembering that they tended to be found in the lower occupational strata. As Richard Ostreicher comments: 'Each of the ethnic working-class cultures included components of mutualism, solidarity, and egalitarian politics which provided the basis for a common ground on which they might come together. . . .'[13] Each also had family structures and strategies that are best explained by their articulation with the industrial system.

The black family, however, despite its almost completely working-class character, requires distinctive treatment, for the position of black workers in the industrial system was qualitatively different from that of other ethnic groups. Their residential patterns, unlike those of the Irish, Germans, and native whites, cannot be explained by their industrial position; they seldom had access to factory jobs except when temporarily imported as strikebreakers; and new immigrant labor, far from pushing native-born Blacks up in the occupational scale, generally pushed Blacks out of the industry or job category entirely. Not surprisingly, Blacks developed some special family patterns which deserve separate consideration. We will return to the black family after examining white working-class families.

Patterns of Work and Family Life in the Working Class

For all the differences outlined above, working-class people shared many common experiences and values which imparted a distinctive cast to their family patterns, despite important variations by occupation and ethnicity. The majority of the working class lived very close to minimum levels of subsistence. Forty per cent of industrial workers fell below the poverty level of $500 per year; another 45 per cent barely stayed above it. Another 15 per cent comprised highly skilled workers, usually Protestant and native-born, who might earn two to three times this amount. But the exceptionally high pay that could be earned by skilled workers did not always compensate for other aspects of the American industrial system – seasonal layoffs, no public social security measures such as pensions or unemployment compensation, no national labor party, unsafe working conditions, and possibly a harsher attitude than elsewhere in the industrializing world toward welfare for men (though not for women and children, who were 'allowed' to be dependent in proportion as men were required to be independent). The cumulative impact of all this, claims Peter Shergold, was that by the early twentieth century even skilled workers' higher pay and greater social mobility still left American workers as a group behind their British counterparts. The British worker

> generally had longer leisure time . . . ; he was far less likely to be killed or maimed while at the workplace; he labored under less pressure: and he was provided with superior social services and facilities – hospital accommodations, city-based unemployment benefits, garbage collection, park space, and so on.[14]

Earnings of male workers, moreover, especially for manual workers but also in the skilled trades, peaked very early, leaving families vulnerable as the father aged and the children left home. A 'man of 23 earned as much as or more than a man two score years his senior.' In Michigan, only 5.2 per cent of the workers surveyed in 1885 had savings accounts to help them through layoffs, illnesses, or old age. In addition to these shared insecurities, most workers also encountered authoritarian or arbitrary treatment on the job, increasing pressure to conform to industrial discipline, and numerous attempts at paternalistic control over their leisure lives. They simultaneously gained common experiences in organizing to resist such control, both at work and in their communities.[15]

Another common experience for American workers was geographic mobility. Population turnover in the cities, small as well as large, seems to have ranged from 40 to 60 per cent in any decade during the nineteenth century. Such high transiency rates may have hampered the consolidation of working-class political and union institutions in some ways, but they also helped to establish a universal working-class culture, marked by an openness to newcomers and a recognition of the need to give and receive aid through associational networks and personal hospitality. Much migration was organized through kinship or ethnic networks, while some was a result of occupational and labor solidarities. Migration was also not simply a one-way, one-time process. Communication and assistance flowed in both directions and set up far-reaching linkages among working-class people.[16]

The effect of these common experiences on working-class family life was twofold. On the one hand, reliance on distinctive family strategies was greatly reinforced; on the other, there was a constant need to look beyond the family for other sources of aid and solidarity. Like the middle-class family, the working-class family in the nineteenth century was the primary source of class reproduction. Working-class status translated directly into specific family strategies and family position greatly influenced an individual's place within the working class. The family, moreover, was the main institution available to cushion the shocks of a deflationary period in which falling profit rates led to cut-throat competition, frequent layoffs, and attempts to impose more control over labor.

Low rates of pay, chronic economic and personal insecurity, and the lack of developed state or trade union institutions to provide social welfare measures ensured that the working-class family had to organize itself as an economic unit, closely coordinating its reproductive and domestic strategies with its position in industrial production. In some factories, especially the mills, families contracted to work together. The male might be paid the wages for the entire family and be held responsible for supervising their behavior on the job. Many industrial enterprises recruited labor through the extended family networks of immigrant males, while in the sweated trades whole families worked together on various parts of a product that was being made on piecework terms. Even in areas where families did not work together, most working-class families required one or more secondary earners in order to make ends meet. Child-rearing strategies and husband–wife interactions had to reproduce 'a collective family economic unit.'[17]

For unskilled and semi-skilled workers, high fertility rates were a rational response to the problem of declining income for an ageing father. Among French-Canadian textile workers, 'one child wage earner could boost the family income, on average, by more than half, and two child wage earners could double it.' Among these workers, large families were the *most* likely to escape poverty.[18] In other industries too the employment of children could allow the family to buy a house, which would then serve as security when the father's income fell off and the children had left the family. It is no wonder that birth rates rose among unskilled and semi-skilled workers in this period, independently of religion and national origin.

In many industrializing cities, 'ethnicity became an increasingly important factor in fertility. The reason, however, rested not in culture but in the dominant class position of different ethnic groups':

> The great rise in Irish Catholic fertility was at least in part a function of its working class character, and the decline among the Scottish Presbyterians, English Methodists, and Canadian Protestants related to the prominence of business-class occupations among them. Ethnicity, in short, served as a mediator between class and fertility.[19]

While most working-class families put their children to work early, they were unlikely to have the wife working outside the home unless the husband were incapacitated in some way. First-generation immigrant wives often worked, but second-generation immigrant families tended to withdraw wives from the paid labor force. Although this is sometimes interpreted as assimilation, it can be more plausibly explained by the exigencies of life in working-class America, where the sharp split between domestic and productive work and the lack of national social security systems or large-scale workers' aid organizations required a full-time worker in the home if wage-earners' returns were to be translated into a minimum level of comfort and long-term security. As Michael Haines observes: 'Child-rearing was apparently an adequate substitute for a wife's labor-force participation outside the home and . . . a good investment for later stages in the life cycle.'[20]

We have already noted Jeanne Boydston's calculation that a woman's work inside the home, prior to the Civil War, had more value than her potential earnings outside. This conclusion would apply equally to the postwar period, given the continuity of wage differentials by gender and the failure of new technology to ease household chores and food preparation. The wife who stayed home, coordinated the schedules of the working members of the family, made their clothes and food, and possibly took in boarders or did home work as the children aged might contribute more to the family economy than one who worked for wages that were often less than a third of men's. As late as 1905, a national survey found that women's wages averaged $5.25 a week. Assuming year-round full employment, seldom possible for women, their average yearly wage would have been $273.00. When one considers that the work week necessary to earn this sum was often sixty hours, it seems likely that the income earned by a working wife would not equal the extra expenditures on clothes, transportation, food, and cleaning that would have been necessary to maintain a barely comfortable living. Unless the family was living substantially below subsistence (as were many Blacks), the family was better off having the wife free to prepare food, keep house, and perhaps earn a little extra money by taking in boarders or doing some piecework on the side.[21]

Homemaking in the nineteenth-century working class was still a full-time job. Many working-class families, even in the cities, had to grow at least part of their own food, because of the prohibitive cost of fresh vegetables. As late as 1890, half the families in the main centers of coal, iron, and steel employment kept livestock or poultry, grew vegetables, or both. Almost 30 per cent grew enough food so that they purchased no vegetables other than potatoes. Of 7,000 working-class families interviewed between 1889 and 1892, fewer than half purchased even prepared bread. Other prepared foods were beyond the means of most working-class families. The housewife, consequently, was involved with food preparation on an almost full-time basis. Workers could seldom afford ice boxes – ice alone cost 42 cents a week in Pittsburgh – nor could they afford to buy larger, theoretically more economical quantities of food, so that marketing and cooking had to be done almost daily. Margaret Byington's 1910 study of the steel town of Homestead found that twenty-one of the ninety families spent less than the 22 cents per person a day estimated to be the rock bottom figure for adequate nutrition. The average expenditure was 24 cents, leaving most families a 'surplus' of only 2 cents. Survival on such budgets required careful, constant work, and a housewife might increase the real income of her family more by staying home and devoting herself to such work full-time than by going out to look for a job.[22]

Susan Strasser has pointed out the limited diffusion of nineteenth-century technology into most American households. Few homes had the mechanical cooking or cleaning devices that were illustrated in popular journals. Laundering was an arduous and time-consuming task, requiring hours of work even for the few who owned machines. The job must have been particularly demanding when the family included workers in heavy industry. In Pittsburgh, working-class homes in the 1880s had no indoor water. Women had to haul water by hand for every task, from cooking to cleaning, and then dispose of it afterwards. Wood and coal stoves required hours of tending and cleaning, while the soot they produced made general housecleaning a formidable undertaking. In 1893 the Commission of Labor revealed that only 47 per cent of New York City's families, 30 per cent of Philadelphia's, 27 per cent of Chicago's, and 12 per cent of Baltimore's had inside toilets. In the New York City tenement district of the 1890s, only 306 of 255,000 residents had access to bathtubs.[23]

In these circumstances, working-class families who wished to maintain a modicum of cleanliness or to eat nutritious and adequate meals would, if they could afford to, assign a full-time worker to household tasks. Given the higher wages of the husband and the earnings advantage of youth, this was most likely to be the wife.

The day-to-day economic dependence of family members upon one another created strong pressures against individualism and toward family solidarity. Such solidarity extended beyond the nuclear family. Contrary to older myths, immigrant extended family networks were not broken up by the process of migration or the transition to industrial work. Such networks were often the impetus to and the means of migration; family connections determined where immigrants would live and helped newcomers adjust to city life, while links with the community of origin were maintained to the extent that many migrants sent remarkably high proportions of their wages back to relatives they had left behind. Evidence suggests that immigrant families were *more* cohesive in America than in the Old World, as they settled together, sought work together, extended the length of parent/child co-residence, and often incorporated other kin into their households. Immigrants, of course, were especially likely to work at piecework or home industry, thus reinforcing extended kinship networks, but extended family networks were important among the entire working class, for males as well as females. Most visiting and vacationing, for example, was done in the homes of relatives.[24]

The same factors that strengthened general reliance on family strategies prevented the nuclear family from operating as an entirely independent unit, even where kin were not present: 'The prevailing native middle-class culture stressed the value of independence and self-reliance, but even workers who fully believed in these virtues could never know when they, too, would need the help of neighbors, friends, or fellow workers.'[25] In consequence, the working-class ethos extended beyond job-related acts of solidarity – supporting strikes, boycotts, and associations – to less formal means of sharing resources, even with newcomers seeking work. As we shall see, working-class families made fewer divisions between family and street life or public and private roles than did middle-class families, though they drew sharper distinctions between work life and personal life. They did accept a clear division of labor on the basis of gender, however, and often formulated it in terms of domesticity.

Working-class Domesticity

The working-class family partook of several elements associated with middle-class domesticity: the wife seldom worked for wages outside the home; a gender-based division of labor prevailed in the family and the workforce, defining men as producers and women as potential wives and mothers; and home-ownership was an important value often linked to ideas about the sanctity of the home. 'Next to being married to the right woman,' editorialized the *Ontario Workman* in 1872, 'there is nothing so important in one's life as to live under one's own roof.' The author then waxed eloquent in his dramatization of what home-ownership meant to a working-class wife:

> We have our cosy house; it is thrice dear to us because it is our own. We have bought it with the savings of our earnings. Many were the soda fountains, the confectionery saloons, and the necessities of the market we had to pass; many a time my noble husband denied himself the comfort of tobacco, the refreshing draught of beer, wore his old clothes, and even patched-up boots; and I, O me! I made my old bonnet do, wore the plainest clothes, did the plainest cooking; saving was the order of the hour, and to have 'a home of our own' had been our united aim. Now we have it; there is no landlord troubling us with raising the rent, and expecting this and that. There is no fear in our bosom that in sickness or old age we will be thrown out of house and home, and the money saved to pay rent is sufficient to keep us in comfort in the winter days of life.[26]

In the absence of social security, home ownership could mean the difference between a comfortable old age and a miserably impoverished one. Since male earnings dropped sharply with age and few pension plans existed, such sacrifices to buy a home were rational and even imperative, despite the fact that they frequently meant pulling children out of school to maximize purchasing power for the home.

This is not to deny a partial acceptance of middle-class values here. Religious and political organizations stressed economic individualism and the possibilities of upward mobility. Upper- and middle-class women influenced working-class women and children in their role as Sunday school teachers, charity workers, or even employers of maidservants.[27] Perhaps even more important was the exceptionally strong and pervasive presence of a lower middle class in America and the real, if limited, possibilities for advancement into white-collar work. The earnings advantage of skilled over unskilled labor created a small group of workers who could afford some of the comforts of middle-class domesticity and who undoubtedly spread such values and aspirations to other sections of the class. It is also worth remembering that middle-class domesticity, in its original form, was critical of excessive accumulation, ambition and individualism – values that would have resonated positively for working-class people.

But it will not do to see working-class family values and organization as a mere reflection or even creative adaptation of middle-class values. First, many working-class family values and practices, such as early employment of children, insistence on the role of active leisure in personal life, and toleration of youthful peer groups outside the family remained remarkably distinct (even though they were later adopted – and reworked – by the middle class). Second, even practices and values that were similar in form possessed a very different content.

The demand for a family wage, for instance, did not necessarily originate in acceptance of middle-class values about woman's sphere. One possibility is that withdrawal of the wife's labor may have been a more or less conscious attempt to resist the exploitation of the family. Hans Medick has commented that the early phases of capitalist expansion rested 'on an increasing exploitation ... of the *total* family labour force.' As competition reduced returns to labor the preindustrial family typically increased its expenditure of labor, falling back on 'self-exploitation' to ensure the subsistence of the family. Although Medick is here talking about handicraft production, so that his remarks apply particularly to home industries in nineteenth-century America, the same principle operated in many early factories, where men could not earn enough to support their family without mobilizing the labor of other family members.[28] Withdrawal of wives from the workplace and the use of domestic ideology to demand a family wage may have represented one attempt to break this pattern, especially as changing technology and increased employer control over work led to a deterioration in the wages and working conditions of industries that had initially offered relatively good opportunities for women workers.

Skilled workers had another reason to oppose the employment of women. It was not simply male prejudice which led to the charge that women were often hired to undercut male wage rates. Women were certainly not hired because employers wished to affirm any commitment to sexual equality or female capacity. They were hired only where and when they could be paid less than men. The employment of women often led to a decline in wage rates for the entire industry involved, as with the transition to a female labor force in the clerical field. Given the craft-union mentality of the time, the logical response of organized workers was to attempt to exclude the cheap competition, and many wives probably acquiesced in this primitive attempt to maintain their husbands' wage rates. The probability that this consideration weighed more heavily than simple male prejudice is supported by the fact that male unionists often worked amicably and showed strong solidarity with women workers who were not directly competitive with them, as in the shoe industry.

Of course, the exclusion of women from jobs was not a long-term solution to employers' attacks on workers' living standards, given the unequal power of craft unions and industrial employers. A craft organization that successfully limited entrance to the trade and maintained high wages was soon likely to find its entire craft obsolete, as employers substituted new jobs or mechanized the task completely. The only long-run solution, as some women and men began to recognize in the 1880s, was to eliminate the source of cheap labor and strikebreakers by achieving equal pay. Nevertheless, in the context of the nineteenth-century labor movement, poorly organized and divided along craft and ethnic lines, most working men responded to the problem of competition from cheap labor by attempting to exclude women (and Blacks or Chinese) from the labor force. The reluctance of men to have their wives work was thus a logical – if ultimately ineffective – response to a real problem, not merely an irrational patriarchal prejudice.

Martha May argues that the demand for a family wage originated among male and female workers, against middle-class, employer, and state opposition. It 'represented a dual claim to subsistence and industrial justice to its early advocates,' as well as a desire to remove the power of economic and social superiors over the working-class household. Clearly the demand did not benefit working women, especially single or widowed ones, in the way it benefited working men: it adopted the limiting theory of the fundamentally different natures of men and women, elevated the male public role, and obscured the productive activity of women in the household. 'But gender divisions remained subordinate to class claims; the working-class family ideology continued to be qualified by its emphasis on subsistence, justice and the demand for better hours and wages,' unlike the middle-class family ideology, which explicitly made domesticity a *substitute* for labor reform or modification of the market system. 'The arguments for the family wage invoked the interests of the entire family, thus going beyond a simple assertion of gender privilege.'[29]

Unlike middle-class domesticity, which reduced morality to gender roles, the working class used gender roles to raise larger issues of industrial justice and social democracy. In the radical union town of Cripple Creek, for example, 'Miners opposed capitalism partly because it forced women to work and destroyed the home'; they justified unionism on the basis that it made a dignified life possible for families. Only in the twentieth century was the family wage demand transformed by Progressive reformers and conservative unionists into a cross-class issue that divided workers on the basis of gender more than it furthered the aims of class autonomy.[30]

Similarly, working-class rhetoric about the sanctity of the home had an entirely different content than did similar sentiments in the middle class. The home, argues Linda Schneider, was 'a symbol of autonomy' for working-class people, a place where workers could assert their own standards of comportment, escape factory regulation, and resist middle-class interference into their leisure life. It was also a counterweight to the opportunities and pressures in industrial society that might lead individuals to abandon class and family obligations.[31]

The sexual division of labor within the working class, and the ideologies of male and female spheres, could actually elevate labor solidarity outside the home. Where men and women were not in competition for jobs, for example, their sense of mutual dependence and complementary roles could heighten labor militancy. In Louisville, male spinners and female weavers cooperated in labor organization and militant strike activity; women's labor efforts garnered strong support from the male labor movement during the 1887 woolen strike. In Troy, ideas about proper work for men and women helped to create an economy based on male labor in the iron foundries and female work in laundering, but the fact that most female industrial workers were single or widowed allowed an ideology of the domestic family to coexist with support for women's economic rights. Many of the predominantly Irish women among the Troy collar laundresses were the sisters, daughters, or in-laws of male ironworkers, and the powerful male union movement in Troy showed them what organization could do. The Troy Collar Laundry Union, organized in 1864 by Kate Mullaney, was strong enough by 1866 to donate $1,000 to the Iron Molders' Association when ironworkers were locked out by their employers. The laundrywomen organized a strike in 1869 and received in their turn substantial financial and organizational support from the Troy Molders and several New York City Unions. (The invention of a new paper collar, however, which threatened the very existence of the collar laundresses, gave employers enough leverage to break the strike.) Carole Turbin suggests that the strong labor community in Troy was supported by the sexual division of labor in both the city and the home:

> Since the city was dominated by two industries, one employing women and the other employing men, when men went out on strike they could rely on the earnings of female family members in the other industry and vice versa. . . . [T]he relationship between industrial structure and family patterns is an important part of the explanation for Troy's strong labor community.[32]

During the latter part of the nineteenth century women proved again and again that acceptance of prevailing gender distinctions did not necessarily moderate militancy. In 1875 the male textile workers at Fall River voted to accept a pay cut announced by the employers.

The women held their own meeting afterwards and voted to strike, on their own if necessary. The men then reversed their decision, joined the women, and together the men and women of Fall River won their strike. In the 1880s, women members of the Knights of Labor led militant strike actions that earned them the praise of Terence Powderly, head of the Knights, as 'the best men in the Order,' a phrase that evidently did not rankle as it would today. Women also used the ideology of gender to shame men into taking part in strikes or to get away with actions for which men might have more readily been shot, such as harassing militia members, crossing military lines to run messages for strikers or bring supplies, and tossing strikebreakers into ditches or subjecting them to the 'water cure' – dowsings in buckets of cold water. Moreover, as we have already seen, where men and women did not manage to cooperate, a shared sense of gender could occasionally reinforce and harden the class solidarity of women workers. 'We are a band of sisters,' wrote a mill operative in the Voice of Industry, 'we must have sympathy for each other's woes.'[33]

Still, it would be wrong to romanticize working-class domesticity any more than middle-class domesticity, or to deny the ultimately conservatizing effects of the Victorian sexual division of labor in the working class. Steven Dubnoff has found that among Lowell mill workers, parents had a much greater tendency to work consistently whatever the wage rate (though women were absent more often then men), than non-parents; single boarders tended to trade extra income for leisure, taking more absences when they received more pay. Parents, in other words, were forced to develop a 'moral orientation' toward work, while boarders, both male and female, were 'strongly calculative' in absenting themselves from work once immediate economic ends were met. Daniel Walkowitz also points to the conservative role of the working-class family in the Gilded Age: it was 'a relatively small private-interest group ... [that] filled the normative role of accommodator, while ... the neighborhood usually remained the arena for collective organization.'[34] The self-sacrifice of the wife at home – some accounts even indicate that women denied themselves food to feed male workers – gave her little of the middle-class woman's 'expanded sphere,' while the 'privileges' of the male worker also forced him into steady employment, limited his mobility, and hampered his ability to stay out on strike.

Parents were not the only ones constrained by family responsibilities. Many young people sacrificed their personal dreams of education or independence to work for the family unit. The role of secondary wage-earners in the family, especially when they were young women, also inhibited labor organization. The majority of the female industrial workforce prior to 1920 was composed of young single women living with their parents. On the one hand, since they were not primary breadwinners, they were not forced to organize in order to survive; on the other inasmuch as their small wages made the difference between family subsistence and absolute poverty, these women faced many pressures to keep on working whatever the conditions and pay. A study of Italian women in industry, undertaken between 1911 and 1913, found that two-thirds of the workers were under twenty-one and more than 80 per cent lived with a parent or parents. Almost all simply turned their pay checks over, unopened, to the head of the family. Such women were unlikely to be able to resist family pressures against striking or other activities that might jeopardize the family's weekly subsistence. Many females shared the situation of thirteen-year-old Fannie Harris, who testified before a New York legislative committee on female labor that she had been earning $2 a week, for sixty hours' work, at a necktie factory:

> Q. What did you do with that two dollars?   A. Gave it to my mamma.
> Q. Did your mamma give you anything to spend?   A. Yes, sir . . . two cents every week . . .
> Q. Have you got any older brothers and sisters?   A. I have an older sister.
> Q. Does she work?   A. Yes, sir.
> Q. Does your mamma work?   A. Now she ain't working because I am working, but before, when I didn't work, she worked . . .
> Q. Does your papa do anything; does he work?   A. Yes, sir; he works, but just now he is not at work – he is sick.[35]

Adopting domesticity was in some ways, then, a defensive maneuver with long-run disadvantages. It was a response partly to the deterioration of working conditions for women, partly to the threat of industrialization to skilled craftsmen, and partly to the failure of middle-class women to address the special needs of women workers. As May points out, 'the family-wage ultimately . . . worked against the interests of working-class men, women and families, by accepting and deepening a sexual double standard in the labor market.' The double standard allowed the state to forestall union demands by granting charity to women without 'providers' and employers to hold down women's wages on the grounds that they worked for 'pin money.' It also gave some women an incentive to act as strikebreakers or non-union workers. Finally, the double standard closed off opportunities to explore alternative family and gender roles within the industrial working-class that might have strengthened working-class solidarity. By the early twentieth century, indeed,

Middle-class social reformers and activists came to embrace the family wage as a means of restoring social stability, while some employers recognized its possibilities as a means to control and divide labor. At the same time, within the ranks of organized labor, the family wage increasingly became a defense of gender privilege. Defense of gender privilege, in turn, was closely connected to a craft exclusiveness that hampered male organizing as well as female.[36]

Working-class Gender Roles and the Limits of Domesticity

The most important thing to grasp about working-class domesticity and family life, however, whatever their pros and cons for labor organizing, is that they had a different social content than did middle-class domesticity and family life. Working-class gender roles were not always as clearly divided, nor were they defined along the same lines, as middle-class ones. Although the separation of paid work and home life appeared earlier in the working class than elsewhere, this was not necessarily equated with the separation of male and female spheres. Home remained a center of important productive activity and of mixed-gender leisure activity for both men and women. The earliest working-class taverns, for example, were often located in private homes, and up through the 1870s much drinking 'remained rooted in the . . . kitchen grog shop. The saloon, as a spatially distinct public and commercialized leisure-time institution, had not yet entirely triumphed.'[37]

City officials increasingly legislated against kitchen taverns and women liquor-sellers, thereby creating the very split between home life and male sociability that they later denounced, and encouraging the male saloon to develop as 'the mirror image of the male factory.' Yet like the factory, the public image of the saloon as a male preserve hid significant participation by women. Perry Duis denies that the saloon was

> a uniquely male preserve. In small 'ma and pa' operations the wife was at home behind the bar as well as behind the stove preparing the free lunch. . . . The crusades against the dance hall and the white slave menace after 1900 also indicate that drinking became less sexually divided as the years passed, while Boston license officials fought a losing cause . . . to enforce temporary segregation-of-sex rules.[38]

Although some working-class wives complained of husbands who ran off to the saloon, in Boston and Chicago at least 'Court statistics ranked drinking low on the list of causes of divorce.'[39] Most working-class women seem to have had no objection to their husbands bringing home a bucket of beer from the local tavern. Home-based beer parties were quite common, with both sexes participating.

Under normal circumstances, the saloon was perhaps less a competitor to the working-class family than a necessary supplement to it. The majority of its regular clients were the bachelors who made up such a high proportion of the working-class city population. It provided these men with food, companionship, a mailing address, often even a place to sleep. Additionally, the saloon served certain functions for married men that were in the interests of the entire family – they provided free lunches or cheap breakfasts, information or even contracts for work, and political patronage. Finally, women also utilized the saloon, which was often rented out for social functions or meetings. Women as well as men bought beer or wine, usually in little pails to take home with them, though German beer gardens were gathering places for the entire family.[40]

Despite an ideology of male production and female domesticity, necessity often blurred the distinctions. Although married working women tried not to work outside the home they did much income-generating work within it, taking in boarders or lodgers, doing laundry, preparing food goods for sale; and the cash raised in these ways was often an important component of the family's budget. Working-class families were also far more vulnerable than the middle class to economic and personal catastrophes that might force a wife into wage-work. Working-class men and women blamed the capitalist, not the woman, when married women had to work. Few derogatory comments about the lack of femininity of women workers, no matter how dirty and arduous their work, are to be found in working-class writings.

Although distinct male and female networks existed in the late-nineteenth-century working class, comments Kathy Peiss, 'there was no simple or rigid gender-based dichotomy between public and private realms of leisure.'[41] Part of the reason for this was the increase in young women working outside the home. By 1890 nearly four million women, almost one in seven, were so employed, one million of them in factories. The proportion of working women in domestic service shrank from 50 per cent in 1870 to 38 per cent in 1890. These women had a period before marriage when they worked and socialized, and might even live, away from their families and in contact with young men of their class.

Ironically, the lack of physical amenities in working-class homes and the greater amount of housework to be done there may also have diminished the distance between male and female responsibilities:

In the 1880s, when the first modern investigations of working-class family life were undertaken by the Massachusetts Bureau of Labor Statistics, one of the findings that most shocked and dismayed the middle-class male investigators was that working-class men would cook, clean, and care for the children while their wives were at work and they were not.[42]

When housewives got sick in urban tenements, someone had to haul water, dump excrement, and tend the fire; the working class did not have servants to protect men from these realities.

Neighbors, Community, and Fellow Workers in the Working-class Family

As we have seen, there were important limits on the privacy of the middle-class family. Male business and female kin networks cut across the couple relationship, while the family often felt it had to live its life on display, proving to neighbors, peers, and social superiors its 'respectability' and conformity to middle-class standards. Yet the middle-class family also emphasized economic privatism, put itself forward as a self-sufficient unit, and sanctioned a degree of ambition for individual mobility, at least for males. The working-class family, by contrast, did not put forward privacy or escape from community obligations as an ideal. The boundaries of the nuclear family, both conceptually and physically, were far more fluid than in the middle class.

Conditions of life in the industrial working class strongly militated against a withdrawal into the nuclear unit. We have already noted the increase in extended families and subfamilies between 1850 and 1880 in urban, industrial areas. Boarding and lodging seem to have increased for the working class as well. Once characteristic of the middle class, these became in late-nineteenth-century cities more of a working-class phenomenon, though particularly associated until the end of the century with native-born Americans. (Newly settled cities in the West, however, tended to follow older patterns, where boarding and extended families were more common among affluent sectors of the population.) The incidence of boarding or lodging at any given census was 15 to 20 per cent (more in the cities), but a substantial majority of native-born workers probably lived in such settings at some time in their life, for boarding was associated with what some authorities call the life cycle but might be more usefully termed the job cycle. Working-class youths tended to lodge when they were selecting among occupations or establishing themselves in the job. After gaining a family, a steady job record, and a home, they were more likely to take in boarders.[43]

The choice of boarding over residence with relatives is sometimes interpreted as preference for an economic transaction over an affective relationship, but this seems dubious, since lower-class families who lived together also had to operate on economic principles in order to survive.

(Family sweatshops in which children as young as four or five had to work all day, pasting roses onto hats or fetching materials, can scarcely be offered as examples of affective relationships.) More likely, the prevalence of boarding among the native-born working class testifies to occupational and ethnic solidarities (the match between boarders and household head was close in both categories) and to the greater income security of these workers: boarding seems to have offered an institutionalized way of progressing from mobile worker to settled household head while receiving the financial benefits of co-residence. Immigrants, on the other hand, until the turn of the century were less likely to take in boarders than to share housing with relatives. The difference is probably related to the divergent job experiences of these members of the working class. Immigrants tended at first to fill low-skilled jobs involving entire families, or to work in preindustrial jobs as family units. Such families would naturally tend to live together. It was also more difficult for low-paid immigrant workers to establish the independence to become or take in boarders.[44]

Although increasing numbers of white-collar workers lived a significant distance from their workplaces, most blue-collar workers continued to live within a mile of their jobs, often within a block or two. With fellow workers nearby, crowded and uncomfortable tenement apartments, and little money to spend on travel even for day trips, working-class men, women, and children did much of their socializing out of doors:

> Streets served as the center of social life in the working-class districts, where laboring people clustered on street corners, on stoops, and in doorways of tenements, relaxing and socializing after their day's work. . . . [O]rgan grinders and buskers played favorite airs, itinerant acrobats performed tricks, and baked-potato vendors, hot-corn stands, and soda dispensers vied for customers. In the Italian community . . . street musicians and organ grinders made their melodies heard above the clatter of elevated trains and shouting pushcart vendors, collecting nickels from appreciative passers-by. Maureen Connelly, an Irish immigrant, remembered listening to the German bands that played in Yorkville. . . . 'Something was always happening,' recalled Samuel Chotzinoff of his boyhood among lower East Side Jews, 'and our attention was continually being shifted from one excitement to another.'[45]

The lack of separation between family and neighborhood life in the working class helps to explain the fact that the sexual division of spheres was different, and often less rigid, than in the middle class. Some areas of recreation were gender-specific (more of these for men than for women). A male leisure culture grew up around cigar stores, barber shops, workingmen's or ethnic societies, and saloons. Women often combined domestic chores with social time by doing laundry in tenement yards or congregating at the pumps and fire hydrants where they got their water; they also simply hung out on stoops or fire escapes while their children played nearby. But the separation of working-class men and women should not be exaggerated. Many men brought beer home for socials with kin and neighbors, and 'workers who were too tired, poor, or temperate [to go to taverns] "congregated in groups on the leeside of some house". . . .' Interestingly, George Bevans's 1913 study of New York workmen found that the higher-paid native-born workers, not the immigrants and unskilled laborers, spent the least amount of leisure time with their families. This contradicts the usual portrayal of immigrant and manual laborers as particularly 'macho' and patriarchal in comparison with more 'enlightened' natives.[46]

For the many working-class couples who spent a majority of their leisure time in each other's company, family recreation was seldom confined to the nuclear unit. When families were not socializing outdoors they might set up evenings at another family's apartment. These often involved shared housekeeping or cooking by the women alongside male card-playing. In an article derived from her detailed investigation of life at Homestead in the early twentieth century, Margaret Byington offers us a glimpse of life in the courtyards of working-class housing, where women exchanged pleasantries as they did their wash and waited to use the pump, men gathered to play cards on summer evenings, and on pay Saturdays households pooled funds to buy beer and socialize.[47]

Boarding and lodging ensured a turnover of unrelated people within the household and seem to have contributed to labor solidarity in working-class communities. In many nineteenth-century labor disputes, for example, the fact that workers boarded in other workers' homes ensured strong community sympathy for a strike and facilitated mutual aid during hard times. Even in expanding rural towns where families were experiencing a contraction in the yards where neighbors had formerly gathered, porches became places of neighborhood sociability. In Middletown, the Lynds found that it was only the 'business class homes' that began after 1900 'to divert the money formerly put into front porches to . . . other more private and more often used parts of the house.'[48] These 'business class' families were to become increasingly worried by the continuing sociability of lower-class households: the turn of the century saw a concerted effort to impose middle-class ideals of privacy on lower-class families.

Meanwhile, however, most working-class families provided little space for privacy and next to no support for personal ambition and individual mobility. Wages were pooled within the household, and the educational prospects or future earnings of children were often sacrificed to the security of the family unit. And not only that of the co-residential family: between 1851 and 1880, Irish immigrants sent $30 million back to the Old Country through the Emigrant Industrial Savings Bank of New York alone. Immigrants also financed local churches with donations that represented an extremely high proportion of their income.[49]

Gender divisions within the working class, moreover, were less connected to the aim of family self-sufficiency than in the middle class, and more rooted in a mutualistic tradition of reciprocity that put group solidarity above family ambition. Where the middle-class cult of domesticity supported rather than challenged the world of business and the free play of the market, the working-class cult of domesticity sometimes complemented and extended union organization or worker resistance to the industrial order. In the 1880s, for example, the Knights of Labor set up cooperative laundries and stores to socialize women's work. The Knights also organized picnics, sociables, and railroad excursions that 'brought the family together within the context of the wider working-class movement. For all their talk of "hearth and home," the Knights of Labor conceived of the family, not as an isolated haven from the world, but rather as the cornerstone of the working-class community.' Leon Fink argues that the Knights

> beckoned both to wage-earning women and workingmen's wives to join in construction of a 'cooperative commonwealth,' which, without disavowing the Victorian ideal of a separate female sphere of morality and domestic virtue, sought to make that sphere the center of an active community life.[50]

If working-class manliness meant, as in the middle class, the ability to work hard to support a family, it also meant meeting one's responsibility to the labor movement and standing up for workers' rights. If working-class womanliness meant – as in the middle class – being a good wife and mother, it could also mean being a dedicated 'union girl.' The female members of the New York Knights of Labor, in a nice blend of gender and class solidarity, passed this resolution:

> whenever the Knights of Labor girls went to a picnic or ball they were to tell all the brother Knights that none of the latter were to walk with a non-union girl in the opening promenade so long as a union girl was without a partner. Should any male Knight violate this rule, all the girl Knights are to step out of the promenade and boycott the entire crowd.[51]

Life versus Labor in the Working Class

One of the major differences between working-class and middle-class family life in the nineteenth century lay in the former's active opposition to industrial values. While the middle class organized its domestic affairs to produce a sanitized, idealized version of the bourgeois work world, the working class pioneered what has become the modern split between personal life and work activities. The split between work and leisure (often formulated as a split between work and life) is not precisely identical with the division between male and female spheres. Indeed, this split has since come to blur many of the older divisions between these spheres.

I have argued that the nineteenth-century middle-class family excluded the cross-class interactions and conflicts of the industrial world but governed its relations according to industrial notions of time, work discipline, property rights, and economic privatism. Children were introduced to wage-work and profit notions through allowances tied to the performance of certain tasks and by rewards for saving. Middle-class authors such as Louisa May Alcott recommended that children be taught the principles of business on a small scale by selling produce from their own garden spots, receiving object lessons on the value of capital accumulation, and acquiring their own little savings banks. Working-class families, age roles, and gender divisions, we have seen, were clearly opposed to such notions. In important ways, working-class personal life ignored time discipline, downplayed private accumulation, and rejected the division of life into separate arenas of work and play, effort and relaxation, competition and cooperation, amateur and expert. The divorce of personal life from work principles raised the possibility that working women could claim a share of personal life; and a mixed-sex leisure culture had begun to develop by the end of the century.

'Long in advance of the hesitant middle-class recognition of the claims of leisure,' comments Daniel Rodgers, 'workers dreamed of a workday short enough to push labor out of the center of their lives.' Two major crusades for the eight-hour day were launched in the late 1860s and 1880s respectively.[52] The second provoked bloody repression and led to a number of changes in class strategy on both sides. Meanwhile, though, workers implemented in daily life what they were unable to win formally.

When workers could no longer drink on the job, they drank on their breaks – as ostentatiously as they could manage. Enterprising young boys picked up 'growlers' from workers, filled them with beer, and carried them back on long poles to the factory gate in time for lunch breaks, receiving a penny each for their efforts. Away from work, working-class leisure activities were characteristically strenuous rather than contemplative, and generally hostile toward middle-class values and practices. Theaters attracted a male, working-class audience quite unlike the female, middle-class audience that patronizes plays today. Audience participation during the acts was the rule, not the exception. Francis Couvares writes that working-class sports such as racing, boxing, bowling, and ball games 'demanded no clear separation between professional and amateur' and that 'most music-making remained amateur through the 1880s.'[53]

Other areas of ethnic/working-class leisure revolved around Fourth of July activities, street festivals, and fairs that were generally far too boisterous and hostile to the rich for middle-class sensibilities. It was working-class and immigrant groups who first adopted participatory and competitive sports. Demands for public play areas also came from the working class, often against vehement opposition from the middle classes. Middle-class reformers responded by banning circuses from public property and positioning 'Keep off the Grass' signs in the parks.[54]

Ironically, many working-class conceptions of leisure were to be adopted by the middle and upper classes around the turn of the century, though only after their implied criticism of bourgeois individualism was blunted. Theodore Roosevelt, for example, was to link working-class notions of active sports to support for imperialism in speeches such as 'The Strenuous Life' (1902). Working-class sports such as baseball and boxing became professional, commercialized businesses. The theater gradually became a respectable place where matinees were attended not by unemployed workers and youngsters playing hooky from school but by middle-class women who politely kept their comments to themselves and saved their applause until the curtain.

Another area of difference between working-class and middle-class families in the nineteenth century was in workers' development and toleration of a youth culture, which seems to have complemented rather than rivaled working-class community and family life. Youth peer groups were hated by civic authorities because they were able to express class hostilities without the restraints faced by their parents: 'During strikes, these gangs would often gather at the factories, break windows, and join in harassing the scabs.' Park reformer Frederick Law Olmstead contrasted the middle-class family scene – a 'tea-table with neighbors and wives and mothers and children, and all things clean and wholesome, softening and refining' – with such a working-class youth group, expressing the blend of fear and distaste they evoked in the middle class:

> Consider how often you see young men in knots of perhaps half a dozen in lounging attitudes rudely obstructing the sidewalks, chiefly led in their little conversation by the suggestions given to their minds by what or whom they see passing in the street, men, women, or children, whom they do not know, and for whom they have no respect or sympathy. There is nothing among them or about them which is adopted to bring into play a spark of admiration, of delicacy, manliness, or tenderness. You see them presently descend in search of physical comfort to a brilliantly lighted basement, where they find others of their sort, see, hear, smell, drink and eat all manner of vile things.[55]

As Olmstead's lurid portrayal reveals, the most visible of these groups were male. Girls tended to be more tightly controlled by their parents, though Kathy Peiss has recently argued that by the end of the century the growth in wage-work for single working-class women had provided them with incentive and opportunity to play a role in developing a newly autonomous leisure culture for working-class youth of both sexes.[56]

The Black Family in the Late Nineteenth Century

Many of these comments about working-class families apply equally to Blacks, who also had a rich community life, a strong youth culture, an orientation toward extended family networks, and values and behaviors clearly opposed to bourgeois individualism. But mention should be made here of the special characteristics of black families in industrializing America, particularly in view of persistent myths that black family and community life was destroyed by slavery and that the resultant 'matriarchal' structure of black communities resulted in a 'tangle of pathology' which prevented Blacks from achieving upward mobility. This alleged 'disorganization' of black culture and family life has been variously attributed to the 'legacy of slavery,' the disruptive effects of migration North, and a 'culture of poverty' caused by severe material deprivation but reinforcing that deprivation by creating 'weak ego structure, confusion of sexual identity, a lack of impulse control, and . . . little ability to defer gratification and plan for the future.'[57]

Attacks on these stereotypes have come from many different angles. First, numerous researchers have demonstrated that Blacks developed their own culture and community both before and after slavery, maintaining group traditions while flexibly adapting and innovating where necessary. The rich community life constructed by Blacks in the period under consideration here is revealed in the list of groups that participated in the 1883 parade celebrating the twentieth anniversary of emancipation in the District of Columbia:

> Hod-carriers Union (500 men), Sons and Daughters of Liberty (50), Fourth Ward Ethiopian Minstrels (26), West Washington Union Labor Association (40), Young Men's Social Club, Washington Star Pioneers (20), Washington Brick Machine Union Association (16), Gay Heart Social Club, Cosmetic Social Club, the Invincible Social Club, Knights of Labor, East Washington Social Club, Knights of Jerusalem, Chaldeans, Knights of Moses, Galilean Fishermen, Sons and Daughters of Samaria, Osceolas, Solid Yantics, Monitor, Celestial Golden Links, Lively Eights, Imperials, Independent Fern Leaf Social Club, The Six Good Brothers, Twilight Social Club, and the Paper Hangers' Union.

A newspaper reporter commented in the same year that there were approximately 100 black societies in Washington, D.C., 'supported almost entirely by the laboring colored people.'[58]

Second, many researchers have argued that the incidence of broken and female-headed families among nineteenth-century Blacks has been exaggerated: two-parent nuclear families were in actuality the normal residential unit. Herbert Gutman reports that between 1855 and 1880, 70 to 90 per cent of black households were male-headed, and at least 70 per cent were nuclear. In Ohio, as well, most black households were nuclear and headed by males.[59]

However, it is important not to overstate the resemblance of black families to what has become the white, middle-class ideal. In Boston, Elizabeth Pleck initially reported that only 18 per cent of black families were headed by just one parent in the late nineteenth century, but more extensive research convinced her that this statistic seriously underestimated the extent of household dissolution. Pleck now estimates that about 25 per cent of black households in northern cities and 34 per cent of those in southern cities were female-headed during this period.[60]

What is at issue is the source of this phenomenon, and this brings us to a third critique of arguments about the legacy of slavery and migration: the important structural differences that did exist between black and white families cannot be attributed to either slavery or migration. In Boston and Philadelphia, the highest proportion of one-parent households was found among long-term residents rather than ex-slaves or migrants from the rural South. In both North and South female-headed families were associated with urban poverty, unemployment, and underemployment rather than with the heritage of slavery or the direct effects of migration.[61]

Between 1880 and 1900 the number of two-parent nuclear families among urban Blacks seems to have declined in at least some areas. Although this change is partly attributable to a rise in the proportion of female-headed households, the greatest single cause was increasing numbers of augmented households or subfamilies – a marked rise in the co-residence of black families and individuals. By 1905, in New York City, one out of 7.9 black households included a subfamily, compared to one in 22.9 for Jews and one in 11.2 for Italians, while female-headed households represented 17 per cent of the black total and 7 per cent for both Jews and Italians. In New York, the proportion of nuclear families among Blacks had declined to 49 per cent by 1905; in Richmond it had fallen to 40 per cent by 1900. The decline in the proportion of nuclear families began earlier in Philadelphia, and centered in the poorest section of the black population. By mid century, almost one-third of the families in the poorest half of the black community were headed by women.[62]

Differences in black family structures, then, were direct consequences of urban poverty. Clearly, the viability of a household dependent upon a central male breadwinner declined for many Blacks during the second half of the nineteenth century. The most probable reason for this development is the increase in unemployment, underemployment, and job discrimination for black males. Job opportunities 'narrowed both relatively and absolutely' for northern and southern Blacks in the latter part of the century. In Buffalo, Blacks were driven out of skilled occupations between 1855 and 1905 and were hit harder than other groups by the depressions of the 1870s and 1890s. In Birmingham, Alabama, Blacks 'were constantly pushed out of various occupations toward the bottom of the occupational hierarchy.' Throughout the South, 'traditional black artisanal skills, which had reached a high point in the late eighteenth century and were maintained throughout the antebellum period by free Negroes, were liquidated in the last decades of the nineteenth century.'[63]

The exclusion of Blacks from skilled trades and even factory work led to poverty and unemployment that undoubtedly made it necessary for many families to pool their resources and for others to split up, as members went different directions in search of work or security. It also produced high mortality rates for black males and led to diseases such as tuberculosis, which caused sterility among black men and women. Childless marriages were more likely than others to be dissolved. The increase in female-headed families also reflected a different consequence of racism: while black men suffered from constant unemployment, black women were able to find jobs in domestic service as white women domestics moved on to more desirable office and manufacturing jobs.

Elizabeth Pleck argues that at least in northern cities, it was the virulence of racist discrimination rather than the failure of Blacks to adopt middle-class values that best explains the high rates of marital dissolution in the late nineteenth century. Indeed, she suggests that the adoption of mainstream values was part of the problem rather than the solution, for the realities of racial discrimination made such values unrealistic guides to family life and caused strain in many marriages.[64]

The distinctive history of Blacks in America, compared to other ethnic groups, illustrates a point made by Eric Wolf about the different functions of racial and ethnic categories in the modern world:

> The function of racial categories is exclusionary. They stigmatize groups in order to exclude them from more highly paid jobs and from access to the information needed for their execution. . . . While the categories of race serve primarily to exclude people from all but the lower echelons of the industrial army, ethnic categories express the ways that particular populations come to relate themselves to given segments of the labor market.

Thus, despite discrimination, ethnic groups in America have over time achieved at least limited job and residential mobility. Segregation and concentrations of poverty, however, have *increased* among Blacks over time, and this has required them to adopt qualitatively different coping strategies than those used by immigrant workers.[65]

We should regard those different coping strategies, however, less as a sign of *disorganization* than *reorganization* of family life. For the final critique to be leveled against the theorists of black family 'pathology' is that their assumptions about what is 'normal' and 'functional' are seriously flawed. Carol Stack and Demetri Shimkin have shown that the extended family networks of both northern and southern Blacks in the twentieth century provide flexible, effective ways of building community while coping with poverty and discrimination. That such networks functioned similarly in the nineteenth century is illustrated by James Borchert's study of alley residents in Washington, D.C. Other studies reveal that black families maintained far tighter and more supportive kin ties than other urban families, more frequently taking care of elders, paupers, and orphans within the family rather than institutionalizing them.[66]

As in other sections of the working class, family life among Blacks, whether one- or two-parent, nuclear or extended, did not develop in isolation from the community; nor did it mirror the fragmentation of life characteristic of industrial capitalist society. Borchert writes that black Washingtonians 'turned the alley into a commons where children could play safely, adults could lounge and talk, and people could even sleep on hot summer nights.' Although 'outsiders were made to feel uncomfortable,' residents developed a strong community life, based on 'clear lines of social order' and expressed in extensive social rituals such as those around death and hospitality:

> Extended kinship networks and the incorporation of friends and neighbors into the family made it difficult to determine where the family ended and neighborhood or community began. The distinction between work and recreation was also unclear in the alleys, if only because there was little time for activities that did not add to the family's limited resources. Children's work was also play, 'Some women regard housework as a form of recreation,' and men fished for both sustenance and pleasure.

Alley dwellers also 'drew no sharp lines between the sacred and the secular. Like everything else in alley life, religion and folklife were intertwined almost completely.'[67]

The ways in which necessary adaptations to poverty interacted with creative innovations in family life and sex roles are well illustrated in the history of black women and children. As Eugene Genovese has pointed out apropos the slave community, far from there being a debilitating black matriarchy, male and female relations may have been healthier than in much of white society. Jacqueline Jones argues that after Reconstruction black women continued to play a leading role in work and community-building, helping black families to develop work patterns that gave them at least some independence from white interference. Nineteenth-century black children's commitment to both work and education suggests that if anyone had a problem with weak ego structure it was the overprotected, passive children of the white middle-class families described by Sennett in Chicago.[68]

In the late nineteenth century many more black wives worked than white: Approximately 20 per cent of married black women worked for wages, in contrast to only 4 per cent of married white women. Elizabeth Pleck has examined different possible reasons for this and suggested as one possibility 'that black women's wage earning was a means of coping with [black men's] long-term income inadequacy.' Although other working men faced low wages and chronic unemployment, they had some possibility of wage raises over time. Jobs available to black men, by contrast, 'were more often dead ends.' Claudia Goldin reports that her research might support either 'the hypothesis that black women worked to enable sons to remain in school or the hypothesis that they worked because their children were discriminated against in the labor market.' The difficulty black children had in finding jobs certainly reinforced an emphasis on education: history bears out modern assertions by Blacks that they have to be twice as qualified as whites to earn almost as much. Even today, for example, Blacks with four years' college education earn an average of $800 less per year than white high school graduates.[69]

Although poverty, discrimination, and commitment to children's education explain much of the tendency for black wives to work, they do not account for all of it. Black wives were more likely to work than white wives from the same income level. This may have been due partly to realistic fear of discrimination and partly to a greater need to protect the family against the strong probability of downward mobility. But it may also have reflected a self-confidence and independence among black women connected to their central role in work and community, as well as an acceptance of and respect for that role by black men.[70]

A final characteristic of black families in the late nineteenth century runs counter to many impressionistic accounts: between 1860 and 1910 the fertility of Blacks was lower than that of their white neighbors in any given region except the South. And 'by 1910 even southern blacks had lower levels of childbearing than did their white neighbors.' Thus the high overall fertility of Blacks in the nineteenth century was a function of the fact that most Blacks lived in the South, a region whose economic and social characteristics tended to foster high fertility among most of its residents. In urban areas, black households were consistently smaller than white ones.[71]

Families in the West

The West is not often associated with the changes in class and family relationships we have been describing. Its image is one of heroic individuals escaping the constraints of both class and culture. Although most of these heroic individuals are male, some females have also begun to receive attention. Calamity Jane (Martha Jane Canary) served as an army scout and a Pony Express rider. Arizona Mary drove a sixteen-yoke oxen team for hire in the Southwest, while Mary Fields, an ex-slave, was a stagecoach driver carrying the US mail through Montana. Belle Starr became an outlaw folk hero. Etta Place, companion of 'The Sundance Kid,' planned many of the holdups in which he was involved and went to Argentina with Sundance and Butch Cassidy. Dona Tules, later known as Señora Dona Gertrudis Barcela, won fame as a gambler and ran her own luxurious gaming salon. Some women sought gold and adventure in such hazardous places as the Klondike. The Northwest Mounted Police reported that between 1897 and 1898, 631 women went through the Lake Tagish Post on the Yukon side of the Chilkoot and White passes.[72]

But these images obscure the central basis of western settlement – the process of capitalist industrialization which enmeshed the West in the same dynamic of class formation and gender roles as was evident elsewhere. The West was opened up by the railroads and the military more than by individual explorers and settlers. The Pony Express may be the outstanding symbol of western individual heroism, but it gave rise to more print than it ever carried, lasting only eighteen months before being replaced by the telegraph. Western settlement was dependent upon and shaped by the spread of industry and international commerce.

People who went West were predominantly middle-class in origin. The cost of moving West rose from about $600 in the 1830s to at least $1,500 at the end of the century. In neither period were these amounts of capital available to the ordinary working person. But the western experience did not re-create the middle-class family farms of the early republican period. Huge mechanized farms appeared almost from the beginning, wealthy ranchers hooked up with railroads and meat-packers to monopolize the best land and transportation centers, and speculators ended up with most of the land opened up by the Homestead Act. Scott and Sally McNall estimate that 'probably less than one acre in nine went to the small pioneers.'[73] Many settlers went broke and moved from failing farm to failing farm before eventually becoming wage-laborers. Those who were successful quickly created a new proletariat by importing Chinese and Mexican laborers.

Although single men predominated among migrants to the West during the first trip along the Overland Trail and during the Gold Rush years, most settlers moved in family groups, and neither the move itself nor the experience of living in the West fundamentally changed Victorian gender roles. The trip itself was probably the most difficult part of pioneering for women. A decision to move was usually made by men, while women dreaded leaving behind the company of friends and relatives, the sphere of religion and sisterhood that was their one source of self-esteem and autonomy in Victorian America. One westbound bride complained: 'Nothing gives me such a solitary feeling as to be called Mrs. Walker. . . . My father, my mother, my brothers, my sister all answer to the name Richardson. The name W. seems to me to imply a severed branch.'[74]

Along the trail women's worst fears were confirmed, as their possessions were the first to fall victim to the harsh exigencies of survival. The trail was littered with the remnants of women's sphere: musical instruments, books, pictures, parlor furniture, knick-knacks, and china were sacrificed as the wagons had to be lightened. The bare necessities retained were, in the eyes of most women, men's things: grain, livestock, tools.

An equally disturbing casualty of the trail was the Sabbath, by this time the one day on which women's concerns and activities received deference. Women diarists invariably recorded their distress at the violation of this day. 'Sabbath!' exclaimed Velina Williams in her diary on 10 April 1853. 'A beautiful morning. The wind lulled and it is decided we must cross the river. The waters . . . seemed to reproach us for disturbing them on this holy day.'[75]

The division of labor that defined male and female identities in Victorian America broke down along the trail, but only partly. While women took on men's tasks, men seldom reciprocated. The result was that women often worked two jobs, fitting in the baking and laundering after camp was made. Kitturah Penton Belknap was uncharacteristically cheery in describing her duties along the trail:

> When we camped I made rising [salt-rising bread] and set it on the warm ground and it would be up about midnight. I'd get up and put it to sponge and in the morning the first thing I did was to mix the dough and put it in the oven and by the time we had breakfast it would be ready to bake. Then we had nice coals and by the time I got things washed up and packed up and the horses were ready the bread would be done and we would go on our way rejoicing.

Other women exhibited more resentment. One, driven beyond endurance, actually set fire to her husband's wagon in an attempt to make him turn back.[76]

As the trip proceeded, women learned tasks generally associated with men in nineteenth-century America. They began to fell trees, make bullets, drive the wagons, help build bridges. The diary of thirteen-year-old Mary Alice Shutes described cherished breaks for fishing with her uncles. Mary Eliza Warner, aged fifteen, reported that she 'drove four horses nearly all day' and played chess with Aunt Celia, 'which Mrs. Lord thought was the first step toward gambling.' Lydia Waters recalled climbing trees with the boys and learning to drive an ox team.[77]

For the older women, however, the addition of men's tasks was simply another burden. Rather than giving women a sense of self-worth and productiveness, sharing work on the trail simply threatened their self-image as women. Because the general social relations and values of Victorian America were not affected or even called into question by the relatively short trip west, the breakdown of women's sphere was experienced as a loss rather than an expansion of woman's role. Women gave up all that made them unique and special without gaining any voice or place of reference in the male world to which they were admitted as temporary laborers, 'draftees rather than partners.' Consequently, women were often embarrassed by their new skills and longed to reestablish the symbols of domesticity that reinforced their image as women. Lydia Waters recalled that an officer and his wife laughed behind her back about her oxen-driving, while Mary Ellen Todd remembered that her pleasure in learning to crack the driving whip was mixed with shame over the unladylike nature of this accomplishment. Women clung to the sunbonnets that kept their faces pale, and tried to prevent their daughters from picking up wild habits. In their role as keepers of life's biological markers, women depressingly catalogued the deaths along the way and wondered who would be next.[78]

The scarcity of women in the West has been exaggerated, but in some places it was severe for a short period. In 1850 rural Oregon had 137 men for every 100 women, while Portland had three times as many men as women. Women were particularly rare in mining areas and frontier towns. California in 1850 had a population that was 90 per cent male. (In all these areas, however, the next twenty years saw the sex ratio come to approximate that in the East.) Some women found advantages in this initial imbalance. One woman recalled of California during the Gold Rush that 'the feminine portion of the population was so small that there was no rivalry in dress or fashion, and every man thought every woman in that day a beauty.' But many women felt deeply the lack of female friends and relatives. As a Nebraska woman complained: 'We do not see a woman at all. All men, single or bachelors, and one gets tired of them.' Moreover, many women discovered that the scarcity of their sex simply meant they had to assume ever more work. Abigail Scott Dunniway described life as a wife in a nineteenth-century Oregon community,

composed chiefly of bachelors, who found comfort in mobilizing at meal times
at the homes of the few married men of the township, and seemed especially
fond of congregating at the hospitable cabin home of my good husband. . . .
To bear two children in two and a half years from my marriage day, to make
thousands of pounds of butter every year for market, not including what was
used in our free hotel at home; to sew and cook, and wash and iron; to
bake and clean and stew and fry; to be, in short, a general pioneer drudge,
with never a penny of my own, was not a pleasant business for an erstwhile
school teacher. . . .[79]

The initial gains of women entrepreneurs soon faded once men,
with more capital and social clout, moved in on their fields. As mining
faded, males displaced women on the job market, even in 'women's
work,' or at least took over ownership of the enterprises, reducing former
proprietors to the status of hired hands. The few early prostitutes who
amassed fortunes and ran their own brothels were replaced by women
who were exploited by pimps and kept only a small percentage of their
earnings. A good example of the transition can be found in the history
of Chinese women in California. They were extremely rare, and a few of
the earliest Chinese women settlers were able to profit from this. Ah-choi,
the second Chinese woman to land in San Francisco, was a prostitute who
became a wealthy businesswoman. Later prostitutes, however, came as
imports under the control of male entrepreneurs who had kidnapped or
enticed them, married them under false pretenses, or actually bought them
from their families.[80]

For a few exceptional women, especially in the fluid early days
of settlement, the West offered special opportunities. For many others,
however, it simply isolated them from the privileges of women's sphere
without giving them the advantages of men's. The contradictory effects
of the West on women are best summed up in a comparison of work
patterns in East and West. Fewer women worked outside the home in
the West than in the East. In 1890, when 17 per cent of all adult
women in the nation were gainfully employed, the percentage was only
13 in the western states. The largest group of employed women in the
West comprised domestics, a fact no longer true by 1890 for the nation
as a whole. Opportunities for factory and office work were far fewer.
Yet western women were more highly represented in the professions
than eastern women. While nationally only 8 per cent of working women
were in the professions, 14 per cent of working women in the West filled
these occupations. Furthermore, both Wyoming and California had laws
requiring equal pay for male and female teachers.[81]

Divorce rates were higher in the West and coeducation was more
frequent. Wyoming was the first state to give suffrage to women. Utah
was next, and by 1914 ten of the eleven western states had granted

women's suffrage, compared to only one eastern state. Yet the leaders of the suffrage movement, even in the West, came from the East, and western newspapers often praised their women as 'angels in contrast with their strong-minded sisters in the East.'[82]

If the move West occasioned little change in Victorian family and gender roles, however, it brought massive disruption to the Indians who lived there. The period from 1870 to 1890 saw the final displacement of the Indians, ending with the shameful massacre at Wounded Knee in December 1890. Whenever possible, Indians were forcibly and destructively 'modernized' through introduction of private property, destruction of communal institutions and rituals, and imposition of the nuclear family. The 1883 Dawes Act broke up Indian tribal lands and allotted them to individuals; the Indians, explained Senator Dawes, 'needed to become selfish.' The Bureau of Indian Affairs attempted to introduce competitive values to Indian children and push Indians into more individualized modes of subsistence. Extended kin networks and communal ties survived, of course, and in some cases were rebuilt in response to poverty and oppression, but the old unity between family ties and social production was broken, with often disastrous results for individual self-image and effective community action.[83]

The role of racism in the settlement of the West can hardly be exaggerated. Not only did it justify war against the Indians, it also worked against Mexicans and Chinese, leading to the Oriental exclusion movement of the 1880s and 1890s. As in the South, racism helped to disguise the area's position as an internal colony of eastern finance; but above all, it cut across potential alliances between farmers and workers as well as hindering unity within the working class. The myth of western individualism also hurt such unity, creating a tendency for farmers' protests to rather vaguely identify 'monopoly' as the enemy and to reject 'class feeling' as *subversive of the social order.*'[84]

The Great Upheaval and its Defeat

There were times, of course, when divergent family strategies, ethnic and racial divisions, and local or regional variations were transcended or fused into a larger expression of class solidarity and united action. In 1878 the Knights of Labor, initially organized as an underground union to avoid repression, came out into the open by holding a national convention. The Knights quickly moved to the forefront of attempts to organize workers across religious, ethnic, and even gender divisions. They tried seriously to build not only a unified working-class culture and movement, but alternative working-class institutions. In addition to the cooperative stores and laundries discussed above, they even set up assemblies that allowed workers to settle domestic and community disputes without depending on the bourgeois court system.[85]

The Knights supported equal pay for equal work and helped to organize a number of female unions and strikes. By 1886 there were about 200 women's assemblies and 50,000 female members. The Knights also organized black workers, recording 60,000 black members by 1886. At the 1886 general assembly the convention set up a women's department to organize women workers, investigate their special problems, and agitate for equal pay. Leonara Barry, an Irish woman who worked in a hosiery mill, became the Knights' General Investigator for women workers, a job that included both education and practical organization. Meanwhile, both the South and the West generated important opposition movements in the 1870s and 1880s: the Granger Movement and Populism. At times these movements seemed on the verge of transcending racism, utilizing the talents of women, and linking up with the industrial working class.

In 1885 the Knights of Labor won a series of strikes in the Southwest and in 1886 they helped to spearhead a national movement for the eight-hour day. In city after city during that year, the working-class 'subculture of opposition' coalesced into stronger organizations, mass marches, huge strikes, and independent political action. Between 1884 and 1886, membership in the Knights of Labor jumped from 50,000 to 700,000. Labor tickets appeared in 189 towns and cities in thirty-four states and four territories, and the Knights claimed to have elected a dozen congressmen in the November election.[86]

Swift and violent repression followed, as the business and middle classes responded in shock and outrage to this evidence of working-class disaffection and potential power. Sean Wilentz has suggested that Haymarket was just the 'beginning of what may some day come to be recognized as the most intense (and probably the most violent) counter-offensive ever waged against any country's organized workers.'[87] The fledgling movement proved unable to withstand the assault. Within a year membership in the labor movement had dropped precipitously; by 1894 the Knights of Labor were effectively finished. With them went many of the institutions and associations that had nourished class solidarity and opposition. These losses were to have momentous long-range consequences for the evolution of working-class family life.

The reasons for labor's defeat were many: ethnic, craft, and ideological divisions played an important role, as did the gap between small-town labor movements and large-city ones, and the lack of a strong reform wing within the middle class. The ability of the American political system to absorb working-class leaders without adopting working-class programs was also a factor; most of the Knights' political victories involved collaboration with one of the major parties. Leon Fink comments that 'the dominant two parties emerged from this period with a stronger grip than ever on the working class. Ironically, a movement that began by defying the contemporary party system may in the end have left workers even more firmly within its confines.' Mike Davis also directs attention to the emergence of a 'spoils system' for local craft unions within the big-city political machines: 'The overall effect . . . was to corrupt labor leadership, substitute paternalism for worker self-reliance, and, through the formation of ethnic patronage monopolies, keep the poorer strata of the working class permanently divided.'[88]

Labor was not wholly crushed. The American Railroad Union led important struggles, culminating in the Pullman strike of 1894; western and southern miners organized; Troy Collar Workers struck successfully; radical German workers in the Midwest and Jewish immigrants in New York built working-class socialist movements; the United Garment Workers was organized; the American Federation of Labor made important gains. There were serious defeats, such as the Homestead and New Orleans strikes of 1892, but important links were forged between the Farmers Alliance and the labor movement, and in 1895 it appeared that a new national coalition between populism and labor might well sweep the country. Yet the coalition was derailed before it had been clearly established. Racism and ethnic divisions were critical determinants of this outcome. The southern elite orchestrated a vicious attack on the Black-white alliance that had begun to emerge in the South, legalizing or extending segregation and whipping up racist fears, while in the North, Law and Order Leagues cooperated with the American Protective Association (founded 1887) to blame immigrants for both economic insecurity and social unrest. At the same time, there was a strong move 'toward depoliticizing reform from above' – 'divesting economic decision-making from locally elected officials to appointed bodies (e.g., planning boards, zoning commissions, or insurance and banking commissions) and to the courts.'[89]

The revival of racial segregation in the South, the diversion of western workers' concerns toward Oriental exclusion, the narrowing of political demands to the call for free silver, and (after 1896) a significant increase in farmers' real income tended to dampen discontent, split the movement along racial lines, and divide farmers from industrial workers. The result was that those left out of the capitalist expansion – in the factories, the South, and the West – did not overcome their differences enough to mount a coordinated challenge to the system that so many of them resented.

The labor movement divided into a dominant reformist and a minority radical wing (itself split along ethnic and ideological lines), while the Populist Party was compressed into the Free Silver campaign.

The working class splintered electorally, some workers supporting the Republicans in reaction to the agrarian and nativist tone of the Democratic Party, others withdrawing from electoral participation entirely (or, as in the case of southern Blacks, being directly excluded from the polls). While workers remained willing to act militantly and to raise issues of working-class solidarity, 'the responses to such appeals to class solidarity were quite mixed. . . . Workers were neither consistently class conscious, nor consistently lacking in class consciousness.' Instead, 'as the excitement passed and the reinforcing network of an oppositional subculture atrophied, class loyalties once again had to compete with other alternatives.'[90]

A revival of working-class organization was to come in the twentieth century, though the declining electoral participation of American workers, the split between radicals and reformists, and the growing dominance of incrementalists in the mainstream labor movement were to change the nature of working-class culture and the role of families within it. In the meantime, one immediate legacy of the Great Upheaval was that recognition of class stratification and conflict was forced upon middle-class consciousness. Middle-class readers rediscovered poverty and exploitation as serious issues; their concerns converged with those of far-sighted businessmen and politicians who realized that some of the most pressing grievances had to be met if larger and more successful social explosions were to be averted. Some of the earliest expressions of this new attitude were heard in cities that had experienced the most powerful outbursts during the Great Upheaval. Chicago civic leader Franklin MacVeagh, for example, 'abandoned his 1870s property-based Tory conception of municipal politics and endorsed "the rational demands of the workingmen. . . . I believe in democracy and democracy is impossible if in the long run workingmen are not a part of its conservative support." '[91]

The attempt to found a conservative support for American democracy in the working class was part of a general transformation of social reproduction that helped to reshape both working-class and middle-class families into a form at once more private and more closely connected to the state. The defeat of the Great Upheaval set the stage for that transformation.

Notes

1. David Montgomery, 'Labor and the Republic in Industrial America, 1860–1920,' *Mouvement Sociale* 111 (1980), p. 204.

2. Ross, *Workers on the Edge*, p.xvi; Montgomery, 'Labor and the Republic,' p. 211.

3. Bruce Laurie and Mark Schmitz, 'Manufacture and Productivity: The Making of an Industrial Base, Philadelphia, 1850–1880,' in Hershberg, *Philadelphia*, pp. 43–92; Katz, *Social Organization*, p. 1; Montgomery, *Beyond Equality*, p. 40; Richard Ostreicher, *Solidarity and Fragmentation: Working People and Class Consciousness in Detroit,*

1875–1900 (Urbana, 1986), pp. 4–13; Rogers, *Work Ethic*, pp. 24, 161, 163, 171; Berthoff, *Unsettled People*, p. 327.

4. David Montgomery, 'Gutman's Nineteenth-Century America,' *Labor History* 19 (1978), pp. 428–9.

5. David Roediger, ' "Not Only the Ruling Classes to Overcome, But Also the So-Called Mob": Class, Skill, and Community in the St. Louis General Strike of 1877,' *Journal of Social History* 19 (1985), p. 227.

6. Leon Fink, *Workingmen's Democracy: The Knights of Labor and American Politics* (Urbana, 1983), p. 57.

7. Ostreicher, *Solidarity and Fragmentation*, p. 60.

8. Lawrence Glasco, 'The Life Cycles and the Structure of American Ethnic Groups,' *Journal of Urban History* 1 (1975); Betsy Caroli, Robert Harney, and Lydio Tomasi, *The Italian Immigrant Woman in North America* (Toronto, 1979); Richard Erlich, ed., *Immigrants in Industrial America, 1850–1920* (Charlottesville, 1977); Charles Mindel and Robert Hubenstein, eds, *Ethnic Families in America* (New York, 1976); Cecyle Neidle, *America's Immigrant Women* (Boston, 1975); Allen Davis and Mark Haller, eds, *The Peoples of Philadelphia: A History of Ethnic Groups and Lower-Class Life, 1790–1940* (Philadelphia, 1973); John Bodnar, *Immigration and Industrialization: Ethnicity in an American Mill Town* (Pittsburgh, 1977); John Bodnar, Roger Simon, and Michael Weber, *Lives of Their Own: Blacks, Italians, and Poles in Pittsburgh, 1900–1960* (Urbana, 1982); Judith E. Smith, 'Our Own Kind: Family and Community Networks in Providence,' in Cott and Pleck, *Heritage of Her Own*; Steven Thernstrom, *Poverty and Progress* (Cambridge, MA, 1964); Virginia Yans-McLaughlin, *Family and Community: Italian Immigrants in Buffalo* (Ithaca, 1977); Claudia Goldin, 'Family Strategies and the Family Economy in the Late Nineteenth Century,' in Hershberg, *Philadelphia*, p. 293; Mfanwy Morgan and Hilda Golden, 'Immigrant Families in an Industrial City: A Study of Holyoke, 1880,' *Journal of Family History* 4 (1979), p. 62.

9. Morgan and Golden, 'Immigrant Families'; Clyde and Sally Griffen, *Natives and Newcomers*; Davis and Haller, *Peoples of Philadelphia*; Tamara Hareven and Maris Vinovskis, 'Marital Fertility, Ethnicity, and Occupation in Urban Families: An Analysis of South Boston and the South End in 1880,' *Journal of Social History* 8 (1975), p. 84; Micaela di Leonardo, 'The Myth of the Urban Village,' in Susan Armitage and Elizabeth Jameson, eds, *The Women's West* (Norman, 1987), p. 279.

10. Hershberg, *Philadelphia*; Anthony Broadman and Michael Weber, 'Economic Growth and Occupational Mobility in Nineteenth-Century Urban America: A Reappraisal,' *Journal of Social History* 11 (1977), p. 69; Ostreicher, *Solidarity and Fragmentation*; Griffens, *Native and Newcomers*, pp. 259–60; Katz, *Social Organization*, pp. 80–81.

11. John Jentz, 'Bread and Labor: Chicago's German Bakers Organize,' *Chicago History* 12 (1983), pp. 24–35; Edward Bunbys, 'Nativity and the Distribution of Wealth: Chicago 1870,' *Explorations in Economic History* 19 (1982), pp. 101–9; Dirk Hoerder, ed., *'Struggle a Hard Battle': Essays on Working-Class Immigrants* (Dekalb, 1986).

12. John Cumbler, *Working-Class Community in Industrial America: Work, Leisure, and Struggle in Two Industrial Cities, 1880–1930* (Westport, 1979); Francis Couvares, *The Remaking of Pittsburgh: Class and Culture in an Industrializing City, 1877–1919* (Albany, 1984); Roy Rosenzweig, *Eight Hours for What We Will: Workers and Leisure in an Industrial City, 1870–1920* (New York, 1983); Bodnar, *Immigration and Industrialization*; Mike Davis, *Prisoners of the American Dream* (London, 1986), p. 43.

13. Ostreicher, *Solidarity and Fragmentation*, p. 61.

14. Trachtenberg, *Incorporation*, pp. 90–91; Peter Shergold, ' "Reefs of Roast Beef": The American Worker's Standard of Living in Comparative Perspective,' in Dirk Hoerder, ed., *American Labor and Immigration History, 1877–1920s: Recent European Research* (Urbana, 1983), p. 101.

15. Michael Haines, 'Industrial Work and the Family Life Cycle, 1889–1890,' *Research in Economic History* 4 (1979), pp. 289–356; Katz, *Social Organization*, p. 280; Ostreicher, *Solidarity*, p. 14.

16. Thernstrom, *Poverty and Progress*; Charles Stephenson, 'A Gathering of Strangers?' in Milton Cantor, ed., *American Workingclass Culture* (Greenwood, 1979); Tamara

Hareven, 'The Dynamics of Kin in an Industrial Community,' *American Journal of Sociology* 84 (1978).

17. Cumbler, *Working-Class Community*, p. 118.

18. Francis Early, 'The French-Canadian Family Economy and Standard-of-Living in Lowell, Massachusetts, 1870,' *Journal of Family History* 7 (1982), pp. 184, 188.

19. Katz, *Social Organization*, pp. 336, 343.

20. Haines, 'Industrial Work,' p. 291; Carol Groneman, ' "She Earns as a Child; She Pays as a Man": Women Workers in a Mid-Nineteenth-Century New York City Community,' in Milton Canton and Bruce Laurie, eds, *Class, Sex, and the Woman Worker* (Westport, 1977).

21. Boydston, 'Her Daily Bread,' p. 19; Strasser, *Never Done*; Elizabeth Butler, *Women and the Trades, Pittsburgh 1907–1908* (New York, 1909), p. 337; Wertheimer, *We Were There*, p. 214.

22. Robert Smuts, *Women and Work in America* (New York, 1974), pp. 11–12; Susan Strasser, 'An Enlarged Human Existence?' and *Never Done*; Susan Kleinberg, 'Technology and Women's Work: The Lives of Women in Pittsburgh, 1870–1900,' *Labor History* 17 (1976); Margaret Byington, *Homestead: The Households of a Mill Town* (Pittsburgh, 1974), pp. 72–4.

23. Strasser, *Never Done*; Ryan, *Womanhood in America*, p. 214.

24. Robert Bieder, 'Kinship as a Factor in Migration,' *Journal of Marriage and the Family* 35 (1973); A. Gordon Darroch, 'Migrants in the Nineteenth Century: Fugitives or Families in Motion,' *Journal of Family History* 6 (1981); Lawrence Glasco, 'Migration and Adjustment in the 19th Century City,' in Hareven and Vinovskis, *Family and Population*; Eugene Litwach, 'Geographic Mobility and Extended Family Cohesion,' *American Sociological Review* 25 (1960); J.S. and L.D. Macdonald, 'Chain Migration, Ethnic Neighborhood Formation, and Social Networks,' *Millbank Memorial Fund Quarterly* 42 (1964); Virginia Yans-McLaughlin, *Family and Community: Italian Immigrants in Buffalo, 1880–1930* (Ithaca, 1977).

25. Ostreicher, *Solidarity and Fragmentation*, p. 16.

26. Katz, *Social Organization*, p. 131.

27. On the role of upper class women as Sunday school teachers, see Wallace, *Rockdale*; for comments on the acculturation patterns connected to the high percentage of young immigrant females living in the homes of native-born employers, see Lawrence Glasco, 'The Life Cycles and Household Structure of American Ethnic Groups,' in Cott and Pleck, *Heritage of Her Own*.

28. Hans Medick, 'The Proto-Industrial Family Economy,' *Economic History Review* 3 (1976), p. 304. For a discussion of how the peasant immigrant family was susceptible to a special exploitation in American industry, see Bodnar, *Immigration and Industrialization*.

29. Martha May, 'Bread Before Roses: American Workingmen, Labor Unions and the Family Wage,' in Ruth Milkman, ed., *Women, Work and Protest* (Boston, 1985), pp. 3, 6.

30. Elizabeth Jameson, 'Imperfect Unions: Class and Gender in Cripple Creek, 1894–1904,' in Cantor and Laurie, *Class, Sex, and the Woman Worker*, p. 175; May, 'Bread Before Roses,' pp. 2–21.

31. Linda Schneider, 'The Citizen Striker: Workers' Ideology in the Homestead Strike of 1892,' *Labor History* 23 (1982), p. 63.

32. Nancy Dye, 'The Louisville Woolen Mills Strike of 1887,' *Register of the Kentucky Historical Society* 16 (1982); Carole Turbin, 'Reconceptualizing Family, Work and Labor Organizing: Working Women in Troy, 1860–1890,' *Review of Radical Political Economics* 16 (1984), pp. 9–11.

33. Foner, *Factory Girls*, p. 90.

34. Steven Dubnoff, 'Gender, the Family, and the Problem of Work Motivation in a Transition to Industrial Capitalism,' *Journal of Family History* 4 (1979); Daniel Walkowitz, *Worker City, Company Town: Iron and Cotton-Worker Protest in Troy and Cohoes, Newark, 1855–1884* (Urbana, 1978), pp. 119–20.

35. Kessler-Harris, 'Where are the Women Workers?' p. 356; Ryan, *Womanhood*, p. 207; Louise Odencrantz, *Italian Women in Industry, A Study of Conditions in New York City* (New York, 1919); Smuts, *Woman and Work*, p. 43.

36. May, 'Bread Before Roses,' pp. 7, 8; Jameson, 'Imperfect Unions'; Andrew Dawson, 'The Parameters of Class Consciousness: The Social Outlook of the Skilled Worker, 1890–1920,' in Hoerder, *American Labor and Immigration History.*

37. Rosenzweig, *Eight Hours,* p. 43.

38. Ibid., p. 45; Perry Duis, *The Saloon: Public Drinking in Chicago and Boston, 1880–1920* (Urbana, 1983), p. 2.

39. Ibid., p. 108.

40. Ibid., pp. 148–9; Jon Kingsdale, 'The "Poor Man's Club": Social Functions of the Urban Working-Class Saloon,' in Pleck and Pleck, *The American Man.*

41. Kathy Peiss, *Cheap Amusements: Working Women and Leisure in Turn-of-the Century New York* (Philadelphia, 1986), p. 26.

42. Zaretsky, 'Place of the Family,' p. 217.

43. John Modell and Tamara Hareven, 'Urbanization and the Malleable Household: An Examination of Boarding and Lodging in American Families,' in Gordon, *Family in Social-Historical Perspective*; Strasser, *Never Done,* pp. 150–52; Hareven, 'Family as Process.'

44. Modell and Hareven, 'Urbanization and the Malleable Household,' pp. 54, 55, 66, n. 10.

45. Sam Bass Warner, *Street Car Suburbs: The Processes of Growth in Boston, 1870–1900* (Cambridge, MA, 1962); Hershberg *et al.,* ' "The Journey-to-Work": An Empirical Investigation of Work, Residence and Transportation, Philadelphia, 1850 and 1880,' in Hershberg, *Philadelphia*; Peiss, *Cheap Amusements,* p. 13.

46. Cumbler, *Working-Class Community,* pp. 155–6; Peiss, *Cheap Amusements,* p. 32.

47. Margaret Byington, 'The Mill Town Courts and Their Lodgers,' *Charities and Commons* 21 (1909), pp. 913–20.

48. Robert and Helen Lynd, *Middletown* (New York, 1929), p. 26. For an example of the role of boarding in creating strike support, see Mary Blewett, 'The Union of Sex and Craft in the Haverhill Shoe Strike of 1895,' *Labor History* 20 (1979), p. 360.

49. Stephen Thernstrom, *Poverty and Progress* (Cambridge, MA, 1964); James Henretta, 'The Study of Social Mobility: Ideological Assumptions and Conceptual Biases,' *Labor History* 18 (1977), p. 175.

50. David Brundage, 'The Producing Classes and the Saloon: Denver in the 1880s,' *Labor History* 26 (1985), p. 39; Leon Fink, *Workingman's Democracy* (Urbana, 1985), p. 12.

51. Montgomery, 'Labor and the Republic,' pp. 204–5.

52. Rodgers, *Work Ethic,* p. 155; Rosenzweig, *Eight Hours.*

53. Couvares, *Remaking of Pittsburgh,* pp. 39, 43.

54. Ibid., pp. 75–9, 108; Trachtenberg, *Incorporation,* pp.146–7; Rosenzweig, *Eight Hours,* pp. 128–30.

55. Cumbler, *Working-Class Community,* p. 44; Trachtenberg, *Incorporation,* pp. 110–11.

56. Cumbler, *Working-Class Community,* pp. 154–5; Peiss, *Cheap Amusements.*

57. Stanley Elkins, *Slavery: A Problem in American Institutional and Intellectual Life* (Chicago, 1959); Oscar Lewis, 'The Culture of Poverty,' *Scientific American* 215(1966); Daniel Moynihan, *The Negro Family: The Case for National Action* (Washington, D.C., 1965); Lee Rainwater and W.L. Yancey, *The Moynihan Report and the Politics of Controversy* (Cambridge, MA, 1967); Nathan Glazer and Daniel Moynihan, *Beyond the Melting Pot: The Negroes, Puerto Ricans, Jews, Italians and Irish of New York City* (Cambridge, MA, 1963). A good review of this literature and other perspectives on black families may be found in William Harris, 'Research on the Black Family: Mainstream and Dissenting Perspectives,' *Journal of Ethnic Studies* 6 (1979).

58. Levine, *Black Culture and Consciousness*; Gutman, *Black Family*; James Borchert, *Alley Life in Washington: Family, Community, Religion, and Folklife in the City, 1850–1970* (Urbana, 1980), pp. 208, 210.

59. Herbert Gutman, 'Persistent Myths About the Afro-American Family,' *Journal of Interdisciplinary History* 6 (1975); Theodore Hershberg, 'Free Blacks in Antebellum Pennsylvania,' *Journal of Social History* 5 (1971–72); Paul Lammermeier, 'The Urban Black Family of the Nineteenth Century: A Study of Black Family Structure in the Ohio Valley, 1850–1880,' *Journal of Marriage and the Family* 35 (1973), p. 455.

60. Elizabeth Pleck, 'The Two-Parent Household: Black Family Structure in Late Nineteenth-Century Boston,' in Gordon, *American Family*, 1st edn, p. 165; Pleck, *Black Migration and Poverty: Boston 1865–1900* (New York, 1979), pp. 182, 194.

61. Pleck, 'Two-Parent Household'; Hershberg, *Philadelphia*, p. 451; Pleck, *Black Migration*.

62. Gutman, *Black Family*, pp. 448, 452, 521–6, 530; Hershberg, *Philadelphia*, pp. 348, 374.

63. Gutman, 'Persistent Myths,' pp. 205–7; Paul Worthman, 'Working Class Mobility in Birmingham, Alabama, 1880–1914,' in Tamara Hareven, ed., *Anonymous Americans: Explorations in Nineteenth-Century Social History*, (Englewood Cliffs, 1971), p. 197; Ira Berlin and Herbert Gutman, 'Natives and Immigrants, Free Men and Slaves,' *American Historical Review* 88 (1983), p. 1194.

64. Pleck, *Black Migration*, pp. 198–200.

65. Eric Wolf, *Europe and the People Without History* (Berkeley, 1982), p. 381; Hershberg *et al.*, 'A Tale of Three Cities,' pp. 461–491.

66. Carol Stack, *All Our Kin: Strategies for Survival in a Black Community* (New York, 1974); Demetri Shimkin, Edith Shimkin, and Dennis Frate, eds, *The Extended Family in Black Society* (Chicago, 1978); Pleck, *Black Migration*, p.196; Borchert, *Alley Life*, p. 81; James and Lois Horton, *Black Bostonians: Family Life and Community Struggle in Antebellum Boston* (New York, 1979).

67. Borchert, *Alley Life*, pp. 196, 220 and *passim*.

68. Genovese, *Roll, Jordan, Roll*, p. 500; Jones, *Labor of Love, Labor of Sorrow*.

69. Elizabeth Pleck, 'A Mother's Wages: Income Earning Among Married Italian and Black Women, 1896–1911,' in Gordon, *American Family*, 2nd edn, p. 502; Jones, *Labor of Love*; Claudia Goldin, 'Family Strategies and the Family Economy in the Late Nineteenth Century: The Role of Secondary Workers,' in Hershberg, *Philadelphia*, p. 305; E.J. Kahn, *The American People* (New York, 1973); Michael Reich, 'The Economics of Racism,' in Richard Edwards, Michael Reich, and Thomas Weisskopf, eds, *The Capitalist System* (Englewood Cliffs, 1972), p. 314.

70. Pleck, 'A Mother's Wages'; Degler, *At Odds*, pp.390–91.

71. Robert Wells, *Uncle Sam's Family: Issues in and Perspectives on American Demographic History* (Albany, 1985), p. 50; Jones, *Labor of Love*, p. 114.

72. Grace Ernestine Ray, *Wily Women of the West* (San Antonio, 1972), p. 66; Laurie Alberts, 'Petticoats and Pickaxes: Who Were the Women that Joined the Klondike Gold Rush?' *Alaska Journal* 7 (1977); Wertheimer, *We Were There*, p. 257.

73. Scott and Sally McNall, *Plains Families: Exploring Sociology Through Social History* (New York, 1983), p. 9.

74. 1838 diary entry of Mary Walker, in Cathy Luchette, *Women of the West* (St George, Utah, 1982), p. 63.

75. Johnny Farragher and Christine Stansell, 'Women and Their Families on the Overland Trail,' *Feminist Studies* 2 (1975); Mrs Velina A. Williams, 'Travel Diary, April-September 1853,' *Oregon Pioneer Association Transactions*, 1919, p. 181.

76. 'Family Life on the Frontier: The Diary of Kitturah Penton Belknap,' ed. Glenda Riley, *The Annals of Iowa* 43 (1977), p. 32; Nancy Wilson Ross, *Westward the Women* (Freeport, NY, 1970), p. 7; Lilian Schlissel, *Women's Diaries of the Westward Journey* (New York, 1982); John Farragher and Christine Stansell, *Women and Men on the Overland Trail* (New Haven, 1979).

77. 'Pioneer Migration: The Diary of Mary Alice Shutes,' part II, in Glenda Riley, ed., *The Annals of Iowa*, pp. 567–92; Lillian Schlissel, 'Diaries of Frontier Women: On Learning to Read the Obscured Patterns,' in Mary Kelley, ed., *Woman's Being, Woman's Place* (Boston, 1979), pp. 57–8; Farragher and Stansell, *Overland Trail*, p. 157.

78. Farragher and Stansell, 'Women and Their Families,' p. 164; Mrs Cecilia McMillen Adams, 'Crossing the Plains in 1852,' *Oregon Pioneer Association Transactions*, Thirty-Second Annual Reunion (1904), p. 290; Lodisa Frizzell, *Across the Plains to California in 1852* (New York, 1915), p. 29.

79. Julie Jeffrey, *Frontier Women: The Trans-Mississippi West, 1840–1880* (New York, 1979), p. 56; Christiane Fischer, 'Women in California in the Early 1850s,' *Southern*

California Quarterly 60 (1978), p. 235; Dee Brown, *The Gentle Tamers: Women of the Old Wild West* (New York, 1958), pp. 64–9; Christiane Fischer, ed., *Let Them Speak for Themselves: Women in the American West, 1849–1900* (Hamden, CN, 1977); Abigail Scott Dunniway, *Path Breaking: An Autobiographical History of the Equal Suffrage Movement in the Pacific Coast States* (New York, 1971), pp. 9–10.

80. Lucie Cheng Hirata, 'Chinese Immigrant Women in Nineteenth-Century California,' in Berkin and Norton, *Women of America*, pp. 223–44; Marian Goldman, 'Sexual Commerce on the Comstock Lode,' *Nevada Historical Society Quarterly* 21 (1978).

81. Wertheimer, *We Were There*, pp. 255–6.

82. Jeffrey, *Frontier Women*, p. 140.

83. D'Arcy McNichols, *Native American Tribalism: Indian Survivals and Renewals* (New York, 1973); Keith Basso, *The Cibecue Apache* (New York, 1970); Richard White, *The Roots of Dependency: Subsistence, Environment, and Social Change Among the Choctaws, Pawnees, and Navajos* (Lincoln, 1983); Albers and Medicine, *The Hidden Half*.

84. C. Vann Woodward, *Origins of the New South, 1877–1913* (Baton Rouge, 1971); Julie Roy Jeffrey, 'Women in the Southern Farmers' Alliance,' *Feminist Studies* 3 (1975), p. 85.

85. Davis, *Prisoners*, p. 31.

86. Ostreicher, *Solidarity and Fragmentation*; Fink, *Working Man's Democracy*, pp. 26–7.

87. Sean Wilentz, 'Against Exceptionalism: Class Consciousness and the American Labor Movement, 1790–1920,' *International Labor and Working Class History* 26 (1984), p. 15.

88. Ostreicher, *Solidarity and Fragmentation*; Couvares, *Pittsburgh*; Montgomery, *Beyond Equality*; Fink, *Workingman's Democracy*, p. 226; Davis, *Prisoners*, p. 33.

89. Fink, *Workingman's Democracy*, pp. 227–8. On the racist counterattack against Black-white alliances, see Joseph Cartwright, *The Triumph of Jim Crow: Tennessee Race Relations in the 1880s* (Knoxville, 1976); Woodward, *Strange Career of Jim Crow* and *Origins of the New South*; Howard Rabinowitz, *Race Relations in the Urban South, 1865–1900* (New York, 1977); David Gerber, *Black Ohio and the Color Line, 1860–1915* (Urbana, 1976); Davis, *Prisoners*, pp. 38–40.

90. Ostreicher, *Solidarity and Fragmentation*, pp. 222, 230.

91. Richard Schneirov, 'Class Conflict, Municipal Politics, and Governmental Reform in Gilded Age Chicago,' in Hartmut Keil and John Jentz, eds, *German Workers in Industrial Chicago: A Comparative Perspective* (Dekalb, 1983), p. 200.

9

Results and Prospects: Toward the Twentieth-century Family

In the second half of the nineteenth century families constituted, for a brief time, the primary means of assigning individuals to work and gender roles within each class, as well as being the main tools for manipulating class position. The sexual division of labor, inculcated and upheld in the family, extended beyond it to organize the *social* division of labor. Gender and family status directed people into work roles in the larger economy and into class-specific associations for solidarity, influence, or mutual aid. Fertility strategies, child-rearing patterns, and domestic roles were critical variables in personal survival and class reproduction, while characteristic decisions about work entry, schooling, marriage, and living arrangements were also associated with different economic and social strata. These distinctive family strategies helped people to cope with and occasionally even to alter their positions in a society increasingly characterized by industrial wage-labor and national incorporation but also still geared in its culture and institutions to small towns or rural areas.

The family played, in addition, a special role in social control during this period, particularly through its repression of individualism. Middle-class families systematically suppressed sexuality, channeled play into lessons on morality and hard work, guarded against behaviors or associations deemed inappropriate to class status, and demanded conformity to proper behavior, attire, personality, and even sentiment according to gender. Working-class families were organized in different ways to inhibit the individualism of their members. Children's schooling was sacrificed to early employment, and family goals such as buying a house were put ahead of personal desires or ambitions. Working-class families reinforced ethnic and class institutions that mandated adherence to group norms, frequently using gender to impose such norms or to ridicule departures from them.

The family has linked personal to social reproduction throughout American history, but the critical importance of distinctive family strategies, organized through the sexual division of labor, was new in the nineteenth century – and, as it turned out, transitional. Among Native Americans the sexual division of labor organized work and social obligations, but there was no separation between private and public spheres or domestic and productive activities, while the nuclear family was embedded within and subordinate to larger kinship networks, whether real or fictive. Among colonial whites, the social and political hierarchy, the local community, and the property-owning household often had more power than the nuclear family over socialization, assignment to work roles, and social control. In the early nineteenth century separate families became more independent, but the emerging middle class linked its new family strategies to religious, social, moral, and political associations beyond the family, while the upper class continued to rely on personal networks and clubs to supplement family alliances and influence the not yet impersonal institutions of banks and employers' associations. Large sectors of the lower classes faced substantial constraints from employers, patrons, and local officials upon their ability to make independent family decisions, while transient or casual workers had few opportunities for family life. Where whole families labored together, they often did so under the paternalistic control of factory owners. Only in the second part of the century did workers begin to inhabit social and residential spaces where they could resist or circumvent upper-class control over their personal life and family arrangements. Only then, too, did middle-class families loosen their commitments to social and religious networks and begin to depend more upon separate familial strategies for social and economic achievement.

The background to these developments was the growing dominance of the market, coupled with the political, geographic, and economic flux in the period and the absence of standardized institutions for regulating class interactions, reproducing class differences, or synchronizing personal life with market behavior. Household, neighbor, and community no longer guided the individual into and through work roles; formal substitutes had not yet been institutionalized. Under these conditions, family strategies were critical in both class formation and in efforts to improve class position (or, more frequently, occupational place within one's class). Gender became the one acceptable hierarchy for legitimizing the social division of labor and ordering the delicate balance between self-control, economic competition, and social order. Ironically, the new centrality of family and gender in regulating social and personal interactions created the impression that these categories were transhistorical, natural, and qualitatively different from the shifting worlds of work and social organization. The idea that the family and the sexual division of labor were presocial and sacrosanct imparted a new sense both of privacy and of universality to family life and gender roles, despite the fact that such privacy was largely illusory and that families varied tremendously in their structures and strategies. Pervasive abstractions about 'the' family and 'the' female mediated among the different classes, providing a common language even when – perhaps especially when – the actual organization of the family and of womanhood was very different in daily life.

But by the end of the 1890s, a further change in the system of social reproduction – the consolidation of a national industrial system in politics and culture as well as production – began to undermine the family's role as main agent for the acquisition of class values and distribution of people on different rungs of the class ladder. At the same time, contradictions and tensions appeared in the system of organizing both family and society through suppression of individualism and delineation of separate spheres for each gender. Paradoxically, erosion of the family's role in directly reproducing the social order laid the basis for the transformation of illusion into reality: families became private, sacrosanct, and superficially similar in structure and strategy as part of the same process whereby they lost many of their nineteenth-century functions to the state, the school, and the market. This process will be the subject of another book, but here I will briefly outline some aspects of this transformation and then examine the implications of the present study for understanding the history of the American family in the twentieth century.

The Transformation of Social Reproduction, 1890–1920

The central thread weaving together nineteenth-century political, economic, and social changes into a new fabric of social reproduction was the shift of the productive system to one based on centralized, national corporations. Industrial output quintupled between 1870 and 1900, and by 1900 the 100 largest companies in America controlled a third of the country's productive capacity. Huge businesses such as the railroads ceased to be exceptions and began to seem the wave of the future. Corporations pioneered mass production, new management techniques, and national advertising campaigns. There was a tremendous increase in the scale of operations, with growing plant size, larger concentrations of workers, and greater integration of different stages of production and distribution under one company. Centralization conferred great economic and political advantages on corporations, though it did not always proceed smoothly. Indeed, a major determinant of social conflict and reform in the early 1900s was the fact that as yet no way had been achieved to coordinate the markets in labor or goods with the possibilities for both increasing and restricting output that accompanied economies of scale. Attempts to solve such problems led to a merger movement after 1897, creating considerable opposition in the middle as well as the working classes and forcing business to rethink traditional methods of exerting power.

The growth of large corporations involved a major restructuring of work: the maturation of specialization and subdivision of tasks; mechanization and mass production; separation of conception from execution, concentrating technological knowledge and skill in management and removing it from the point of production; expanded control over the steps and timing of the work process, including multiplication of foremen and other supervisors; and standardization of jobs to make workers at each level interchangeable. While many unskilled workers moved up to higher pay and greater responsibility, skilled workers lost autonomy and status. Employers sought to counteract the homogenizing effect of this mechanization and standardization, with its ominous possibilities for wider worker solidarity, by what has been called the 'balkanization' of the workforce – the creation of new ethnic divisions and artificial distinctions among jobs.

As late as 1871, two-thirds of the American population had been self-employed; by 1900 a majority depended upon wage-labor. This involved not just a closure of working-class avenues to self-employment: increasingly, middle-class security meant permanent white-collar employment rather than a shop or profession of one's own. Clerical work became a lifetime job rather than a temporary stop on the way to self-employment. The spread of wage-labor also drew new workers into the market. Between 1890 and 1910, the number of women workers doubled to more than eight million, or 20 per cent of the labor force. A steadily decreasing proportion of the female workforce worked in domestic settings.

Industrial centers such as Pittsburgh, Cleveland, Detroit, and Chicago became huge cities in this period. By 1900, the largest 200 cities in America accounted for one-third of the country's population and two-thirds of its industrial production. Between 1890 and 1920, small towns in America doubled in number and lost the distinctive character they had retained through the 1880s, becoming integrated into larger industrial and political networks and orienting more toward national news, mass media, popular events, and advertising than to local issues or personalities. By 1920 a majority of the population was urban. Larger cities assumed their modern pattern, as affluent people left the city centers for suburban areas, while new ethnic groups crowded into deteriorating housing in the center. Fewer and fewer people lived at or near work. Instead, there was a rise in ethnic and class concentrations in various neighborhoods and a hardening of the barriers between work zones, political arenas, recreational centers, and residential neighborhoods. Work and leisure as well as classes and ethnic groups were more strictly segregated.

Schooling became a more important conduit through which workers were funneled into different levels of the work process. Teachers tried to inculcate in groups the values that middle-class families had been laboring to develop at home – punctuality, honesty, tidiness, respect for property, and 'Americanism.' Public schooling spread rapidly throughout the 1890s, and attendance laws were enforced more strictly. Older crude distinctions between those who had schooling and those who had not became more finely calibrated and more determinant of where people entered the job market.

The government by courts and political parties that had characterized nineteenth-century America seemed no longer sufficient, and from the 1890s the state created more administrative arms to help regulate trade, the financial system, and social welfare. The upper class was far in advance of the working class in organizing to shape state policy. The National Association of Manufacturers (1895), National Chambers of Commerce (1912), and American Association of Advertisers (1917) only formalized an already advanced coordination of national business interests. Workers made some gains in local school boards but increasingly lost access to larger institutions of civic government after 1900, a date which also marked the start of decreasing lower-class participation in presidential elections. Middle-class women, however, expanded their participation in civic organization in the 1890s, founding settlement houses and consumer leagues to deal with some of the urban problems that male reformers and businessmen still ignored.

The working class, moreover, despite its paltry representation in urban government, continued to organize in this period. Even though labor divided into separate components after the 1886 defeat – a dominant craft unionism and minority movements of industrial syndicalists, ethnic radicals, and socialists – it was by no means clear that business unionism would prevail. Many craft unions retained radical definitions of equality and opposed new controls over the work process, while any coordinated action of syndicalists, ethnic radicals, and socialists threatened to be very difficult to control. Although it failed, the Homestead Strike of 1892 mobilized previously unorganized unskilled workers alongside skilled craftsmen to fight Pinkerton strikebreakers. The militant Western Federation of Miners began organizing unskilled workers and promulgating socialist ideas. By 1898 it was so successful that its threat to sponsor a new national labor organization spurred the American Federation of Labor to undertake new organizing drives. For the first time, depression did not set off a long-term decimation of the ranks of organized labor: between 1897 and 1904 union membership increased by 300 per cent; strikes in the early 1900s involved broader sectors of the work force and a wider range of establishments than formerly. By 1904 the American Federation of Labor had more than 1.5 million members. The Industrial Workers of the World, or the Wobblies, founded in 1905, rejected collaboration with the employing class and organized militant strikes that often won widespread public sympathy.

The increased visibility and durability of the labor movement created a new factor to be reckoned with in American life. Together with the need to coordinate economic and political policies and develop an apparatus favoring national – even international – economic expansion, it convinced growing numbers of businessmen and politicians that some limits to competition and aggrandizement were necessary. The 'friends of property,' as Teddy Roosevelt argued, had to come to terms with at least some sections of the labor movement. A new social attitude toward labor was evident in the Great Coal Strike of 1902. As late as 1894, in the Pullman Strike, President Grover Cleveland had followed the established government policy of breaking strikes outright. In 1902, however, widespread sympathy for the strikers – and their powerful position in controlling the basic fuel of most eastern cities – led President Roosevelt to pressure the mine owners to negotiate. The upshot was the first case of government strike arbitration.

But this was hardly a workers' victory. With considerable justice, Clarence Darrow, representing the workers before the Anthracite Coal Strike Commission, called the commission's recommendations cowardly. Cautious governmental mediation of this sort went hand in hand with a massive offensive against radical working-class demands, especially those that resisted new management prerogatives. The importation of southern Blacks as strikebreakers grew, and private police continued to terrorize strikers. Nevertheless a key tactical shift had taken place in governmental and corporate policy: recognition of the limits of laissez-faire capitalism and of the need to grant limited reforms in order to facilitate industrial expansion. Some corporations and politicians even undertook a modest rapprochement with the conservative wing of the American Federation of Labor.

These economic changes made the old notion of the republic anachronistic – and not just in the domestic sense. If the republic was no longer based on self-sufficient households, regulated by their own equality rather than by larger economic and political forces, it had equally ceased to be a self-sufficient, isolationist part of the world that could afford to turn up its nose at European rivalries. By 1898 many politicians, businessmen, and journalists had embraced a new world role for America. A raucous national chauvinism and jingoism appeared, with a complementary enthusiasm for military intervention; debates over imperialism and anti-imperialism began to divide businessmen as well as workers.

A number of these factors worked to strengthen the hand of reformers: the growth of unionization; new divisions between corporations and smaller capitalists; the homogenization of the labor force in key industries; the growing social weight of the cities and visibility of urban poverty; and the new requirements for rationalizing the political and economic system. There were countervailing forces, however, which thwarted direct translation of these conditions into a united working-class movement or program: the employers' offensive against radical unions; increasingly rigid job and residential segregation of new immigrants; the revived racism and exclusionism that were consequences of the failure of the populist–labor alliance. Another important factor was the dilution of traditional working-class and ethnic cultures by a new national, commercialized culture. Mass-circulation dailies strove to win readers away from specialized labor or ethnic presses, seeking human interest stories that could appeal across ethnic and class lines. National companies began the process of what Susan Strasser describes as the 'branding' of American production, creating products that were independent of local distributors or personal references.[1] Department stores expanded the boundaries of acceptable consumption by associating their wares with different aspects of the home and suggesting that wise shopping could place a proper home – or at least some standardized aspect of such a home – within anyone's reach.

These economic, political, and cultural changes prompted adjustments in the role assignments and strategies of middle- and working-class families. In turn, their responses deepened and added new elements to the transformation of social reproduction. It does not seem too far-fetched to suggest that the years 1890 to 1920 saw a crisis of family identity and gender roles, followed by a decisive shift in their patterns.

Many of the changes between 1890 and 1910 lessened the incentives or possibilities for families to be the central source for the transmission of specific, class-based values and skills. Changes in work patterns made individual initiative and personal repute less important: supervisors, audits, and formal job ladders monitored the behavior and progress of workers on the job. Suppression of the kind of individualism that might disrupt the economic or social order was now built into the job experience and did not need such vigilant attention at home. The spread of schools created formal channels for placing people onto different rungs of the occupational ladder and produced more commonalities in the lives of children. Other changes in the economy lessened the demand for child labor. All this eroded the special role of the family in deciding the timing of entry into work. Age grading and age congruence in major life transitions began to spread. Child labor declined after 1900, even in areas not affected by the growing movement to legislate it out of existence. One study of Irish families found a substitution of income from lodging for that of working children after 1900, even for children not covered by child labor laws. Lodging itself changed in nature. Lodging and boarding became less familial after 1900: they were now casual, urban phenomena no longer dependent upon close occupational and national identities, though associated with larger class similarities.

The growth of suburbs and residentially homogeneous neighborhoods freed middle-class families from the discipline and constraints of street life, which had prevailed in neighborhoods where classes and functions were mixed. It lessened the urgency for family supervision over peer-group associations and mitigated the need to teach rigid boundaries between personal life and work life: those boundaries were now established in social space rather than in the psyche; less energy had to be put into internalizing boundaries now that they were so sharply drawn in work, school, and neighborhood.

At the same time as these developments reduced the pressure on the family to coerce individuals into certain set behaviors, people were actively struggling against such repression, heeding the blandishment of advertisers to consume, demanding leisure time and personal life, and rebelling against thrift, caution, and convention. Attempts by middle-class reformers in the 1880s to eradicate working-class recreation and leisure activities had failed. Rather, genteel culture and leisure began to crumble. Increasingly, popular middle-class books emulated, if they also diluted, working-class dime novels and Westerns. More serious authors expressed their disdain for Victorian hypocrisy and sentimentality in a new kind of novel. Yellow journalism gained an avid middle- as well as working-class readership, and imitations of working-class and black culture became the rage: middle-class people listened to ragtime, did the cakewalk, copied the tough dancing pioneered by urban working youth, embraced competitive sports, and started going to amusement parks and nickelodeons.

Old divisions by gender ceased to operate in the same way, either at work or in the home. Young working women abandoned domestic service and sewing to work in industrial or office jobs. They pioneered new mixed-sex recreation patterns in the cities and broke old gender barriers by organizing on the job. Even middle-class women workers left traditional women's fields (albeit only to create new ones in the long run). By 1900, women were a quarter of the clerical workforce; they would become a majority by the 1930s. In the federal bureaucracy female clerks worked alongside males, meeting potential marriage partners outside the family or actually competing with men for promotions and jobs. Middle-class housewives faced yet another difficulty connected to changing work patterns: a 'servant crisis.' Where there had been one servant per eight households in 1870, there was one in ten or eleven in 1890 and only one in eighteen by 1920. Mother–daughter bonds weakened as new alternatives in work and recreation opened up for daughters, challenging the priority of female kin networks with new heterosocial ties. Yet the period from 1890 to 1920 also saw a tremendous extension of female ties in the political arena, as women entered clubs, professional associations, and political action committees in unprecedented numbers.

Governmental bodies increasingly took over many of the functions of social control, socialization, welfare, and political or economic regulation that had formerly been practiced by families or associations organized along familial gender lines. At the turn of the century, Edward Ross noted the growing role of the schools in promulgating morality and social control, announcing that the schoolmaster was replacing the priest. With the disestablishment of religion, he declared, came the establishment of education. What Ross ignored here, of course, was the fact that there had been a transitional moral authority between priest and teacher: the disestablishment of religion had seen the establishment of the Victorian mother; establishment of the schools was also the disestablishment of domesticity.

Internal contradictions within domesticity had also surfaced by the 1890s. The debilitating side-effects of Victorian constraints on women were noted by authors William Dean Howells, Henry James, and Thorstem Veblen as well as by women activists in the 1890s. Widespread curtailment of births in the middle class led to polarized responses. The Comstock Laws and other repressive measures of the late nineteenth century were symptoms of the crisis posed by the dissociation of sex from reproduction; but repression only stimulated some women to claim as a right what they had formerly merely exercised on the sly. The relatively respectable movement for voluntary motherhood was soon rivaled by advocates of mechanical birth control aids and by opponents of the sexual double standard. By the early 1900s, even the conservative *Ladies Home Journal* was advocating sex education, though for quite conservative ends. The triumph of ideals about companionate marriage and the new social freedoms being exercised by women also exacerbated discontent when a marriage failed to work. By the end of the 1890s divorce was growing three times faster than the population, while the percentage of people who never married had reached an all-time high.

Mobilizations of women around suffrage and temperance, though based on many conservative, small-town values and on an acceptance of the ideology of separate spheres, could not be contained within domesticity. The radical nature of women's demand for equal participation in even one aspect of the public realm could not be disguised by assurances that their political work was merely 'enlarged housework.' While the Women's Christian Temperance Union reflected fears of urbanization, immigration, and industrialization and was associated with nativism, by the 1890s it also supported suffrage, prison reform, restrictions on child labor, and an amelioration of working conditions. During the 1890s many of the elitist biases of the suffragists were challenged by practical experience. In 1896 Susan B. Anthony and Ida Husted Harper examined the defeat of woman suffrage in California and concluded that it could not be attributed to the lower classes or to the foreign-born. In San Francisco, they noted, the largest percentage of the opposition came from 'the district containing the so-called best people.'

Men had their own identity crisis in this period. As an impersonal work and political order ignored men's individual values, skills, and reputation, masculinity lost its organic connection with work and politics, its material base. The loss of opportunities for middle-class men to succeed to self-employment and the growing subordination of skilled workers to management contradicted traditional definitions of manliness. The qualities men now needed to work in industrial America were almost feminine ones: tact, teamwork, the ability to accept direction. New definitions of masculinity had to be constructed that did not derive directly from the work process.

The Possibilities and Limits of Reform

The transformation of social production, the erosion of separate sexual spheres as the organizing principle in society, shifts in sources of female and male identity, and the resultant identity crisis of both state and family unleashed new possibilities as well as new problems. Progressivism was as complicated a response to the early-twentieth-century crisis of social reproduction as evangelism had been to the early-nineteenth-century crisis. Like evangelism, Progressivism contained conservative and liberal wings, with a smattering of radicals, and comprised a remarkably contradictory combination of ideas and interests, often in the same individuals. The convergence and conflict of many different social forces and individual actors, with a wide range of goals and strategies, produced a movement that cannot be neatly categorized.

Revisionist historians have stressed the participation of businessmen and politicians in reforms designed to rationalize the economy, co-opt dissent, and align the political system with the needs of corporations. Certainly the 'efficiency craze' of 1900–15 and the drive for 'scientific management' were often code names for speed-ups and served corporate interests. Yet many aspects of incorporation produced middle-class opposition and divided the capitalist class itself. The increased visibility of urban poverty and industrial repression provoked sincere outrage. Such divisions helped socialists and radical unionists to get a national hearing and even win allies within the middle class. For some people, efficiency did not automatically mean enhancement of profits; social efficiency could also stand for the possibility of ending the tremendous waste of human lives and talent characteristic of laissez-faire industrialism. Similarly, incorporation was not the only possible response to the inefficiency of individual enterprise: collectivization or communalism seemed equally logical alternatives to many reformers.

Whatever the eventual ability of the corporate system to bend reforms to its ends, it should not be forgotten that many reforms were won against business opposition and represented significant limits on the economic and political prerogatives of the corporations. Even where reformers began with fairly conservative values, the dynamics of working for reform often radicalized them. The inadequacy of established political, economic, and familial channels forced people to use other means of organization and communication, from muckraking to mass demonstrations to new kinds of issue-oriented coalitions, and many radically revised their political ideals and social values in the process.

The period from 1900 to World War I, in consequence, saw an outpouring of new organizations, alliances, and ideas. The dynamism of Progressive reform can be seen clearly in the activities of women. Middle-class women founded settlement houses and groups such as the Immigrants Protective League to aid the urban poor; they organized consumer leagues to improve working conditions and product standards. Women from all classes and ethnic backgrounds campaigned for minimum wage legislation for women and youths, as well as for limits on child labor. Working-class women like IWW leaders Mary Harris, 'Mother' Jones and Elizabeth Gurley Flynn pioneered innovative forms of labor protest and organization, using tactics designed to mobilize maximum public support. Free-speech battles brought workers from around the country to pressure company towns into allowing organizing drives. Miners' wives took their children to jail when they were arrested for picketing, then sang to them all night until nearby residents clamored for their release. In 1903, campaigning against child labor, Mother Jones organized a children's march from Philadelphia to New York. Working women founded Working Girls Clubs in the 1880s and the National League of Women Workers in 1897.

Women took the lead in organizing important, if ultimately limited, instances of cross-class collaboration. While working women benefited from the publicity and financial resources middle-class women could bring to strikes and organizing drives, middle-class women benefited perhaps even more from learning to rely on mass organization and independent action. The National Women's Trade Union League, formed in 1903, brought wealthy reformers and prominent social workers – women known as 'allies' – together with labor organizers like Leonara O'Reilly of the ILGWU, Mary Fiertas of the Textile Workers, Mary Kenney O'Sullivan of the Bindery Workers, Rose Schneiderman of the Cap Makers' Union, and Mary Anderson, a shoeworker who later became director of the Women's Bureau of the United States Department of Labor.

The WTUL sought to organize women workers, secure equal opportunity for women on the job and within the unions, lobby for legislation improving working conditions, and gain general public support for the trade union movement. WTUL members held open-air street meetings, organized picket lines, set up health inspections for women workers, raised money for strikers, issued educational leaflets for both the general public and the male-dominated trade unions, and trained women as organizers and public speakers. The WTUL also endorsed woman suffrage and by 1910 was heavily involved in the suffrage movement, helping to tilt it toward the mass mobilizations and uncompromising organizing that eventually secured its victory.

Among the most important areas of collaboration between women workers and middle-class supporters were the garment districts in New York and other major cities. On 8 March 1908, New York garment workers marched for an eight-hour work day, woman suffrage, and an end to child labor. In 1909 a strike began after two shirtwaist shops in New York locked out their workers for attempting to join the International Ladies Garment Workers Union. The company then hired thugs to beat up the strikers and had picketers arrested. At this point the WTUL became involved, and the arrest of its socially prominent members on the picket lines helped to publicize the union's cause. The strike spread throughout the garment industry and developed into a general strike, which became known as the 'Uprising of the 20,000.' Activities such as these – especially those after the Triangle Shirtwaist Company fire in 1911, where 146 workers died – led to the growth of the ILGWU and formation of the Amalgamated Clothing Workers of America, as well as garnering significant middle-class support. Telephone operators, candy-makers, and hotel maids began to organize.

Socialists were active supporters of unionization and women's rights. In 1907 the Socialist Party launched a journal called *The Socialist Woman*, which propagandized for women's rights from a non-racist, pro-working-class position. As a party whose presidential candidate, Eugene Debs, polled more than 6 per cent of the vote in 1900 and in

1912 won up to 40 per cent in some urban working-class districts, the Socialist Party certainly had an effect in countering some of the racist and nativist elements within the suffrage and labor movement. Thus the WTUL, more heavily influenced by the socialists than were the male-led unions, refused to join the American Federation of Labor in the Oriental exclusion campaign.

All this ferment led to an array of new ideas and proposals for reorganizing society. Many well-known Progressives considered themselves socialists in at least some sense, while public outrage against political corruption and business chicanery challenged many of the basic tenets of Social Darwinism and private profit. It was no longer possible to argue that the US was a society of rugged individualist males and protected domestic females, and this threw into question former justifications of both laissez-faire politics and sexual segregation. If individual enterprise was no longer the basis of production, why should not businesses be regulated by the public? And if men no longer protected women from the economic and political forces of the new era, why should men represent women in the public world? People began to rethink sex roles as well as relations between government and industry. Although many adulated Teddy Roosevelt, who sought to re-create masculinity in sports and imperialism, there were also serious critiques of such sex role divisions. Female scientists disputed biological determinism, anticipating modern research on the equality of the sexes. Henrietta Rodman, Charlotte Perkins Gilman, and others criticized the restrictiveness of the nuclear family, pointed to the artificiality of many gender distinctions, and saw mechanization and efficiency as requiring the socialization of housework. Book titles and magazine articles drew attention to The Unrest of Women and The Marriage Revolt.

The impact of such radical ideas was felt in the mainstream suffrage movement, and significant sectors of it moved away from the racism and elitism of the 1880s and 1890s. During the Homestead Strike, Lucy Stone had blithely advised workers to start their own businesses if they did not like their jobs, but by 1901 Ida Husted Harper and others were criticizing the suffrage movement for its lack of sensitivity to the problems of workers and for its failure to recruit working women. The Boston Equal Suffrage Association, founded in 1901, began to experiment with new kinds of campaigning. Its members went door to door in ethnic and working-class neighborhoods. They also held outdoor soapbox rallies and street meetings. By 1909 the Boston women were able to report that 235 unions had endorsed woman suffrage. In 1907 Harriet Stanton Blatch organized the Women's Political Union, an association of factory and professional women that began to hold mass parades in New York. In 1911 the Illinois State Woman Suffrage Party explicitly linked suffrage with improvement of working conditions for wage-earning women, as did the Ohio Woman Suffrage Association in 1915.

Attitudes toward immigrants also changed. Urged on by feminist social reformers, suffragists increasingly began to work among immigrants, holding block parties in Irish, Italian, Syrian, and Polish neighborhoods. A new repugnance against racism emerged among some sectors of the suffrage movement, although the pervasive racism of the period continued to shape the ideas of most suffragists. In May 1913, Elizabeth Freeman reported in *The Socialist Woman* that white suffragists at the St Louis and Chicago conventions had refused to recognize the racial barriers set up by the hotels, forcing the hotel managers to back down. W.E.B. DuBois wrote a suffrage pamphlet that was published by NAWSA, and during the last years of the campaign many black women joined northern suffrage organizations or formed their own clubs. Racism continued to mar the suffrage movement throughout its history, but for the first time since the 1860s anti-racist ideas were visible in the movement. When Ida B. Wells was asked not to march with the Chicago contingent at the protest on Wilson's inaugural day but to join a separate black contingent, she simply stepped out into the Illinois delegation during the parade. Two white women then closed ranks beside her and she completed the march without incident as part of an interracial delegation.

These were heady times. Innovative ideas were raised for the reorganization of social and personal reproduction, and it was by no means obvious that the conservative strain of Progressivism in general or the women's movement in particular would triumph. The air seemed full of possibilities.

But not all possibilities were equally attainable, given the relation of forces in early-twentieth-century capitalism, the increasing leverage of giant corporations, and the limits to most reformers' understanding of or willingness to confront the structural props of the system. Ignoring the realities of struggle between the two dominant classes in America – capital with its control over the instruments and decisions of production, labor with its ability to halt the process of production – many reformers fancied they could play a mediating role between capital and labor, as consumers. Maud Nathan of the National Consumers' League claimed that when consumers organized, their power would be greater than that of either capital or labor.

But the power of consumers could be exercised only indirectly and secondarily, after production had already taken place under existing class relationships. Failing to challenge the economic, political, and legal supports for the private exercise of economic power, reformers ended up having their somewhat vague demands defined and implemented by those with structurally based power in America. Thus efficiency came to be defined in terms of profit rather than natural or human resources; interdependence came to be conceived in terms of the factory's division of labor rather than the reciprocity and mutual responsibility of a commune; new administrative bodies were attached to existing political and legal power structures rather than replacing them; and regulation of social life propped up the system of private property and wage-labor. Necessary reform of medical care helped to establish a corporate–medical alliance; the reduction in authoritarianism and standardization in the schools shaded into tracking, or educating children, as Charles Eliot put it, in accord with 'their evident or probable destinies.' Because reformers did not challenge the fundamental power relations of society, or even the dominant ideology, their humanitarian innovations were often put to work in the service of streamlining the corporate system and perpetuating social control. It is in this sense that Gabriel Kolko has called Progressivism 'the triumph of conservatism.'[2]

The conservative aspects of Progressivism came to the fore after the outbreak of World War I. The war boom brought many smaller capitalists into the camp of the large corporations, while nationalism and xenophobia undercut reform sentiment. Funds for the Immigrants Protective League, which had serviced 12,000 immigrants in 1912, had dried up by 1919. Socialists and Wobblies were harassed and jailed during the war; new patriotic and racist societies were founded. The Russian Revolution raised middle-class fears that reform might threaten their own privileges, as did the prospect of a postwar strike wave, which was clearly on the agenda. Conservatives and journalists used the Seattle General Strike and the Steel Strike of 1919 to fan those fears into hysteria. The Ku Klux Klan and American Legion grew rapidly after 1919, the Palmer raids broke up several radical organizations and intimidated thousands of activists, and a manufacturers' open shop crusade gained momentum. The victory of woman suffrage was a product of the previous years' mobilizations and a courageous final push by the Woman's Party, but the women's movement had no program beyond the vote; it promptly splintered and declined, helped along by vicious red-baiting.

I will explore elsewhere the evolution and outcome of the Progressive movement, especially in relation to the family. Here I simply wish to note that the limits of Progressive reformers and the growing weight of business leaders ultimately made many of the era's achievements highly ambiguous in their effects. Substantive slum reform was tied to a campaign to eradicate the street life and 'promiscuous' communal habits of the poor. Housing reform broke up lower-class kin networks and boarding practices, imposing middle-class behaviors and family forms on poor families. Birth control activists helped poor women to gain greatly desired control over their bodies, but also developed unsavory connections with the eugenics movement. Sincere attempts to help needy children were interlaced with 'the invention of delinquency,'[3] which suspended many civil rights for youth, allowing reformers to penalize behaviors they found unacceptable even when no laws had been broken.

Rebellion against Victorian repression had similarly ambiguous outcomes. Certainly, the effort was personally liberating for many individuals. But in seeking freedom, women and youth often simply moved onto the unoccupied turf of capitalism, rather than trying to rebuild its edifices. That unoccupied turf was consumerism, which turned out to be fully compatible with corporate expansion and quite limited in the emancipation it conferred. The liberation of personal life through commercial recreation also meant the standardization of amusement and the incorporation of personal life into the market. Sexual freedom came to be defined in competitive, consumerist terms. Rebellion against genteel culture was often channeled into the purchase of packaged imitations of working-class and black culture, imitations that were sanitized, mass-produced, and shorn of social rebellion. When working-class sports were adopted by the middle class they were also professionalized. They became, as Francis Couvares has commented, 'at once more alluring and more distant from everyday life'[4] – and more divorced from self-organization or group assertion.

Consolidation of a Corporate Social Order

The conservative evolution of Progressivism did not, of course, turn back the clock. It merely confirmed that the new system of social reproduction, despite important reforms, would serve the needs of an expanding corporate society. By the 1920s the outlines of a modern industrial pattern of social reproduction, including a new family system, were in place. The hallmark of the new system was an economic dominance of corporations so complete as to allow big business, under normal circumstances, to utilize rather than be governed by the concomitant expansion of the state administrative apparatus. A system of mass production and distribution evolved in which corporate decisions about labor control and marketing became major determinants not only of what was produced but also of where people lived, what areas of the country were developed, where roads were built, what laws were proposed and what political reforms implemented. Government regulation never challenged the right of newly incorporated businesses to maintain the private prerogatives of 'individual enterprise'; it merely dealt with casualties or serious malfunctions of the corporate production/private profit system. Even the most radical twentieth-century reforms did not so much limit property rights as expand them to encompass new aspects of life – the right to recreation, the right to privacy, the right to make choices in the marketplace. These rights were seen as individually owned properties, not aspects of social interdependence, and their important benefits should not obscure the ways in which their development reinforced economic individualism.

Relations between labor and capital came to be characterized by state or corporate destruction of autonomous centers of working-class production and organization, whether on the job or in the larger culture, but acceptance, occasionally even encouragement, of expanded working-class consumption. On the one hand, the 1920s were marked by a major offensive against radicals, independent expressions of ethnic or working-class culture, and demands for worker control on the job. Militant unions were broken; civil rights of dissenters were abrogated. New zoning laws and more efficient public regulation restricted traditional expressions of working-class culture in local community celebrations and peer-group associations. The roundup of thousands of suspected radicals in the Palmer raids of 1919 was followed by the Centralia massacre, the conviction and execution of Sacco and Vanzetti, institution of teacher loyalty oaths, a full-scale purging of textbooks, and the deportation of Marcus Garvey (whose massive black nationalist movement could not be packaged and sold to middle-class America as a naughty little foray into a marginalized culture). All these measures were aimed at individuals and groups that held alternative conceptions of the basic structure of twentieth-century America.

But this repression was complemented by social and economic concessions that undercut the radicalism of the petty bourgeoisie and some sectors of the working class. America emerged from World War I an international power that had begun to exploit the resources of its Latin American neighbors and gain entry to untapped markets and supply areas such as China. Between 1913 and 1920, America moved from the world's largest debtor nation to the world's largest creditor nation. GNP doubled during the same period. A profit surge in the 1920s allowed many corporations to grant wage increases, while the cheapening of production brought many new goods within the reach of workers. Although corporations moved ruthlessly against workers who resisted new management techniques, they showed an increased willingness to bargain over wages. The concept of the family wage was accepted by most corporate and political leaders, as well as by conservative unionists who welcomed the excuse to avoid organizing women workers. It allowed a new stabilization of social relations whereby destruction of independent centers of working-class activity and contraction of labor demands to 'bread-and-butter' issues were offset by an expansion of personal consumption and a reaffirmation of male privilege.

A mass-production economy took off as the housing, electrical appliance, and automobile industries boomed. By 1925, the cosmetics industry was a $141 million business. By 1929, there were more than twenty-five million automobile registrations in America and almost 70 per cent of American homes had electricity. Prices did not rise as fast as production, which meant that real wages increased despite the attack on unions. In 1909 a factory worker had to work 22.2 months, almost two years, to earn the cost of a basic Model T. By 1923 it took him only three months. Radio sales rose 1,400 per cent between 1922 and 1929, reaching nearly a billion dollars. Movies or nickelodeons were accessible, at least occasionally, to nearly every family. If workers could no longer take over their local community for Fourth of July celebrations, they could buy train or bus tickets to amusement parks and sports arenas carefully built on neutral territory.

The combination of higher living standards for those safely encased in the wage system and repression against the rest led to a serious contraction of the radical movement and organized labor. The 1921 telephone operators' strike was broken and membership in the International Ladies Garment Workers Union fell from 250,000 to 40,000 during the 1920s. Between 1921 and 1923 alone, the organized labor movement lost more than a million workers. Unions increasingly fought simply for a greater share of the wealth that their members created, accepting the corporate structure of America and deemphasizing independent political action or demands for workers' control. There was also a tremendous decline in social activism. The NAWSA became the League of Women Voters and its membership dropped by 90 per cent. Settlement house workers complained later that the 1920s were the ten worst years they had ever known.

An economic and political system emerged in which control of work and politics was more completely vested in corporations than in any other capitalist nation at a comparable level of development, but where workers had more material benefits available to them while they were employed than in any other nation. The family wage was one of the props of this system; American workers consistently had a lower rate of labor-force participation by married women than any other industrial nation. Mass consumerism was another mainstay. Working-class culture was partly legitimized and absorbed into mainstream America; but it was also injected with bourgeois patterns of individualism. Separate working-class and ethnic cultures were homogenized into mass audiences. The mass movements of the early 1900s had been created by activists who organized to produce common goals and collective deeds; the mass audiences of the 1920s were created by entrepreneurs who provided forums in which the largest number of people could satisfy private needs. The idea that mass production involved 'giving people what they want' ignores the fact that corporations only tried to ascertain and supply the private and individual desires held by the greatest number of people, redirecting the give and take of collective *organization* into simultaneous *consumption* by individuals. Business interests no longer tried to force workers to accept middle-class culture; instead they became suppliers of a commercialized, standardized mass culture that incorporated, but abstracted from their original context, working-class patterns of recreation and leisure.

The only reforms to maintain momentum during the 1920s were those associated with this new stabilization around consumerism and the family wage system. Working class people obtained goods and amusements formerly denied them. Youth of all classes found new possibilities for personal choice in dating, shopping, and consuming mass-produced entertainment. The push to convert the working class to economic and political individualism was softened by social regulation designed to provide for those who most obviously could not obtain individual freedom through wage-labor and whose misery might undermine the argument that individualism provided a rational base for organizing the economy. As compensation for America's insistence that able-bodied men did not need government aid or regulation of their working conditions, government and business were willing to offer such assistance to widows, infants, and even working women. The same courts that struck down other Progressive reforms in the 1920s consistently upheld protective legislation, limiting female access to many fields of work, defining women as temporary workers unable to bargain over their terms of employment, and re-creating in the workforce and union movement a sexual division of labor that had been challenged in the early 1900s. Reformers explicitly advocated protective legislation and the family wage as ways of stabilizing the workforce and compelling the man 'to do his duty as breadwinner.'

Elements of a New Family System

These developments combined with changes in schooling and work to alter functions, roles, and expectations within American families. A detailed account of the evolution of modern families will be the subject of a sequel to the present study. For now, let me just suggest that the qualitative shift away from the Victorian family occurred in the 1920s and that the basic patterns and contradictions of modern family life took shape in this period. The axis of relationships within the family underwent a decisive shift from the mother–child relationship to the couple relationship, while the axis *between* the family and larger social institutions also pivoted sharply. Work, religion, class, kin networks, and gender-based voluntary associations had limited the privacy of nineteenth-century families and inhibited any attempt to carve out an arena of personal expression and self-fulfillment within the family. In the early twentieth century, however, families lost their organic connection to such intermediary groups. In proportion as they related more directly to the state and the market (or to new religious figures who utilized the mass media, bypassing local congregations) they also developed a new cult of privacy, along with heightened expectations about the family's role in fostering individual fulfillment. This change was inextricably bound up with the same forces that have made fulfillment through the family so problematic ever since: rejection of social and political obligations transcending the family even while the family became more dependent on state institutions; the expansion of rights on the basis of self-ownership rather than social obligation; the growth of consumerism; a new focus on romantic love and sexuality; and a youth and leisure culture explicitly opposed to the Victorian categories of male work and female morality.

It is often said that the spread of mass production and consumption in the early twentieth century eroded the economic functions of the family. In some arenas, certainly, industry took over productive tasks formerly located in the home. The mass production of food, clothes, and medicine, for example, shifted the housewife's role from production to consumption of these goods. Fewer and fewer of the basic necessities of life were produced at home.

Yet as Clair Brown and Ruth Cowan have pointed out,[5] mass production had two other effects. First, it created new goods and services that had *never* been produced in the home – electricity, sewer systems, movies, household appliances, articles of mass communication and transportation. Second, mass production also involved a *decrease* in the provision of certain goods and services from outside the home. Peddlers, ice merchants, milkmen, knife-sharpeners and other people who used to deliver goods and services door to door were steadily driven out of business; local stores gradually gave way to centralized shopping districts and recreation centers, forcing the consumer to take over transportation and distribution tasks that had once been an extension of production.

The effects of mass production on the family, and particularly on the housewife's role, were complex. The removal of productive tasks from the home did not immediately pull family members out of it in separate directions. Some industrial products – such as electricity, mechanical cleaning devices, the radio, and the telephone – allowed new activities to take place within the home. Housework could produce many more services and conveniences in less time. Some amusements could now be consumed at home. Children could study or play there to an extent not possible before. Although other new products took people out of the home – the automobile, for example, commercial amusement parks, or the movies – they also increased the frequency of family excursions, breaking down some older recreation patterns that had cut across the family or reached beyond it. Thus mass production in some ways augmented the unity, or at least the self-sufficiency, of the nuclear family *vis-à-vis* neighbors and extended kin networks. It also enlarged the family's responsibility for seeking out and transporting to the home many goods and services that either used to be delivered or could never before be consumed there. In the early-twentieth-century context, of course, such jobs were likely to devolve upon the wife.

Brown contends that technology brought expanded options for consumption but no increased flexibility to the family, for it magnified the family's reliance on wage-work, mass-produced commodities, and municipal services. Similarly, it brought more luxuries but no increase in power to wives not engaged in paid labor: their contribution to the family's accumulation of goods declined while their 'unproductive' tasks, such as picking up and delivering goods or family members, multiplied. As Cowan argues, time saved by the greater efficiency of household technology tended to be replaced by time spent transporting goods and people or by meeting the greater need to demonstrate the value of homemaking. There was a sentimentalization and elaboration of cooking and cleaning tasks that once had been seen as dirty work, delegated to servants if feasible or otherwise embarked on as seldom as possible. At the same time, an inherent incentive existed for housewives to seek paid work, at least on occasion, in order to expand the family's consumption. The family wage system and protective legislation were only fragile peacekeepers in the growing conflict between woman's roles as guardian of the family hearth and contributor to the family larder.

The growth of the state similarly took some roles away from families and women but added others. The expansion of social welfare programs and the professionalization of much traditional women's work into the home economics movement, the helping professions, and teaching probably undermined the authority of mothers and female volunteers. Yet these fields provided many new jobs for women and offered some opportunities for the exercise of authority by employed women. The state may have intervened more in family life, but also increasingly guaranteed it. As Eli Zaretsky points out, the modern liberal state reconstituted the private nuclear family by redefining its basis as wage-labor and stepping in to shore up families without wage-earners.[6] There was *more* concern than in the nineteenth century for avoiding institutionalization of the poor, especially children, keeping them in their original families if possible or creating substitute, foster families. Government policies also made state aid for food or housing dependent upon poor families assuming a private, nuclear form.

The growing role of non-familial institutions in placing individuals into work, school, and welfare hierarchies was quickly recognized by most families. Accordingly, the early twentieth century saw a general redefinition of family and gender in terms of consumerism. Dating was organized around the consumption of recreation, and marriage prospects were increasingly defined in market terms. Girls put popularity above morality, or reduced morality to an aspect of their value on the marriage market; once she was married, a woman's role was, as one advertisement put it, to serve as 'purchasing agent' for the home. Successful masculinity became connected more with a pay check or, for boys, a liberal allowance than with skill or independence at work. The activity of parents became directed less at ensuring that their children should *be* more than themselves than that they should *have* more than themselves.

Another early-twentieth-century innovation was the acceptance of sexuality in personal life. The 1920s experienced a sexual revolution every bit as shocking to contemporaries as that of the 1960s, as young people dated without chaperones, attended petting parties, and made sexual attraction a prime quality in choosing mates. Yet despite the tensions in family life introduced by peer groups, new dating customs, and the 'discovery of adolescence,' the growth of heterosexual romance by no means undermined the centrality of family ties. Sexual intimacy became an important aspect of the couple relationship, and demands were made for the integration of eroticism, companionship, and mutual support into a relationship with one adult of the opposite sex. The elevation of heterosexual couple relationships to a central place in self-fulfillment undermined the intense female networks of earlier years. Indeed, a growing chorus of politicians, educators, and physicians denounced female friendships and associations as unnatural and began to discern in them ominous signs of lesbianism.

The sexualization of society, then, did not constitute an attack on the family but in some ways made the family more central to people's lives. Freud portrayed all society as organized around the satisfaction and frustration of needs generated in the family. The sense that the family was the wellspring of all social institutions deepened in other areas as well. If youths demanded new freedoms, they connected those to their search for a mate; indeed, the age of marriage fell in this period. If advertisers appealed to individualism, they also oriented more and more of their advertisements to portraying shared recreation and deep intimacy within the nuclear family circle. Mother's Day is a twentieth-century invention. Higher standards for family life were expressed by both youth and elders. Mass media made marriage *the* happy ending for all stories of adversity or conflict. Holidays became less oriented toward civic, patriotic, neighborly, or ethnic events and more toward the celebration of family life. Family planning was seen as a way of improving the quality of family life itself.

The increased centrality of family life as an arena for personal expression and emotional satisfaction applied to all classes. A twentieth-century trend that emerged in the 1920s has been the convergence of family strategies, behaviors, and values, despite the continuation or acceleration of inequality in other arenas of life. As we have seen, nineteenth-century families took very class-specific forms. Fertility, housework, gender roles, and the experience of childhood and youth all varied widely according to a family's needs for reproducing or improving its position within a particular class. In the twentieth century the family continued to confirm and reproduce class differences, but it began to do so by channeling people into institutions, values, and behaviors that were largely similar. Objective conditions and institutions began to reproduce class associations, work habits, and entry into jobs; the family increasingly concerned itself with consumption habits. And while a family might recognize the need to coordinate its consumption of good and services (whether from the market or the state) with its economic and social place, the fundamental goals of families lost their qualitative differences, while many behaviors converged.

By the 1920s, young people had begun to exhibit *less* diversity in the age at which they embarked on various stages of the life course or the order in which they proceeded through education, work and marriage than did nineteenth-century youths. Transitions between life stages have become more tightly scheduled in the present century, while family decisions or variations have become less important determinants of those transitions. Twentieth-century housewives also exhibit less variation in their work, leisure, and life course than did their late-nineteenth-century counterparts. Researchers returning to Muncie, Indiana – the 'Middletown' studied by Robert and Helen Lynd in 1924–25 – found that the steady convergence of 'lifestyles' among different social groups has continued: despite the maintenance or increase of inequality in occupational prestige, job security, and wealth, there are more similarities today in home furnishings, types of housework done, parental relations to children, rate of paid-labor-force participation by wives, and so on.[7] Values concerning family life, even if they cannot always be strictly observed, have been homogenized across different social strata. Indeed, the sharp increase in 'abnormal' families over the past twenty years may well be a result not of new pluralistic values but of economic and social factors that make commonly held standards and practices more and more difficult to maintain.

Contradictions of the New Familialism

For all the new 'expressivism' of twentieth-century families, there was also a new 'instrumentalism' implicit in the acceptance of self-fulfillment as a proper goal of family formation and interaction. If the family was not obliged to neighbors, class associations, or larger social responsibilities, why should family ties be based on anything broader than self-interest? Theoretically, it was women who mediated between family autonomy and interpersonal obligations, but their new immersion in consumerism muddied their moral authority. Women's role in consumption interacted with the continued emphasis on sexual virtue, for example, to create a peculiarly schizoid image of female self-control: women were jelly when it came to resisting material temptation, but could be stone when it came to withholding sex.

Acceptance of consumerism within families fostered a certain confusion about the commensurability of things and emotions, creating a tendency to define one's individuality in terms of one's neediness for both: market individualism, David Levine has argued, created 'a social hierarchy of neediness,' in which people learned to seek self-fulfillment by embracing new needs and discovering new discontents.[8] These discontents stimulated a demand for new personal relationships as well as new products, inadvertently introducing planned obsolescence into the very love relations that were now held to be the most stable sources of personal identity.

Other contradictions were embedded in the new family values and practices. The simultaneous broadening of demands for emotional fulfillment and narrowing of its sources to the couple relationship generated marital strains. Women's changing roles as wives created more incentives for them to expand family consumption, including taking paid work if necessary; conversely, expanded aspirations about the possibilities of improving living standards through housework might keep women home but also raised their stress levels. Inflated expectations about married life led to bitter disappointments, so that divorce rates in the 1920s made the greatest percentage leap, aside from 1946, in American history. Elaine Tyler May argues that many of these divorces were connected to new ambiguities about what constituted an adequate standard of living and a proper level of support for one's spouse.[9]

At the same time as these tensions were introduced into the couple relationship, new generational conflicts mounted. Women's relationships with their children became more problematic as nineteenth-century maternalism clashed with twentieth-century romance and the cult of youthful independence. The basis of paternal authority also became less clear. The widening gap between an increasingly intimate, affectionate family life and a more bureaucratized work and political world required intermediary institutions such as peer groups, which injected a kind of ritual youth rebellion into family relationships. Notions of deferred gratification clashed with demands for expanded consumption. Conflicts between parents and children over these issues were only exacerbated by the growing literature on childcare, which vacillated between advocating indulgence and repression at different stages of the child's development.

But most of the forces that undermined family harmony were integrally connected with those that elevated family unity to a central value for twentieth-century Americans. The nineteenth-century view of the family as refuge seems modest compared to emerging twentieth-century demands that the family provide a whole alternative world of satisfaction and intimacy. Where a family succeeded in doing so, people might find previously unimagined pleasures in family life. But the new ideals also increased the possibilities for failure: even the rudest shelter can provide a refuge; the personal relations and material furnishings required to construct an alternative world within the home are harder to come by, especially given the expectations raised by commercial amusements.

The recurring sense of 'crisis' in the twentieth-century American family is inseparable from the century's establishment of the private family as the preeminent site for satisfaction of the emotional needs of men, women, and children. Ambiguity about the future of 'the family' was inherent in the triumph of a cultural symbol system in which the establishment of a new family became *the* happy ending for every story.

Perspectives on American Family History: The Difficulty of Generalization

American families have changed considerably over time, and in certain patterned ways, but pronouncements about unilinear and irreversible outcomes of such changes are difficult to defend. Barbara Laslett, for example, has argued that the central historical trend has been the increasing privacy of American family life.[10] We have already seen that preindustrial records reveal an astounding interference in domestic matters by church groups, servants, neighbors, and community, while nineteenth-century families put serious limits on the privacy of family life and family members. The authority of grandparents, especially male, intruded into the nuclear family during colonial days, while in the nineteenth century female kin networks and the practice of visiting in the homes of relatives cut across the self-sufficiency of the nuclear unit. Not until the present century did nuclear families envision themselves as capable of meeting all the emotional needs of husband

and wife and refusing interference from neighbors, same-sex networks, and other kin.

Yet Christopher Lasch and Jacques Donzelot have argued that the privacy of modern family life is largely illusory, pointing to the penetration of families by state agencies and the mass media.[11] And even extended family networks have survived to a surprising extent: twentieth-century individuals, simply because of falling mortality rates, have more kin alive than ever before; and though in most cases we live further from them, modern transportation and communication technology may well have *increased* the likelihood of contact with extended family networks.

The expansion of autonomy and privacy for middle-class families in early-twentieth-century America rested on a constriction of autonomy for parts of the working class. Privacy that was eagerly sought by many middle-class families in this period was *imposed* on working families through the campaign of reformers and police against boarding, lodging, lower-class peer-group associations, and neighborhood sociability. On the other hand, the loss of autonomy for working-class families in work and community life was also associated with creation of the first possibilities for a working-class family life in recreation and consumption.

Even within the family, the trend toward privacy has by no means been uniform. While parents have ceased to demand total obedience from their children, offering them the opportunity to make many of their own decisions as well as to inhabit private rooms, they have become more and more insistent that children share their thoughts and feelings. One author has commented that the nineteenth-century image of the family as refuge gave way in the twentieth to the model of the 'family as encounter group';[12] the right to remain silent seems to have become a thing of the past. Any mother who has bought into the periodic hypes about 'super babies' can testify to the almost total lack of personal privacy between infant and mother, as each interaction is turned into a 'growth experience.' It is hard to say whether the net effect of the decline in authoritarianism and the increase in demands for communication has expanded or diminished privacy for family members.

What of the family's social centrality? The family has lost many of the productive, religious, and political functions it filled during the eighteenth and nineteenth centuries, but this should not be confused with eradication of its social and economic role. Family background still accounts for most economic and educational success in America, and the 1966 Coleman Report found that the family resources children brought to school affected their rates of learning more than the resources at the school itself.[13] The evolution of work roles has eroded the ongoing importance of family for such members of the middle class as professionals and managers, who need to make frequent moves to follow promotions and job opportunities. Yet most Americans have become *less* rather than more mobile in terms of residence and occupation during the twentieth century. The recent expansion of professional jobs requiring mobility has been accompanied by an increase in the need for family solidarity among other middle-class and working-class groups. Deterioration of their economic position has forced many families into lengthened co-residence of parents and young adults: between 1970 and 1984, the number of young adults aged eighteen to thirty-four living with parents increased by 84.8 per cent.

Furthermore, even as the family has lost some older functions, it may have gained new ones such as serving as a unit of consumption or a source of emotional sustenance. For every family whose members go their way in pursuit of 'A Sony of my owny,' there is another that organizes all its major decisions around the need to make payments on the home. Carl Degler has argued that the family has become a more specialized institution, concentrating on childcare, but one can also see it as losing specifically defined functions like education only to gain a more generalized function of measuring personal happiness. John Demos suggests that 'while the family is now less important from a social standpoint, it may be *more* important from a psychological one.'[14] Certainly the amount of emotional satisfaction demanded, if not always obtained, from husband–wife and parent–child relations in the twentieth century would have astounded previous generations.

The historical relation between family 'autonomy' and state 'interference' is also more complicated than is commonly thought. As we have seen, colonial authorities and neighbors had little respect for the sanctity of the nuclear family, routinely intervening to enforce social norms. Even at the height of laissez-faire capitalism, both informal associations and state institutions often cut across family relations and limited the family's freedom of action. In the present century, the state's 'usurpation' of family functions has gone hand in hand with – and was necessitated by – its destruction of intermediary units in society and its insistence that the wage-earning nuclear family be the basic economic cell of capitalism. Mothers' Pensions and Aid to Dependent Children policies, which have often forced families to split up as a condition for receiving aid, are not as contradictory as one might think: in one sense the state destroys nuclear families here; but it also reinforces the norm and social functions of the private nuclear family by making an 'abnormal' family a condition for receiving help. The policy justifies all kinds of additional state intervention on the grounds of a 'family pathology' its own actions have fostered, but it also implicitly grants the sanctity of a so-called normal family.

The increase in the state's ability to monitor and regulate families that are dependent on welfare programs has been matched by its growing willingness to allow more privileged families to make their own decisions about formerly prohibited practices such as birth control and abortion. But the state has hardly followed a laissez-faire attitude toward such families. The 'self-sufficient' middle-class family has become increasingly reliant on state-financed employment, education subsidies, Veterans' Administration loans and federal tax breaks for home ownership, and tax monies being spent on the road and sewer systems that make suburban living possible. Total federal tax subsidies for 'independent,' primarily 'intact,' home-owning families came to $42.4 billion in 1986, dwarfing the $14.3 billion in housing assistance for low-income households.

The impact of state policies on age and gender roles has also been mixed. Expansion of the state's ability to limit parental rights in the interests of the child has been accompanied by growing reluctance to place children in non-familial settings. In the early twentieth century, the creation of a 'foster family' system imposed dominant nuclear family norms on deviant families without abrogating parental rights, giving the state quite a bit of power to temporarily intervene in families but leaving foster families very vulnerable to sudden assertions of rights by the 'natural' parents. State intervention has clearly undermined some traditional male prerogatives within the family, and state employment has created numerous little niches for women to earn a livelihood or even exert a modicum of power over others. Yet the total dependence of women upon men may well have increased, if it is remembered that women constitute the bulk of welfare cases and males dominate the top levels of the social welfare hierarchy.

Relationships between the family and the market have been equally multifarious. American advertisers from the 1920s to the present have used images of family life to sell products, and numerous innovations of the mass market, as we have seen, elevated the centrality of the family in people's lives and self-definition. On the other hand, a primary growth sector of the economy today is the provision of goods and services to singles, and these have a considerable dissolving effect on family ties. Still, the people most likely to divorce or not to marry are those least likely to have illusions that they can afford the beckoning single life: people married in their teens or before completing their education.

Conservative discussions of the family often focus on the ways in which small businesses are the backbone of 'traditional' family life, teaching hard work, deferred gratification, thrift, and intense maternal investment in child-rearing. Yet one of the main spheres left for individual entrepreneurship in modern corporate America is personal life, which can be only incompletely standardized to provide a market for mass production. It is difficult to see the qualitative economic difference separating Amway distributors, Avon representatives, fitness centers and other small businesses catering to local personal and family needs from the entrepreneurs who set up surrogate-mother clinics, provide divorce advice, open singles bars, or begin booking pornographic movies into their small theaters when they cannot compete with the new mega movie houses.

The early years of this century saw a moderation of separate spheres in the organization of work and personal life; the activities of women have since further broken down many rigidities in the sexual division of labor. A fixed connection between gender, family status and social role is less acceptable, and somewhat less visible, than formerly. Since 1950, the number of working wives has doubled to 52 per cent of all wives, while the number of working mothers has quadrupled. Yet many of these women work only part-time, and their work is still likely to be interrupted by or geared to family commitments. As of 1983, 80 per cent of all working women were concentrated in just twenty of the 420 occupational categories listed in the US census.

Divorce rights have not destroyed some Golden Age of feminine security, but neither have they liberated women. The unequal distribution of wealth and power according to gender that used to be produced through the dynamics of family relations is now often produced through the dynamics of family break-up. Slogans such as 'the feminization of poverty' ignore the ways that women have historically born the brunt of poverty *within* the family, 'taking up the slack' by expanding their housework hours to compensate for decreased income or actually denying themselves food in order to feed the male 'breadwinner.' Today, however, divorce rather than marriage has become a means to such privilege for some men. One California study found that after the first year of divorce the man's standard of living rose by 49 per cent, while the woman's fell by 74 per cent. Divorce is now the greatest single predictor of poverty for women and children, leaving them the fastest-growing poverty group in the country and ensuring their entry into the low-paid, part-time work that reinforces their personal dependence as well as their economic marginalism: such employment constitutes the main growth area of the modern economy. Because of their concentration in these jobs, women continue to earn only 60 per cent of male income and to cluster disproportionately in 'female' sectors of the economy.

Ironically, many of the gains that middle-class professional women have made in non-traditional or higher paid employment have only increased the demand for traditional female labor – from cleaning women to fast-food workers to surrogate mothers. While the husbands of more privileged working women now profess to the pollsters a willingness to help around the house, it appears that most of the housework and childcare these women have given up has actually been taken over by poorer working women. Once again, the moderation of sexual inequality in some spheres has resulted in its aggravation in others.

Some authors claim to have discovered a growing concern for children in the history of American family life. They point to the brutal suppression of children's individuality by colonial parents, the seeming indifference to the disposition of children in colonial divorce proceedings, the use of child labor in the nineteenth century, and the acceptance of harsh physical punishment until relatively recently. Others, however, argue that the trend since the beginning of the twentieth century has been quite different: children have lost childhood itself, as they have increasingly been exposed too early to the complications of sex, the sordidness of adult pains and conflicts, and the materialism of the adult world.

As with most of the other generalizations, unilinear trends are hard to discern. John Demos argues convincingly that despite different standards for emotional and physical treatment of children, no pattern of child abuse as we know it today can be discerned in colonial New England. Although there has been a marked decline in the overall acceptability and frequency of physical punishment, an apparent rise in the incidence of child-battering and sexual abuse has also occurred. Yet Christine Stansell has found some evidence of sexual abuse of children in early-nineteenth-century American cities, and we have already seen that prolonged childhood in nineteenth-century middle-class families depended on the early exploitation of working-class girls, who were also sometimes forced into prostitution to supplement their inadequate wages.[15] Colonial children were less protected from knowledge of sexuality, death, and poverty than most modern middle-class youngsters, but their behavior was more tightly controlled by parents and authorities.

Some observers point to the failure of modern parents to supervise their teenagers or cite the five to seven hours a day that children spend watching television as signs of the disengagement of American parents. The 'Middletown' researchers, however, found that both working-class and 'business-class' parents 'spent more time with their children in 1978 than in 1924.'[16] Yet we need to beware making invidious comparisons in either direction. Are, for example, the reports of Middletown parents in 1924 and 1978 strictly comparable? It may be that these reports reflect different definitions of time spent with children. It is hard to believe that mothers in 1924, who seldom worked outside the home, spent less total time in the presence of their children than modern women. They may well, however, have spent smaller amounts of time devoting themselves exclusively to their children, and therefore reported this as less time. On the other hand, modern reports of time spent with children may include time that has little to do with actual interactions: the statistics on television viewing can be interpreted as reflecting a historical trend toward *greater* dependence on but less intensity within the family; television may have become a functional – which is not to say desirable – substitute for apprenticeship, childcare by neighbors, shared family tasks, and so forth.

Undoubtedly, some of the contradictory evidence for historical trends is due to different trajectories in different classes. If the middle-class child has grown up earlier since the beginning of the twentieth century, many sections of the working class only first gained the possibility of childhood in that same period. Other seeming contradictions may in fact be part of the same process: intense idealization of childhood may involve erotic or narcissistic undertones that can shade into incest or abuse as people compete to see who will be best 'taken care of' by the family. Indulgence of their own children was for many people in twentieth-century America part of a turning inward to the family that involved repudiation of responsibility for other people's children. As the old woman in Tillie Olsen's 'Tell Me A Riddle' taunts her husband when he fusses over their grandchildren and tells her that their advantages should make her happy: 'And are there no other children?'

The difficulties of unilinear generalizations about the past of American families are compounded when people begin to project the trends they discern into the future. Some argue that the family is a dying institution. The United States, for example, has the highest divorce rate in the world, and the expansion of single-person and other non-family households is occurring at a much faster rate than the formation of new families. In 1984, 25.7 per cent of families with children under eighteen were headed by a single parent (90 per cent of these women). This had risen to 26.3 per cent in 1986, and some observers predict that by 1990 one in three families will be headed by a single parent.

But the US also has the highest marriage and remarriage rate in the world, and proportionally fewer persons remain single all their lives today than in the eighteenth and nineteenth centuries. The fall in mortality over the past hundred years has tended to negate the overall effect of high divorce rates, so that more couples live together longer than perhaps at any time in history. One hundred years ago, the average marriage lasted only twelve years. People who *are* married report high levels of satisfaction. The latest US statistics, moreover, show a drop in both the rate and the absolute numbers of divorces. The depth of our pessimism about family life in the recent period and the enthusiasm of the much-heralded 'return to family values' may merely reflect the inevitable oscillations in our attachments to the family that flow from our lack of alternatives to it. Whether we measure ourselves by the family's success in our lives or by the shadow cast by its failure we are still testifying to its emotional centrality in twentieth-century America.

This is not to say that there are not some stunning new problems associated with family life in America; and neither the AIDS scare, the new boom in popular celebrations of family values, nor hysterical movies about the homicidal outcomes of extramarital affairs are likely to end them. Many, perhaps most, of the problems are associated with poverty. The number of single-parent families doubled between 1970 and 1985; a majority of these families fall below the poverty line. Twenty per cent of American children – 50 per cent of black American children – will experience poverty for at least a few years of their life, and a growing number of American families are permanently poor. Between 1978 and 1984 the median income for a two-person family fell by 3 per cent, while that of families with seven or more members fell by 16 per cent. As of 1987, families with children made up 33 per cent of the homeless population in America's cities. Teenage illegitimacy rates have soared, and teachers working in every class and region of the country report problems with drugs, discipline, and educational commitment among their students. More dramatic pathologies abound. A 1985 national poll by *The Los Angeles Times* found that 22 per cent of Americans had been victims of child abuse, with 55 per cent of the incidents involving sexual intercourse and 36 per cent sexual fondling. Twenty-three per cent of the abusers were relatives and 41 per cent friends or persons involved with a child's parent.

These problems, however, cannot be blamed on some supposed rejection of 'traditional' family values. Divorce is not caused by working wives or feminism; it is most frequent among women who marry in their teens or who have left their education incomplete. (However, among women who work, those who earn the highest incomes are most likely to face divorce, which seems less a problem of women working than of male inability to accept women working on equal terms.) The pressures that prevent family formation or create incentives for family dissolution are more economic than cultural: young men's earnings have dropped by almost a third in the past ten years, young black men's by almost 50 per cent. In 1963, 60 per cent of men aged twenty to twenty-four earned enough to keep a family of three above the poverty line; by 1984 only 42 per cent could do so. At the other end of the age spectrum in earnings, things also worsened. Between 1949 and 1973, the earnings of a man passing from age forty to age fifty increased by 30 per cent; between 1973 and 1984 they decreased by 14 per cent. As for teenage pregnancies, the peak year was 1957, when 97 out of every 1,000 girls aged fifteen to nineteen gave birth, compared to 52 of every 1,000 in 1983. The rise in illegitimate births among teenagers probably reflects a decline in the viability of young families more than a rejection of traditional expectations about marriage.

Nor can these problems be solved by a return to some mythical Golden Age of the family or adoption of some 'correct' model of family life. No family system is always and everywhere suited to the best development of personal or social life. Nuclear families that cosset their children may, as Sennett argued of nineteenth-century Chicago, create fearful individuals incapable of risk-taking or forging wider social ties. Yet the same family that is an effective tool of class or ethnic interests may achieve this by ruthless suppression of its individual members, as so many working-class and immigrant youths, pulled out of school to finance a family home, could testify. Ghetto kin networks that pool and circulate resources to even out the effects of poverty and discrimination are adapting intelligently to the exigencies of social, not familial, pathologies, but their leveling mechanisms often hamper individual achievement in education and work. On the other hand, the conditions for promoting such achievement in youth have often been the abnegation of personhood by the mother and the severance of ties with extended kin or community networks.

American history provides no model for those who seek to recover some perfect family from our past. People who like the parental authority and male dominance of colonial families would be horrified by their routine acceptance of sexual discussions, the invasion of privacy by neighbors and community officials, and the relative indifference to privileging the nuclear unit. Those who are attracted by the corporate limits on individual enterprise among colonial households, on the other hand, are unlikely to be enamored of the insistence on hierarchy and acceptance of social inequality. People who turn to the nineteenth-century middle-class family for their model of domesticity and maternalism tend to forget that this family was the main arena for the development of birth control and, frequently, the exercise of abortion. They might also be surprised by the extent to which this family downplayed private, heterosexual relations, endorsing intimacies among women that would scandalize them today. Those who would embrace the sisterhood of nineteenth-century women, on the other hand, are likely to detest the shared assumptions that created this female solidarity.

The family that emerged in the 1920s provides no more satisfactory answers for most people. Those attracted by its romanticizing of the couple relationship have been slow to see the other consequences of stressing coupled intimacy as the main source of emotional satisfaction: demands for divorce or for legitimation of gay and lesbian unions stem partly from acceptance of the idea that there are no substitutes for couple relationships and the correlative conclusion that an unsatisfactory couple relationship is intolerable. The liberation of sexuality and consumerism within marriage has led to a jading of tastes and a search for new thrills that tempt many to venture outside the marital relation. Wearing false eyelashes and different-colored wigs to bed, as Tammy Bakker found out, may only feed the appetite for variety.

Many people are attracted by the images of self-contained suburban families that multiplied in the 1950s; but they tend to forget the dependence of the suburban family on state employment and the expansion of federal debt (not to mention the frequent confusion of this family with its idealized portrayal in television serials of that period). From a different political perspective, other people admire the expansion of personal rights since the 1960s – freedoms for youth, legislation against discrimination on the basis of gender, birth control, abortion, repeal of laws restricting personal choice. But these same people often fail to recognize that claiming such rights on the basis of ownership of one's body, home, or credit card leads to a denial of reciprocity and obligation, as well as to the dilemmas of surrogate-mother contracts.

This brief summary of the complexities in family history suggests that we need to avoid cataclysmic pronouncements about the 'breakdown' or 'resurrection' of family life and seek a more nuanced evaluation of trends in American families. I suggest that the family has become both more and less intense for its members, at the same time and as part of the same process. The urge to escape commitment is inseparable from the demands that commitment makes, which is why America's 'womanless' novels and manless diaries appeared at the same instant and in the same social milieu as did the romantic paeans to married love. No sooner did the idea appear that the family should be the source of all emotional satisfaction than the rage for failing to meet those emotional needs welled up against it. The right to divorce had its origins in the emphasis on the need for married love, and divorce rates have climbed steadily ever since heterosexual love was heralded as the primary outlet for our emotional and sensual needs. So too has the glorification of childhood and insistence on its central place in American life been accompanied by the growth of child pornography and an apparent rise in the incidence of child abuse.

Yet both the disappointment with and the withdrawal from family life contribute to a yearning for the 'perfect' family that reinforces its primacy in our emotional self-identification. The tensions and blow-ups of modern family life only highlight the decline of community and civic alternatives to family-centeredness. The rise of individualism, which constantly challenges the daily operation of the family, nevertheless had its origins in the idea that a family could detach itself from the constraints of social or geographic community and relate directly to the political and economic marketplace; though individualism regularly undermines the unity of the family, it also re-creates private family arrangements by rejecting more collective sources of mutual aid and solace.

Perhaps the main lesson here is to eschew simplistic value judgments about changes in family relationships over time. Instead of heralding the advent of 'affective individualism' or lamenting the loss of a broader sense of community, instead of condemning the overemphasis on marriage for women or enthusing over women's new autonomy within marriage, instead of embracing the new family 'pluralism' or bemoaning the loss of traditional commitments, we must develop a more balanced evaluation of family history. Changes in families have resolved some tensions only to create new ones. Old patterns of equality and inequality have given way to new patterns of autonomy and control. Losses for some family members have been gains for others, while gains for some family units have been losses for others. To be a guide for understanding and action in today's world, family history must neither lull us into complacency by celebrating what we have gained, nor distract us from the present by romanticizing what we have lost. It must show us how the combination of gains and losses fits into the larger pattern of social reproduction. The 'crisis of the family' is part of the historical predicament facing modern society: it revolves around the question of which decisions should or can be private, and which can and should be social. It raises the issue of what kinds of dependence and independence we can tolerate, and what social obligations we should strive to forge. We have to deal on a daily basis with this predicament in our own families; but we will have to solve it in society as a whole.

Notes

1. Susan Strasser, *Satisfaction Guaranteed: The Genesis of the American Mass Market* (New York, forthcoming).

2. Sol Cohen, 'The Industrial Education Movement, 1906–17,' *American Quarterly* 20 (1968); Gabriel Kolko, *The Triumph of Conservatism* (New York, 1963).

3. Anthony Platt, *The Child-Savers; The Invention of Delinquency* (Chicago, 1969).

4. Couvares, *Remaking of Pittsburgh*, p. 125.

5. Clair (Vickery) Brown, 'Home Production for Use in a Market Economy,' in Thorne and Yalom, *Rethinking the Family*; Ruth Schwartz Cowan, *More Work for Mother: The Ironies of Household Technology from the Open Hearth to the Microwave* (New York, 1983).

6. Zaretsky, 'Place of the Family.'

7. Theodore Caplow and Bruce Chadwick, 'Inequality and Life-Styles in Middletown, 1920–1978,' *Social Service Quarterly* 7 (1979).

8. David Levine, *Economic Theory: The Elementary Relations of Economic Life* (New York, 1978), p. 299.

9. Elaine Tyler May, *Great Expectations: Marriage and Divorce in Post-Victorian America* (Chicago, 1980).

10. Barbara Laslett, 'The Family as a Public and Private Institution: An Historical Perspective,' *Journal of Marriage and the Family* 35 (1973).

11. Lasch, *Haven in a Heartless World*; Jacques Donzelot, *The Policing of Families* (New York, 1979).

12. John Demos, *Past, Present, and Personal: The Family and the Life Course in American History* (New York, 1986), p. 38.

13. Christopher Jencks, *Who Gets Ahead? The Determinants of Economic Success in America* (New York, 1979); James Coleman, 'Towards Open Schools,' *The Public Interest* 5 (1967). For summaries and discussions of the Coleman Report, see Frederick Mosteller and Daniel Moynihan, eds, *On Equality of Educational Opportunity* (New York, 1972). For discussion of the ways that a ruling class based primarily on family inheritance functions in a politically democratic society, see G. William Domhoff, *Who Rules America?* (Englewood Cliffs, 1967) and 'New Directions in Power Structure Research,' Special issue of *The Insurgent Sociologist* 5 (1975).

14. Degler, *At Odds*; Demos, *A Little Commonwealth*, p. 183.

15. Demos, *Past, Present, and Personal*, pp. 68–91; Stansell, *City of Women*.

16. Caplow and Chadwick, 'Inequality and Life-Styles,' p. 381.